EVERYDAY LIFE

a reader

From the reference
library of

_____

EVERYDAY LIFE

a reader

Lorne Tepperman
University of Toronto

James Curtis
University of Waterloo

McGraw-Hill Ryerson Limited

Toronto   Montreal   New York   Auckland   Bogotá   Caracas
Lisbon   London   Madrid   Mexico   Milan   New Delhi   Paris
San Juan   Singapore   Sydney   Tokyo

Everyday Life: A Reader

ISBN: 0-07-551285-8

(Reprint code)   3 4 5 6 7 8 9 0 D 0 9 8 7 6 5 4 3 2

Printed and bound in Canada

Canadian Cataloguing in Publication Data

Main entry under title:

Everyday life

Rev. ed. of: Readings in sociology : an introduction.
Includes bibliographical references and index.
ISBN 0-07-551285-8

1. Sociology.   2. Canada — Social conditions.
I. Tepperman, Lorne, date — .   II. Curtis,
James E., date — .   III. Title: Readings in
sociology : an introduction.

HM51.E84 1992   301   C91-094889-5

Sponsoring Editor: Catherine A. O'Toole
Senior Supervising Editor: Carol Altilia
Copy Editor: Gail Marsden
Permissions Editor: Norma Christensen
Cover and Text Design: Stuart Knox / Matthews Communications Design
Technical Artist: Stuart Knox

This book was manufactured in Canada using acid-free paper.

Contents

Preface

We were pleased when McGraw-Hill Ryerson asked us to prepare a brief edition *Readings in Sociology: An Introduction*. This prompted us to do some very interesting reading, far and wide, in Canadian sociology that we might otherwise have postponed. Also, we were pleased to prepare this volume because instructors had requested it. Given the many differences between this book and our earlier one, the new reader has been given a name of its own — *Everyday Life: A Reader*.

In preparing this book, we have made use of two years of informal feedback on the first edition, and much preliminary thinking about the changes we might make for instructors requesting a shorter volume. The result is quite a different book. The first edition was a representative and systematic portrayal of trends in studies in Canadian sociology. The new edition gives greater emphasis to recent, not classic, writing and is much more fast-paced reading, intended for introductory sociology students. As it turned out, different instructors using the first volume were divided in reporting that they preferred a textbook just like that one *or* that they preferred a book like the present one. The difference of opinion was rooted to a great extent in whether the course was one or two semesters in length. To their credit, McGraw-Hill Ryerson decided to provide both books in their offerings.

We have maintained the emphasis on variety and quality from the original reader in this edition, but we have reduced the size of the volume significantly. Also, we have set aside articles that introductory instructors found difficult for their first-year students, and introduced new topics and articles that deserve wider attention among these undergraduate students. Accordingly, the new reader is down to 27 articles from 71 in the other edition. And, among these articles in *Everyday Life* are many selections or excerpts not included in the earlier book — over 40% new material.

This new reader continues to cover most of the topics included in the earlier one. Five sections (on "social interaction and social organization," "political and economic organization," "education and the schools," "work and occupations," and "community and region") have been eliminated. However, we believe this new arrangement best reflects the use many instructors have been making of the earlier reader.

Each section of the book begins with a brief introduction intended to link that section with those that precede and follow it, and to integrate the excerpts contained in the section. As before, all the articles are closely edited for brevity and clarity. Also, a biographical sketch of the author(s) still precedes each piece.

For those who will acquire an appetite for further fare in Canadian sociology from reading the material in this volume, the biographical sketches show good places to begin additional reading. The same is true of the other biographical sketches and articles provided in *Readings in Sociology*.

We trust readers of *Everyday Life* will find this book a refreshing and exciting introduction to Canadian sociology. We hope you will receive as much enjoyment and yield from it as we did in putting it together.

Acknowledgements

We want to express our appreciation to several people who provided valuable assistance with this volume. First level thanks must go, of course, to the authors of the selections in this book — for producing the material, permitting its inclusion in this book, allowing our abridgement of their work (in many instances), and providing, on short notice, brief biographical sketches to accompany their contributions. Second, Al Wain, a freelance editor, skillfully shortened many of the selections to allow more items and authors to be included and to make for fast-paced reading. Third, Denise Baker and Lorraine Albrecht, at the University of Waterloo, gave much help with correspondence and manuscript preparation. Fourth, teaching colleagues at various universities and McGraw-Hill Ryerson's reviewers gave helpful suggestions for the contents of this volume. Fifth, Catherine O'Toole and Norma Christensen at McGraw-Hill Ryerson gave us strong support. Catherine O'Toole saw the merit of this brief edition and pressed for its preparation. Norma Christensen handled, with dispatch and grace, the onerous tasks of all correspondence around permissions requests.

As was the case with our earlier volume, *Readings in Sociology* with McGraw-Hill Ryerson, the present project proved to be very difficult because of the many excellent pieces of work and many exceptional scholars who could not be included. The length requirements for this volume were very reasonable on the grounds of manageable reading, but they made for hard constraints on the number of selections that could be offered. Indeed even the two books, this one and *Readings in Sociology*, do not have enough space to allow us to capture the full richness of current Canadian sociology.

We again applaud this wealth of Canadian research. We dedicate this volume to our colleagues in Canadian sociology who have given us so many avenues of understanding everyday social life in Canada.

EVERYDAY LIFE

a   reader

What Is Sociology?

This section contains articles about the nature of sociology and, in this way, sets the stage for the rest of the book. In this introduction, we define and describe sociology. The first article in the section distinguishes between sociology and other social sciences; while the second article discusses three of sociology's classic concerns.

Sociology is the science that produces theories about social relations. To sociologists, the word "science" means much the same as it does to physicists or biologists. Science makes and tests theories about the real world. A science of social relations is more complex than other sciences, because people are more complicated than atoms and amoebae. Still, all sciences have the same goals.

For sociologists, just as for physicists, theories are tentative explanations of the world we can see and measure. We base predictions of future events on such theories. Then, we judge each theory against competing theories to see how well they predict the future. We also use theories to explain social life in the present and the past. A science tests its theories over and over to improve and even discard them in favour of better ones.

Social relations are relationships between people that are somehow binding. The subject matter of sociology is the social bond that connects individuals in groups and societies. In turn, *societies* are collections of social relations. A society includes all the understandings (for example, values and rules) that its members share, all the bonds that are based on these understandings, and all the organizations (from friendships and families up through businesses and governments) that grow out of these bonds.

Drawing the boundaries of a society is no easy matter. Many social relationships cross international borders, like the one between Canada and the United States. Some researchers even wonder whether Canada and the United States, which are distinct nation-states, are really distinct societies. For similar reasons, others wonder whether the two are distinct economies. Trade and the flows of capital and migrants tie these two countries together. Yet the idea of a "Canadian society" still has value. It helps us understand why life is different in Halifax and Boston, Toronto and Buffalo, Winnipeg and Minneapolis, Vancouver and Seattle.

Sociological theories have certain common characteristics. Good theories are tentative, thorough, and economical. They are tentative because disproof is always a possibility: indeed, scientists seek to disprove, not prove, theories. They are thorough because scientists want to explain as much of reality as they can with a single theory. Yet they are also economical — other things being equal, we seek to explain as much as we can with as few assumptions as possible.

Theories should also be true or "valid," as far as we can tell. Like other humans, sociologists can be blind to what is true and false. Personal interests and biases may mislead them. Agreed-upon methods of discovering, testing, and communicating their findings reduce the risk of error due to such bias.

Sociological theories should not be circular or true-by-definition. A theory that "satisfied workers are happy with their jobs" is circular if all that we mean by "satisfied" is "happy with their jobs." A circular theory, though true, has no value to science because it can never be proved false and adds nothing to our stock of knowledge.

We can test a theory that is *not* circular for validity. Scientists, including sociologists, never prove a theory absolutely right; they only prove contending theories less right. We consider the theory that best survives many attempts at disproof, and shows itself most thorough and economical, to be the most valid, *for the time being*.

All sociological theories, like all of science's theories, must be tested against the world we can observe and measure. Some of Einstein's theories in physics had to wait for decades until sensitive enough equipment could test their mathematically derived predictions. Likewise, sociological theories may not be immediately testable. Some, like Marx's (for example, 1967) theories about the coming of communism to industrial societies, predict future events. Marxists might argue that conclusive data are not available yet: we cannot judge yet whether these theories are valid. Others might say that Marx's theories have been judged and found wanting.

Whatever the difficulties, a sociologist must always seek validation for his/her theories. Every theorist must sooner or later appeal to the evidence that our senses offer for support. Reason must prevail over intuition, emotion, and good intention. None but the court of empirical evidence will decide a theory's fate in the long run.

Two other aspects of sociological theories need mentioning. First, sociological theories should help us understand *everyday life*. Historically, sociologists have always paid special attention to the public problems of their times. Much work has been done by "middle range" researchers moving back and forth between theory and an active concern with current events.

We call sociology that directly influences the way some portion of society functions *applied sociology*. Many North American universities now teach applied sociology, because the application of sociological knowledge plays an ever larger part in sociologists' professional work. Every year more graduate sociologists take jobs outside universities and apply their knowledge to decision-making in government and corporate organizations and interest groups.

Sociologists apply their knowledge in a wide variety of ways. For example, political polling — one type of applied sociology — analyzes the popular support for particular candidates or policies. By understanding the results of polls, political parties can modify their positions and the way they present these positions to the public.

Another type of applied sociology — market research — analyzes consumer preferences and public perceptions of different products. With such information, manufacturers and advertisers decide which new products to introduce. They learn how to change old products, and how to focus their advertising to maximize sales.

Sociologists also carry out a wide variety of *policy research*. Policy research aims at determining the need for new policies and likely public reactions to these policies. One kind of policy research, social impact assessment, tries to anticipate the ways a policy will change society if put into practice. Another type of applied sociology, evaluation research, assesses whether a new policy is achieving what policy-makers hoped it would.

The main activity of sociologists is not knowledge application, however; it is theory-making. Without good theory, applied sociology can never achieve the results we desire. To this end, sociological theory must give us back more than we already know. By connecting previously unconnected facts, a good theory yields insights no one anticipated. It leads us *beyond* the obvious to the unexpected, the paradoxical and contradictory. The more sociology succeeds in making non-obvious predictions, the more mature a science sociology has become.

The essence of sociology is its "classical tradition." In his paper in this section, Robert Brym shows that the classic concerns that motivated sociology's founding figures include questions like: (1) "What is the relationship between the individual and society?" (2) "Are the most important determinants of social behaviour cultural or economic?" and (3) "What are the bases of social inequality?" Like all good questions, these ones allow many answers. Over the course of time, sociologists from different schools of thought have answered the central questions of sociology in many ways. Yet, the classic questions emerge time and again, demanding new answers. Today, they remain as fresh and challenging as they were a century ago.

Sociology is not only the asking and answering of these classic questions: it is also what living people who call themselves "sociologists" do. In fact, the discipline has developed differently in different countries. In some places (as in the USA), sociology has been more influenced by social psychology; in others, by anthropology (as in Great Britain); and in other places still, by philosophy (as in Germany). In Canada, all of these disciplines have influenced the development of sociology.

As well, history and political economy have shaped the development of Canadian sociology. In English-speaking Canada, sociology's connection with history and political economy began with the work of political economist Harold Innis (see, for example, Innis, 1923; 1930; 1940) and his protégés, especially S.D. Clark (see, for example, Clark, 1962; 1966; 1976) at the University of Toronto. Yet other schools have drawn on other influences, At McGill University, Carl Dawson and Everett Hughes taught the "Chicago School's" ecological approach, which focused on the geographic dispersion and interaction of competing groups (see, for example, Hughes, 1943). This approach linked Canadian sociology with mainstream American work.

The British socialist tradition made itself felt in work by Leonard Marsh (see, for example, 1940) in the 1930s and 1940s. Later work by John Porter (see, for example 1965) in the 1950s-1970s set the enduring character of Carleton University's "school" of sociology. It set the groundwork for Marxist-oriented sociology as practised today by Wallace Clement, a student of John Porter's (see, for example, Clement, 1975; 1977), and many others.

Despite historical, national, and regional variation, sociology *is* distinguishable from the other social sciences (e.g., psychology, anthropology, political science, and economics); from the more speculative or deductive disciplines (e.g., philosophy); and the less systematic inductive fields (e.g., journalism and social work).

An article by Kenneth Westhues in this section helps us see the defining features by comparing sociology with other disciplines. Of course, fields of study making up the humanities and social sciences can never be entirely distinct. They all study human behaviour and must, therefore, often talk about the same things. Yet, as Westhues shows, they do this differently using (often) different language, rules of proof, and different kinds of data to support their arguments.

As well, the various disciplines have somewhat different purposes. Some pay more attention to theorizing, others to describing, prescribing, or even taking action. By comparison, sociology has always inclined towards theorizing about *social structure* with the help of data. ("Social structure" is the regular patterning of relations among individuals and groups.) This inclination is clear enough so that sociologists around the world can readily understand one another and make use of one another's findings. There is probably more similar thinking among the world's sociologists than there is between the sociologists and economists, or sociologists and psychologists, or sociologists and anthropologists, of any given country.

Nonetheless, social theorizing always reflects a particular time and place in history. Sociological theories must take appropriate notice of such influences as geography, economy, political struggle, and demographic change. Differences in sociological approach inevitably arise out of genuine social differences between Canada and the USA, for example.

As well, differences in sociological theorizing reflect differences in the outlook and background of the theorists. Much as we might wish social science to be free of subjectivity, our biases are likely to intrude nonetheless. For example, work by male researchers has tended to vary quite considerably from work by female researchers, in terms of the questions asked and hypotheses tested.

Is there a more general problem here? If gender biases intrude when the researchers belong to one sex (typically, male) rather than another, will racial biases intrude if most research is done by white people? And will the monopolization of research by college-educated middle class people cause class biases in the research as well?

These are very important questions. On the one hand, all research tells us something about the researcher — his or her biases, background and associations, for example. On the other hand, researchers have struggled with these questions for many decades and are still doing so. They have made some headway by being aware of the potential problem of bias and trying to guard against it. You will want to remain alert to possible researcher biases as you read the articles in this book.

References

Clark, S.D. *The Developing Canadian Community*. Toronto: University of Toronto Press, 1962.

_____. *The Suburban Society*. Toronto: University of Toronto Press, 1966.

——. *Canadian Society in Historical Perspective*. Toronto: McGraw-Hill Ryerson, 1976.

Clement, Wallace. *The Canadian Corporate Elite: Economic Power in Canada*. Toronto: McClelland and Stewart, 1975.

——. *Continental Corporate Elite: An Analysis of Economic Power*. Toronto: McClelland and Stewart, 1977.

Hughes, Everett C. *French Canada in Transition*. Chicago: University of Chicago Press, 1943.

Innis, Harold A. *A History of the Canadian Pacific Railway*. Toronto: University of Toronto Press, 1923.

——. *The Fur Trade in Canada: An Introduction to Canadian Economic History*. Toronto: Oxford University Press, 1930.

——. *The Cod Fisheries: The History of an International Economy*. New Haven, CT: Yale University Press, 1940.

Marsh, Leonard C. *Canadians In and Out of Work: A Survey of Economic Classes and their Relations to the Labour Market*. Toronto: Oxford University Press, 1940.

Marx, Karl. *Capital*. New York: International Publishers, 1967.

Porter, John. *The Vertical Mosaic*. Toronto: University of Toronto Press, 1965.

ONE

Sociology Compared to Other Fields

Kenneth Westhues

KENNETH WESTHUES, Professor of Sociology at the University of Water-loo, specializes in the sociology of religion, social movements, and sociological theory. His publications include *Society's Shadow: Studies in the Sociology of Countercultures* (1972); *Village in Crisis*, with Peter Sinclair (1974); *First Sociology* (1982); and "Defensiveness and social structure: The ideology of separate school trustees" (1983). Professor Westhues has served as Department Chairman at the University of Waterloo and was recently awarded the Distinguished Teacher Award there; he has also taught as a Visiting Professor at Fordham University and Memorial University of Newfoundland. He has served as associate editor of the *Canadian Journal of Sociology*, *Review of Religious Research*, and *Sociological Analysis*.

HOLISM

In universities that abound with disciplines we need to distinguish sociology from the rest. Five characteristics are relevant for this purpose, the first of which is sociology's goal of providing holistic social analyses. In the writings of nearly all the founders of the field there is an unmistakable attempt to understand social life as a whole. Marx, for instance, had no intention of writing simply about the economy. He stressed it only because for him it was the basis of political, religious, and all other dimensions of the whole, the society, which ever remained his fundamental concern. When Durkheim wrote about suicide, or Weber about bureaucracy, it was not as specialists in these areas but in order to shed light on the social order in general. An emphasis on the whole, an attempt to integrate knowledge about social life, is almost the hallmark of the discipline.

The lesson of the founders has not been lost on their descendants in the present day. Major contemporary sociologists like Peter Berger at Boston College, Amitai Etzioni at George Washington University, the late Talcott Parsons (1903–1979) at Harvard, or the late John Porter (1921–1979) at Carleton, among many others, have aspired to write holistic analyses of the societies confronting them. The sociology curriculum continues to be wide open, with almost no subject matter excluded in principle. A glance through a few university calendars reveals courses regularly taught in the sociology of art, bureaucracy, conflict, death, education, family, gangs, housing, ideology, Jews, knowledge, law, music, nationalism, occupations, politics, Quebec, religion, sport, technology, values, and youth. . . . Societies as integral wholes are sociology's subject matter, and from this vantage point, any part of the whole merits study.

Its holism distinguishes sociology from economics, political science, and some other fields. Economics limits itself to *that aspect of* a society which concerns the production, distribution, and consumption of goods and services. Political science focuses only on *that aspect* related to governmental institutions and the structure of power. The various "studies" — religious, black, leisure, family, and so on — similarly restrict themselves to a particular part or institution of the societal whole. One need only look at typical curricula in these disciplines to see how much more narrowly than sociology they define their aims. One should also note the anger of economists, for example, when they observe in the sociology syllabus something called "The Sociology of the Economy." Their anger is a price sociologists pay for trying to understand how the whole social enterprise fits together.

In actuality, of course, not all sociologists use their study of particular scenes in the drama of social life to understand the drama in its entirety. Encouraged by the overspecialized organization of the discipline, many researchers look no farther than their specific areas of study, whether drug use or divorce, prostitutes or priests. Thus is created the regrettable misconception that economics and political science study the important aspects of social life, sociology the more piddling ones. But fortunately the overspecialized sociologists are balanced out by those economists and political scientists who exceed the nominal limits of their disciplines, use them instead as windows on the whole, and attempt to write holistic works of social analysis. Economists like John Kenneth Galbraith, Kenneth Boulding, Milton Friedman, or Paul Sweezy come to mind; so do political scientists like C.B. Macpherson, Ralph Miliband, or the late Hannah Arendt. Among the best practitioners, the boundaries separating these latter disciplines from sociology break completely down. Among the rest, however, and in the organization of these disciplines in North America, the distinction between holism and specificity is apt.

THEORY BUILDING

A second characteristic of sociology is its emphasis on interpretation and theory building. Thus is sociology distinguished from journalism and history, both of which share with the first an attentive scrutiny of the events in social life. In the main, journalists chronicle the present, and historians the past. In both cases the emphasis is on accuracy of factual detail, and this is a special strength of both disciplines. There is in journalism an implicit concept of a certain universe of newsworthy events, and reporters are dispatched to city halls, hockey arenas, scenes of crime, and so on for the purpose of "covering" as many such events as possible. For historians the events of the past constitute a comparable universe. One professor is said to "cover" those of the Renaissance period, another those of pre-Civil War America, and so on. Neither journalists nor historians customarily feel obliged, however, to separate rigorously the events of importance from those of little consequence. Doing so is not a high priority for them, nor is tying events together with theoretical glue. Whether for the past or present their goal is to provide, as *The New York Times* puts it, "all the news that's fit to print."

It is a poor sociologist who does not devour newspapers and history books. The facts they provide, though never indisputable and always seen through their authors' mirrors, are the necessary beginnings of good sociology. Journalists and historians provide in a sense the pieces for the puzzle sociologists would solve. Sociology must assume acquaintance with events, for its purpose is to separate the significant from the trivial ones and then to weave the first kind together into a picture of how and why things happen in social life. The goal of sociology is not to chronicle but to interpret, not to record but to analyze, not to describe but to explain. Inevitably the pursuit of this goal entails disregard for some well-documented facts. Historians often complain that sociologists overgeneralize and fail to make room for exceptions. They voice the same complaint against members of their own discipline, like Oswald Spengler or R.H. Tawney, who became more interested in analyzing history than in chronicling it. Without doubt the world needs both chroniclers and analysts, but sociology fits better in the latter category.

INTELLECTUAL PRIMACY

A third and critical quality of sociology is that its purpose is knowledge, not action. This is not to say that sociology is irrelevant to action, only that it remains distinct from it. It is one thing to come up with ideas about the structure of a society, ideas even which imply that something should be done, and quite another

actually to set about doing it. The former is the task of sociologists and other social scientists, the latter that of social workers, legislators, lawyers, planners, reformers, community organizers, and anyone else who takes up the challenge of acting upon the status quo. If sociologists distill history into theories, people in the active professions distill theories into plans of action and into action itself. An undergraduate major in sociology is a common route to professional schools of social work, law, and planning, but the business of making the ideas that make change is nonetheless distinct from making change directly.

A sociologist is or ought to be an intellectual, one who reflects on the experience of contemporary life and tries to put into words its enduring regularities. A certain detachment from immediate social concerns is for this reason a necessary part of the sociologist's work. In order to perform well the task of the intellectual, he or she stands a little to one side of the class structure and the arena of conflicting interests in the society at large. The more sociologists can emancipate themselves from indebtedness to particular class and ethnic interests, including those of their personal backgrounds, the better their work becomes. Contrariwise, sociologists who do their work in the interests of particular groups cannot thereby fulfill the mission of their discipline. Hired-hand intellectuals, even those engaged by the underprivileged, are not intellectuals at all.

Standing apart is not, of course, the same as running away. The sociologist need not act in order to be concerned with action. Indeed, the sociologist has to be concerned because even in our time people suffer. All kinds of them. Dependent mothers whose husbands have disappeared but whose children still need to eat. People laid off from their jobs and left wondering whether they are good for anything. Adolescents who doubt that the world or even their own parents need them. People made to feel ashamed of their language or the color of their skin. Old people vegetating on pensions in the deathly, parasitic quiet of old-age homes and retirement villages. Even prosperous people trapped in the suburban quest for consumer goods, acquiring more but enjoying it less. It is the obligation of the sociologist to speak to them all with compassion and with an analysis that will help them regain control over their lives. In meeting this obligation, sociologists can be sure of opposition from the advantaged classes, those who fear to lose their advantage if history is diverted from its present path. If there were no such opposition, sociologists would surely be failing in their intellectual task.

SENSE EVIDENCE

A fourth characteristic of the discipline is its attempt to ground ideas in the evidence that meets human eyes and ears, in the social world as perceived by bodily senses, in the data given by experience. . . .

Sociology's reliance on the evidence of the senses, what is sometimes called the empirical method of research, distinguishes this discipline also from certain kinds of philosophy. Jean-Jacques Rousseau (1712–1778), one of the greatest French philosophers, wrote at the start of his *Discourse on the Origin and the Foundation of Inequality Among Mankind*, "Let us begin, therefore, by laying aside facts, for they do not affect the question."[1] Rousseau was actually more respectful of facts than this line

suggests, but some contemporary philosophers show great disdain for the kind of sense evidence sociologists closely attend to. They seek to create logically coherent systems of ideas, but systems so abstract as to be irrelevant to happenings in everyday life. At many universities one can take a perfectly secular course on ethics, for example, and learn a great deal about how people ought to behave, but scarcely even look at how they actually are behaving. It is a kind of learning that tends to baffle sociologists, except for its value as an exercise in mental discipline. Other philosophers define their goal differently and try to create sets of ideas which are at once logically consistent and relevant to practical affairs. The ties of their work to sociology are quite close.

AN EXPLICITLY SOCIAL FOCUS

To state clearly the last of the five attributes of sociology relevant here, I should recall an analogy of variously distorted mirrors. Those of religion and philosophy we can set to one side since they lack the particular warp of evidential methods. The mirrors of economics and political science we can set to another side, since they have the empirical warp but are not, as it were, full-strength. To still another side should be placed those of history and journalism, since they reflect the empirical world but in the manner of a set of dots in a child's colouring book — the dots have still to be connected before a picture of something emerges. Social work and planning we shall not count as mirrors, since they are plans of action abstracted from various mirrors. At last we are left with the full-length, interpretive mirrors bent by the evidence of the senses. In contemporary universities only two such mirrors are in common use. Sociology is one, psychology the other. Distinction between them is important because for all their closeness they are immensely far apart. . . .

When a psychologist looks at people, what he or she sees in the mirror of that discipline is so many individual persons. A group or society appears only as a collection of these individuals and can be understood according to the kinds of personalities they have. Psychologists assess individual personality through a vast array of tests, measuring intelligence, aptitude, vocational interest, self-concept, motivation, moral development, creativity, insight, adjustment, leadership, machiavellianism, impulsiveness, authoritarianism, and hundreds of other qualities they have conceptualized. Indeed, I think psychology has more tests than sociology has specialities. Some psychologists reject testing, however, preferring simply to record individuals' behaviour in laboratory settings or to interview them one by one. In any case an understanding of the regularities in how individuals act remains the basic goal of the discipline. It is as if the psychologist's mirror reveals the human person as what is fundamentally real; people may join together in groups but the individual always comes first.

In sociology it is exactly the other way around. For us the group is prior. The reality displayed in our mirror is always some kind of social system, whether a dyad (two-person group) of lovers, a family, a nation, or at the most general level the human community. In a sense sociology does not focus on individuals at all, but only on the roles they play in groups. We sociologists spend little time testing personalities. When confronted with an individual our first inclination is to ask which groups the person belongs to: which class, ethnic group, sex, occupation, religion, marital status, age category, income category, civic associations, community of residence, place of origin, and so on. We in sociology approach the individual through the mediation of the roles he or she plays in groups. Qualities of personality, insofar as they are independent of social order, escape our attention. For me at least there are no such qualities, only those many which derive from participation in groups and those few which will leave their mark on social life in the future.

The difference between psychological and sociological perspectives appears most clearly in their practical applications.[2] For what the detached scholar conceptualizes as the object of analysis, the corresponding applied practitioner regards as the object of change. Applied psychologists therefore use knowledge about individuals to help individuals change. The market for their services is large. Clinical psychologists try to help their clients overcome excessive shyness, aggressive tendencies, anxiety, dependency, depression, or other disorders of personality. Personnel psychologists design employee training programs and try to boost workers' motivation and morale. Counseling psychologists help individuals cope with the transition from youth to adulthood and later from adulthood to old age. In all these and many other applications of the academic discipline, the problem is located in the individual and the solution requires some kind of individual transformation. Success is measured by the degree to which the client becomes able to adapt to life in the society at hand.

In the eyes of an applied sociologist it is not the individual who needs to change. The problem inheres in the structure of social life and only social change can solve it. The shift in perspective has occurred in the life of many social activists who once considered that something must be wrong with *them* and who later concluded otherwise. Allen Ginsberg, for instance, a poet-hero of the 1960s youth movement, sought psychological counseling in his youth, trying to help himself adapt to the world around him. The therapy did not work and Ginsberg shifted the blame angrily to his society: "I saw the best minds of my generation destroyed by madness, starving hysterical naked."[3] Betty Friedan, the noted American leader of the women's movement, recalls a similar shift in perspective in her life. Eventually she concluded that her frustration in the conventional women's role called not for better coping on her part but for change in the social role assigned to women.

As might be expected, the job market for applied psychologists is much larger than for those who would apply sociological knowledge. The latter are more interesting, however, and the impact of their work lasts longer than a lifetime. People educated in sociology, for instance, were well represented in the socialist and separatist government which gained power in Quebec in the elections of 1976. David Barrett, the reform-minded premier of British Columbia from 1972 to 1975, had been trained as an applied sociologist. "This job is just an extension of social work," he told a reporter. "Social workers have more business in politics than lawyers do."[4] It bears mention also that two leftist contenders from the American presidency in recent times, former senators George McGovern and Eugene McCarthy, both have backgrounds in sociology. The application of sociology, almost invariably involves political action, because it is not individuals but the society itself which is

to be acted upon. Those who use sociology in a practical way do not ask whether people are coping with their milieu but whether their milieu is bringing out the best in them.

The contrast between psychology and sociology is nowhere more apparent than in the field of social work, which draws on both perspectives in devising concrete programs for the alleviation of human suffering. Not surprisingly, both as students and as practitioners, social workers tend to be divided into two camps. The majority adopt a psychological perspective and become caseworkers; each person or family is a "case," to be interviewed, counseled, and helped to adjust to the conditions of contemporary life. A minority of social workers (like Mr. Barrett) adopt instead a more sociological perspective, avoid the casework routine, and apply themselves to community organizing, social policy formulation, and the design of preventive social programs. Their goal is to modify the conditions of contemporary life in such a way that coping comes naturally. Between them and the caseworkers or clinicians there is an inevitable tension, but one which must be expected in light of the divergent theoretical postures with which they approach the task of helping people.

Like any distinction, of course, that between psychology and sociology admits of exceptions. Especially is this so in the United States, where popular culture is on the side of psychology, enshrining individualism as a national value. As a result there is an individualistic bent to sociology in the United States, where the discipline's ties to psychology are much closer than elsewhere in the world. An important movement in American sociology, led by George Homans at Harvard University, has even built a conception of society on the principles of behaviorist psychology. But this movement is clearly aberrant in the context of sociology more generally. It is balanced, moreover, by a contrary trend in social psychology toward the adoption of a more sociological outlook. Albert Pepitone, a psychologist at the University of Pennsylvania, has criticized his discipline sharply. In a 1976 article in the *Journal of Personality and Social Psychology*, he argued that "the social behaviour we observe in the real world and laboratory ... is normative, in being more characteristic of definable groups, organizations, and other socio-cultural collectives than of individuals observed at random."[5] Pepitone's point is as novel in psychology as Homan's writings are in sociology; each documents in a backhanded way the distinctive perspective of his discipline.

SUMMARY

A fear sometimes voiced in sociology is that the progressive demise of positivism has left the discipline too much up in the air, too nebulously defined, without coherence or a sense of unified purpose. But the five characteristics reviewed above show that the field is indeed distinctive and coherent, even as it is actually practiced today. For sociologists after all differ from other thinkers by their unique combination of five qualities: an integration of economic, political, and other social insights; emphasis on theory; commitment to the intellectual life; reliance on sense evidence; and focus on groups rather than individuals. Sociology can therefore be defined in summary as the disciplined, intellectual quest for holistic, empirical interpretations of the structure of social life. . . .

Notes

[1] Jean-Jacques Rousseau, *The Social Contract and Discourse on the Origin and Foundation of Inequality Among Mankind*, (New York: Pocketbooks, 1967), p. 177.

[2] For a splendid and readable case study of this difference see Joseph Helfgot, "Professional Reform Organizations and the Symbolic Representation of the Poor," *American Sociological Review* 39: 475–91, (1974).

[3] Allen Ginsberg, *Howl*, Part 1, line 1, *Howl and Other Poems*, (San Francisco, California: City Lights, 1956.)

[4] David Barrett, quoted in *Colombo's Canadian Quotations* (Edmonton: Hurtig, 1974), p. 36.

[5] Albert Pepitone, "Toward a Normative and Comparative Bio-Cultural Social Psychology," *Journal of Personality and Social Psychology*, 34: 641–53 (1976).

TWO

Foundations of Sociological Theory

Robert J. Brym

ROBERT J. BRYM is Professor of Sociology and an Associate of the Centre for Russian and East European Studies at the University of Toronto. He has written widely on Canadian and Soviet societies. His latest books are *From Culture to Power: The Sociology of English Canada* (1989, with Bonnie Fox), *The Capitalist Class: An International Study* (1989, with Tom Bottomore) and *The Social Condition of Humanity*, Canadian edition (1991, with Irving M. Zeitlin). He is former Sociology Editor of the *Canadian Review of Sociology and Anthropology* and is now Editor of Sage Studies in International Sociology.

INTRODUCTION

Sociology will inevitably appear a confusing enterprise to students just beginning to study it. Sociologists occupy themselves with problems that also concern political scientists, economists, psychologists, and social workers, urban planners, psychiatrists and lawyers. In what sense, then, is sociology distinct from these other disciplines?

The answer has more to do with the unique *approach* of sociologists to their subject matter than with the nature of the subject matter itself. While many kinds of scholars are interested in, say, crime, economic development, elections and mental disorders, sociologists ask relatively distinct questions about these and other social issues.

I shall examine three of the main questions that have animated the discipline since its origins in the nineteenth century: (1) What is the relationship between the individual and society? (2) Are the most important determinants of social behaviour cultural or economic? (3) What are the bases of social inequality?

The debates surrounding these questions are recurrent. It is the tenacity and longevity of these disputes that permits us to characterize them as key issues in sociology. But the enduring character of these disputes may also be a source of some frustration to the introductory student. It may appear that nothing ever gets resolved in sociology. However, careful study of the discipline should demonstrate that sociological knowledge is, to some degree, cumulative. In other words, although sociologists ask much the same questions today as they did a century ago, their answers are now much more precise, complex and enlightening than they were then; the classic questions of sociology continue to engage lively minds in a debate that gets more and more sophisticated over time.

14

Let us begin by examining Emile Durkheim's *Suicide*, which, nearly a century ago, set out a highly controversial idea about the individual's relationship to society.

INDIVIDUAL AND SOCIETY

a. Durkheim on "Social Facts" and Suicide

Usually we are inclined to think of any act — a suicide, a marriage, a revolution, the achievement of extraordinary economic success in life — as the outcome of an individual's (or many individuals') motives. Features of society are, in turn, usually viewed as the result of many individual passions and decisions. Durkheim, however, turned this conventional wisdom on its head. He argued that individual passions and decisions are the result of certain features of society, that the social whole is greater than the sum of its individual parts. And, according to Durkheim, the study of how social patterns influence individual behaviour is what sociology is all about (Durkheim, 1966 [1895]).

Consider, for example, the act of suicide. For two reasons, no act appears to be more personal than the taking of one's own life. First, common sense suggests that suicide is the outcome of some profound disorder in the mind of the *individual*. Second, suicide seems the most *anti-social* act imaginable: it negates — indeed, destroys — society, at least for one person.

Yet in 1897 Durkheim proposed the controversial idea that the causes of suicide are not at all personal. If suicide rates are high in one group of people and low in another, this is due, said Durkheim, to the operation of "social facts."

Before specifying what Durkheim meant by a social fact, let us briefly see how he disposed of psychological explanations of suicide.[1] For different groups, Durkheim examined the association between rates of suicide (the number of suicides among 100,000 people) and rates of psychological disorder (the number of cases of psychological disorder among 100,000 people). The notion that psychological disorder causes suicide is supported, Durkheim reasoned, only if suicide rates tend to be high where rates of psychological disorder are high, and if suicide rates tend to be low where rates of psychological disorder are low.

But Durkheim's examination of European government statistics, hospital records and other sources revealed nothing of the kind. For example, he discovered that: (1) There are slightly more women than men in insane asylums. But there are four male suicides for every female suicide. (2) Jews have the highest rate of psychological disorder among the major religious groups in France. But they also have the lowest suicide rate. (3) Psychological disorders occur most frequently when a person reaches maturity. But suicide rates increase steadily with age.

Clearly, suicide rates and rates of psychological disorder do not vary directly; in fact, they appear to vary inversely. Why, then, do males commit suicide more frequently than females, the aged more than the young, Jews less than Catholics, Catholics less than Protestants? Durkheim saw these regularities as results of variations in the degree of "social solidarity" in different categories of the population. Groups whose members interact more frequently and intensely are, accordingly, expected to exhibit lower suicide rates. For example, married adults are half as likely as unmarried adults to commit suicide, because marriage creates social ties that bind the individual to society. Where these ties are absent, suicide is more likely. Likewise, large families provide their members with more social ties than do small families; the suicide rate is thus lower in large families. In general, wrote Durkheim, "suicide varies with the degree of integration of the social groups of which the individual forms a part. . . . The more weakened the groups to which he[2] belongs, the less he depends on them, the more he consequently depends only on himself and recognizes no other rules of conduct than what are founded on his private interests," the greater the chance that an individual will take his or her own life (Durkheim, 1951 [1897]: p. 209).

b. The Phenomenological Response

Many contemporary sociologists continue to argue that the proper focus of the discipline is the study of social pressures that constrain or influence the minds of individuals. Today, using advanced statistical techniques, researchers can measure the independent and combined effects of many social "variables" on many types of behaviour. The choice of a marriage partner may, for example, seem to be a question of love. But even love is constrained by social facts: research reveals that a very large proportion of marriages join partners from the same ethnic groups and classes.

However, not all marriages take place within ethnic and class groupings. This, opponents of the Durkheimian position argue, points to an important flaw in the theory. They argue that Durkheim paints an altogether too mechanical and deterministic view of the individual in society, making it seem as if people behave like

billiard balls, knocked about on predetermined trajectories, unable to choose to alter their destinations. But, Durkheim's critics continue, we know from our everyday experience that this is not the case. People *do* make choices — often difficult ones — about what career to follow, what country to live in, whether and in what form they will adopt an established religion, whether to engage in heterosexual or homosexual relationships (or both), and so forth. Two people with similar social characteristics may react quite differently to similar social facts because, according to Durkheim's detractors, they may *interpret* the same social facts differently. In the opinion of such "phenomenological" sociologists, an adequate explanation of social phenomena requires that we understand the *subjective meanings* people attach to social facts and the ways in which people actively *create* these social facts.

In order to understand better the phenomenological school of thought let us return to the problem of suicide. If a police officer discovers a dead person at the wheel of a car which has run into a tree it may be very difficult to establish with any certainty whether the death was accidental or suicidal. Interviewing friends and relatives in order to find out the dead person's state of mind immediately before the crash may help rule out the possibility of suicide. But, as this example illustrates, understanding the intention or motive of the actor is critical to explaining or labelling a social action. Suicide, then, is not just an objective social fact, but an inferred, and therefore subjective, social fact. A state of mind must be interpreted — usually by a coroner — before the dead body becomes a suicide statistic (Douglas, 1967).

Because social stigma is attached to suicide, coroners are inclined to classify deaths as accidental whenever such an interpretation is at all plausible. Experts believe that, for this reason, official suicide rates are about one-third lower than actual suicide rates. The phenomenological study of social life reveals many such inconsistencies between objective and subjective reality. For instance, when increased crime rates among native Canadians are reported in the newspapers this may reflect more crimes being committed by native Canadians. But the phenomenological sociologist is unlikely to accept such reports at face value. The higher crime rate may result from a politically motivated change in the official definition of what constitutes a crime, or increased police surveillance in areas where native people reside. Here, inquiry into the subjective underside of the official picture may deepen our understanding of how society works.

Most modern sociologists think it makes more sense to combine the Durkheimian and phenomenological approaches. Thus, most sociologists analyze how men and women interpret, create and change their social existence — but within the limits imposed upon them by powerful social constraints. This synthetic approach is found in the work of Karl Marx and Max Weber, who, along with Durkheim, established the groundwork of modern sociology. It is to an examination of their work that we now turn.

STRUCTURE VERSUS CULTURE

a. Marx's Legacy

Both Marx and Weber stressed the importance of analyzing subjective social actions *and* objective social constraints (compare Marx, 1972 [1932]: p. 118 with Weber, 1947 [1922]: p. 103; see also Gerth and Mills, 1946: pp. 57–8). They also had compatible (though different) ideas about the *nature* of these constraints.

Marx, like Weber, recognized that the external determinants of behaviour consist of economic, political and cultural forces. Marx tended to assign overwhelming causal priority to the economic realm. Weber did not deny the primacy of economic arrangements; but he rounded out Marx's analysis by showing how the political and cultural facts of life can act as independent, important causes of many social phenomena.

In the middle of the nineteenth century Marx proposed a sweeping theory of the development of human societies. In this theory the engine of change is economic organization — more precisely, society's class structure and its technological base. In 1859 Marx succinctly put his argument as follows:

> At a certain stage of their development, the material forces of production in society come into conflict with the existing relations of production, or — what is but a legal expression for the same thing — with the property relations within which they had been at work before. From forms of development of the forces of production these relations turn into their fetters. Then occurs a period of social revolution. With the change of the economic foundation the entire immense superstructure is more or less rapidly transformed (Marx, 1904 [1859]: pp. 11–12).

How then does Marx's theory apply to the rise of capitalism? In European feudal society peasants tilled small plots of land which were owned not by the peasants themselves but by landlords. Peasants were legally bound to the land, obliged to give landlords a set proportion of their harvest and to continue working for their landlords under any circumstances. In turn, landlords were expected to protect peasants against poor economic conditions and marauders.

By the late fifteenth century, certain processes had been set in motion that eventually transformed feudal society into a modern capitalist system. Most important was the growth of exploration and trade, which increased the demand for many goods and services in commerce, navigation and industry. By the seventeenth and eighteenth centuries some urban dwellers — successful artisans and merchants — had accumulated sufficient capital to expand their production significantly. In order to maximize their profits these capitalists required an abundant supply of workers who could be hired in periods of high demand and fired without obligation during slack times. It was therefore necessary to induce and coerce indentured peasants from the soil and transform them into legally free workers who would work for wages (Marx and Engels, 1972 [1848]: pp. 336 ff.).

In Marx's view, the relations of production between wage labourers and capitalists at first facilitated rapid technological innovation and economic growth. Capitalists were keen to adopt new tools, machines and production techniques. These changes allowed capitalists to produce more efficiently, earn higher profits and drive their competitors out of business. Efficiency also required that workers be concentrated in larger and larger industrial establishments, that wages be kept as low as possible, and that as little as possible be invested in improving working conditions. Thus, according to Marx, workers and capitalists would stand face-to-face in factory and mine: a large and growing class of relatively impoverished workers opposing a small and shrinking class of increasingly wealthy owners.

Marx argued that in due course all workers would become aware of belonging to the same exploited class. This sense of "class consciousness" would, he felt, encourage the growth of working class organizations, such as trade unions and political parties. These organizations would be bent on overthrowing the capitalist system and establishing a classless society. According to Marx, this revolutionary change was bound to occur during one of the recurrent and worsening "crises of overproduction" that characterized the capitalist era. The productive capacity of the system would, Marx said, come to far outstrip the ability of the relatively impoverished workers to purchase goods and services. Thus, in order to sell goods and services, capitalists would be forced to lower their prices. Profits would then fall, the less efficient capitalists would go bankrupt and massive unemployment of workers would result — thus deepening the economic crisis still further. The capitalist class system had originally encouraged economic growth. Eventually the crises of overproduction it generated would hinder such growth. At that time the capitalist class system would be destroyed and replaced by socialism, Marx argued.

As this thumbnail sketch shows, beliefs, symbols and values — in short, culture — play a quite minor independent causal role in Marx's theory. Marx analyzed how, under some circumstances, ruling class ideology could form a legitimizing cement in society and how, under other circumstances, subordinate class consciousness could become an important force for change. But in his work it is always the material circumstances of existence that ultimately determine the role ideas play.

b. Weber on Capitalism and the World Religions

Weber, like Marx, was interested in explaining the rise of modern capitalism. And, like Marx, he was prepared to recognize the "fundamental importance of the economic factor" in his explanation (Weber, 1958 [1904–51]: p. 26). But Weber was also bent on demonstrating the one-sidesness of any *exclusively* economic interpretation. After all, the economic conditions Marx said were necessary for capitalist development existed in Catholic France during the reign of Louis XIV; but the wealth generated in France by international trade and commerce tended to be consumed by war and the luxurious lifestyle of the aristocracy rather than invested in the growth of capitalist enterprise. In Weber's view, what prompted vigorous capitalist development in non-Catholic Europe and North America was a combination of (1) propitious economic conditions such as those discussed by Marx and (2) the spread of certain moral values by the Protestant reformers of the sixteenth century and their followers in the seventeenth century.

For specifically *religious* reasons, followers of the Protestant theologian John Calvin stressed the need to engage in intense worldly activity, to demonstrate industry, punctuality and frugality in one's everyday life. In the view of men like John Wesley and Benjamin Franklin, religious doubts could be reduced, and a state of grace assured, if one worked diligently and lived ascetically. This idea was taken up by Puritanism, Methodism and other Protestant denominations; Weber called it the "Protestant work ethic" (Weber, 1958 [1904–5]: p. 183.

According to Weber, this ethic had wholly unexpected economic conse-quences: where it took root, *and* where economic conditions were favourable, early capitalist enterprise grew robustly. In other words, two *independent* developments — the Protestant work ethic (which derived from purely religious considerations) and the material conditions favouring capitalist growth (which derived from specifically economic circumstances) — interacted to invigorate capitalist development. Weber made his case even more persuasive by comparing Protestant Western Europe and North America with India and China. He concluded that the latter cases differed from the former in one decisive (but certainly not exclusive) respect: Indian and Chinese religions inhibited capitalist economic action. In contrast to ancient Judaism and later Christianity, Asiatic religions had strong otherworldly, magical and antirational components that were inimical to worldly success in competition and accumulation. As a result, capitalism developed very slowly in India and China (Zeitlin, 1987 [1968]: pp. 135–50.

Subsequent research has demonstrated that the association between the Protestant ethic and the strength of capitalist development is very much weaker than Weber thought (on Western Europe and the United States, see Samuelsson, 1961 [1957]; on Canada, see Brym, 1986: pp. 24–7). In some places, Catholicism has co-existed with vigorous capitalist growth and Protestantism with relative stagnation. Nonetheless, even if Weber was wrong about this particular case, his *general* view — that religious developments cannot be reduced to economic developments, and that religious ideas have economic consequences — are still widely regarded as brilliant and valid insights.

Just as some Marxist sociologists have adopted a strict economic determinism, others have misinterpreted Weber's ideas in a way that supports a sort of cultural determinism. But the plain fact is that Weber assigned about the same relative weight to economic and cultural forces as did Marx; and there is nothing in Marx's work that is incompatible with Weber's insights into the relative autonomy of religious developments. This aspect of the controversy between orthodox Marxists and Weberians may thus be as specious as the disagreement between rigid Durkheimians and phenomenologists.

THE BASES OF SOCIAL INEQUALITY

Thus far I have singled out areas of similarity or compatibility in the thought of Marx and Weber. However, in Weber's "long and intense debate with the ghost of Karl Marx" (Albert Salomon, quoted in Zeitlin, 1987 [1968]: p. xi), there also emerged some ideas that are incompatible with those of Marx. This is especially obvious in Weber's work on social inequality.

Marx regarded ownership or non-ownership of property as the fundamental basis of inequality in capitalist society. In his view, there are two main classes under capitalism. Members of the *capitalist* class, or *bourgeoisie*, own but do not work means of production. Members of the *working* class, or *proletariat*, work but do not own means of production. In addition, Marx discussed some minor classes that are vestiges of pre-capitalist times. Most important, members of the *petite bourgeoisie* own and work means of production (e.g., farmers, owners of small family businesses). Marx also analyzed various divisions within the major classes. These class segments were distinguished from one another by their sources of income (e.g., financial and industrial capitalists) or skill level (e.g., skilled and unskilled manual workers).

In defining classes in this way, Marx was *not* trying to account for gradations of rank in society. Instead, he sought to explain massive historical change. The major classes, in his view, were potentially self-conscious groups engaged in conflict that would eventually result in societal transformation.

Weber agreed that " 'property' and 'lack of property' are . . . the basic categories of all class situations" (Weber, 1946 [1922]: p. 182). But his analysis of inequality differed from Marx's in three main ways. First, he was profoundly skeptical about Marx's interpretation of historical development. As a result, he stressed that members of classes do not necessarily become class-conscious and act in concert. Second, Weber argued that property relations are just one aspect of a more general "market situation" that determines class position. For example, expertise acquired through formal education is a scarce commodity on the labour market. Such expertise increases one's advantage or "life-changes" and is therefore an important factor structuring the class system. On this basis, and in addition to the capitalist and manual working classes, Weber distinguished large and growing classes of technical/managerial personnel and white collar workers who perform routine tasks.

Third, Weber was less concerned than Marx with the sources of conflict between discrete classes and more concerned than Marx with the bases of complex social hierarchies. For this reason he showed that the bases of social inequality are not exclusively economic.

One non-economic source of inequality is the way honour (or esteem or prestige) is distributed in society. Weber referred to groups distinguished from one another in terms of prestige as *status groups*. For example, line of descent (including ethnic origin) may account for the level of esteem in which a status group is held, and esteem affects the life-chances of status group members. A second non-economic source of inequality derives from the formation of political parties. A party, in Weber's definition, is an association that seeks to gain control over an organization — ranging all the way from, say, a sports club to a state — for purposes of implementing specific policies. Parties may recruit members from specific classes or status groups, or both. As such, and to the degree they achieve organizational control, parties bestow more advantages on their supporters than on non-supporters.

If parties and status groups are independent bases of social inequality, then, according to Weber, they are not wholly independent, especially in capitalist societies. There is an association between status group and party membership, on the one hand, and class position on the other. The structure of class inequality helps shape status group and party membership; in fact, "today the class situation is by far the predominant factor" (Weber, 1946 [1922]: p. 190).[3]

Much of modern sociology has been devoted to exploring the ramifications of Weber's refinement of Marx's stratification model. What are the economic determinants of class that do not derive from ownership versus non-ownership of property? How do the concentration of ethnic and other status groups in particular class locations reinforce status group cohesion? How do ethnic and other forms of status group identification serve to reinforce patterns of inequality? To what degree do classes serve as recruitment bases for political parties? To what degree do different types of political parties enact policies that redistribute income? These are among the most popular questions asked by modern sociologists, and they are all indebted to Weber's elaboration of the Marxian schema.

Recent years have also witnessed an important addition to the stratification model. It is now generally acknowledged that *gender* is a basis of social inequality quite on a par with status groups, parties and classes. Thus, in Canada and elsewhere, gender is as important a determinant of annual income as class (Ornstein, 1983), because women in the paid labour force tend to be segregated in low-pay, low-prestige jobs (Fox and Fox, 1986). Even if one matches a group of Canadian men and a group of Canadian women in terms of education, occupation, amount of time worked each year, and years of job experience, one discovers that the women earn only 63 per cent of what the men earn (Goyder, 1981: p. 328). Meanwhile, the great bulk of household labour continues to be performed by women, even if both spouses work; one study conducted in Vancouver found that, when their wives entered the paid labour force, husbands did on average only one hour more housework per week (Meissner *et al.*, 1975).

Classical theories teach us little about the causes of such gender inequality. That is, while Marx and Weber may have been able to account more or less well for the expansion and contraction of particular locations in the stratification system, they "give no clues about why *women* are subordinate to *men* inside and outside the family and why it is not the other way around" (Hartmann, 1984 [1978]: p. 174).

Over the past fifteen years or so, biological, cultural and structural theories of gender inequality have been proposed. Accumulated research seems to indicate that while biological factors — especially women's childbearing function — may have encouraged some division of labour between the sexes in primitive societies, there is no biological reason why male and female jobs should have been rewarded differently, let alone why they continue to be rewarded differently today. Cultural theories, which locate the causes of gender inequality in the way people learn established practices, cannot account either for the origins of gender inequality or the sources of variation in such inequality. Explanations that root gender inequality in social structure appear more promising. While the subordination of women is evident in virtually every known society, it takes on different forms and degrees in different times and places. Unravelling the relationship between social structure, on the one hand, and the form and degree of gender inequality, on the other, is a complex task which lies at the cutting edge of contemporary research on social inequality (see, for example, Coontz and Henderson, 1986).

CONCLUSION

In this brief essay I have set out three questions that lie at the foundations of classical sociology. I have emphasized that the significance of these questions derives from their proven ability to continue provoking the sociological imagination. The remainder of this book demonstrates the soundness of my assertion. As will be seen, the value of many of the readings in this volume derives in part from their indebtedness to the first practitioners of the discipline.

Notes

I would like to thank Jim Curtis, Jim Richardson and Lorne Tepperman for helpful comments on a draft of this article.

[1] Durkheim actually analyzed several types of suicide and disposed of several types of explanations. However, strict space limitations preclude a full discussion of these.

[2] For the most part, classical sociology (as well as history, political science, economics, and so forth) virtually ignored the existence of women in society. This was reflected not only in the use of sexist language, but in major oversights and imbalances in sociological theorizing, as will be illustrated later in this essay.

[3] Unfortunately, many modern sociologists, particularly in the United States, have trivialized Weber — and rendered him much more "anti-Marxist" than he in fact was by exaggerating the independence of the various bases of inequality, unnecessarily multiplying the number of bases, regarding inequality as a continuous ranking of statistical categories, and highlighting the subjective evaluation of prestige as the major basis of inequality. For a critique of these tendencies, see (Parkin, 1972 [1971]: esp. pp. 13–47).

References

Brym, Robert J. "Anglo-Canadian Sociology," *Current Sociology*, Vol. 34, No. 1 (pp. 1–152), 1986.

Coontz, Stephanie and Henderson, Peta, eds. *Women's Work, Men's Property: The Origins of Gender and Class*, S. Coontz and P. Henderson, eds. London: Verso, 1986.

Douglas, John D. *The Social Meaning of Suicide*. Princeton: Princeton University Press, 1967.

Durkheim, Emile. *The Rules of the Sociological Method*, 8th edn., G. Catlin, ed., S. Solovay and J. Mueller, trans. New York: The Free Press, 1966 (1895).

Durkheim, Emile. *Suicide: A Study in Sociology*, G. Simpson, ed., J. Spaulding and G. Simpson, trans. New York: The Free Press, 1951 (1897).

Fox, Bonnie J. and Fox, John. "Women in the labour market, 1931–81: exclusion and competition," *Canadian Review of Sociology and Anthropology*, Vol. 23 (pp. 1–21), 1986.

Gerth, H.H. and Mills, C. Wright. "The Man and his work", in *From Max Weber: Essays in Sociology*, H. Gerth and C. Mills, eds. and trans., pp. 1–74. New York: Oxford University Press, 1946.

Goffman, Erving. *The Presentation of Self in Everyday Life*. Garden City, N.Y.: Anchor, 1959.

Goyder, John C. "Income differences between the sexes: findings from a national Canadian survey," *Canadian Review of Sociology and Anthropology* Vol. 18 (pp. 321–42), 1981.

Hartmann, Heidi I. (1984 [1978]) "The unhappy marriage of Marxism and feminism: towards a more progressive union," in *Feminist Frameworks: Alternative Theoretical Accounts of the Relations between Women and Men*, 2nd edn. edited by A. Jaggar and P. Rothenberg, pp. 172–189. New York: McGraw-Hill, 1984 (1978).

Marx, Karl. *A Contribution to the Critique of Political Economy*, N. Stone, trans. Chicago: Charles H. Kerr, 1904 (1859).

Marx, Karl. "The German ideology: part I," in *The Marx-Engels Reader*, R. Tucker, ed., pp. 110–64. New York: Praeger, 1972 (1932).

Marx, Karl and Engels, Friedrich. "Manifesto of the Communist Party," in *The Marx-Engels Reader*, R. Tucker, ed., pp. 331–62. New York: Praeger, 1972 (1848).

Meissner, Martin *et al.* "No exit for wives: sexual division of labour and the culmination of household demands," *Canadian Review of Sociology and Anthropology* Vol. 12 (pp. 424–39), 1975.

Ornstein, Michael D. "Class, gender and job income in Canada," *Research in Social Stratification and Mobility*, Vol. 2 (pp. 41–75), 1983.

Parkin, Frank. *Class Inequality and Political Order: Social Stratification in Capitalist and Communist Societies*. London: Paladin, 1972 (1971).

Samuelsson, Kurt. *Religion and Economic Action*, E. French, trans. Stockholm: Scandinavian University Books, 1961 (1957).

Weber, Max. "Class, status, party," in *From Max Weber: Essays in Sociology*, H. Gerth and C. Mills, eds. and trans., pp. 180–95. New York: Oxford University Press, 1946 (1922).

Weber, Max. *The Protestant Ethic and the Spirit of Capitalism*, T. Parsons, trans. New York: Charles Scribner's Sons, 1958 (1904–5).

Weber, Max. *The Theory of Social and Economic Organization*, T. Parsons, ed. New York: The Free Press, 1947 (1922).

Culture

This section of the book is about *culture* and contains articles on differences between Canadian and American culture, differences between Canadian and American approaches to religion, and culture as ideology.

"Culture" is one of the main concepts in social science. In anthropology, a sister discipline, the concept of "culture" is as central as "social structure" is to the study of sociology. In political science (where it comes to be known as "political culture") and management science (where it comes to be known as "organizational culture"), the concept is useful in explaining collective behaviour. And in sociology, "culture" helps to explain how individuals and groups fit together.

"Culture" takes in all the shared ways of thinking, feeling, and behaving that characterize a group or society and distinguish it from another. Culture is uniquely human; learned, not genetically programmed; and transmitted by "socialization," about which we say more in the next section. The concept is important because it helps us think about sociology's classic questions; especially, how societies change and what happens when they do.

In the nineteenth and twentieth centuries, the entire Western world modernized. With industrialization and the growth of cities, social relations changed markedly. No longer based on tradition and blood ties, social relations became impermanent, impersonal, and narrow.

Social, political, and economic life all changed; but they changed at different rates. Uneven change proved that social, political, and economic life are all distinct, even though related. This realization stimulated a systematic study of social order, what establishes and what disrupts it. In short, it set the stage for sociology to emerge as a discipline. It also forced sociologists to take note of the role of culture in this complex process.

Modernization grows out of industrialization, urbanization, complex science and technology, secular religion, mass literacy, and a new public awareness of the world. According to researchers like sociologist Alex

Inkeles and Smith (1974), modern cultures produce people who are more likely to plan, reason, treat others as equals, and interest themselves in other parts of the world. Modernization expands human horizons beyond past and present to the future; beyond a narrow interest in self, family, and community to an interest in nation, world, and cosmos.

Other images of modernization are less rosy. Karl Marx (1818–1883) and Max Weber (1864–1920) thought modern society was exploitive, alienating, impersonal, overorganized but without enough concern for human beings, obsessed with technology and efficiency, faddish and overcrowded with meaningless gadgetry. Modernity, in this view, is a worldwide consumer's market obsessed with the need for material possessions as a proof of personal value.

Whichever assessment is more accurate, and both seem to apply, Western culture has changed significantly in the last two centuries. Culture is the context of shared ideas about how to do things, within which a society changes or maintains order. Accordingly, with cultural modernization, the relations that make up societies also change significantly.

In the last section we noted that, historically, sociologists have been concerned with answering the question, "Are the most important determinants of social behaviour cultural or economic?" This question is misleading because culture and economy are not so neatly separated. People learn to think and do what is economically necessary. Some writers argue culture and economy fit together because the ruling economic class promotes ways of thinking and behaving that serve their own interests. Sociologists call culture produced in this way an *ideology*.

Others argue that shared ways of thinking and acting arise naturally out of daily experience. They are not the result of efforts by a ruling class to protect its own interests. Cultural patterns arise and persist because they actually help people make sense of their everyday lives. Sociologists following Karl Mannheim (see, for example, 1936) have adopted this second point of view, and also refer to their object of study as "ideology."

Culture does not only reflect economic relations, it also shapes them. This theme finds its strongest expression in the writings of Max Weber and his followers (like Alex Inkeles) who have studied modernization. What goes on in people's minds — their thoughts about the meaning of life, the purpose of money-making, the predictability of nature and our ability to harness it — all affect people's willingness to play economic roles or change them. Even Karl Marx, the strongest believer that economic forces explain social life, knew that people's thinking could change history. People's thoughts had to change before revolutions could make significant political and economic changes. Undermining the "legitimacy" of an economic and political order prepares people to make a revolutionary change.

"Culture" is fundamental to two other classic concerns of sociology noted in the first section. First, culture is important in the relationship between individuals and society. After all, every society is a set of individuals who share common ways of thinking and behaving — that is, a common culture. People produce social structures to attain their cultural goals. Therefore, culture and social structure must fit together.

As well, research shows that sharing values and practices with other people is basic to personal well-being. A shared, consistent culture not only makes a society possible: as Durkheim (see, for example, 1933) showed, it makes human life meaningful and tolerable. The acculturated human being is a miniature version of the society and culture of which he/she is a member.

Of course, this view of human life is oversimplified (or suggests an "oversocialized" image of people), as many sociologists have remarked. It is fairer to say that, just as the culture makes society's members, so do members of society make the culture they share.

"Culture" and "society" are related but distinct concepts. For a variety of reasons we shall start to explore below, even such similar societies as Canada and the United States can have different cultures. Often, cultural views on inequality are central to cultural differences between nations. For example, Seymour Martin Lipset has analyzed cultures to explain why (and how) Canadians are different from Americans: how and why they do not behave similarly in many important ways. In answering this question in this section, Lipset focuses on the different ways Canadians and Americans respond to inequality.

In a different vein Reginald Bibby, in his article in this section, focuses on the different ways Canadians and Americans (and British people) respond to the supernatural. Specifically, Bibby contrasts the attitudes to religion we find in Canada with those commonly held in the United States and Great Britian. By looking at how people in different nations respond to similar important issues, we learn a lot about the core elements of their culture.

This comparison has practical, as well as theoretical, importance. Indeed, the question of what makes Canada different from the United States is important for a number of reasons. Almost every Canadian has remarked at some time on differences between the United States and Canada, and between Americans and Canadians. Lipset tries to think about this commonly asked question systematically by focussing on cultural differences. As we discover, answering this question is central to understanding the uniqueness of Canadian society. Further, any answer about Canada's uniqueness implies an answer to the other old question of whether Canada and the United States can or should be distinct nations.

The answer is no clearer today, in an age of free trade with the United States, then when Goldwin Smith addressed the issue of union between Canada and the United States a century ago or William Lyon MacKenzie looked longingly at American democracy fifty years earlier. Is Canada really different from the USA? Can it continue to be different? Should it be different? These are questions we cannot answer without thinking seriously about cultural differences between Canada and the United States.

In doing so we must avoid assuming that Canadians (or Americans) think, feel, or behave more uniformly than they really do. Experience tells us that Canadians vary significantly. Sociologists deal with this variation by studying and writing about *subcultures.* Subcultures arise within subgroups of the society whose members have certain common experiences or concerns that differentiate them from the rest. These special concerns are important enough to serve as the foundations for somewhat distinct life patterns. This is why sociologists study ethnic subcultures, deviant or criminal subcultures, and even regional subcultures.

Within Canadian society, regional subcultures are particularly important. Ways of thinking and behaving differ considerably between English-speaking Canadians and French-speaking Canadians, and within English Canada, between people in Ontario, the Maritimes, and the West. The greater the inequality between groups, the larger a subcultural difference we typically find. Subcultures often express social uniqueness in the face of outside domination and help a group to resist assimilation.

We have already hinted at the relevance of "culture" to another of sociology's classic questions; namely, the bases of social inequality. People's shared ways of thinking and acting tend to keep a system of inequality in place. This is clear in the mass acceptance of ideologies about economic inequality, discussed in the following article by Patricia Marchak. It is also clear in the harder-to-explain but equally significant practices of gender inequality and racial discrimination we discuss in later sections. These forms of inequality are hard to eliminate even in communist societies where, presumably, class inequality no longer exists.

Cultures, then, include a generalized attitude toward social inequality and, often, detailed notions about the bases and justifications for inequality. For example, they may specify who (i.e., what types of people and what types of social roles) we ought to consider most worthy. Sociologists study the ways in which such ideas come into being, but their answers do not always agree. On the one hand, "functionalists" argue that ideas about inequality reflect dominant concerns or values of society and the relative scarcity of certain valuable skills. On the other hand, Marxists argue that different evaluations of people (and skills) come after the fact of social inequality. The most vulnerable and powerless people are most likely to be labelled "worthless" and deprived of rewards. They cannot prevent such labelling.

We must take both arguments into account when we study particular cases of inequality. What is important here is, simply, to note the significance of "culture" in framing the terms of the debate. It is often hard to change a system of inequality because doing so means changing an important part of the cultural system.

References

Durkheim, Emile. *The Division of Labor in Society*. Translated by George Simpson. New York: Free Press, 1933 (1893).

Inkeles, A. and Smith, D.H. *Becoming Modern: Individual Change in Six Developing Countries*. Cambridge, Mass.: Harvard University Press, 1974.

Mannheim, Karl. *Ideology and Utopia*. New York: Harcourt, Brace and World, 1936.

THREE

Value Traditions in Canadian and U.S. Cultures

Seymour Martin Lipset

SEYMOUR MARTIN LIPSET is the Caroline S.G. Munro Professor of Political Science and Sociology at Stanford University. His first teaching post was at the University of Toronto; and before going on to Stanford in 1975, he was the George Markham Professor of Government and Sociology at Harvard University. His work has included analyses of Canadian politics and society, particularly his study, *Agrarian Socialism: The Cooperative Commonwealth Federation in Saskatchewan* (1950). He has dealt extensively with comparative analyses of values and institutions in Canada and the United States, in his books *The First New Nation* (1963), *Revolution and Counterrevolution* (1968) and *Continental Divide: The Values and Institutions of the United States and Canada* (1990). Two of his books have received awards: *Political Man* (1960) was given the MacIver Award and *The Politics of Unreason* (1970) was awarded the Gunnar Myrdal Prize. He has also been elected to membership in the National Academy of Sciences, the American Academy of Arts and Sciences, and the American Philosophical Society.

THEORY AND APPROACH

There is much to be gained, both in empirical and analytic terms, from a systematic comparative study of Canada and the United States. They have many of the same ecological and demographic conditions, approximately the same level of economic development, and similar rates of upward and downward social mobility. And alongside the obvious distinctiveness of francophone Quebec, anglophone Canadians and Americans have much in common in cultural terms as well. Yet, although overall these two people probably resemble each other more than any other two nations on earth, there are consistent patterns of difference between them. To discover and analyze the factors which create and perpetuate such differences among nations is one of the more intriguing and difficult tasks in comparative study.[1]

In this essay I shall focus on value differences between the two countries, that is, differences in that set of attitudes which tends to characterize and permeate both the public and private ethos in each country. The central argument of the paper is that Canada has been a more elitist, law-abiding, statist, collectivity-oriented, and particularistic (group-oriented) society than the United States,[2] and that these fundamental distinctions stem in large part from the defining event which gave birth to both countries, the American Revolution. . . .

A brief characterization of the essential core, or organizing principles, of each society may help clarify the type of difference being referred to here. With respect to the United States, the emphases on individualism and achievement orientation by the American colonists were an important motivating force in the launching of the American Revolution, and were embodied in the Declaration of Independence. The manifestation of such attitudes in this historic event and their crystallization in an historic document provided a basis for the reinforcement and encouragement of these orientations throughout subsequent American history. Thus, the United States remained through the nineteenth and early twentieth centuries the extreme example of classically liberal or Lockean society which rejected the assumptions of the alliance of throne and altar, of ascriptive elitism, of mercantilism, of *noblesse oblige*, of communitarianism. Friedrich Engels, among other foreign visitors, noted that as compared to Europe, the United States was "purely bourgeois, so entirely without a feudal past" (Engels, 1942: 467).

By contrast, both major Canadian linguistic groups sought to preserve their values and culture by reacting against liberal revolutions. English-speaking Canada exists because she opposed the Declaration of Independence; French-speaking Canada, largely under the leadership of Catholic clerics, also sought to isolate herself from the anti-clerical, democratic values of the French Revolution.[3] The leaders of both, after 1783 and 1789, consciously attempted to create a conservative, monarchical and ecclesiastical society in North America. Cana-

dian elites of both linguistic groups saw the need to use the state to protect minority cultures, English Canadians against Yankees, French Canadians against anglophones. In the United States, on the other hand, the Atlantic Ocean provided an effective barrier against the major locus of perceived threat — Britain — which helped sustain the American ideological commitment to a weak state that did not have to maintain extensive military forces. As with the United States, however, these initial "organizing principles" in Canada served to structure subsequent developments north of the border. Although the content and extent of the differences between the two countries have changed over time, the contemporary variations still reflect the impact of the American Revolution. . . .

Given all of the differences distinguishing the Canadian historical experience from the American, it is not surprising that the peoples of the two countries formulated their self-conceptions in sharply different ways. As an ideological nation whose left and right *both* take sustenance from the American Creed, the United States is quite different from Canada, which lacks any founding myth, and whose intellectuals frequently question whether the country has a national identity. Sacvan Bercovitch has well described America's impact on a Canadian during the conflict-ridden sixties.

> My first encounter with American consensus was in the late sixties, when I crossed the border into the United States and found myself inside the myth of America . . . of a country that despite its arbitrary frontiers, despite its bewildering mix of race and creed, could believe in something called the True America, and could invest that patent fiction with all the moral and emotional appeal of a religious symbol. . . . Here was the Jewish anarchist Paul Goodman berating the Midwest for abandoning

the promise; here the descendant of American slaves, Martin Luther King, denouncing injustice as a violation of the American Way; here, an endless debate about national destiny, . . . conservatives scavenging for un-Americans. New Left historians recalling the country to its sacred mission. . . .

Nothing in my Canadian background had prepared me for that spectacle. . . . To a Canadian skeptic . . ., it made for a breathtaking scene; a pluralistic pragmatic people openly living in a dream, bound together by an ideological consensus unmatched by any other modern society.

Let me repeat that mundane phrase: *ideological consensus*. . . . It was a hundred sects and factions, each apparently different from the others, yet all celebrating the same mission. . . . (Bercovitch, 1981: 5–6, emphasis in original)

Although interpreted in a variety of ways by different groups and individuals, the ideology of the American Revolution provides for each of them a *raison d'être* for the Republic — it explains why the United States came into being, and what it means to be American.

The contrast with Canada is a sharp one. Canada could not offer her citizens "the prospect of a fresh start, . . . because (as the Canadian poet Douglas Le Pan put it) Canada is 'a country without a mythology' " (Bercovitch, 1981: 24). To justify her separate existence, both linguistic cultures deprecated American values and institutions. As Frank Underhill once noted, Canadians are the world's oldest and most continuing anti-Americans (Underhill, 1960: 222; for an elaboration, see Kendall, 1974: 20–36). This stance was reflected in the writings of various Canadian observers in the 1920s, who "discerned and condemned an excessive egalitarian quality derived from notions of independence and democracy that had been set free during the [American] Revolution" (Weaver, 1973: 80). Further evidence of such attitudes

was gathered during the 1930s when the first efforts at a systematic sociological investigation of opinions in Canada concerning themselves and Americans were launched. One of the most important and prolific contributors to the research was S.D. Clark, then starting his scholarly career. He summarized the findings in the following terms:

> Canadian national life can almost be said to take its rise in the negative will to resist absorption in the American Republic. It is largely about the United States as an object that the consciousness of Canadian national unity has grown up. . . .
>
> Constantly in the course of this study we shall come across the idea that Canadian life is simpler, more honest, more moral and more religious than life in the United States, that it lies closer to the rural virtues and has achieved urbanization without giving the same scope to corrupting influences which has been afforded them in the United States. (Clark, 1939: 243, 245)[4]

As Clark suggests in this passage, Canadians have tended to define themselves, not in terms of their own national history and tradition, but rather by reference to what they are *not*: American.

These differences between Canada and the United States can be seen, not just in history or in the findings of social science research, but also in the novels, poems, and stories created by writers in each country. In fact, of all artifacts, the art and literature of a nation should most reflect, as well as establish, her basic myths and values. And many analysts of North American literature have emphasized the continuing effects of the "mythic and psychic consequences of founding a country on revolution or out of the rejection of revolution" (Brown, n.d.: 2). . . .

RELIGION

... The majority of Canadians adhere to the Roman Catholic or Anglican churches, both of which are hierarchically organized and continued until recently to have a strong relationship to the state. On the other hand, most Americans have belonged to the more individualist "nonconformist" Protestant sects. . . .

Religion in both countries has become more secularized in tandem with increased urbanization and education. For instance, Canadian Catholicism, particularly in Quebec, has modified the nature of its corporatist commitment from a link to agrarian and elitist anti-industrial values to a tie to leftist socialist beliefs. These variations, of course, parallel the changes in French Canadian nationalism. Public opinion research suggests that francophone Catholics have given up much of their commitment to Jansenist puritanical values, particularly as they affect sexual behaviour and family size. This secularizing trend, although generally observable in both countries, has been less noticeable in the United States, particularly among evangelical Protestants. Americans, according to data from sample surveys presented below, are much more likely to attend church regularly than Canadians, and to adhere to fundamentalist and moralistic beliefs. And the continued strength of Protestant evangelical, sectarian and fundamentalist religion south of the border has meant that traditional values related to sex, family and morality in general are stronger there than in Canada.

A large body of public opinion data gathered in the two countries bear on these issues. Most findings are not precisely comparable because of variations in question wording. Fortunately, a research organization linked to the Catholic Church, CARA, has conducted a systematically comparative study of values in 22 countries, including Canada and the United States, where the data were collected by the Gallup Poll at the start of the eighties.[5] The two tables which follow on page 34 present some of the relevant CARA findings.

There is a consistent pattern in these data: Americans far outnumber Canadians generally in giving expression to Protestant fundamentalist beliefs, with anglophones more likely to hold such views than francophones. And, congruent with the variations in religious practice and belief, Americans appear to be more puritanical than Canadians, with francophones the most tolerant with respect to sexual behaviour. . . .

LAW AND DEVIANCE

The difference in the role of law in the two countries is linked to the historical emphases on the rights and obligations of the community as compared to those of the individual. The explicit concern of Canada's founding fathers with "peace, order, and good government" implies control and protection. The American stress on "life, liberty, and the pursuit of happiness" suggests upholding the rights of the individual. This latter concern for rights, including those of people accused of crime and of political dissidents, is inherent in the "due process" model, involving various legal inhibitions on the power of the police and prosecutors, characteristic of the United States. The "crime control" model, more evident in Canada, as well as Europe, emphasizes the maintenance of law and order, and is

TABLE 3-1   Religious Beliefs and Values 1980–81, in Percent

	Americans	English Canadians	French Canadians
How important is God in your life? (1 = not at all; 10 = very important) Percentage choosing 9 or 10	59	44	47
Believe "there is a personal God"	65	49	56
Believe the Ten Commandments apply fully to themselves	83	76	67
Believe the Ten Commandments apply fully to others as well	36	28	23
Believe in "the Devil"	66	46	25
Believe in "Hell"	67	45	22
Believe in "Heaven"	84	73	58
Believe in life after death	71	61	63
Believe in a soul	88	80	80

Source: CARA, Center for Applied Research in the Apostolate, *Values Study of Canada* (code book) Washington, D.C.: May 1983.

TABLE 3-2   Family Values 1980–81, in Percent

	Americans	English Canadians	French Canadians
Agree that "marriage is an outdated institution"	7	11	19
Believe that "individuals should have a chance to enjoy complete sexual freedom without being restricted"	18	18	24
Disapprove of idea of a woman wanting a child but not a stable relationship with one man	58	53	34
Agree that sexual activity must subscribe to certain moral rules	51	49	34

Source: CARA, Center for Applied Research in the Apostolate, *Values Study of Canada* (code book) Washington, D.C.: May 1983.

less protective of the rights of the accused and of individuals generally.[6] . . .

Property rights and civil liberties are also under less constitutional protection in Canada than in the United States. John Mercer and Michael Goldberg note:

In Canada . . . property rights are not vested with the individual but rather with the Crown, just the opposite of the U.S. where the Fifth and Fourteenth Amendments to the U.S. Constitution guarantee property rights. Interestingly, in the [recently enacted] Canadian Charter of Rights and Freedoms property rights (as distinct from human rights) were explicitly not protected. . . . Such a state of affairs would be unacceptable in the United States where individual rights and particularly those related to personal and real property are sacrosanct. (Mercer and Goldberg, 1982: 22)

The Canadian government has greater legal power to restrict freedom of speech and to invade personal privacy. Acting through an order-in-council, it may limit public discussion of particular issues and, as in 1970 during the Quebec crisis, impose a form of military control (see Callwood, 1981: 333–334, 341–342; Bell and Tepperman, 1979: 83–84; Smith, 1971). Comparing American and Canadian public reactions to violations of privacy by the government, Alan Westin writes:

> [I]t is important to note that in Canada there have been some incidents which, had they happened in the United States, would probably have led to great *causes célèbres*. Most Canadians seem to have accepted Royal Canadian Mounted Police break-ins without warrants between 1970 and 1978, and also the RCMP's secret access to income tax information, and to personal health information from the Ontario Health Insurance Plan. If I read the Canadian scene correctly, those did not shock and outrage most Canadians. (Westin, 1983: 41)

That Canadians and Americans differ in the way they react to the law is demonstrated strikingly in the aggregate differences between the two with respect to crime rates for major offenses. Americans are much more prone than Canadians to commit violent offenses like murder, robbery, and rape and to be arrested for the use of serious illegal drugs such as opiates and cocaine. They are also much more likely to take part in protest demonstrations and riots. Although the United States population outnumbers the Canadian by about ten to one, the

ratios for political protest activities have ranged from twenty to one to forty to one.

Evidence from national opinion surveys in the two countries indicates that lower rates of crime and violence in Canada are accompanied by greater respect for police, public backing for stronger punishment of criminals, and a higher level of support for gun control legislation. For example, when asked by the Canadian Gallup poll in 1978 to rate the local, provincial, and Royal Canadian Mounted Police, a large majority (64 percent, 64 percent, and 61 percent, respectively) said "excellent or good." The corresponding percentages reported by Harris survey for local, state and federal law enforcement officials in 1981 were 62, 57, and 48.[7] In the early eighties, the CARA surveys conducted by Gallup found more Canadians (86 percent) than Americans (76 percent) voicing a great deal or quite a lot of confidence in the police. There was no significant difference between the two Canadian linguistic groups on this item. . . .

The lesser respect for the law, for the "rules of the game" in the United States, may be viewed as inherent in a system in which egalitarianism is strongly valued and in which diffuse elitism is lacking. Generalized deference is not accorded to those at the top; therefore, in the United States there is a greater propensity to redefine the rules or to ignore them. The decisions of the leadership are constantly being questioned. While Canadians incline toward the use of "lawful" and traditionally institutionalized means for altering regulations which they believe are unjust, Americans seem more disposed to employ informal and often extralegal means to correct what they perceive as wrong.

The greater lawlessness and corruption in the United States may be attributed in part to the greater strength of the achievement value in the more populous nation. As Robert Merton has pointed out, a strong emphasis on achievement means that "[t]he moral mandate to achieve success thus exerts pressure to succeed, by fair means if possible and by foul means if necessary" (Merton, 1957: 169). Merton accounts for the greater adherence to approved means of behavior in much of Europe compared to the United States as derivative from variations in the emphasis on achievement for all. And the same logic implies that since Americans are more likely than their Canadian neighbors to be concerned with the achievement of ends — particularly pecuniary success — they will be less concerned with the use of the socially appropriate *means*; hence we should expect a higher incidence of deviations from conventional norms in politics and other aspects of life south of the forty-ninth parellel.

Although the cross-national behavioral and attitudinal variations with respect to law and crime have continued down to the present, Canada has been involved since 1960 in a process of changing her fundamental rules in what has been described as American and due process directions. The adoption of a Bill of Rights in 1960, replaced by the more comprehensive Charter of Rights and Freedom in 1982, was designed to create a basis, absent from the British North America Act, for judicial intervention to protect individual rights and civil liberties.

While these changes are important, it is doubtful that they will come close to eliminating the differences in legal cultures. Canadian courts have been more respectful than American ones of the rest of the political system. As Kenneth McNaught concluded in 1975,

our judges and lawyers, supported by the press and public opinion, reject any concept of the courts as positive instruments in the political process. . . . [P]olitical action outside the party-parliamentary structure tends automatically to be suspect — and not least because it smacks of Americanism. This deep-grained Canadian attitude of distinguishing amongst proper and improper methods of dealing with societal organization and problems reveal us as being, to some extent, what Walter Bagehot once called a "deferential society." (McNaught, 1975: 138; see also Whyte 1976: 656–657; Swinton, 1979: 91–93)

Beyond these general distinctions there are specific provisions in the new Charter of Rights and Freedoms which set it apart from the American Bill of Rights. For example, to protect parliamentary supremecy, the Canadian constitution provides that Parliament or a provincial legislature may "opt out" of the constitutional restrictions by inserting into any law a clause that it shall operate regardless of any part of the Charter. In addition, the new rights do not include any assurance that an accused person shall have a lawyer, nor that he has the right to remain silent, nor that he need not answer questions which may tend to incriminate him in civil cases or in investigatory proceedinsg (Pye, 1982: 221–248; McWhinney, 1982: 55–57, 61; Westin, 1983: 27–44; see also McKercher, 1983). . . .

THE ECONOMY: THE PRIVATE SECTOR

The United States, born modern, without a feudal elitist corporatist tradition, could create, outside of the agrarian South, what Engels described as the purest example of a bourgeois society. Canada, as we have seen, was somewhat different, and that difference affected the way her citizens have done business.

According to Herschel Hardin, Canadian entrepreneurs have been less aggressive, less innovating, less risk-taking than Americans.[8] Hardin seeks to demonstrate that private enterprise in Canada "has been a monumental failure" in developing new technology and industry, to the extent that Canadian business has rarely been involved in creating industries to process many significant inventions by Canadians, who have had to go abroad to get their discoveries marketed (see also Brown, 1967; Bourgault, 1972; Hardin, 1974; 102–105).

This has been partly due to traditional management values and organization processes (McMillan, 1978: 45).[9] Also important is the fact that, compared to Americans, Canadian investors and financial institutions are less disposed to provide venture capital. They "tend consistently to avoid offering encouragement to the entrepreneur with a new technology-based product ... [or to] innovative industries" (Science Council of Canada, 1972: 123).

The thesis has been elaborated by economists. Jenny Podoluk found that "investment is a much more significant source of personal income in the United States than in Canada. ... When Canadians have invested, the risky new Canadian enterprise has not been as attractive as the established American corporation."[10] Kenneth Glazier, in explaining the Canadian tendency to invest in the U.S. rather than in Canada, argues that

One reason is that Canadians traditionally have been conservative, exhibiting an inferiority complex about their own destiny as a nation and about the potential of their country. ...

Thus, with Canadians investing in the "sure" companies of the United States, Canada

has for generations suffered not only from labor drain and a braindrain to the United States, but also from a considerably larger capital drain. (Glazier, 1972: 61)

Data drawn from opinion polls reinforce the comparative generalizations about the greater economic prudence of Canadians. Studies of English and French speaking Canadians indicate that on most items, anglophones fall between Americans and francophones. When asked by the American and Canadian Gallup Polls in 1979 (U.S.) and 1980 (Canada) about usage of credit cards, 51 percent of Canadians said they never used one, as compared to 35 percent of Americans. The latter were more likely than Canadians to report "regular" usage, 32 percent to 16 percent. Francophones made less use of credit cards (64 percent, never) than anglophones (44 percent, never). English speakers were also more likely to be regular users than French speakers.[11]

THE ECONOMY: THE PUBLIC SECTOR

The proportion of the Canadian GNP in government hands as of the mid-seventies was 41 percent, compared to 34 percent in the United States; as of 1982 the ratio was 44 to 38 percent (Nelles, 1980: 132, 143 n.28; United Nations, 1983: 22). Subtracting defense spending, roughly 2 percent for Canada, and 5 to 6 percent for the United States, widens the gap between the two countries considerably (see U.S. Arms Control and Disarmament Agency, 1982: 42, 71). Taxes as a share of total domestic product were 35 percent in Canada as compared to 30 percent in the United States in 1982 (*U.S. News and World Report*, 1984: 65).[12] Unlike "the

United States, [Canada] has never experienced a period of pure unadulterated *laissez-faire* market capitalism" (McLeod, 1976; Aitken, 1959). The period since 1960 has witnessed a particularly rapid expansion in the number of crown corporations: fully 70 percent of them were created in the past quarter of a century (Chandler, 1983: 187). . . .

Research based on opinion poll interviews indicates that Canadians, at both elite and mass levels, are more supportive than Americans of state intervention. Summarizing surveys of high level civil servants and federal, state and provincial legislators, Robert Presthus reports:

> [a] sharp difference between the two [national] elites on "economic liberalism," defined as a preference for "big government." . . . Only about 17 percent of the American legislative elite ranks high on this disposition, compared with fully 40 percent of their Canadian peers. . . . [T]he direction is the same among bureaucrats, only 17 percent of whom rank high among the American sample, compared with almost 30 percent among Canadians. (Presthus, 1974: 463)

Differences related to party affiliation in both countries emphasize this cross-national variation. Canadian Liberal legislators score much higher than American Democrats on economic liberalism and Canadian Conservatives score much higher than Republicans. Conservatives and Republicans in each country are lower on economic liberalism than Liberals and Democrats, but *Canadian Conservatives are higher than American Democrats* (Presthus, 1977: 15).

Mass attitudinal data reinforce the thesis that Canadians are more collectivity oriented than Americans and therefore are more likely to support government intervention. In the 1968–70 studies of American and English Canadian attitudes discussed earlier, Stephen Arnold and Douglas Tigert found that, compared to Canadians, Americans are more opposed to big government and less likely to believe that government should guarantee everyone an income. They also reported that Americans are more likely than Canadians to take part in voluntary communitarian activities which, according to the authors, contradicts my assumption that Canadians are more collectivity oriented (Arnold and Tigert, 1974: 80–81). However, I would argue that the findings support this contention, since they demonstrate that Americans are more likely to take part in voluntary activity to achieve particular goals, while Canadians are more disposed to rely on the state. And in fact, a subsequent article by Stephen Arnold and James Barnes dealing with the same findings concluded: "Americans were found to be individualistic, whereas Canadians were more collectively oriented," more supportive of state provisions of medical care or a guaranteed minimum income (Arnold and Barnes, 1979: 32).

The existence of an electorally viable social-democratic party, the New Democrats (NDP), in Canada, has been taken by various writers as an outgrowth of the greater influence of the tory-statist tradition and the stronger collectivity orientation north of the border. Conversely, the absence of a significant social movement to the south is explained in part by the vitality of the anti-statist and individualist values in the United States. There is, of course, good reason to believe, as Louis Hartz, Gad Horowitz, and I, among others, have argued, that social democratic movements are the other side of statist conservatism, that Tories and socialists are likely to be found in the same polity, while a dominant Lockean liberal tradition inhibits the emergence of socialism, as a political force (see Hartz, 1955; 1964: 1–48; Horowitz, 1968: 3–57; Lipset, 1977: 79–83; 1983: 52–53). . . .

However, there are other plausible explanations for the difference in the political party systems of Canada and the United States which suggest that the contrast in socialist strength should not be relied on as evidence of varying predispositions among the two populations. As I noted in an article on "Radicalism in North America," one of the main factors differentiating the United States from Canada and most other democratic countries has been its system of direct election of the President. In America, the nation is effectively one constituency and the electorate is led to see votes for anyone other than the two major candidates as effectively wasted. Seemingly, the American constitutional system serves to inhibit, if not to prevent, electorally viable third parties, and has produced a concealed multi-party or multi-factional system, operating within the two major parties, while the Canadian focus on constituency contests is more conducive to viable third, and even fourth, parties (Lipset, 1976: 36–52).[13] And many, such as Michael Harrington, former national chairman of the Socialist Party of the U.S., have argued that there is a social democratic faction in America that largely operates within the Democratic Party (Harrington, 1972: 250–269).[14]

Evidence, independent of the effect of diverse electoral systems, that the forces making for class consciousness and organization, linked to collectivity orientations, are more powerful in Canada than the United States may be found in trade union membership statistics. Canada not only has had much stronger socialist par-

ties than America since the 1930s, but workers in the northern country are now much more heavily involved in unions than those in the south. By 1984, only 18 percent of the non-agricultural labor force in the United States belonged to labor organizations compared to almost 40 percent in Canada (Troy and Sheflin, 1985; Department of Labour, Canada, 1984: Table 1).[15] In the United States, the percentage organized in unions has fallen steadily from a high point of 32.5 in 1954, while in Canada the figure has moved up from 22. . . .

ELITISM AND EQUALITARIANISM

. . . Elitism is presumed to be reflected in diffuse respect for authority, and in Canada contributes to the encouragement of a greater role for the state in economic and social affairs. Equalitarianism can be perceived as the polar contrast to elitism, in Tocquevillian terms as generalized respect for "all persons . . . because they are human beings" (Lipset, 1970: 38). Equalitarianism, however, has many meanings, not all of which are incompatible with elitism. Conceptualized as "equality of result," it enters into the political arena in efforts to reduce inequality on a group level. And, reiterating the arguments just presented, it may be said that Tory stimuli, elitist in origin, produce social democratic responses, efforts to protect and upgrade the position of less privileged strata.

Conceptualizing equalitarianism in this fashion leads to the expectation that nations which rank high with respect to the value of achievement, "equality of opportunity," will be less concerned with reducing inequality of condition. If the United States is more achievement oriented and less elitist than Canada, then she should place more emphasis on educational equality as the primary mechanism for moving into the higher socio-economic positions. Canada, on the other hand, should be more favorable to redistributive proposals, thus upgrading the lower strata, as, in fact, she is.

Robert Kudrle and Theodore Marmor note that "the ideological difference — slight by international standards — between Canada and the United States appears to have made a considerable difference in welfare state developments" (Kudrle and Marmor, 1981: 112). Canadian programs were adopted earlier, "exhibited a steadier development," are financed more progressively and/or are more income redistributive in the areas of old age security, unemployment insurance, and family allowances (nonexistent in the United States), and medical care (Kudrle and Marmor, 1981: 91–111). . . .

As of 1979, the percentage of Canadians aged 20-24 in higher education had risen to 36, but the comparable American figure had increased to 55.[16] The proportion of Canadians enrolled in tertiary education jumped by 125 percent; that of Americans by 72 percent. Americans, however, moved up more in absolute terms, 23 percent to 20 percent for Canadians.

Some analysts of recent changes in Canadian universities have referred to them as "Americanizations" (Bissell, 1979: 198). Canada not only sharply increased the number of universities and places for students, but her higher education institutions, following public policy, have changed. They have incorporated practical and vocationally relevant subjects, expanded the social sciences and graduate programs, and placed greater emphasis on faculty scholarship. . . .

The changes in size and content of higher education in Canada should lead to a reduction in the proportion of persons without professional training who hold top jobs. Comparative data indicate that Canada has differed from America, and resembled Britain, in disproportionately recruiting her business and political administrative elites from those without a professional or technical education. As Charles McMillan reports, "Canadian managers tend to be less well educated than their counterparts in any other industrialized country with the possible exception of Britain" (McMillan, 1978: 45).[17]

This conclusion is documented by Wallace Clement's studies of business elites which reveal that the Canadians not only have less specialized education than the Americans, but also that the former are much more likely to have an elitist social background. As Clement reports, "entrance to the economic elite is easier for persons from outside the upper class in the United States than it is in Canada. . . . [T]he U.S. elite is more open, recruiting from a much broader class base than is the case in Canada" (Clement, 1977: 183, 209). Sixty-one percent of the Canadian top executives are of upper class origin compared to 36 percent of the Americans (Clements, 1977: 215–250, esp. 216; see also Safarian, 1969: 13).

Similar cross-national differences among top civil servants are reported by Robert Presthus and William Monopoli from studies done during the late sixties and early seventies (Presthus and Monopoli, 1977: 176–190). These revealed that a much higher proportion of Canadian than of American bureaucrats have been of upper class origin. Presthus explains the phenomena "both in industry and government" as reflecting strong traces of the "generalist", amateur approach to administration. The Canadian higher civil service is patterned rather closely after the British administrative class, which even today tends to symbolize traditional and charismatic bases of authority. Technical aspects of government programmes tend to be de-emphasized, while policy-making and the amateur-classicist syndrome are magnified. . . . (Presthus, 1973: 34, 98)

As with many other Canadian institutions, the civil service has been changing. A more recent survey of bureaucrats in central government agencies by Colin Campbell and George Szablowski finds that in "the past decade Canada has seen a remarkable influx of bureaucrats representing segments of the populace traditionally excluded from senior positions in the public service," and that many of those interviewed had "experienced rapid upward mobility" (Campbell and Szablowski, 1979: 105, 121). These developments may reflect the documented decrease in educational inheritance in Canada as the higher education system has grown (Manzer, 1974: 188–206).

Cross-national surveys conducted in recent years have explicitly sought to estimate support for meritocracy when contrasted with equality of result. Their findings point to strong differences between Americans and Canadians on these issues. In the fall of 1979, national samples in the two countries were asked by a Japanese research group to choose between the two in fairly direct fashion:

Here are two opinions about conditions existing in our country. Which do you happen to agree with?
A. There is too much emphasis upon the principle of equality. People should be given the opportunity to choose their own economic and social life according to their individual abilities.
B. Too much liberalism has been producing increasingly wide differences in peoples' economic and social ife. People should live more equally.

Forty-one percent of the Canadians chose the more egalitarian and collectivity-oriented option B. The proportion of Americans responding this way was 32 percent. Clearly the pattern of responses suggests that Canadians value equality of result more than Americans, while the latter are more achievement oriented (Hastings and Hastings, 1982: 519, 520, 525). . . .[18]

If greater commitment to equality of result leads Canadians to voice a higher preference for equality over freedom or liberty, as they do in the CARA study, the assumption that Canada is more elitist than the Unites States implies, as I noted in an earlier comparison of the two societies, that Canadians should be more tolerant toward deviants or dissidents than American, (Lipset, 1970: 46–48). I suggested that even without a due process system, the greater tolerance and civil liberties for unpopular groups in elitist democracies, such as Britain and Canada, as compared to populist ones reflected the ability of elites in the former to protect minority rights. Opinion studies from many democratic societies indicate that educated elites invariably are more tolerant than the less educated; hence the tyranny of the majority is less of a problem in a more elitist system. And the CARA data bear out the anticipation that Canadians would, therefore, be more tolerant than their southern neighbors. . . .

MOSAIC AND MELTING POT: CENTER AND PERIPHERY

In an earlier paper, I asserted that "Canada is more particularistic (group-attribute conscious) than the seemingly more universalistic United States" (Lipset, 1970: 55). These differences are reflected (a) in the Canadian concept of the "mosaic," applied to the right to cultural survival of ethnic groups, as compared to the American notion of the "melting pot"; (b) in the more frequent recurrence and survival of strong regionally based third parties in Canada than in the United States; and (c) in the greater strength of provinces within the Canadian union, compared to the relative weakness of the states. . . .

The origin of these cross-national differences, as with those previously discussed, can be traced to the impact of the Revolution. American universalism, the desire to incorporate diverse groups into one culturally unified whole, is inherent in the founding ideology, the American Creed. Canadian particularism, the preservation of subnational group loyalties, an outgrowth of the commitment to the maintenance of two linguistic subcultures, is derivative from the decision of the francophone clerical elite to remain loyal to the British monarchy, as a protection against the threat posed by Puritanism and democratic populism from the revolutionary south. Given the importance of the French-speaking areas to British North America, the subsequent Canadian federal state incorporated protections for the linguistic minority, and the provinces assumed considerable power.

These differences could be expected to decline with modernization. Most analysts have assumed that industrialization, urbanization, and the spread of education would reduce ethnic and regional consciousness, that universalism would supplant particularism.

The validity of the assumption that structural modernization would sharply reduce ethnic and regional diversity and the power of federal sub-units has been challenged by development both within and outside of Canada. From the sixties on the world has witnessed an ethnic revival in many countries. In Canada, even prior to the revival, the values underlying the concept of the "mosaic" meant that various minorities, in addition to the francophones, would be able to sustain a stronger group life than comparable ones in the United States. As Arthur Davis points out:

> [E]thnic and regional differences . . . have been more generally accepted, more legitimized [in Canada] than they have been in our southern neighbour. There has not been as much pressure in Canada for "assimilation" as there has been in the United States. . . . Hutterite communities unquestionably are granted more autonomy in Canada than in the United States. Likewise, the Indians of Canada, however rudely they were shunted onto reservations . . . were seldom treated with such overt coercion as were the American Indians (Davis, 1971: 27). . . .

The greater autonomy and coherence of ethnic groups north of the border is the result, not just of a different set of attitudes, but also of explicit government policies which reflect them. Ever since the publication in 1969 of the fourth volume of the *Report of the Royal Commission on Bilingualism and Biculturalism*, the country has been committed to helping all ethnic groups through a policy of promoting "multiculturalism" (*Report of the Royal Commission on Bilingualism and Biculturalism*, 1969). The extent of the government's willingness to support this policy was reflected in the 1973 establishment of a cabinet ministry with the exclusive responsibility for multiculturalism. In addition, the government has provided funding to ethnic minorities for projects designed to celebrate and extend their cultures.

During the past two decades blacks have assumed a role within the American polity somewhat similar to that which the Québécois play in Canada. The call for "Black Power," in the context of demands for group, as distinct from individual, rights through affirmative action quotas and other forms of aid, has led the United States to explicitly accept particularistic standards for dealing with racial and ethnic groups. Much as francophones have legitimated cultural autonomy for other non-Anglo-Saxon Canadians, the changing position of blacks has enabled other American ethnic groups and women to claim similar particularistic rights. In effect, the United States has moved toward replacing the ideal of the "melting pot" with that of the "mosaic. . . ."

CONCLUSION

Canadian provinces have become more disposed than American states to challenge the power of the federal government. Movements advocating secession have recurred in this century, not only in Quebec, but in part of the Maritimes, the Prairies, and British Columbia as well. The tensions between Ottawa and the provinces and regions are not simply conflicts among politicians over the distribution of power. Public sentiment in Canada remains much more territorial than in the United States, reflecting more distinct regional and provincial interests and values. In a comparative analysis of "voting between 1945 and 1970 in seventeen western nations, Canada ranked among the least nationalized, while the United States was the most nationalized . . ." (Gibbins, 1982: 158). . . .

Few Canadian scholars are ready to agree, as John Porter was, that the difference is derived from the continued influence in Canada of counterrevolutionary traditions and institutions, or that the variations represent a choice of different sets of values, as the choice between a preference for the maintenance of group identities or for the diffusion of individual universalism" (Hueglin, 1984: 22).[19] Rather, they discuss a variety of relevant factors: "*societal* (economic, demographic, and international forces) and *institutional*)" (Esman, 1984; Smiley, 1984).

Two variables, both of which may be linked to the outcome of the American Revolution, appear to be most important. One is the role of the French Canadians discussed earlier. The other is the effect of the variation between the Presidential-Congressional divided-powers American system and the British parliamentary model. As Roger Gibbins emphasizes, "the Quebecois . . . have used the Quebec provincial government as an instrument of cultural survival and, because the stakes are so high, provincial rights have been guarded with a vigor unknown in the United States" (Gibbins, 1982: 192). . . .

. . . I have paid more attention here than in my earlier writings to variations between the two Canadian linguistic cultures. The evidence indicates that francophone Canadians vary more from their anglophone co-nationals than the latter do from Americans. Quebec, once the most conservative part of Canada, has become the most liberal on social issues and had a quasi-socialist provincial government from 1976 to 1986. Clearly, as John Porter and others have emphasized, there are Canadian styles and values that differentiate both linguistic cultures from the American one.

The cultural and political differences

between the two North American nations suggest why they occasionally have some difficulty understanding each other in the international arena. There are the obvious effects of variations in size, power, and awareness of the other. Canadians object to being taken for granted, and to being ignored by their neighbor. As citizens of a less populous power, they sympathize with other small or weak countries who are pressed by the United States. But beyond the consequences of variations in national power and interests, Canadians and Americans, as I have tried to spell out here, have a somewhat different *Weltanschauung*, world-view, ideology. . . .

The United States and Canada remain two nations formed around sharply different organizing principles. As various novelists and literary critics have emphasized, their basic myths vary considerably, and national ethoses and structures too are determined in large part by such myths. However, the differences in themes in the two national literatures have declined in the past two decades. Ronald Sutherland and A.J.M. Smith, two Canadian literary critics, have both called attention to a new nationalism north of the border, one which has pro-

duced a more radical literature (Sutherland, 1977: 413; Smith, 1979, 236–237). But ironically, as Sutherland points out, these changes are making Canada and her fiction more American, involving a greater emphasis on values such as pride in country, self-reliance, individualism, independence and self-confidence.

It may be argued, however, that these changes, while reducing some traditional differences, have enhanced others. The new nationalism, often linked among intellectuals both to socialism and Toryism, seeks to resist takeover of Canada's economy and increased cultural and media influence by Americans, and its weapon in so doing is the remedy of state action. As Christian and Campbell have observed in this context: "Toryism, socialism, and nationalism all share a common collectivist orientation in various forms" (Christian and Campbell, 1983: 209).

Although some will disagree, there can be no argument. As Margaret Atwood has well put it: "Americans and Canadians are not the same, they are the products of two very different histories, two very different situations" (Atwood, 1984: 392).[20]

Notes

[1] My initial treatment of this subject was presented in Lipset (1963: ch. 7). The arguments presented there were elaborated in Lipset (1965: 21–64). This article was subsequently updated and incorporated as a chapter in Lipset (1970: 37–75). The page references to the article here are to the 1970 edition, which has the widest circulation of the three. The current article is both an extension on the theoretical level and a condensation of the empirical content of a recent analysis (Lipset, 1985: 109–160).

[2] For a review of propositions in the literature see Arnold and Barnes (1979: esp. 3–6). See also Vallee and Whyte (1971: 556–564) and Archibald (1978: 231–241).

[3] Northrop Frye notes that English Canada should be "thought of . . . as a country that grew out of a Tory opposition to the Whig victory in the American Revolution. . . . [Quebec reacted against] the French Revolution with its strongly anti-clerical bias. The clergy remained the ideologically dominant group in Quebec down to a

generation ago, and the clergy wanted no part of the French Revolution or anything it stood for" (Frye, 1982: 66). For a discussion of Canada's three founding nationalities, the English, the French and the Scots (those who settled in Nova Scotia were Jacobites) as defeated people, see MacLennan (1977: 30).

4 For a comparable report by a historian of the 1930s in Canada see Neatby (1972: 10–14).

5 See CARA (1983). The percentages for the United States are based on 1,729 respondents; for English-speaking Canadians, 913 respondents; and for French-speaking Canadians, 338 respondents.

6 These models are taken from the work of Packer (1964).

7 Data from the Roper Center, Storrs, Connecticut. A comparison of the attitudes of a sample of the public in Calgary in 1974 with those in Seattle in 1973 also indicate more positive attitudes towards police in Canada than in the United States (Klein, Webb, and DiSanto, 1978: 441–456).

8 As economist Peter Karl Kresl puts it: "Canadians have been described as a nation of 'sufficers.' By this it is meant that economic decision makers tend to be content with a pace of economic activity and a degree of efficiency that is not the maximum possible but is rather one that is 'adequate,' or that suffices. . . . Hand in hand with this is . . . the frequently observed lack of aggressiveness and competence on the part of much of Canadian industrial leadership" (Kresl, 1982: 240).

9 Canadian novelist Mordecai Richler has bemoaned Canada's lack of "an indigenous buccaneering capitalist class," suggesting that Canadians have been "timorous . . . circumspect investors in insurance and trust companies" (Richler, 1975: 32; also Friedenberg, 1980: 142).

10 As summarized in Hiller (1976: 144). John Crispo also notes the "propensity among Canadians to invest more abroad" (Crispo, 1979: 28; Kresl, 1982: 240–241).

11 Data computed at my request from Gallup studies in files at the Roper Center, Storrs, CT.

12 The source is the Organization for Economic Cooperation and Development.

13 The argument that the difference in the voting strength of socialism is largely a function of the varying electoral systems has been challenged by Robert Kudrle and Theodore Marmor. They emphasize that the Canadian labor movement "is more socialist than is the U.S. labor movement and always has been" and conclude that "a real but unknown part" of the greater strength of the social democratic New Democratic Party, as compared to that received by American socialists, "may be reflecting a different underlying distribution of values from the United States" (Kudrle and Marmor, 1981: 112; see also Rosenstone, Behr, and Lazarus, 1984).

14 Norman Thomas, the six-time candidate of the Socialist Party for President, also came to believe that the electoral system negated efforts to create a third party, that socialists should work within the major parties (Harrington, 1972: 262).

15 In both countries, unions are much stronger in the public sector than in the private one. See also Rose and Chaison (1985: 97–111).

16 The data are from World Bank, 1983: 197; UNESCO, 1982: 111–143, *Statistical Abstract of the U.S.*, 1982–83: 159.

17 Writing in 1978, he suggested the gap still existed in spite of the growth in numbers of business students.

18 Further evidence that Americans emphasize achievement more than Canadians may be found in Geert Hofstede's (1984: 155–158, 186–188) multinational comparison of work-related employee attitudes.

19 This is Hueglin's characterization of the predominant perspective on this question, with which he disagrees.

20 For an excellent statement by a Canadian historian detailing the relationship between the diverse histories and contemporary North American societies in terms highly similar to those presented here, see McNaught (1984).

References

Aitken, H.G.J. "Defensive expansionism: the state and economic growth in Canada." In H.G.J. Aitken, ed., *The State and Economic Growth*, pp. 79–114. New York: Social Science Research Council, 1959.

Archibald, W. Peter. *Social Psychology as Political Economy*. Toronto: McGraw-Hill Ryerson, 1978.

Arnold, Stephen J. and Barnes, James G. "Canadian and American national character as a basis for market segmentation." In J. Sheth, ed., *Research in Marketing*. Vol. 2 (pp. 1–35). Greenwich, Conn: JAI Press, 1979.

Arnold, Stephen J. and Tigert, Douglas J. "Canadians and Americans: a comparative analysis." *International Journal of Comparative Sociology* 15 (March-June, 1974): 68–83.

Atwood, Margaret. *Survival: A Thematic Guide to Canadian Literature*. Toronto: Anansi Press, 1972.

————. *Second Words: Selected Critical Prose*. Boston: Beacon Press, 1984.

Beer, Samuel. "The modernization of American federalism." *Publius: The Journal of Federalism* 3 (Fall, 1973): 49–95.

Bell, David and Tepperman, Lorne. *The Roots of Disunity: A Look at Canadian Political Culture*. Toronto: McClelland and Stewart, 1979.

Bercovitch, Sacvan. "The rites of assent: rhetoric, ritual and the ideology of American consensus." In Sam B. Girgus, ed., *The American Self: Myth, Ideology and Popular Culture*, pp. 5–42. Albuquerque: University of New Mexico Press, 1981.

Bissell, Claude. "The place of learning and the arts in Canadian life." In Richard A. Preston, ed., *Perspectives on Revolution and Evolution*, pp. 180–212. Durham, N.C.: Duke University Press, 1979.

Bourgault, Pierre L. *Innovation and the Structure of Canadian Industry*. Ottawa: Information Canada, Science Council of Canada, 1972.

Brown, J.J. *Ideas in Exile, a History of Canadian Invention*. Toronto: McClelland and Stewart, 1967.

Brown, Russell M. "Telemachus and Oedipus: images of tradition and authority in Canadian and American fiction." Department of English, University of Toronto, n.d.

Bruckberger, R.L. "The American Catholics as a minority." In Thomas T. McAvoy, ed., *Roman Catholicism and the American Way of Life*, pp. 40–48. Notre Dame, Ind.: University of Notre Dame Press, 1960.

Bryce, James. *Modern Democracies* vol. 1. New York: Macmillan, 1921.

Brym, Robert J. "Social movements and third parties." In S.D. Berkowitz, ed., *Models and Myths in Canadian Sociology*, pp. 29–49. Toronto: Butterworths, 1984.

Burke, Edmund. *Selected Works*. Oxford: Clarendon Press, 1904.

Callwood, June. *Portrait of Canada*. Garden City, N.Y.: Doubleday and Co., 1981.

Campbell, Colin and Szablowski, George J. *The Superbureaucrats: Structure and Behavior in Central Agencies*. Toronto: Macmillan of Canada, 1979.

Careless, J.M.S. *Canada: A Story of Challenge*. Cambridge: Cambridge University Press, 1963.

Center for Applied Research in the Apostolate. *Values Study of Canada*. Code book. Washington, D.C. May, 1983.

Chandler, Marsha A. "The politics of public enterprise." In J. Robert S. Prichard, ed, *Crown Corporations in Canada*, pp. 185–218. Toronto: Butterworths, 1983.

Christian, William and Campbell, Colin. *Political Parties and Ideologies in Canada*, 2nd ed. Toronto: McGraw-Hill Ryerson, 1983.

Clark, S.D. In Angus, H.F. ed., *Canada and Her Great Neighbor: Sociological Surveys of Opinions and Attitudes in Canada Concerning the United States*. Toronto: The Ryerson Press, 1938.

_____. *Church and Sect in Canada*. Toronto: University of Toronto Press, 1948.

_____. "The Canadian community." In George W. Brown, ed., *Canada*, pp. 375–389. Berkeley: University of California Press, 1950.

_____. *The Developing Canadian Community*. Toronto: University of Toronto Press, 1962.

Clement, Wallace. *Continental Corporate Power*. Toronto: McClelland and Stewart, 1977.

Crispo, John. *Mandate for Canada*. Don Mills, Ontario: General Publishing Co., 1979.

Curtis, James. "Voluntary association joining: a cross-national comparative note." *American Sociological Review* 36 (October, 1971): 872–880.

Davis, Arthur K. "Canadian society and history as hinterland versus metropolis." In Richard J. Ossenberg, ed., *Canadian Society: Pluralism, Change and Conflict*, pp. 6–32. Scarborough, Ontario: Prentice Hall, 1971.

Department of Labour. *Information*, Ottawa, June 26, 1984.

Engels, Friedrich. "Engels to Sorge." February 8, 1890. In Karl Marx and Friedrich Engels, *Selected Correspondence*, pp. 466–468. New York: International Publishers, 1942.

_____. "Engels to Sorge," September 10, 1888. In Karl Marx and Friedrich Engels, *Letters to Americans*, pp. 203–204. New York: International Publishers, 1953.

Esman, Milton J. "Federalism and modernization: Canada and the United States," *Publius: The Journal of Federalism* 14 (Winter, 1984): 21–38.

Friedenberg, Edgar Z. *Deference to Authority*. White Plains, N.Y.: M.E. Sharpe, Inc., 1980.

Frye, Northrop. "Letters in Canada: 1952. Part 1: Publications in English." *The University of Toronto Quarterly*, 22 (April, 1953): 269–280.

_____. *Divisions on a Ground: Essays on Canadian Culture*. Toronto: Anansi, 1982.

Gibbins, Roger. *Regionalism: Territorial Politics in Canada and the United States*. Toronto: Butterworths, 1982.

Glazer, Nathan and Moynihan, Daniel P. "Introduction." In Nathan Glazer and Daniel P. Moynihan, ed., *Ethnicity: Theory and Experience*, pp. 1–26. Cambridge: Harvard University Press, 1975.

Glazier, Kenneth M. "Canadian investment in the United States: 'Putting your money where your mouth is'." *Journal of Contemporary Business* 1 (Autumn, 1972): 61–66.

Grant, John Webster. " 'At least you knew where you stood with them': Reflections on religious pluralism in Canada and the United States." *Studies in Religion* 2 (Spring, 1973): 340–351.

Griffiths, Curt T., Klein, John F., and Verdun-Jones, Simon N. *Criminal Justice in Canada*. Scarborough, Ontario: Butterworths, 1980.

Hagan, John and Leon, Jeffrey. "Philosophy and sociology of crime control." In Harry M. Johnson, ed., *Social System and Legal Process*, pp. 181–208. San Francisco: Jossey-Bass, 1978.

Hardin, Herschel. *A Nation Unaware: The*

Canadian Economic Culture. Vancouver: J.J. Douglas, 1974.

Harrington, Michael. *Socialism*. New York: Saturday Review Press, 1972.

Hartz, Louis. *The Liberal Tradition in America*. New York: Harcourt, Brace, 1955.

———. *The Founding of New Societies*. New York: Harcourt, Brace, and World, 1964.

Hastings, Elizabeth H. and Hastings, Philip K. ed., *Index to International Public Opinion, 1980–1981*. Westport, Conn.: Greenwood Press, 1982.

Hiller, Harry H. *Canadian Society: A Sociological Analysis*. Scarborough, Ontario: Prentice-Hall of Canada Ltd., 1976.

Hofstede, Geert. *Culture's Consequences: International Differences in Work-Related Values*. Beverly Hills: Sage Publications, 1984.

Horowitz, Gad. *Canadian Labour in Politics*. Toronto: University of Toronto Press, 1968.

Horowitz, Irving Louis. "The hemispheric connection: A critique and corrective to the entrepreneurial thesis of development with special emphasis on the Canadian case." *Queen's Quarterly* 80 (Autumn, 1973): 327–359.

Hueglin, Thomas O. "The end of institutional tidiness? Trends of late federalism in the United States and Canada." Kingston, Ont.: Department of Political Science, Queen's University, 1984.

Innis, Harold A. *Essays in Canadian History*. Toronto: University of Toronto Press, 1956.

Kendall, John C. "A Canadian construction of reality: northern images of the United States." *The American Review of Canadian Studies* 4 (Spring, 1974): 20–36.

Klein, John F., Webb, Jim R. and DiSanto,

J.E. "Experience with police and attitudes towards the police." *Canadian Journal of Sociology* 3(4) (1978): 441–456.

Kresl, Peter Karl "An economics perspective: Canada in the international economy." In William Metcalf, ed., *Understanding Canada*, pp. 227–295. New York: New York University Press, 1982.

Kudrle, Robert T. and Marmor, Theodore R. "The development of welfare states in North America." In Peter Flora and Arnold J. Heidenheimer, eds., *The Development of Welfare States in Europe and America*, pp. 81–121. New Brunswick, N.J.: Transaction Books, 1981.

Lipset, Seymour Martin. "Democracy in Alberta," *The Canadian Forum* 34 (November, December, 1954): 175–177, 196–198.

———. "Revolution and counterrevolution: the United States and Canada." In Thomas R. Ford, ed., *The Revolutionary Theme in Contemporary America*, pp. 21–64. Lexington: University of Kentucky Press, 1965.

———.*Revolution and Counterrevolution*. Revised paperback edition. Garden City, N.Y.: Anchor Books, 1970 [New York: Basic Books, 1968].

———. "Radicalism in North America: a comparative view of the party systems in Canada and the United States." *Transactions of the Royal Society of Canada* 14 (Fourth Series) (1976), pp. 19–55.

———. "Why no socialism in the United States?" In S. Bialer and S. Sluzar, ed., *Sources of Contemporary Radicalism*, vol. 1, (pp. 31–149), Boulder, Colorado: Westview Press, 1977.

———. "Value differences, absolute or relative: the English speaking democracies." In *The First New Nation: The United States in Historical Comparative Perspective*. Expanded paperback edition, pp. 248–273. New York: W.W. Norton, 1979 [New York: Basic Books, (1963)].

_____. "Socialism in America." In P. Kurtz, ed., *Sidney Hook: Philosopher of Democracy and Humanism*, pp. 47–63. Buffalo, N.Y.: Prometheus Books, 1983.

_____. "Canada and the United States: the cultural dimension." In Charles F. Doran and John H. Sigler, eds., *Canada and the United States: Enduring Friendship, Persistent Stress*, pp. 109–160. Englewood Cliffs, N.J.: Prentice-Hall, Inc., 1985.

_____. "North American labor movements: a comparative perspective." In Seymour Martin Lipset, ed., *Unions in Transition: Entering the Second Century*. San Francisco: Institute for Contemporary Studies, 1986.

MacLennan, Hugh. "A society in revolt," in Judith Webster, ed., *Voices of Canada: An Introduction to Canadian Culture*, pp. 29–30. Burlington, Vt.: Association for Canadian Studies in the United States, 1977.

Manzer, R. *Canada: A Socio-Political Report.* Toronto: McGraw-Hill Ryerson, 1974.

Matthews, Ralph. "Regional differences in Canada; social versus economic interpretations." In Dennis Forcese and Stephen Richer, eds., *Social Issues: Sociological Views of Canada*, pp. 82–123. Scarborough, Ontario: Prentice-Hall, 1982.

McDougall, Robert L. "The dodo and the cruising auk." *Canadian Literature* 18 (Autumn, 1963): 6–20.

McInnis, Edgar W. *The Unguarded Frontier.* Garden City, N.Y.: Doubleday, Doran & Co., 1942.

McKercher, William R. *The U.S. Bill of Rights and the Canadian Charter of Rights and Freedoms.* Toronto: Ontario Economic Council, 1983.

McLeod, J.T. "The free enterprise dodo is no phoenix." *Canadian Forum* 56 (August, 1976): 6–13.

McMillan, Charles J. "The changing competitive environment of Canadian business." *Journal of Canadian Studies* 13 (Spring, 1978): 38–48.

McNaught, Kenneth. "Political trials and the Canadian political tradition." In Martin L. Friedland, ed., *Courts and Trials: A Multidisciplinary Approach*, pp. 137–161. Toronto: University of Toronto Press, 1975.

_____. "Approaches to the study of Canadian history," *The (Japanese) Annual Review of Canadian Studies* 5 (1984): 89–102.

McWhinney, Edward. *Canada and the Constitution, 1979–1982.* Toronto: University of Toronto Press, 1982.

Mercer, John and Goldberg, Michael. "Value differences and their meaning for urban development in the U.S.A." Working Paper No. 12, UBC Research in Land Economics. Vancouver, B.C.: Faculty of Commerce, University of British Columbia, 1982.

Merton, Robert K. *Social Theory and Social Structure.* Glencoe, Ill.: The Free Press, 1957.

Michalos, Alex C. *North American Social Report: A Comparative Study of the Quality of Life in Canada and the USA from 1964 to 1974*, vol. 2. Dordrecht, Holland: D. Reidel Publishing Co., 1980.

Neatby, H. Blair. *The Politics of Chaos: Canada in the Thirties.* Toronto: Macmillan of Canada, 1972.

Nelles, H.V. "Defensive expansionism revisited: federalism, the state and economic nationalism in Canada, 1959–1979." *The (Japanese) Annual Review of Canadian Studies* 2: 127–145, (1980).

O'Toole, Roger. "Some good purpose: Notes on religion and political culture in Canada." *Annual Review of the Social Sciences of Religion*, vol. 6. (1982) The Hague: Mouton, pp. 177–217.

Packer, Herbert. "Two models of the criminal process." *University f Pennsylvania Law Review* 113 (November, 1964): 1–68.

Porter, John. *The Measure of Canadian Society: Education, Equality and Opportunity.* Agincourt, Ontario: Gage Publishing, 1979.

Presthus, Robert. *Elite Accommodation in Canadian Politics.* Cambridge: Cambridge University Press, 1973.

_____. *Elites in the Policy Process.* Toronto: Macmillan of Canada, 1974.

_____. "Aspects of political culture and legislative behavior: United States and Canada." Robert Presthus, ed., *Cross-National Perspectives: United States and Canada,* pp. 7–22. Leiden: E.J. Brill, 1977.

Presthus, Robert and Monopoli, William V. "Bureaucracy in the United States and Canada: social, attitudinal and behavioral variables." In Robert Presthus, ed., *Cross-National Perspectives: United States and Canada,* pp. 176–190. Leiden: E.J. Brill, 1977.

Pye, A. Kenneth. "The rights of persons accused of crime under the Canadian Constitution: a comparative perspective." *Law and Contemporary Problems* 45 (Autumn, 1982): 221–248.

Richler, Mordecai. "Letter from Ottawa: The sorry state of Canadian nationalism." *Harper's* 250 (June, 1975): 28–32.

Rose, Joseph B. and Chaison, Gary N. "The state of the unions: United States and Canada," *Journal of Labor Research* 6 (Winter, 1985): 97–111.

Rosenstone, Steven J., Behr, Roy L. and Lazarus, Edward H. *Third Parties in America: Citizen Response to Major Party Failure.* Princeton, N.J.: Princeton University Press, 1984.

Royal Commission on Bilingualism and Biculturalism. *Report.* Book 4. *The Cultural Contribution of the Other Ethnic Groups.* Ottawa: Queen's Printer, 1969.

Safarian, A.E. *The Performance of Foreign-Owned Firms in Canada.* Washington, D.C.: National Planning Association, 1969.

Schoenfield, Stuart. "The Jewish religion in North America: Canadian and American comparisons." *Canadian Journal of Sociology* 3(2): 209–231, (1978).

Schwartz, Mildred A. *Politics and Territory: The Sociology of Regional Persistence in Canada.* Montreal: McGill-Queen's University Press, 1974.

Science Council of Canada. "Innovation in a cold climate: 'impediments to innovation'." In Abraham Rotstein and Gary Lax, eds., *Independence: The Canadian Challenge,* pp. 120–131. Toronto: The Committee for an Independent Canada, 1972.

Smiley, Donald V. "Public sector politics, modernization and federalism: the Canadian and American experiences." *Publius: The Journal of Federalism* 14 (Winter, 1984): 52–59.

Smith, A.J.M. "Evolution and revolution as aspects of English-Canadian and American literature." In Richard A. Preston, ed., *Perspectives on Evolution and Revolution.* Durham, N.C.: Duke University Press, 1979.

Smith, Denis. *Bleeding Hearts . . . Bleeding Country: Canada and the Quebec Crisis.* Edmonton: M.G. Hurtig, 1971.

Statistical Abstracts of the U.S. 1982-83. 103rd edition.

Sutherland, Ronald. *The New Hero: Essays in Comparative Quebec/Canadian Literature.* Toronto: Macmillan of Canada, 1977.

_____. "A literary perspective: the development of a national consciousness." In William Metcalfe, ed., *Understanding Canada,* pp. 401–414. New York: New York University Press, 1982.

Swinton, Katherine. "Judicial policy making: American and Canadian perspectives." *The Canadian Review of American Studies* 10 (Spring, 1979): 89–94.

Tarrow, Sidney. "Introduction." In Sidney Tarrow, Peter J. Katzenstein and Luigi Graziano, eds., *Territorial Politics in Industrial Nations*. New York: Praeger, 1978.

Taylor, Charles Lewis and Jodice, David A. *World Handbook of Political and Social Indicators*, vol. 2, 3rd ed. New Haven: Yale University Press, 1983.

Tepperman, Lorne. *Crime Control: The Urge Toward Authority*. Toronto: McGraw-Hill Ryerson, 1977.

Thomas, Ted E. "The gun control issue: a sociological analysis of United States and Canadian attitudes and policies." Oakland, California: Department of Sociology, Mills College, 1983.

Tocqueville, Alexis de. *Democracy in America*, vol. 1. New York: Vintage Books, 1945.

Troy, Leo and Sheflin, Leo. *Union Sourcebook*. West Orange, N.J.: IRDIS Publishers, 1985.

Underhill, Frank. *In Search of Canadian Liberalism*. Toronto: Macmillan of Canada, 1960.

UNESCO 1982 *Statistical Yearbook*. Paris: UNESCO, 1982.

United Nations. *World Economic Survey, 1983* (supplement). New York: United Nations, 1983.

U.S. Arms Control and Disarmament Agency. *World Military Expenditures and Arms Transfers 1971–1980*. Washington, D.C., 1982.

U.S. News and World Report, "How big is government's bite?" August 27, 1984: 65.

Vallee, Frank G. and Whyte, Donald R. ed. *Canadian Society: Sociological Perspectives*. Third edition. Toronto: Macmillan of Canada, 1971.

Weaver, John Charles. "Imperilled dreams: Canadian opposition to the American Empire 1918–1930," Ph.D. dissertation, Department of History, Duke University, 1973.

Weber, Max. *The Methodology of the Social Sciences*. Glencoe, Ill.: The Free Press, 1949.

Weller, Geoffrey R. "Common problems, alternative solutions: a comparison of the Canadian and American health systems." Thunder Bay, Ont.: Department of Political Science, Lakehead University, 1984.

Westhues, Kenneth. "Stars and Stripes, the Maple Leaf, and the Papal Coat of Arms." *Canadian Journal of Sociology* 3(1): 245–261, (1978).

Westin, Alan F. "The United States Bill of Rights and the Canadian Charter: A socio-political analysis." In William R. McKercher, ed., *The U.S. Bill of Rights and the Canadian Charter of Rights and Freedoms*, pp. 27–44. Toronto: Ontario Economic Council, 1983.

Whyte, John D. "Civil liberties and the courts." *Queen's Quarterly* 83 (Winter, 1976): 655–663.

World Bank. *World Development Report 1983*. New York: Oxford University Press, 1983.

FOUR

Religion in Canada Versus the U.S. and England

Reginald Bibby

REGINALD W. BIBBY, Ph.D., Professor of Sociology at the University of Lethbridge, is one of Canada's best-known analysts of social trends. He is the author of *Fragmented Gods: The Poverty and Potential of Religion in Canada* and *The Emerging Generation: An Inside Look at Canada's Teenagers* (the latter written with Don Posterski).

WE ARE NOT LIKE THE AMERICANS

... What I want to stress is that history has produced two very different religious marketplaces. Canada is neither a replica nor an underdeveloped version of its southern neighbour. We both have continuing markets for the supernatural, and we are both opting primarily for fragments. But the rules and the companies are different.

The Market

Life experience and the limitations of science create a market for supernatural explanations. The question is not, "*Will* people believe and practise?" but rather, "*What* will they believe and practise?" The United States — generally regarded as the world's most advanced nation — shows no signs of a diminished interest in the supernatural.

Religious Fragments

The extensive religion surveys carried out by the Gallup organization[1] reveal that Americans readily endorse the central traditional beliefs concerning the existence of God (95%), the divinity of Jesus (70%), and life after death (71%). Some 87% say they pray at least sometimes, while 72% recognize the Bible as "the Word of God" (37% endorse the view that it is to be taken literally). As for weekly service attendance, Americans have what many regard as a world-leading level of about 40%. The figure for Catholics is 51%, for Protestants 39% — in both cases about ten percentage points above their Canadian counterparts.

But the signs of fragment adoption are readily evident. Despite the way they view the Bible, only 51% say they read it daily (25% never). They, like us, stumble on fairly simple knowledge questions: fewer than half know who delivered the Sermon on the Mount (42%) or the names of the four gospels (46%). While 40% of all Americans claim to be "born again," just 56% say religion is "very important" in their lives, a ... drop from 75% in 1952.

Further, all is far from well on the attendance front. The current Catholic level of 51% represents a significant drop from 74% in 1958; the Protestant figure in the same year was 44%. Fewer than one in two Americans are regular attenders. The regional variations are notable, with attendance being far higher in the predominantly Baptist South than in the East and Midwest, and lowest in the West.

Like Canadians, Americans readily "buy" less conventional ideas and practices at the supernatural shopping market. More than two in ten think they have seen a ghost or spirit; six in ten report ESP or *déjà vu* experiences; more than 20% believe astrological predictions are correct.[2] The ability of Americans to combine the conventional and the unconventional was suggested to me on a recent trip to Nashville, the headquarters of the nation's largest denomination, the Southern Baptist Convention. In its Saturday issue, the local newspaper's church page included the daily horoscope offerings, along with Ann Landers' column!

No one has compiled American survey data on religion like George Gallup Jr. Drawing upon fifty years of research, Gallup recently made the following observations about the current religious scene. Catholics who in the 1960s might have left the Church today "feel they can disagree on [various] issues and still be part of the Church."[3] Even so, the 1978 study, *The Unchurched American*, has revealed that for many Protestants and Catholics, believing has become divorced from belonging.[4] According to his own scale, Gallup rates the commitment of only about one in ten Americans as high,

four in ten as moderate, and five in ten as low.[5] He further depicts a consumer type of faith:

> While high levels of religious belief and activity are found in U.S. society, there is ample evidence of a self-centered kind of faith ... stated in terms of "it makes me feel good." ... The religious-motivated behaviour ... is more often in the nature of a passive "live and let live" philosophy than in the nature of selfless and heroic action on behalf of others.[6]

Religion has come to have a highly specialized place in American society. Robert Bellah and his associates note in *Habits of the Heart* that "diversity of practice has been seen as legitimate because religion is perceived as a matter of individual choice"; there is, however, "the implicit qualification that the practices themselves accord with public decorum and the adherents abide by the moral standards of the community."[7] ...

The Rules

But the rules of the religious marketplace are different. In Canada, a pluralistic ideal means that religious groups are expected to co-exist for servicing. In the United States, the pursuit of truth means that religious groups are allowed to compete for truth.

... In contrast to the Americans, "we did not separate violently from Europe," Pierre Berton reminds us, "but cut our ties cautiously in the Canadian manner — so cautiously, so imperceptibly that none of us is quite sure we actually achieved our independence."[8] Our religious groups did not compete for truth but serviced the immigrants in the French and English expressions to which they had grown accustomed, aided in whole or in part by public funds.

Americans, on the other hand, made their dramatic break with England and set out to establish a distinctive nation. Their "charter myth" included the belief that the country had been founded by God to give leadership to the world. The key to its development was the creation of a milieu of liberty, an environment in which individuals could have freedom of expression and the freedom to pursue truth.

The constitutional guarantee of religious freedom accordingly separated Church and State, giving individuals the opportunity to explore and proclaim truth as they understood it. As with the other sectors of American life — the economy, education, and politics, for example — the religion market was technically "up for grabs."

Thus it is that the American religion market is, and has always been, a dynamic one, characterized by aggressive, persistent claims to truth, a style quite foreign and frankly rather repugnant to pluralistically minded Canadians. . . .

. . . Variations on the normative Judeo-Christian theme are welcome in the U.S. The American obsession with pursuing and disseminating truth legitimizes "new and improved" truth claims. A natural outcome of this free-enterprise emphasis in a rewarding environment is religious innovation. In the mid-1970s, there were 223 distinct religious bodies in the U.S., compared with only 63 in Canada.[9]

There is also little doubt that American soil has been the base for a large number of new religious movements which . . . have spread to Canada and . . . other parts of the world.[10] From a market-model point of view, what is being reflected is not only a greater American receptivity to new religions but also a competitive and lucrative milieu in which religion — primarily within Judeo-Christian limits — is a robust and potentially profitable product, financially and otherwise.

The search for truth produces a lively market. Pluralism, insisting as it does on respect for diversity, either kills the ability to make market inroads or dulls the inclination.

The Companies

. . . U.S. Conservative Protestants, primarily . . . Baptists, constitute the largest Protestant grouping (more than 20%; see Table 4-1). They have had this status since about 1950. Before that time, they were exceeded in numbers only by the Methodists, now the second-largest Protestant denomination (9%). Lutherans (7%) stand third, followed by Episcopalians (3%), and Presbyterians and United Church of Christ (2% each). . . .

These findings show that four "religious companies" — the Roman Catholics, Baptists, Methodists, and Lutherans — hold down 64% or almost two-thirds of the American religious market. . . .

Nevertheless, from the standpoint of sheer affiliation, these have been the dominant religious denominations now for some time. The U.S. market may be open to "religious entrepreneurs" and indeed appears to have been a hotbed of religious innovation. Yet the market is clearly monopolized by four main companies.

It is important to keep in mind . . . that the dominant companies are different in the two countries. Most striking is the strength of the Conservative Protestants in the U.S. — more than 20%, compared with 7% in Canada.

Consequently, there is little basis for assuming that because a program "works" in the U.S. it will "work" in Canada. In the case of Conservative Protestants, for example, the difference in numbers has important implications for possibilities of growth. In Canada, as in

TABLE 4-1   Religious Affiliation of Americans: 1947–84 *(In %s)*

	1947	1957	1967	1976	1984
ROMAN CATHOLIC	20	26	25	27	28
PROTESTANT	69	66	67	61	57
Baptist	••	••	21	21	20
Methodist	••	••	14	11	9
Lutheran	••	••	7	7	7
Presbyterian	••	••	6	5	2
Episcopalian	••	••	3	3	3
Other	••	••	16	14	16
JEWISH	5	3	3	2	2
OTHER	1	1	3	4	4
NONE	6	3	2	6	9

Source: Derived from *The Gallup Report*, May 1985.
Note: Because of rounding, some percentage columns do not equal 100.

other societies where they constitute a numerical minority, expansion is very difficult, especially if the other dominant religious groups provide an evangelical menu offering of their own. The only path to significant proportional growth is "the tough path" of proselytization; birth and immigration — much easier means of numerical expansion — do not produce sufficient numbers of new members to alter the evangelicals' percentage.

In the United States, on the other hand, the numerical prominence — indeed, dominance — of evangelicals means that considerable growth occurs through birth and retention. Proselytization is consequently neither particularly common nor necessary. In Canada it is a necessity, though it is a path less travelled. . . .

Canadians taking their cues from the United States in trying to understand current religious developments or plan effective programs have mistaken a window for a mirror.

MAYBE A LITTLE LIKE THE ENGLISH

. . . England's religious setting is similar to ours in that a market for the supernatural exists, fragment adoption abounds, and the rules of the competition are fairly similar. We differ significantly, however, when it comes to our respective religious companies.

The Market

England had historically been characterized by a pervasive interest in the supernatural. In addition to the visible role played by Christianity over the centuries, interest in magic, superstition, spiritualism, and psychic phenomena has been high. . . .

Religious Fragments

The English exhibit a wide range of supernatural beliefs and practices. Belief in God or a Supreme Being is high (72%), while belief in the divinity of Jesus and heaven is held by about half the population.[11] Close to one in three people say they engage in daily private prayer,[12] and claims of religious experiences are very common.[13] A University of Leeds researcher, Robert Towler, further reports that "folk religion," characterized by a wide variety of heterogeneous beliefs and practices, is widespread.[14]

As noted, the English have not lacked an interest in less conventional phenomena either. David Hay and Ann Morisy have reported widespread claims of paranormal and ecstatic experiences.[15] Other surveys have found that one in six continue to believe in ghosts, while one in ten assert belief in reincarnation.[16] . . .

It is also very clear, however, that fragment adoption rather than commitment has been widespread. Only one in four describe their religious beliefs as very important to them.[17] The smorgasbord-like combinations of beliefs and practices are described by researchers who examined a London borough:

> Of the doubters, agnostics and atheists, over a quarter say they pray on occasions to the God whose existence they doubt. . . . Of those who say they believe in a Deity, one in five are definite in their assertion that they do not believe in life after death; one half say they never go to church. . . . Of those who attend Church of England services regularly or intermittently, one-quarter do not believe in an after-life — on the other hand, one-fifth of those who don't go to church at all do believe.[18]

Martin comments that English culture, far from being secular, "wobbles between a partially absorbed Christianity" and a strange mixture of values like fate and luck.[19]

Fragment adoption is also evident in weekly service attendance. Levels have declined from 36% in 1851 to a current level of about 10%.[20] The general pattern has been for attendance to be lower in the larger cities and among the working classes. In Liverpool, for example, the drop has been from 70% in 1831 to about 30% in 1891, 20% in 1934, to a current level of under 10%.[21] Attendance is, however, higher than the national level for Roman Catholics (close to 40%), and Nonconformist groups (some 25%).[22] . . .

English churches, like their North American counterparts, have found themselves dealing with a selectively minded clientele. Donald Reeves, Rector of St. James' Anglican Church, Piccadilly, maintains that "religion is just another commodity to be consumed," regarded "on the same level as playing golf or washing the car or belonging to Rotary."[23]

The churches, faced with this downturn in attendance, have sought to make changes, to update and upgrade. David Jenkins, the Church of England's Bishop of Durham, became a household name when he declared on the eve of his consecration that he had grave doubts about the virgin birth and Jesus' resurrection. The magnitude of the negative reaction spoke volumes about the Church's theological diversity. . . .

The Rules and the Companies

From the year 1531, when Henry VIII defied the Pope and declared himself the head of the Church of England, "the Anglicans" have enjoyed the monopoly that goes along with being a state religion. . . . Following a century and a half of severe persecution, religious freedom, officially at least, came into being with the passage of the Toleration Act in 1689 [but] . . . the Roman Catholic hierarchy was not restored in England until 1850.

The Church of England has been and continues to be the official state church. British sovereigns are the supreme governors of the Church and in turn are crowned at their coronation services by the Archbishop of Canterbury (The Primate of All England and leader of the worldwide Anglican communion). The senior Bishops are entitled to sit as members in the House of Lords. Clergy, however, are not paid by the state unless in its employ.[24]

For three hundred years, other non-Catholic religious groups have been allowed to compete for whatever part of the market they find it possible to garner. The market results have never been in doubt. Aligned with the state, in 1900 the Church of England was the Church with which almost seven in ten people in Britain claimed affiliation. Today it continues to be the choice of some six in ten (see Table 4-2). . . .

This historical move in the direction of semi-pluralism has created a market mood not dissimilar to Canada's. Groups primarily service their own; they do not aggressively raid each others' ranks. Further, the proportional market shares of Anglicans and Roman Catholics are essentially reversed in the two countries (10% and 46% respectively in Canada). . . .

. . . The tendency towards a fairly stable religious market is not attributable only to semi-pluralism. Its sources also include dominant cultural traits. I am thinking specifically of reserve and non-aggressive competitiveness. . . . The hype associated with Americans' promotion of the religions of their choice [is] foreign — and, I would suggest, unacceptable — to most of the English. . . .

The attendance drop-off in England has been much greater than that experienced, at least to date, in Canada. Nevertheless, as in our country, sheer religious affiliation has power in England. It continues to be related to a strong demand for rites of passage.[25] In addition, it carries with it emotional weight. Reeves writes that "we are not just a nation of lazy agnostics or cool rationalists. There are many who have jettisoned the dogma but cherish the music or admire the buildings inspired by faith. . . ."[26]

Affiliation, while usually falling short of commitment, may also be commonly associated with endorsement, making defection unlikely. Edward Bailey, for example, maintains that people who appear

TABLE 4-2   Religious Affiliation of the British: 1900, 1970, 1980* *(In %s)*

	1900	**1970**	**1980**
Anglicans	66	57	57
Other Protestants	25	18	16
Roman Catholics	6	14	14
Other	1	3	4
None	2	8	9

Source: Derived from Barrett, 1983: 699.
* These figures are for Great Britain (i.e., England, Scotland, Wales, and Northern Ireland).

to have unclear personal faiths nonetheless frequently affirm "Christianity" itself. When they make reference to terms like "Christ," "God," or "the Church," they may be clumsy theologically. But the more important thing for them is that these terms stand for this "Christianity" to which they subscribe.[27] . . .

Our examination of . . ., the United States and England, reveals that interest in supernatural phenomena persists. . . . Yet the nature of modern life in all three societies, with its emphasis upon role and institutional specialization, has limited the influence of religion. At the personal level, people are opting for fragments. . . . Religious groups are typically relegated to the role of interest groups.

Canadians do not differ from Americans in either their inclination to embrace the supernatural or their tendency to adopt religious fragments. What is different is that we live in a society that values pluralism over competition and has a religious market dominated not by Conservative Protestants but by Roman Catholics and denominations of British descent.

When we compare ourselves with the English, we find they, too, embrace the supernatural, primarily in fragment form. They also have a stability fostered by a belated religious pluralism. But the religious market knows the legacy of giving one company a major advantage for a long time. . . .

Notes

1 The American data here are drawn from Gallup, 1985.
2 Cited in McGuire, 1987: 92, 94.
3 Gallup, 1985: 12.
4 Gallup, 1985: 10.
5 Gallup, 1985: 12.
6 Gallup, 1985.
7 Bellah et al., 1985: 225.
8 Berton, 1982: 36.
9 Cited in Fallding, 1978: 145.
10 See, for example, Wilson, 1970; Hiller, 1978; Stark and Bainbridge, 1985.
11 Sigelman, 1977: 290.
12 Martin, 1967: 55.
13 Hay and Morisy, 1978 and 1985.
14 See, for example, Towler, 1985.
15 Hay and Morisy, 1978 and 1985.
16 Martin, 1967: 55.
17 See Gallup, 1986: 2 and Sigelman, 1977: 290.
18 Cited in Martin, 1967: 53.
19 Martin, 1967: 76.
20 Barrett, 1982: 700; Martin, 1967: 19.
21 Martin, 1967: 44.
22 Barrett, 1982: 700; Martin, 1967: 40.
23 Reeves, 1986: 194.
24 Barrett, 1982: 702–5.
25 See, for example, Martin, 1967: 51.
26 Reeves, 1986: 191.
27 Bailey, 1986.

References

Bailey, Edward. "The Religion of the People." In Tony Moss (ed.), *In Search of Christianity*, pp. 178–88. London: Firethorn Press, 1986.

Barrett, David B. (ed.). *World Christian Encyclopedia*. Nairobi: Oxford University Press, 1982.

Bellah, Robert, Madsen, Richard, Sullivan, William M., Swidler, Ann and Tipton, Steven M. *Habits of the Heart*. New York: Harper and Row, 1985.

Berton Pierre. *Why We Act Like Canadians*. Toronto: McClelland and Stewart, 1982.

Fallding, Harold. "Mainline Protestantism in Canada and the United States of America: An Overview." *Canadian Journal of Sociology* 3 (1978): 141–60.

Gallup, George, Jr. *Religion in America, 50 years: 1935–1985*. May, Report No. 236. Princeton: The Gallup Report, 1985.

_____ . *Emerging Trends*. October, Vol. 8, No. 8. Princeton: Princeton Research Center, 1986.

Hay, David, and Morisy, Ann. "Reports of Ecstatic, Paranormal, or Religious Experiences in Great Britain and the United States: A Comparison of Trends. *Journal for the Scientific Study of Religion* 17 (1978): 255–68.

_____ . "Secular Society, Religious Mean-ings: A Contemporary Paradox." *Review of Religious Research* 26 (1985): 213–27.

Hiller, Harry H. "Continentalism and the Third Force in Religion." *Canadian Journal of Sociology* 3 (1978): 183–207.

Martin, David. *A Sociology of English Religion*. London: SCM Press, 1967.

_____ . *A General Theory of Secularization*. London: Harper Row, 1978.

McGuire, Meredith B. *Religion: The Social Context*. Belmont, Calif: Wadsworth, 1987.

Reeves, Donald. "Radical Christianity." In Tony Moss (ed.), *In Search of Christianity*, pp. 192–200. London: Firethorn Press, 1986.

Sigelman, Lee. "Multi-nation Surveys of Religious Beliefs." *Journal for the Scientific Study of Religion* 16 (1977): 289–94.

Stark, Rodney, and Bainbridge, William Sims. *The Future of Religion*. Berkeley: University of California Press, 1985.

Towler, Robert. *The Need for Certainty: A Sociological Study of Conventional Religion*. Boston: Routledge and Kegan Paul, 1985.

Wilson, Bryan. *Religious Sects*. New York: McGraw-Hill, 1970.

FIVE

Ideology and Social Organization

Patricia Marchak

M. PATRICIA MARCHAK, Dean of the Faculty of Arts and Professor of Sociology at the University of British Columbia, Vancouver, specializes in the study of ideology and political economy. Her books and articles include *Ideological Perspectives on Canada* (1975, 1981); *In Whose Interests: An Essay on Multinational Corporations in a Canadian Context* (1979); *Green Gold: The Forest Industry in British Columbia* (1983); *Uncommon Property: The Fishing and Fish Processing Industries in British Columbia*, co-edited with Neil Guppy and John McMullan (1987); "Canadian Political Economy" (1985); and *The Integrated Circus: The New Right and the Restructuring of Global Markets* (1991). As well as writing numerous scholarly papers and giving many presentations, Professor Marchak has served as President of the Canadian Sociology and Anthropology Association, as Book Review Editor for the *Canadian Review of Sociology and Anthropology*, and on the editorial boards of *Studies in Political Economy and Current Sociology*.

IDEOLOGIES

Dominant and counter-ideologies grow out of the same social organization. They take the same economic arrangement, the same territorial boundaries, the same population as their units of analysis. But they posit different relationships between these units and different organizations within them. Although the two major ideologies of our time — which we will label liberalism and socialism — claim to explain society in historical and comparative perspective, they both originate in the period of the European Industrial Revolution, and both are unmistakably locked into industrial society as it emerged in Europe at that time.

Because they grow out of the same organization, they have much in common. They are the two sides of a single coin: one describing how the entire structure looks to one who accepts it and expects it to survive; the other, how it looks to one who rejects it and anticipates its demise. . . .

Ideologies are explanations for the social organization, but they are, as well, evaluations of it. These evaluations tend to be circular: the social organization gives rise to certain beliefs about what is right, appropriate, and desirable, that is, to certain values. These values are then assumed, and the society judges itself by those values. The liberal democracy gave rise to positive evaluations of equality, individualism, material prosperity, and personal freedom. The society is then judged within that framework: does it allow for the realization of these values? The dominant ideology rests on an affirmative answer: yes, this society provides the necessary conditions for equality, material prosperity, and personal freedom. Where there are deficiencies, these are often not recognized. Where the deficiencies are recognized, they are explained not as symptoms of a system that fails but as aberrations or temporary problems in a system that succeeds.

Widespread acceptance of an ideology creates an incapacity for judgment of its truth. There is comfort in believing what so many others appear to believe, in accepting conventional wisdom. There is fear in doing otherwise. Sometimes there are, as well, serious social consequences. To many minds, the person who admits to a deviant perspective is out of bounds, somehow dirty and unacceptable.

Counter ideologies involve a good deal of imagination. They provide a critique of the present society and a creative vision of an alternative. Both socialism and the "new right" provide these critiques and creative visions; and whether we agree with them or despise them, we are indebted to their proponents for enabling us to imagine other ways of doing things.

Counter ideologies generally begin with a critical perspective which arises from recognition of inconsistencies between what the dominant ideology portrays as truth and what the senses suggest is reality. They begin, then, as reform movements and their members are social critics. Equality, material prosperity, and personal freedom may be assumed as "right" values, but the society is judged as deficient in providing for their realization. The negative judgment leads to an analysis of social organization which diverges from that propagated by those who hold the dominant ideology and believe it to meet its own objectives. Gradually the analysis turns into a fully developed counter ideology, an entirely different way of viewing the society.

———

Some people think that ideology is something that happens to others, and generally to somewhat deranged others. That is not the sense in which the term is used here. We are all immersed in ideological understandings of our world.

We define ideology as: shared ideas, perceptions, values, and beliefs through which members of a society interpret history and contemporary social events and which shape their expectations and wishes for the future.

A dominant ideology is defined as that particular set of ideas, perceptions, values, and beliefs which is most widely shared and has the greatest impact on social action at any particular time in any particular society.

A counter ideology is defined as a set of ideas, etc., which is held by a substantial minority and which has noticeable impact on social action. There may be many or few counter ideologies in any society at any historical period.

There is another definition of ideology: the ideas and values of the ruling class, disseminated through agencies controlled by that class in ways that obfuscate class realities for subservient classes. We are not using this definition here.

Ideology and theory are different entities, though they grow out of the same womb. Theory consists of explicit assumptions, a reasoning by which the assumptions are demonstrated to be linked to conclusions on the one hand, and such material evidence as can be gathered on the other. It is, by definition, open to challenge through the presentation of more complete or contesting evidence, or by a refutation of the logic that links assumptions to conclusions. It is not a faith. It is not unexamined.

In some ways, theories are rivals and enemies of ideologies because they tend to dissect them. Someone begins by saying, "Hmm, I believe this and that, I think I'll write it all down in some systematic way so that others will think as I do." Then, in the writing of it, the author begins to see some inconsistencies, some flaws in logic, some mismatch between theory and evidence. And the reader, perusing the manuscript, says, "but this isn't good enough." Theories evolve over time, moving further and further away from their ideological base, becoming more sophisticated, more logical, more consistent — but often moving so far from their beginnings that they leave the majority of believers far behind.

Ideologies normally attract some people who want to make them public and systematic. In addition to theorists, there are scribes and prophets who define ideologies, trying to demonstrate how their particular beliefs are unique and true. For this reason, we can examine such ideologies through the writings of the scribes and the speeches of the prophets. And, as we begin to see which values they emphasize, which utopian visions they advance, we can label the ideologies and identify them relative to one another with reference to specific values. But for the same reason that we need to distinguish between theory and ideology, we need to recognize the possible differences between what the scribes and prophets say and what a majority of believers accept.

Ideologies may be phrased in terms we would recognize as political, that is, they are about the political world and how the public arena should be governed. Other ideologies may also have political implications but may be phrased as religious belief systems. Although the language of discourse may seem very different, there are usually close ties between what people believe about the meaning of human existence or the properties of nature and gods, and what they believe about political governance in the temporal world.

We are concerned here with the major ideologies of our society, the dominant and the counter ideologies which motivate large numbers of people. And we are concerned primarily, though not exclusively, with how these ideologies link up with economic and political events. There are, in addition to these central ideologies, other versions of the world espoused by smaller numbers of people. Some of these other versions take political forms, some take religious forms.

Political ideologies ultimately boil down to the relative emphasis placed on individualism versus collectivism, and on egalitarianism versus elitism. It is in these terms that we can identify the difference between one ideology and another. We have political labels for various positions in our own society, along two continuums: the first, from extreme individualists (society has absolutely no claims on the individual, and there should be no rules, government, or constraints on individual actions) to extreme collectivists (society always has precedence over individuals, and the right to demand conformance with rules for the public good); and the second, from extreme elitism (there should be rulers and the rulers should have complete power) to extreme egalitarianism (all people should be absolutely equal in condition, not just opportunities). The differences between these labelled positions can be noted by referring to the theories, scribes and prophets, but as observed above, we must be wary of assuming that all adherents to labelled positions are consistent in their beliefs.

INDIVIDUALIST AND MARKET-BASED IDEOLOGIES

Anarchism, libertarianism, and to a lesser degree, liberalism, treat society as a collection of individuals. Society does not exist in and of itself, it is not an organic whole. Individuals each strive to manufacture the necessary conditions for life, and the market mechanism has emerged as a means of coordinating their separate strivings without applying force. The preservation of individual liberty and of the "free market" become the major concerns of advocates of these positions.

Anarchism and Libertarianism

The individualist position is taken to the extreme in anarchist and libertarian ideologies; all other values become subordinate. Anarchists would do away with all government and social restrictions on personal liberty; libertarians (though with some differences between various groups) generally accept the necessity of government, but would restrict its functions to the defence of persons and property. Anything which prevents individuals from fully exercising their initiative, entrepreneurial skills, and talents is harshly judged: thus democracy and the welfare state are deemed to be impediments to individual growth. Inequality is viewed as inevitable because

people are genetically unequal, and as necessary because the most talented provide the leadership which permits others to survive. Libertarians believe that "pure" capitalism is an ideal social and economic system because it includes a genuinely free market for absolutely all goods and services.

Liberalism

Liberalism has a somewhat different meaning in Canada than in the United States. In Canada, it is an approach which emphasizes the individual but combines that emphasis with concern for the preservation of law, order, and public well-being in the society, and includes some concern for equality between citizens. In the United States, its connotation is more strongly connected to social and collective values, closer to what Canadians would regard as "social democratic." It differs from the Canadian social democratic view in that while both take equality to be a positive value, the liberal view is that equality of opportunity is sufficient, and that such equality is largely achieved within the present social system. Social democrats argue in favour of greater equality of condition and perceive great inequalities of both opportunity and condition in the present social system.

Like libertarians, liberals believe in the virtues of a free enterprise market, in which all sellers and buyers compete on equal terms for the attention of consumers. Unlike libertarians, liberals temper this belief by acknowledgment of some services and goods which "ought" to be in the public realm. The free enterprise market is rarely called "capitalism" in liberal ideology; the phrase "free enterprise" becomes the euphemism for capitalism. Consonant with the belief that society is made up of individuals, liberals deny the existence of classes in capitalist society. A great deal of emphasis is placed on the education system because liberals believe that individuals have equal opportunity in that sphere, each achieving there what their innate talents and hard work permit and thus moving upward or downward in the social system according to ability.

The role of government is to regulate the market place and ensure that the rules are fair and equitable; government is not itself an economic actor in a truly "free" enterprise system. Further, since there are no classes, government cannot be seen as the agent of any particular class; and since there is no ruling class, it cannot be seen as acting on behalf of that class.

Liberalism has been the dominant ideological perspective adopted by Canadians throughout the past 40 years. One political party is called "Liberal" but when we speak of liberalism, we do not refer exclusively to this party. In fact, throughout this period, the two major alternative parties, the Progressive Conservative and the New Democratic Parties, have shared much of the liberal version of Canadian society.

COLLECTIVIST POSITIONS

Collectivist positions begin with the argument that the society is an organic whole. Society exists independent of the individuals who happen to live in it at any time. But there is enormous difference in the conclusions and policy positions taken by collectivists of the "left" and of the "right." The basic difference occurs between those who believe that society

ought to be more egalitarian (social democratic, socialist, communist) and those who believe it should be more hierarchically ordered (conservative, corporatist, and fascist).

Social Democratic

Social democrats accept the basic values of liberalism but place more emphasis on equality. As well, they recognize the existence of classes, of class barriers, and of governments acting in the interests of a dominant or ruling class. They thus share some of the understandings of socialists. They are committed to the gradual and democratic evolution of a socialist society, which they understand to be a more egalitarian organization within which workers have decision-making control over production, and private ownership rights over industrial units and natural resources are abolished. This is the position of various democratic socialist parties throughout the world, and of the CCF and NDP parties.

Socialist

Socialists perceive capitalism as a system where a ruling class extracts wealth from a subordinate class (or classes), sells products made by labour, and uses the profits to invest in more properties and new technologies which displace or further enslave labour. Classes exist, inequalities are essential to the system, and individual freedom is highly circumscribed by the fundamental requirement that labour must produce goods and services for capital. For the socialist these conditions are unacceptable.

Socialism involves a version of the future which differs markedly from that liberalism. For liberals, the future is a continuum of the past and present. It is a highly optimistic ideology, assuming eternal progress and gradual elimination of imperfections in the social system. But socialism, identifying capitalism as an oppressive and exploitative system, involves the belief that only through the destruction of capitalism can a more egalitarian and humane system emerge. Capitalism is expected to self-destruct, because its internal contradictions must eventually cause a fatal blockage in the capacities of capitalists to continue accumulating new profits (this is called "a crisis of accumulation" in the socialist literature).

For the liberal, capitalism is necessary reality and critiques of it are ideology. For the socialist, the liberal version of capitalism is ideology. It is understood by socialists as an essential feature of the capitalist system, because it induces workers to consent to their own exploitation. They are persuaded, rather than forced (though force may on occasion also be necessary), to believe that the system is fair even if it leads to extremely unequal distributions of material wealth and economic power. Part of the key to this persuasion is, in the opinion of socialists, the nature of democratic governments. These are either so constrained by the economic decisions of private capital or so instrumentally attached to private capital (there are different theories on this) that they can do little more than facilitate private accumulation. They mediate class conflict by developing rules for employment, hours, welfare and the like, because the system could not continue with persistent or violent class conflict, but the appearance is of governments acting in the general public interest. As well, since governments are formally elected by the population at large, there is a widespread belief in their neu-

trality and representative character. The ideology of democracy, then, and the mechanics of democratic elections are important features of capitalism because they "legitimate" the economic system and provide the pretence of impartiality.

Conservatism

Conservatism — like liberalism not to be interpreted as necessarily coincident with a particular political party — shares with socialism a belief that there are classes, that capitalism necessarily involves inequality, and that the marketplace should not be the locus of most important social decisions. But unlike socialism, conservatism gives a high positive value to class inequalities: they are necessary because society requires leadership, and well established leaders look after less well established workers. Conservatism thus values a "natural" hierarchy, paternalistic relations between capital and labour. For the conservative, government properly has the right to establish norms for the conduct of social life, though it should have a restrained role in the economy.

The chief difference between conservatism and liberalism is in their respective views of society: conservatives viewing it as an organic whole within which individuals have assigned places; liberals as a collection of individuals each striving for personal goals. Thus true conservatives should be concerned with the collective moral fabric as well as the permanence of a dominant class. Logically, liberals would be less concerned with social and moral issues except where society infringes on individual rights.

Corporatism

Corporatism shares with conservatism the belief in a natural hierarchy of human beings, the importance of planning the economy and the positive evaluation of social classes. It goes beyond conservatism in arguing that economic units — corporations — should make the decisions about the conduct of economic life. Democratic procedures typical of liberal societies are viewed as unacceptable, because they allow uninformed and unpropertied individuals and groups to choose leaders and policies and thus inhibit social progress.

This position is associated with Italy under Mussolini, and has not had much of a history in Canada though some Canadians flirted with it during the 1930s. At the present time, some Canadians are again flirting with it, and there are curious alliances between some of its advocates and libertarians.

Fascism

Fascism is an extreme form of corporatism, going beyond it in accepting the necessity for force in controlling dissidents. We usually associate it with Nazi Germany in the 1930s and 1940s, but there was a fascist party in Canada during the 1930s, and a very small group of followers have persisted throughout this century.

DOMINANT IDEOLOGY

If we identify the dominant ideology as the values and beliefs held in common by a majority, we would include the liberal, social democratic, and conservative positions as falling within its compass. Although they differ in the degree to which they emphasize individualism and egalitarianism, they share a number of assumptions. To begin with, proponents of these positions assume the legitimacy of private property rights but at the same time recognize legitimate constraints on these. They accept (with varying degrees of approval) the economic drive for profits, but again, place limits on its capacity to drive the entire social system. They accept differential rewards for work associated with numerous social factors (education, skills, talent, etc.), but reject differences associated with gender, ethnicity, religion, or other "non-economic" attributes of individuals. Although both the conservative and social democratic positions include acknowledgement of the reality of class divisions in capitalist society, and liberalism does not, all three tend to explain social events in terms of individuals or non-class groups (e.g., men and women, ethnic groups, particular interest groups) more than in terms of classes. All positions involve notions of social progress toward a "better" society to be achieved through gradual evolution.

Political parties espousing these points of view make many more distinctions between the positions. It is in their interests to do so, of course, since they have to make their party appear to be the unique champion of individual rights or equal opportunity or whatever.

All societies arrive, whether through conscious political activity or tacit agreements and traditional activities, at some position between individualism and collectivism, egalitarianism and elitism. There is another set of values which cross-cuts these, providing a third dimension to social organization. It is attitudes toward nature.

Societies dependent on hunting and gathering, and some societies dependent on cultivation of foods, have developed understandings of people as components of nature on the same level with other animate beings. Most such societies also hold the view that there are unseen spirits guiding and judging their activities. Within these perceptions, animals and land are highly valued, and destruction of either is unacceptable behaviour. Thus the hunter must apologise to the beast he has killed, explaining his need for food and his sincere appreciation for the sacrifice made by the animal.

By contrast, the industrial society treats animals and humans as qualitatively different entities, with humans having the right to kill and conquer all other living things. Land is but a space where human activity takes place: it has no spiritual quality.

Within the past decade, new social movements have arisen within industrial societies opposed to the destruction of our environment. Some of these have taken on political aspects, organizing as political parties or as pressure groups. The anti-nuclear movement, the Green Party, and numerous groups devoted to the saving of particular territories are among these. To date, these groups have not developed consistent positions on individualism-collectivism, egalitarianism-elitism. They are, in a sense, outside the mainstream of public discourse, and adherents to environmentalist ideologies could, conceivably, place themselves anywhere within the other political spectrums.

Similarly, religious movements sometimes exist outside the main discourse of industrial society. While the major religions in Canada — Christian Catholicism and Protestantism and Judaism — have generally adopted and supported the dominant ideology, smaller and often sectarian groups have challenged these views. Some support highly individualistic positions (salvationist religions), others more collectivist positions (cultural renewal religions).

The industrial society is not a static social organization. The processes set in motion by the development of urban populations and competitive capitalism destroyed the feudal aristocracy and the peasantry. They created new forms of government. They destroyed societies and created new ones in far-off colonies. Change occurred at many levels simultaneously: at the level of the family unit, at the level of education. The liberal ideology explains these changes as cumulative growth. Society is always progressing, always adjusting to new conditions. Its growth is limitless, its perfection is a viable goal. The analogy is to a wheel turning over new territory and adding always to its conquest of distance.

Marx posited quite a different kind of change — cumulative, still, but fraught with internal contradictions. The growth in competitive capitalism would give rise to monopoly capitalism. The growth of wealth at the top would create the growth of poverty at the bottom. The more successful the capitalists were in developing technology and organizing the workforce for their own ends, the faster they brought about their own demise by an organized, efficient proletariat. The wheel in this analogy spins ever faster only to break down from over-use, and its riders are obliged to make a new wheel out of the parts. Marx envisioned the final stages in these words:

One capitalist always kills many. Hand in hand with this centralization, or this expropriation of many capitalists by few, develop, on an ever-extending scale, the co-operative form of the labour process, the conscious technical application of science, the methodical cultivation of the soil, the transformation of the instruments of labour into instruments of labour only usable in common, the economizing of all means of production by their use as the means of production of combined, socialized labour, the entanglement of all peoples in the net of the world-market, and with this, the international character of the capitalistic regime. Along with the constantly diminishing number of the magnates of capital, who usurp and monopolise all advantages of this process of transformation, grows the mass of misery, oppression, slavery, degradation, exploitation; but with this too grows the revolt of the working-class, a class always increasing in numbers, and disciplined, united, organized by the very mechanism of the process of capitalist production itself.[1]

Whether one takes the progressional view of history or the dialectic view, one is struck by the observation that cumulative growth in any respect of social organization eventually becomes destructive of that organization. Whether we eventually arrive in a different town by riding the wheel from one place to another, or whether the journey itself transforms the travellers, the fact is that the industrial society of the 1980s is not the industrial society of the 1920s or the 1880s. It is qualitatively a different society. The technology has changed dramatically. The social organization has changed. The population balance has changed. The relations between nation states have changed. What has noticeably failed to change is the ideology.

The ideologies at the popular level are very much the same as they were in these other times. Speeches to the Chamber of Commerce reflect the same abiding faith in progress, material prosperity, and general affluence; the same evaluation of private property, individualism, and achievement; the same belief in the existence of equality and opportunity. The slogans of the Left are remarkably similar to those uttered in the trade union struggles of the turn of the century. There is the same belief in massive exploitation by a ruling class, the same faith in the nobility of labour, the same conviction that pervasive equality is both yet to come and highly desirable.

In Canada, for example, feudalistic values remained into the early 20th century. While these were tinged by the values of liberalism as it was expressed in the United States and Britain, liberalism in its classic form did not emerge as a dominant ideology until very late in history by comparison with these other countries. Nearly a century after the American War of Independence had spawned the notion that individuals should pursue happiness and that this was a legitimate basis for social organization, as long again after the French Revolution had bannered the words "liberty, equality, fraternity," Canada continued to be ruled by a landed aristocracy which gained its wealth through the fur trade, export-import businesses, and banking. Its values were not those of industrial capitalists. It was not engaged in competitive enterprise, and was not generating new wealth out of the production of goods for a market. At the other end of the social scale, the larger part of the population was engaged in farming rather than manufacturing, and Canada was largely a rural country before World War I; indeed, it remained predominantly rural until the 1930s. The slow development of industry and of an industrial urban labour force retarded the development of liberalism as an ideology.

Conservatism, then, has not been absent in Canada, but in the past half-century it has not been a dominant ideology either.

Liberalism and socialism can interpret one kind of society, one form of industrial organization. This is the society in transition within the political framework of nation states. Neither is suited to providing a popular interpretation or appropriate set of values for maintenance of a multi-national or non-national capitalism in which wage work is not available to many people, surplus is not created out of labour, communications technology becomes more central to political control, and corporations are the chief social as well as economic organizations. Those of us who continue to live in the "old world," like the peasant of the feudal period or the colonials of an imperial empire, are unable to envision or make sense of the developments around us which lead in such a direction. We attempt to interpret them through the ideological perspectives of a society already in decline. Subtly, scarcely intruding on our consciousness, a new set of perceptions and beliefs and their appropriate justifying values will develop around the new technologies and within the corporate empires. Some of this will be transmitted to the generations now living out what may well be the last stage of national states and a social organization which divides the political, economic, and religious realms. These transmissions are phrased clumsily, to fit existing belief systems. Thus we have insights on what might be called "liberal corporatism" and we are puzzled by where the Soviet form of corporatism fits in to our theories of history. But if the past is an indication of the future, it will not be the case that liberalism as an ideology imperceptibly becomes corporatism; nor that socialism becomes totalitarianism; but rather that both are superseded by new ideologies emanating from a new society that has already grown within the old and destroyed its foundations.

Notes

[1] Karl Marx, *Capital* (1867), translated by Samuel Moore and Edward Aveling. (New York: International Publishers, 1967). Vol. 1, pp. 762–763.

Socialization

This section is about *socialization*, the process by which people learn social skills and other aspects of their culture. This learning makes humans different from animals, which mainly act on instinct. Through socialization humans learn to be effective members of the society, class, region, and family into which they are born, and come to understand the social relations that surround them.

Though easy to define, socialization is a complicated process and hard to explain fully. The process goes on throughout life, but in childhood the changes are most dramatic and visible. A child is born without any knowledge of social rules. By the time he or she begins school, a child has learned to follow the commands of people in authority, cooperate with peers, accept responsibility, and carry out tasks at home.

Typically, the rules children learn through socialization fit the values of our culture. For example, children learn to believe that they must obey authority. They are trained to associate authority with parents, grandparents, teachers, and police officers, among others. Peers, on the other hand, have no such cultural claim to authority; they must compete for it. None of the learned bases for authority seem to apply, so children establish rules among themselves by fighting, as animals do. Once they have created a rough hierarchy, children know their place in the playground just as they do in the classroom. For the time being, order prevails.

Like schoolyards, many social situations lack a clear "definition of the situation." Every group must hammer out rules, then learn and obey them. In other cases, rules already exist and people must learn to follow them, even if they conflict with earlier learning.

For example, the worker promoted to supervisor experiences a conflict of values. As a worker, the person may have felt loyal to the union and opposed to management. As supervisor, he or she must feel loyal to management and oppose the union. The antagonistic worker/supervisor relationship creates a conflict within the person who is changing roles. People resolve conflicts such as these through *resocialization*. Research shows that most people make the change satisfactorily, if not always smoothly. Indeed, socialization goes on throughout life and people prove almost infinitely capable of learning and unlearning social roles.

Role is a commonly used word. Its special meaning for sociologists lies in the view that social life is like drama. This approach assumes that "all the world's a stage,/And all the men and women merely players./They have their exits and their entrances,/And one man in his time plays many parts/His act being seven ages." (Shakespeare, *As You Like It*. Act II, Scene VII, lines 139–143.).

Shakespeare's lines remind us of the changeability of human identity and the many difficult transformations that come with aging. Finally, Shakespeare says, we are "sans teeth, sans eyes, sans taste, sans everything" (line 166). Sociologists who take the dramaturgical approach see human beings playing parts on the "stage" of life. People pass from one role to another and retrain themselves as often as necessary to play their assigned parts.

This approach seems to suggest that people are guided mainly by the immediate chances of reward — not scruples, ethics, or a life purpose. It fails to separate the self from the role and ignores what people "really" are when not on stage. Sociologist Erving Goffman, who has not ignored this issue, calls behaviour that slips out of a role "backstage behaviour" (see, for example, Goffman, 1959).

From a dramaturgical standpoint, interactions between people are determined by an agreed-upon "script." For example, the ways a doctor and patient will interact are largely prescribed in the roles "doctor" and "patient." Doctors learn their part of the script in medical school. Patients learn theirs in the mass media, or by interacting with doctors.

Cross-cutting roles often complicate our interactions. For example, in the Canadian North, the interaction between a native doctor and white patient may differ from the interaction between a white doctor and native patient. The doctor may expect deference from the patient, and the white person may expect deference from the native. When these two scripts — doctor-patient and white-native — are in conflict, confusion can result. Many of our social interactions are complicated in similar ways, yet predictable. People come into a world of fairly stable pre-existing relations. In a world they never made, people must learn to play their assigned parts. This "top-down" theory is more likely to emphasize persistent inequalities of power. Such inequalities favour certain roles and interactions over others. In general, top-down theory fits the observed persistence of social order. Change and conflict are everywhere, but we see them most clearly against the backdrop of order that characterizes most of our lives.

Yet, even under the simplest conditions, interactions are more than a performance of scripted social roles. People repeatedly meet new situations and create new roles and rules. This creative process particularly interests the sociologists known as "symbolic interactionists." They hold that, whether they realize it or not, people often negotiate social relations from "the bottom up," through interaction. For these theorists, sociological research means understanding how people make sense to one another, reach agreements, and manage to make their agreements work. It is this negotiation process that creates and re-creates, what we call social structure.

Creativity and spontaneity are evident in all newly forming ethnic communities and movements to protest social inequality, to name only two examples we discuss in later sections. The resurgence of neighbourhoods, networks, and informal communities all show human creativity despite the supposed "death of community." In the end, power is always exercised from both above *and* below. The struggle for power between those at the bottom and those at the top is precisely what accounts for social conflict and change. People are always "bargaining" about order and power — in business, family, or politics.

Thus, all social organizations display top-down socialization *and* bottom-up creativity; and all respond to pressures for change. Socialization influences the forms spontaneity and creativity may take, and the patterns of change that finally emerge.

Theories about socialization change with time; but the same issues keep coming up, just as in other areas of sociological research. We never manage to completely answer the central questions, and keep raising them anew with each generation.

Take the issue of "nature" versus "nurture." Scholars have long debated whether certain human characteristics are natural or learned. Are cooperation and creativity more natural than selfishness and destructiveness, for example? Karl Marx addressed this question in his manuscripts of 1844, when discussing the alienating effects of work under capitalism ([1932] 1961). Whether people naturally tend in one direction or the other makes a profound difference, especially if we are arguing in favour of socio-economic systems that depend on cooperation, as socialism and communism do.

Similar concerns about cooperation and selfishness are addressed by sociobiologists, not represented in this volume. These researchers try to understand the roots of human behaviour by observing animals similar to humans on the evolutionary scale of development.

The nature versus nurture debate gets farther from resolution the more we learn about the genetic origins of human behaviour. For example, leadership and competitiveness may be determined (in part) by genes, as some paired twin studies suggest. If so, small group dynamics are not an exclusive concern of psychology and sociology. In future, scientists may be able to genetically engineer such traits as leadership and competitiveness.

Future research may even prove that cultural variation between societies is due in part to genetic variation between them, and is not as responsive to social engineering as many sociologists have believed in the past. At this point, it is safest to say that our behaviour is neither all nature nor all nurture. It is a combination of the two. All of this raises interesting ethical questions about the impact of genetic engineering on society. The nature/nurture debate has left us with an open challenge for the future.

Another debate concerns the relative importance of childhood versus adult socialization. Early theorists like Sigmund Freud (see, for example, 1962) held that parent-child interaction in the first few years of life fundamantally shaped personality. Adult life plays out infantile fantasies and traumas that only intensive therapy can hope to modify.

A later way of thinking holds that personal identity and social behaviour continue to change over time. They also change with the environment: we are what we do and we are who others think we are. Sociological ideas like the "looking glass self," the "self-fulfilling prophesy," and the "labelling theory" of deviance all suggest that we begin and continue life as socializable creatures. Our malleability, use of symbols, and ability to communicate ideas makes us different from all other animals.

A third major debate is about the way we are socialized. Is it by reward and punishment (or imitation) — largely a matter of vicarious gratification or self-reward? Do we learn to be macho males and simpering females, for example, because we are punished if we behave like (male) sissies or (female) tomboys? Is it because the mass media and observation of the adult world prove that conforming to these gender stereotypes brings more rewards than deviating from them? Or is there a reactive kind of socialization, as the Freudians suggest? Do we become cruel or racist if we are insecure and unloved as children? Some research on authoritarianism (Adorno et al., 1958) has pointed in that direction.

As with all the important and interesting questions in sociology, this one is far from resolution. More skilful and ingenious analysts will have to find ways of combining their insights to yield better explanations.

What about the purposiveness of socialization, as teaching and learning? The article in this section by Nancy Mandell shows that much learning takes place without teaching. Even little children playing in a sandbox are learning a social "script," a set of rules for interaction. In certain senses, daycare is where children first learn to "do a job" — to master and practice certain skills. Of course, much of what goes on is also pure creativity: the emergence of new skills by surprise, of new roles through negotiation. All of these processes of socialization occur in childhood and continue throughout life.

We seem to learn language by listening, or trial and error. As we do, we learn a hidden code of meanings (or idioms) of which neither we nor our teachers are completely aware. Is that how we learn social roles and values? That question certainly comes to mind when we read the article by Bernd Baldus and Verna Tribe presented below. They show that children learn class distinctions well before adolescence, probably unconsciously. Little children quickly learn to distinguish and verbalize the common prejudices of our culture. What's more, they learn them without purposeful teaching by parents, teachers, or the mass media.

Yet not all socialization is unconscious or unintended. Formal education will receive more attention in a later section of this book. Note, however, that in our own and most modern industrial societies, formal education is a centrally important socializing process. Education helps middle-class families to program their children for success in society's status wars. Such preparation is no simple matter. Both parents and teachers feel ambivalent about competitive education. They see merits in both education for personal development, on the one hand, and for socio-economic success, on the other. The Parent Teachers Association is one place where parents and teachers regularly debate this issue.

Later purposeful socialization takes place in colleges, universities, and professional schools. The selection from Jack Haas and William Shaffir's study of the education of medical students shows that not all of this socialization is skill-oriented. Of course, students must learn job skills: how to cut meat (if a butcher), how to pour cement (if a construction worker), and so on. Just as important, they must also learn subcultural codes of behaviour: how they will have to talk, dress, and deal with colleagues, bosses, or clients.

Much of what passes for professional training, as a lawyer, doctor, or manager, for example, is training in comportment — in how to appear competent. Learning how to do the actual job (for example, how to cure a sick patient or win a court case) comes later with experience at the workplace.

In the professions, style and comportment are particularly important. To succeed, professionals must establish and maintain a particular kind of relationship with the client or purchaser of services. This relationship is a kind of dominance based on scarce expertise and perceived (as much as real) competence. Professionals maintain their dominance through a professional mystique learned in professional school and reinforced on the job, often with the assistance of professional associations.

Developing the needed "cloak of competence" may be just as important as developing competence itself. The competent professional whose cloak of competence has slipped may have more trouble getting his clients to purchase services than the less competent professional with a better bedside manner.

Socialization teaches us, then, how to function reasonably effectively in the real world.

References

Freud, Sigmund. *Civilization and Its Discontents*. London: The Hogarth Press, 1962 (1930).

Goffman, Erving. *The Presentation of Self in Everyday Life*. Garden City, New York: Anchor, 1959.

_____. *Asylums: Essays on the Social Situation of Mental Patients and Other Inmates*. Garden City, New York: Anchor, 1961.

Marx, Karl. *Economic and Philosophical Manuscripts of 1844*. Moscow: Foreign Language Publishing House, 1961 (1932).

SIX

Role-Taking Among Preschool Children

Nancy Mandell

NANCY MANDELL, Associate Professor of Sociology at York University, Toronto, specializes in the study of socialization processes; childhood; women, work and family; and education. Her books include *Reconstructing the Canadian Family* (1988) with Ann Duffy; *Few Choices: Women, Work and Family* (1989) with Ann Duffy and Norene Pupo; and a forthcoming book with Stewart Crysdale and Alan King, *Canada's Resilient Generation: Young Adults' Transition from School to Work* (1992), analyzing data collected from a large, three-year Social Sciences and Humanities Research Grant on the transitional experiences of vocational and nonvocational youth in four metropolitan centres in Canada. She has also published articles on childhood history, "The Child Question: Links Between Women and Children" (1988); childhood negotiation of institutional structures, "Children's Negotiation of Meaning" (1984); and on studying children, "The Last Adult Role in Studying Children" (1988). Currently, Professor Mandell coordinates the Faculty of Arts undergraduate Women's Studies Programme and continues to work in the areas of educational streaming, women, work and family.

George Herbert Mead considered role-taking central to social communication. Role-taking refers to taking the attitude of others, becoming aware of others' thoughts and feelings, and putting oneself in their place (Cooley, 1922; Mead, 1934; Vygotsky, 1962). Mead assumed that we constantly strive to put ourselves in other people's shoes and to imagine what they are thinking. As a result, we are able to see ourselves as others see us. According to Mead, role-taking is only possible if we have the capacity to communicate symbolically through the use of verbal language and nonverbal gestures. The self emerges with this ability to take the role of the other and with the development of language.

Mead suggested that the development of self takes place in three stages. In the preparatory stage, infants imitate others, playing patty-cake or "reading" for example, without understanding what they are doing. In the play stage, children play actual roles. They pretend to be Ninja turtles, princesses, and robbers by taking on the roles of particular others they have observed. In the game stage, children learn to take the role of a number of others. By playing games and interacting in a variety of settings, children take on the roles of the generalized other rather than the role of a single, particular other. Through their involvement in role-taking, children's self-identity and knowledge of others emerges. Role-taking is seen as limited, nonreflexive, and solitary in the play stage, and as holistic, reflexive, and participatory in the game stage. Role-taking is presented as a linear and sequential process.

This study of preschool children fulfills two objectives. First, role-taking among preschoolers is revealed as a more gradual, negotiable, and intricate piecing together of joint acts than a linear reading as Mead suggests. Rather than sorting children's behaviour into play and games stage categories, my focus is on the process by which children pick up on another child's behaviour and situational use of objects and work that line of action into their own on-going conduct. Second, opportunities for involvement with others are shown to differ according to whether children engage in highly structured, semi-structured, or unstructured environments within day-care centres. Structure imposes real limitations on behaviour and leads to the emergence of certain types of behaviour. An understanding of the interplay of structure with behaviour provides adults with a greater understanding of what children are learning in particular situations.

Highly adult-structured environments, such as activity tables, provide children with excellent opportunities for observing the work patterns of others and for evolving group definitions of work. An activity table refers to an area in a day-care centre where children carry out teacher-designed tasks such as pasting, cutting, stringing, measuring, mixing, and colouring various physical objects. Such settings encourage children to adapt their responses to fit into clearly differentiated tasks. Learning to work is a significant social skill teachers assume children have accomplished by kindergarten. Practice in day-care settings offers children the chance to learn these skills.

In contrast, child-structured interactions within both semi and unstructured settings offer the most opportunities for creative peer involvement. Here I am considering both ritualized scripts within physical locales, such as sandboxes, and free play episodes occuring within the outdoor play area and inside the playrooms of the centres. In both these relatively unsupervised environments, children explore the flexibility and expansiveness of play. Tasks are clearly undifferentiated. The children must decide on a mutually agreeable interactive focus and produce the rules, routines, and rituals that sustain interaction. In the most open-ended settings, children engage in interpersonal problem solving and reflexive behaviour due to the considerable degree of conflict that arises. Conflict emerges as children create structures for interaction rather than mold themselves to preexisting rules, practices, and rites.

What emerges then is a continuum of interaction among preschoolers according to the degree to which children either fit into existing contexts or create social activity. In highly structured environments, children are both conforming to adult definitions of appropriate behaviour and learning to evolve unique peer episodes. In child structured interactions, within semi and unstructured settings, children engage in creative involvements ranging from habitualized, predictable exchanges to flexible, imaginative affairs.

Role-taking is defined as the act of interpreting, knowing, and comprehending the meaning intended or expressed by another. For children, their task in building joint encounters is to find ways to express their views of the joint act that are meaningful to others. Role-taking occurs then through this gradual process of translating, describing, and piecing together the meanings of another's actions and placing these actions within a totality whose meaning is mutually shared. In peer involvement, children are afforded opportunities to learn to role-take by practicing routinized scripts and by enacting novel episodes.

THE SETTING AND METHODS

The data accumulated comes from a sample of sixty-two children, aged two to four, in two different centres in two different countries. Between 1976 and 1978, I conducted observations for a period of 15 months at a private, parent cooperative day-care center in Boston, Massachusetts. During 1978–79, I did fieldwork in Hamilton, Ontario for ten months in a day-care centre that was publicly sponsored by an established Canadian nonprofit organization. In both settings, I assumed a "least adult role" (Mandell, 1988), following the children as they pursued their interests, doing whatever they were doing, and, when invited, interacting with them as an older playmate might. I neither corrected nor directed their actions. Rather, I tried to learn their ways of greeting one another, building social exchanges, and leave taking. I analyzed the data separately and, finding few negative cases (Geer, 1967), collapsed them into one analytic model.

ROLE-TAKING IN STRUCTURED SETTINGS

In adult-structured environments, children are introduced to teachers' definitions of work. "Learning to work" refers to the process by which children learn what teachers expect and how, as a group, they should respond to their demands. It involves engaging in negotiation with adults and other children, learning to strike a reasonable bargain between rival perspectives on how much work to do, when to do it, and how to do it. Most of these aspects of the work bargaining process are likely to be new experiences for preschoolers.

Through careful monitoring of others' behaviour, children acquire a sense of how tasks should be accomplished. Monitoring takes two forms: staring, by strategically placing oneself in a position to scan the behaviour of others, and physically following others around, cautiously maintaining social distance. At the activity tables, only the first type of monitoring is possible.

During their time together at activity tables, children routinely observe, monitor, and build on the actions of others. By jointly engaging in tasks, children establish group definitions of the work process. For example, in the following excerpt, two boys mutually determined how to carry out an assignment of making a barn using precut pieces.

> *Derek and Micah are at the art table. Derek says to Micah "What's these for?" (pointing to the cut out pieces). Micah responds, "Building a barn. Here's the piece for the barn." He places a cut out piece on his paper. "You paste this on here. Here's the rest of the farm (pointing to the other*

cut out)." Derek begins pasting pieces on it.

One of the children's main techniques for creating projects is to focus on their own acts and use the other child's actions as a stimulus to continue with their own participation. In the above example, we see children hesitate, stare at each others' work, and follow leads in choosing and manipulating materials. While the end results may be dissimilar, the process is one of joint construction.

Teachers and children differ over the nature of working. Teachers define work assignments as solitary tasks that take place beside other children. Children, however, watch others to see how tasks should be carried out and then build on the behaviour of relevant others. In this way, individual assignments become group efforts. Throughout my observations, no incidents of solitary performances were observed. As indicated in the next example, for children, working is a group event involving the constant and careful observation of others.

Often the early morning art activities are highly structured. The children make things that the teachers have predesigned and then they often put this artwork up on the wall. For example, all the fire hats go on the wall and pieces of fruit are made for the fruit trees. Jennifer is sitting at the art table cutting out items from a magazine. She is not talking but is listening to Lydia and Zoe, who are at the same table also trying to cut with the scissors.

Group observation is particularly necessary in educational work settings since the workers, the children, are not provided with clear production standards. In teaching, the ends are ill defined and consequently mistakes are equally so (Hughes, 1971). Children must observe others at work in order to evolve standards of work.

In learning to work, children are learning to express individual interpretations of their assignments that are meaningful to others. There are three tactics that children use to accomplish this: joint manipulation, making public announcements, and working around territorial constraints.

Since work is an interpretive process, the social goals of children is to make connections with their peers. One of their main techniques is to jointly manipulate objects with others. In this field work example, the goal of manipulating playdough is to create recognizable shapes. The teachers interpret this as a small muscle coordination task. The children see this as an opportunity to interact with others.

I sat down at the playdough table. Brock and Ryan arrive almost immediately after I do. Brock looks at Ryan and says, "Want to play with me?" Ryan looks back at him and hands him a piece of playdough. Each boy starts to mash up the playdough and stick plastic fingers into it. Ryan picks up a plastic man, runs him around saying, "Robot, robot. Buzz, buzz." Brock hands Ryan another man and announces, "Mommy." Ryan smiles and repeats "Mommy?" He hides it under the playdough. Brock leans over and helps him hide it. They both smile and giggle together.

The teachers insist that the children

are to remain seated at the table, work independently, and complete the project by creating recognizable shapes. In conforming to these demands, the children evolve their own definitions of how to work. Working requires interaction. Objects provided by the teachers become props. In one of the centres, playdough became ice cream, bones, airplanes, robots, birthday cakes, and other food. These objects are essential for social interaction since it is in the joint manipulation of objects that children come to know and understand the behaviour of others.

Another technique children use in working together is to make public announcements. Public announcements consist of children defining their social object for others at the table. In the following example, children initiate a joint exchange by announcing that their beads had become monsters.

Nadine, Susan, and Aaron are sitting at an activity table with beads on their fingers. (The task is to string beads.) Nadine waves one at Susan growling and saying, "Here's a monster." Susan screams, "Ah, ah!"

Public announcements direct others to attend to their work. In constrained settings, they also become invitations to interact.

Interactions are limited by territorial constraints. Territoriality refers to children's attempts to delimit and to protect both a physical and a social arena for peer interaction (Adler and Adler, 1984; Joffe, 1973). Adult structured situations limit children's choice of social partner, constrain their emotional expressions, and set interactional boundaries.

Children's choice of social partner is

limited to children sitting near them. As an involuntary activity, children are forced to work with their neighbours at the activity tables. Day-care centres function as preparation for elementary school since involuntary participation is a chief characteristic of schoolwork.

Emotional expressiveness is limited in adult structured situations by a set of normative rules. Children are to be eager to work, but reserved. Emotional display above an acceptable "work" level was a noise signal to teachers that "nonwork" behaviour was occurring. The following example indicates that children learn to display interest and eagerness to their peers in an appropriately subdued fashion.

I sit down at the paint table. Alan, Tracey, and John are painting. They are all concentrating on their work, judging by the lack of noise and conversation, and their disinterest in my arrival and each other. Their motions are very slow and deliberate and they all seem to be painting with great caution. Their faces are serious and they are all involved with their work.

Further, there are territorial limits to children's interactions. Children's social space is limited and premised on mutual monitoring of their momentary playmates' behaviour. Children coach each other by making continual comments about their involvement objects, by constantly watching their neighbours, and by occasionally questioning them on what they are doing. In contrast, the children are mute when asked for formulaic assessments by the teachers. Adult clarification requests such as "That's nice Alex. What is it?" receive neither facial nor verbal response. Clearly, these questions miss the meaning that such acts hold for children.

In summary, activity tables are highly structured situations encouraging a pattern of "fitting into" structures created by adults. The direct and indirect effects of adult structure on peer interaction include altering children's affective states, restricting or expanding the boundaries of the environment, inhibiting or facilitating behaviour, affecting the choice of social partner, and serving as alternative social objects (Rosenblum and Plimpton, 1970).

ROLE-TAKING IN SEMI-STRUCTURED SETTINGS

In contrast with the limited involvements children experience at activity tables, semi-structured settings, such as sandboxes, home centres, gym equipment, and building block areas, represent some of the best opportunities to learn and to practice involvement with others. These locales impose physical and social limits on children's behaviour but are structurally open and flexible enough to allow spontaneous negotiation.

Within these settings, two characteristic behaviours emerge: interpretive observation and ritualized role enactment. First, sandboxes are excellent vantage points from which to interpretively observe mini-situations without being vulnerable to the exclusion tactics used to establish territorial boundaries in free play episodes. Often I used the sandbox in the same manner as did the children, as convenient and protected locations from which to observe the actions of others before active attempts to align actions with others were made. In this example, children seem to be idly pouring and sifting sand when, all the while, they are interpretively observing.

Jordanna, Lynn, Nolan, Kim, Cathy, and Jennifer are all playing with the sand alone. They are digging, pouring, and patting into containers. They are all quiet and unobtrusively keeping tabs on what the others are doing. I sit down in the sandbox and start to pour sand into a container. After I repeat this action a dozen times, Lynn and Jordanna turn to me and start to talk.

Semi-structured settings, such as sandboxes, provide prearranged social scripts in which children fill in expected role activity. Garvey (1977) calls these non-person, or functional roles in which there is an action plan, but no definite role or person is assumed. The children perform ritualistic action or perform customary functions. For example, in the sandbox, children repeatedly engage in cooking and building themes. The cooking theme entails using sand as food. A particular favourite is to use sand as birthday cakes. The building theme involves patting, heaving, and lugging sand into various shapes. This process provides children with a joint object focus through which continued interaction is sustained.

Alissa, Megan, and Courtney are in the sandbox, each holding a container and a shovel. Alissa is singing to herself. They are all putting sand into the containers, walking over to the climber, and dumping it out. Jason arrives with a toy wheelbarrow and runs it into the sandbox. The other children start piling their sand containers into the wheelbarrow. This repetition proceeds for ten minutes or more.

Cooking and building scenes do not involve preexisting social roles. For example, the children do not tend to take on the role of mother, father, fireman, or monster as soon as they enter the sandbox. When these roles emerge, if they do, they are not necessary to continue the joint interaction of the children. Rather, their enactment represents the emergence of novel behaviour more characteristic of free play situations.

In building ritualized encounters, children use repetition and turn taking. Repetition establishes common ground with others and provides a strategy for accessing involvement with others. Initial overtures are often made through mutual object manipulation. This takes the form of children pouring sand on others' piles, patting others' sand arrangements, and mutually digging holes. By repeating these actions, children indicate their desire to join in with the others. Repetition of overtures also induces the other child to take a turn, as this example indicates.

Dove begins to "play" with me by putting his sand on top of my pile. Together we take turns filling the container.

Repetition is a vehicle by which children structure shared understandings and achieve dialogue. Through repetition, children also acknowledge turns, maintain contact, and mark the event as a social enterprise. This example shows that often repetition consists of a nonverbal conversation.

Sally, Keith, Leah, and I are in the

sandbox. As soon as I sit down, Leah offers me some sand. I take it and put it on her pile. We pour sand back and forth on each other's piles for several minutes. Brad arrives, surveys the situation, and starts to pour sand into our pail. We all continue to take turns. Eventually Leah holds out her hand with sand in it and says to me, "Cakes?" I take it and offer it to Brad saying, "Cake?" Brad eats the sand. Kelly shouts, "Brad, don't eat the sand. Look, he ate it. It tastes awful. This is a pretend cake!"

This particular scene, like many others I observed, continued for some minutes with children taking turns, picking up sand, and labelling it as food. By repeating their actions, the children are providing themselves time to evaluate the actions of others and to figure out their next step. Eventually, the children place their repetitive behaviour within a familiar context by labelling sand as "cake." This labelling then suggests further action.

Repetition also serves as a way to incorporate more players. In this example, verbally repeating the traditional birthday song provides a familiar script children can easily fit into.

As soon as I sit down in the sandbox, Cindy arrives. She looks at me and asks, "Do you want some cake?" She puts her face to mine and rubs noses. I ask, "Is it chocolate?" Cindy replies, "It's my birthday." She makes a sand cake and starts to sing "Happy Birthday" to me. Nicole comes riding up on her big wheel, gets into the sandbox, and joins in with the song, patting Cindy's cake. Roy ar-

rives by riding his big wheel right into the sandbox, pats the cake, and says to Cindy, "Blow out the candles."

Short, abbreviated sentences help children retain the ongoing social script (birthday songs) and practice their interactive skills of building exchanges. Slobin (1975) suggests that for exchanges to be fully developed, they must be semantically clear, processible in ongoing time, quick and easy to process, and contextually expressive. Repetition and turn taking help children achieve these conditions.

Turn taking provides children with an opportunity to coordinate their behaviour. Turn taking also follows a ritualistic course. For example, in sandbox encounters, once a child has manipulated the sand and perhaps verbally marked the event by labelling it, the child's turn ends. Yielding a turn is accomplished by staring at one's partner while remaining completely still. This immobility functions like silence in a conversation by signaling the other's turn (Goldman and Ross, 1978).

In semi-structured situations, repetition and turn taking serve as peer socializing devices, filling in pauses and sequencing action. With practice, children learn to build more complex interactive scenes so that other techniques are used in conjunction with repetition and turn taking. In unstructured settings, the construction of novel scripts employs quite distinct tactics.

ROLE-TAKING IN UNSTRUCTURED SETTINGS

When external structures provide little structure, children create their own (Carpenter, 1983). They place their own framework of rules, norms, and expectations on activities. In creating structures, children often apply familiar and practiced schemes to new situations and objects. They rely on old scripts, rules, and action plans from previous experiences. Interactional rules, plans, and problems are not formulated in advance but emerge in coordinated peer play.

The potential for conflict is high in free play situations due to numerous interactional demands — including the process of creating structure, the ways in which objects are used, the age and experiences of the participants, and the use of specific negotiative strategies. Establishing a shared object focus represents a major interactional difficulty. Often negotiation among children for a shared object focus takes on a trial and error appearance, as this example demonstrates.

William is on the floor busily putting blocks together. Chris is beside him assembling his own. Matthew comes over to the blocks with a wooden truck. He's running it up and down William's ramp making car noises. William allows him to do this and joins Matthew in assembling a ramp. Don sits on the floor beside Matthew and tries to run his boat up the ramp. Matthew pushes him away saying, "This is not water."

Free play is unpredictable, novel, and fragile. Children constantly define and redefine their use of objects. In this next example, children begin interacting together by creating a fire truck episode in the yard. The script changes to one in which they drive off in their fire truck to South America, pick up an assortment of monsters, return to their original locale, the climber, and resume putting out fires.

Denny, John, and Sally are sitting on the climber in the yard. Denny has a fire engine hat and is "driving" the fire truck (the climber) and yelling, "Fire! Fire!" John says, "Let me drive, Den. You be the fireman and I'm the chief." Den doesn't say anything, which John takes to be agreement. I sit down beside the boys and ask, "Where are we going?" Denny replies, "To the fire. You sit here. John is the chief." Sally says, "I want to go to the fire," and she moves closer. Den shouts "Get away Sally, only me, John and Mark can go." Sally stays still and no one says anything to her. I ask, "Where's the fire?" Denny replies, "In South America. We have to go there and in the end of July and there are monsters. Big, hairy monsters you can pick up and put in your pocket."

The three-year-olds in this example are using a physical object the climber, as a substitute for an imaginary object, a fire truck. Objects-as-substitutes is one way young children accomplish joint acts. Older children aged five and up are, following Piaget (1962), more likely to use objects as replicas, such as using an iron for ironing. They seem to prefer the greater freedom of action provided by play themes that do not depend on the enactment of specific roles (Connolly, 1983). Their elaboration of play frames is more organized around action sequences with whatever objects are immediately available.

In unstructured, free play situations, interaction cannot proceed without children staking out ecological boundaries (Cavan, 1970). This includes careful monitoring of others, physical and/or verbal signaling of openness to joining or being joined in play, and agreeing on a shared object focus once both partners have agreed to interact. Having assessed what others are doing, children attempt to join in with others' acts by jointly manipulating the object of attention. Children flop down beside others, handle toys, build blocks, and rapidly pursue others on bikes. These physical actions are accompanied by statements such as, "This is my bus," "Get out of the water," and "Come into my house." Both actions and statements indicate children's willingness to be joined in creating novel scripts. Nonverbal openers are also indicators of children's willingness to either join or be joined by others (Goffman, 1963). Children stand closer than normal to the other person, gaze directly at their new partner, and express joy and excitement. Laughter, giggling, and grinning are so common in free play episodes that some researchers (Bamberg, 1983) suggest these are automatic prerequisites, as well as products of peer involvement.

Having agreed on what social objects they will jointly manipulate, children are faced with the task of creating mutually enjoyable and agreeable action plans. Sometimes action plans emerge from a literal and stereotypical use of objects. Bikes are ridden, cars are pushed along the floor, and gym equipment is climbed. Other times, action plans ensue from children's adoption of character roles, including well-known ones such as policemen, mothers, and bus drivers, and fictional roles such as monsters, superheroes, and robots. Adopting roles requires interpreting, rather than replicating, life events. Children announce to others their exact transformation by saying, "You be the baby," "Let's go to the fire," and "Your car is out of gas." Or else children signal their new identity by growling like monsters or animals, "shooting" with pretend guns, or "flying" through the air like superheroes. A combination of gestures, actions, attitudes, tone of voice, and speech style announce children's roles and intentions.

Unstructured episodes are distinguished by the number of times the object focus or theme changes. Characteristically, there are four ways in which children switch themes. These include: (1) redefining the context within which the action is interpreted ("I'm the doctor so stop fighting, Ned"); (2) offering a new interpretation of an act by redefining it ("This isn't a cake. It's a blueberry.") or through negating the theme ("I'm not fishing anymore."); (3) redefining their presentation of self ("I'm too young to do that."); and (4) explaining the meaning of an action through clarification ("That's a monster, not a dog.") and territorial protection ("You can't be the baby.").

Free play situations are intolerant of newcomers, suggesting this form requires more explicit boundary drawing to sustain it over numerous thematic shifts. In contrast, involvement in the sandbox builds on increasingly repetitive and correct turn taking responses and is dependent on children acknowledging its expansion through participation. Similarly, at the activity tables, group redefinition of adult demands relies on the consensus of the majority. More highly structured and semi-structured episodes thus sustain the inclusion of newcomers more easily than unstructured situations.

CONCLUSION

Activity tables are examples of highly adult-structured settings encouraging a pattern of children fitting into structures determined by adults. They provide children with opportunities to observe work patterns of others, to evolve group definitions of work, and to jointly produce finished pieces. Semi-structured environments are ideal places for children to practice role-taking skills within a frame skeletal enough to include reliable and customary scripts, but negotiable and open enough to allow for the emergence of novel acts. Unstructured settings allow children to create original events by applying their own schemes, both familiar and practiced, to new objects in the environment. Compared with structured and unstructured episodes, unstructured interactions appear more interpersonally demanding since sequences are less explicit and children are required to be more clear in their communication.

References

Adler, Patricia and Adler, Peter. "The carpool: a socializing adjunct to the educational experience." *Sociology of Education* 57 (1984): 200–210.

Bamberg, Michael. "Metaphor and play interaction in young children." Pp. 127–143 in Frank Manning (ed.), *The World of Play*. New York: Leisure Press, 1983.

Carpenter, C. Jan. "Activity structure and play." Pp. 117–45 in Marsha Liss (ed.), *Social and Cognitive Skills; Sex Roles and Children's Play*. New York: Academic Press, 1983.

Cavan, Sherri. "The etiquette of youth." Pp. 554–564 in Gregory Stone and Harvey Farberman (ed.), *Social Psychology through Symbolic Interaction*. Waltham, Mass.: Xerox, 1970.

Connolly, Jennifer, Doyle, Anna-Beth and Ceschin, Flavia. "Forms and functions of social fantasy play in preschoolers." Pp. 71–92 in Marsha Liss (ed.), *Social and Cognitive Skills: Sex Roles and Children's Play*. New York: Academic, 1983.

Cooley, Charles. *Human Nature and the Social Order*. New York: Charles Scribner's Sons, 1922.

Garvey, Catherine. *Play*. Cambridge, Mass.: Harvard University Press, 1977.

Geer, Blanche. "First days in the field." Pp. 372–398 in Phillip Hammond (ed.), *Sociologists at Work*. New York: Basic, 1967.

Goffman, Erving. *Behavior in Public Places*. New York: Free Press, 1963.

Goldman, B.D. and Ross, H. "Social skills in action: an anaylsis of early peer games." Pp. 177–212 in Joseph Glick and K. Alison Clarke-Stewart (eds.), *The Development of Social Understanding*. New York: Gardiner, 1978.

Hughes, Everett C. *The Sociological Eye. Selected Papers*. Chicago: Aldine, 1971.

Joffe, Carol. "Taking young children seriously." Pp. 101–116 in Norman Denzin (ed.), *Children and their Caretakers*. New Brunswick, New Jersey: Transaction, 1973.

Mandell, Nancy. "The Least Adult Role in Studying Children." *Journal of Contemporary Ethnography* 16 (1988): 433–467.

Mead, George Herbert. *Mind, Self and Society*. Edited by Charles Morris. Chicago: University of Chicago Press, 1934.

Piaget, Jean. *Play, Dreams and Imitation in Childhood*. New York: Norton, 1962.

Rosenblum, L.A. and Plimpton, E.H. "The effects of adults on peer interactions." Pp. 195–217 in M. Lewis and L. Rosenblum (eds.), *The Child and Its Family: The Genesis of Behavior* (Vol. 2). New York: Plenum, 1979.

Slobin, Dan I. "Language change in childhood history." Language behavior research laboratory working paper, No. 41:1–37, University of California, Berkeley, 1975.

Vygotsky, L.S. "Play and its role in the mental development of the child." *Soviet Psychology* 12 (1966): 1–18.

SEVEN

Children's Perceptions of Inequality

Bernd Baldus and Verna Tribe

BERND BALDUS, Professor of Sociology at the University of Toronto, received his undergraduate and graduate training in the German Federal Republic and in the United States. His research and publications have been primarily concerned with the origins and the persistence of social inequality in human societies. The following article is one of several that explore social control processes that legitimate inequality structures and stabilize them over time. At present, Professor Baldus is working on an evolutionary history of social inequality.

VERNA TRIBE, who assisted Professor Baldus with the following study, does not work in the field of Sociology.

... Our study is part of an effort to find out when and in what form views about social inequality develop. Since previous research (e.g., Hess and Torney, 1967; Easton and Dennis, 1969) indicated that related political beliefs appeared during — though not necessarily as a result of — primary schooling, we chose children from Grades 1, 3, and 6 from three public schools in the Toronto area for the study. We wanted to see at what age children began to use social inequality as a criterion for the identification and the ordering of their environment. We also wanted to examine whether the children's sex, the occupation of their fathers (divided into blue collar and white collar/professional categories), or the school they attended had any influence on their use of inequality as a criterion of orientation. Finally we wanted to find out whether the children made evaluative judgments in conjunction with their perceptions of social inequality. More specifically, we were interested to see whether there was any predisposition to see high class or low class figures as likely to engage in morally approved or disapproved behaviour, or to succeed or fail in competitive tasks. ...

PROCEDURE

The three schools in which our study was carried out were chosen from residential areas with widely differing income characteristics in order to maximize the chance of identifying school-specific differences in the perception of social inequality, one of our independent variables. In each school we selected a sample of 36 children, 12 each from Grade 1, Grade 3, and Grade 6, for a total of 108 cases. Their age ranged from five to twelve years, the majority in each grade being six, eight, and eleven years old. Each child was interviewed individually and the interviews were taped and later transcribed. During the first part of the interview, we used five sets of photos taken in Toronto. They consisted of two pictures of a man, one well dressed and named Mr. Gordon, the other in casual clothes and named Mr. Ellis, (set 1); two pictures of a house, one taken in the high income Rosedale area, the other in an old working class district of Toronto (set 2); two pictures of a living room, one in a Rosedale home, the other in a rented apartment and furnished with used and worn furniture (set 3); a photo of a small old car and one of a Lincoln Continental (set 4); and two more pictures of individual men, one well dressed and addressing a meeting, the other in older clothing and sitting on a porch. We introduced each interview as a game of matching pictures of people, houses, living rooms, and cars. We also explained the use of the tape recorder and asked a few questions about name, age, and grade. We then showed the children the pictures of Mr. Gordon and Mr. Ellis and asked for any differences they noticed when comparing the two men. Following that the children were handed the pictures of the two houses and were asked to tell us who in their opinion lived in which house. After that, they matched the living rooms with the houses, and the cars with the two men. Before we showed them the last set of pictures we told them that both Mr. Gordon and Mr. Ellis were giving a party at their house. We then showed them set 5 and asked them which of the men in the picture Mr. Gordon and Mr. Ellis would invite to their party. The children had the option of making no choice at all, but none of them used it. After assigning each set the children were asked why they had made their choice.[1]

The picture matching served also as an introduction to the second part of the study. The sets of pictures were designed in such a way that they could provide cumulative information on status symbols such as houses, cars, or funiture which distinguished the two men and which approximated as much as possible visual impressions of class differences which the children might encounter in their day to day experience. When the picture matching was completed each child was told that Mr. Gordon and Mr. Ellis both had children. We then read four short stories and asked each child whose son or daughter the hero in the story was likely to be. The first of the stories involved a boy who swore and started an unprovoked fight in the schoolyard. The second story was about a boy who received more valentines than anyone else and was liked best by his classmates. Story three told of a girl who could not read as well as the other children. The last story was about a boy who lied to his mother. The first and last stories thus described the transgression of a generally accepted norm. Stories 2 and 3 portrayed a boy who was held in high regard by others, and a girl who was relatively unsuccessful in a competitive task. The stories had been tested in a pilot study, and even the youngest children had no difficulty in comprehending the problem which they presented.

All interviews took place during regular school hours. The children had no apparent problem with the questions and seemed to enjoy the task. All were used to being recorded on tape, and many of them know one of the interviewers who frequently worked in the classrooms.

RESULTS

Findings from the first part of the study, the picture-matching tasks, appear in Table 7-1. The data indicate that with increasing age there is a clear and significant increase in the children's ability to identify the common inequality dimension in the pictures and to order them accordingly. This is evident both in the total number of correct matches for each question, and in the number of children in each grade who are able to match all pictures correctly. Only 7 of the 36 children in Grade 1 did so, while 22 children in Grade 3 and 25 children in Grade 6 completed all 4 matching tasks correctly. Data for Grade 2 which do not appear in Table 7-1 show that the progression between Grades 1 and 3 is continuous, and that there is no particular time period during these three years where most of the change occurs.

An analysis of variance with the summated scores of the picture matches as dependent variables, and grade, sex, father's occupation, and school as independent variables shows grade as the only significant source of variation of the matching scores ($DF = 6$, $F = 7.955$, $P = 0.001$). Neither the children's sex, nor their school environment nor the oc-

cupational position of their father seem to have a significant effect on their ability to order the pictures on the basis of social inequality between the two main figures.

The numerical evidence is supported by an analysis of the transcripts of the taped interviews. They indicate the same gradual development of the ability to verbalize one's choice. Grade 6 students explained their choices with considerably more complex vocabulary and with more differentiated references to social inequality than their counterparts in Grades 3 and 1.

The initial question about differences between Mr. Gordon and Mr. Ellis was answered by the Grade 1 children primarily in terms of such easily noticeable criteria as the different shirts the two men were wearing, that one had curly hair, or that one was standing and the other one was sitting. Only four of the children made the evaluative comments, for instance that Mr. Gordon "looked happy" or was wearing "good clothes." In Grade 3, such evaluative descriptions became more frequent. Mr. Gordon was described as "dressed up" and as "looking nicer" than Mr. Ellis, while the latter appeared as "old" or wearing "work clothes." One of the children made social

TABLE 7-1   Picture-Matching, by Grade

	Set 1 (House)		Set 2 (Living Room)		Set 3 (Car)		Set 4 (Party)	
	Correct Matches	Incorrect Matches	Correct Matches	Incorrect Matches	Correct Matches	Incorrect Matches	Correct Matches	Incorrect Matches
Grade 1	18	18	20	16	27	9	24	12
Grade 3	31	5	27	9	35	1	33	3
Grade 6	34	2	27	9	35	1	35	1

Kendall's Tau c. for Set 1: -0.39506 ($p < 0.0001$); for Set 2: -0.17284 ($p = 0.0385$); for Set 3: -0.19753 ($p = 0.001$); for Set 4: -0.27160 ($p - 0.0001$)

inequality the first and only identifying criterion: Mr. Gordon "looks like he has more money," while Mr. Ellis "looks like he doesn't have a job." The majority of the children in Grade 3 continued to identify differences between the two men in factual terms. By contrast, inequality-related criteria were the first things mentioned by roughly one-half of the children in Grade 6: Mr. Gordon looks like a businessman, and Mr. Ellis doesn't. "He (G) looks like an executive. He (E) could be a worker in a plant, or drive a truck." Many of the children drew inferences to other aspects of the men's life which were not visible in the pictures: "He (G) has a good business job, and he (E) is the sort of guy that watches football. He (G) cares more about his dress." "Mr. Ellis looks like he is not a good salesman. Mr. Gordon looks like a salesman, with a suit and a tie. Mr. Ellis looks like an ordinary guy who lives in an apartment, a pop-corn salesman with enough pennies." "One (E) is rather mean-looking. This one (G), looks like he would come from a rather well-fashioned family compared to this one (E)." Only a few of the Grade 6 children still used factual criteria when identifying differences between the two men.

A similar progression toward a more articulate and more frequent use of social inequality as an ordering criterion was evident in the picture-matching. Children in Grade 1 matched the houses with the pictures of the two men by commenting that "it looks right," or that one house looked "bigger" or "older" and therefore went with Mr. Gordon or Mr. Ellis. Only two of the children based their choices on some idea of the men's social position; one paired the large house with Mr. Gordon "because he works in an office" while the other child paired Mr. Ellis with the small house because it "looks like a working house." Generally,

comments were short and hesitant. About one-half of the children in Grade 1 could give no explanation at all. In Grade 3 the majority of comments made reference to differences in wealth as a basis for matching the houses with the two men. "Because I think this man (G) looks as if he has lots of money and he should have a bigger house, and this man (E) doesn't have neat clothes like this man, and he should have a house like this." "He (G) looks like a big businessman and this looks like a fancy house." Only a few of the children used factual criteria such as age or facial expression as a basis for matching the pictures. In Grade 6, almost all the children identified social inequality as the common dimension of the pictures. Mr. Gordon was described as rich, as a big businessman, as someone who made much money, and who therefore could afford a big or fancy house. Many of the comments not only described, but evaluated: "This man (G) is a real man, like he is rich and that, and this man (E) is just like a normal man and this is a normal house." "Mr. Gordon looks kind of rich. I don't know why. But he slicks up his hair. Mr. Ellis looks like he is tough, maybe a big mouth. These (E) houses are close together. Mr. Gordon's house looks really like a mansion."

Reasons for matching the pictures of the two living rooms with those of the houses were factual in Grade 1: similarities between the windows in house and living room, similarities in colour or the impression that house and living room had the same curtain. These observations were not always correct — some of the children were clearly guessing. Grade 3 children began to identify the furniture in the living room as expensive, rich, valuable, or shabby, and these attributes usually accompanied correct matches. In Grade 6, inequality-related observations became detailed and showed a comprehension not only of the relationship between income and lifestyle, but of a relatively wide variety of items which were taken as symbolic indicators of social class. "Well, it's sort of the same thing as with the houses. He (G) is a big businessman, and if you are a big businessman you get more money and you can afford more things. Not too many people can afford fireplaces in their house, or an antique table, and this thing, whatever it is, just looks like an ordinary house in which everybody can live, because this couch looks like anybody can afford it. This house looks average."

The question which of the two cars Mr. Gordon and Mr. Ellis were driving produced the largest number of correct matches in all grades. Cars appear to be one of the first symbols of social position which the children learn, girls just as much as boys. . . . In Grade 6 almost all children thought that Mr. Gordon would drive the large car because he was richer and looked "fancier. . . ."

The last matching task asked children to pair the pictures of Mr. Gordon and Mr. Ellis with those of two other men who were to be invited to their party. The children in Grade 1 based their choices primarily on their impressions of physical characteristics such as age, facial expression, or dress. Some of the judgments bore no apparent relationship to the pictures — as in other tasks, many Grade 1 children had obvious difficulties in explaining their choice. The conceptual problems of finding a common dimension in the pictures, as well as their still relatively small verbal repertoire, imposed constraints even on those children who made expected choices and seemed to know why.

Many of the Grade 3 children also based their choice on the appearance of similar age; Mr. Ellis was generally seen as older; and so was the man on the porch. Some of the Grade 3 answers, however, suggested quite explicitly that Mr. Gordon was likely to associate only with someone who was as rich or as well dressed as he was. In Grade 6 most of the children considered the perceived social position of the men as the criterion that brought them together at a party, and they drew detailed inferences as to what the men had in common. "He (G) looks like a politician, and so does he, the way they dress. The way they look, they are sincere and perfect. This looks like an ordinary street person who is looking for work and couldn't get it." "This man is dressed nice and that man is not dressed nice. And that man is at a convention and he is talking, and he has to be pretty important and Mr. Gordon is pretty rich, so he would know important people. That man is sort of old and hangs around the street, so Mr. Ellis meets him sometimes and they become friends, and so he invites him to his party."

Three more general conclusions can be drawn from the verbal replies of the children. First, children become more articulate and more certain in their choice as they progress from Grade 1 to Grade 6. This is indicated by the number of children who are not able to give any explanation at all. Such children comprise as many as one-half of the children in Grade 1, while only very few of the children in Grade 6 cannot state any reasons why they made a particular choice.

Second, there is a clear increase in the use of explicit inequality-related criteria in explaining picture matches as one proceeds through the grades. Explanations were classified as inequality-related when they made explicit references to differences in wealth between Mr. Gordon and Mr. Ellis. Comparative explanations comprised all other comparisons of the two men, such as that Mr. Gordon looked "happier," "younger," or "cleaner" than Mr. Ellis. Factual explanations involved the use of noncomparative observations of details in the pictures as an ordering criterion; for example, that there was a chimney in the large house and a fireplace in the living room. Factual choices were not always correct. Many of the factual details were inaccurate and reflected the younger children's difficulties in identifying common properties of the pictures.

The third conclusion concerns the increasingly evaluative language employed by the children as they explain their choice. Evaluative components of the replies are particularly evident in Grade 6 and reveal the outlines of an ideological image of social inequality which is shared by many of the children. Mr. Gordon and his possessions evoke admiration, respect, and sometimes awe for a person and lifestyle which most of the children find clearly desirable. These feelings are not necessarily connected to details in the pictures. Instead, the pictures recall for the children schematic images of social models which are already part of their cognitions and fantasies. Mr. Gordon and Mr. Ellis become recognizable because of their affinity with such existing images. Once they have been identified in these terms the children freely draw inferences which go substantially beyond what is visible in the pictures. The "classy," "important," "rich" and "well dressed" Mr. Gordon is for most children a fixture in a social environment which appears invariant and of which people like Mr. Gordon are a natural and desirable part. Money is the general source of Mr. Gordon's attractiveness. He most likely obtained it by being a "businessman." Conversely, Mr. Ellis is described less frequently, and when he is described it is usually done in derogatory terms. It is possible that such judgmental elements appear already in many of the answers in Grade 3. Terms such as "new" or "young" used in connection with Mr. Gordon often suggested an evaluative meaning, though their more limited verbal repertoire provided the Grade 3 children with fewer ways of expressing their judgment.

The second part of our study was designated to investigate the evaluative dimension of children's perception of inequality more closely. We wanted to find out whether there was a consistency in the way in which behaviour described in each of the four stories was attributed to the child of the low class or the high class figure in the pictures, and thus indirectly to them. The results are summarized in Table 7-2. Unlike the picture matches, the attribution of the stories to the children of Mr. Gordon or Mr. Ellis does not show much variation between the grades. An analysis of variance of the added scores showed that none of the independent variables, grade, sex, father's occupation, or school, caused any significant variance of the story matches. Instead, Table 7-2 shows a relatively high number of correct matches in all grades, with a small but not statistically significant increase in Grades 3 and 6. Even in Grade 1 a majority of the children considered it more likely that Mr. Gordon's child would be liked by his classmates, and that the child of Mr. Ellis would get into an unprovoked fight, perform badly in a reading task, or lie to his mother. . . .

While there is only a small increase in an already initially high number of correct matches, we found a clear progression in two other areas. The first is the number of children in each grade who attribute all four stories correctly to the

TABLE 7-2   Story-Matching, by Grade

	Story 1		Story 2		Story 3		Story 4	
	Correct Matches	Incorrect Matches	Correct Matches	Incorrect Matches	Correct Matches	Incorrect Matches	Correct Matches	Incorrect Matches
Grade 1	28	8	27	9	25	11	20	16
Grade 3	30	6	30	6	26	10	28	8
Grade 6	29	7	29	7	29	7	26	10

The level of significance for Kendall's Tau c is larger than 0.06 for all stories.

hypothetical children of Mr. Gordon and Mr. Ellis. Of the 36 children in Grade 1 only 10 did so. In Grade 3 that figure increases to 19, and in Grade 6, 23 out of 36 children assigned the attractive role to Mr. Gordon's child, and the morally reprehensible or unsuccessful behaviour to the children of Mr. Ellis. These figures suggest an increase in the children's capacity to find common properties such as the class differences between the two men, and to categorize information on moral and performance behaviour accordingly as they grow older. The change between Grade 1 and 3 reflects the same transition from Piaget's preoperational to concrete operations stage which we found earlier in the picture matches.

A similar progression is evident in the frequency with which children rely on perceived class differences between the two men as a basis for attributing the behaviour described in the stories to their children. An analysis of the verbal explanations indicates that the higher the grade the more likely the children are to express prejudgments. Transcripts from the Grade 1 interviews show that a large number of children could not provide an explanation for their choice, or phrased it in terms of some simple and not always correctly observed external characteristic such as that Mr. Ellis had

curly hair, or that Mr. Gordon was sitting down. These observations bore no obvious relationship to the matching task, and reflect the same difficulties of the youngest children to give verbal accounts of what they had done that were already evident in the first part of our study. A few children explained their (correct) choices by stating that Mr. Gordon "looks happy," is "bigger," or "smiles," or is "unhappy." The transcripts do not allow any conclusion whether such statements were based on some rudimentary perception of social inequality between the two men.

Some of this is also characteristic of the Grade 3 answers. There is, in particular, still a relatively high proportion of children who cannot give explanations for their choices, even if these were in the expected direction. At the same time there are the first clearly preconceived explanations. Mr. Ellis' son fights and swears "because Mr. Ellis looks rough, and his son would fight, and Mr. Gordon is richer, and his son wouldn't fight," or "cause I don't think Mr. Gordon's kids would swear because he doesn't swear around the house and his kids wouldn't learn those words." Mr. Gordon's son is liked better by his classmates "because Mr. Gordon looks like he is a happy man, and his son would be a nice boy, and everyone would like him." Or, "Everybody liked him because he was rich, because his father was rich." Mr. Ellis' daughter cannot read well "because he (E) looks like his daughter hasn't very much education." And the boy who lies to his mother that he had to stay in school while he was in fact playing football is Mr. Ellis' "because he (G) looks like his son would come home and he doesn't play ball and has good clothes, and his (E's) son wears rough clothes and would go out and play ball."

In Grade 6 almost all answers reveal the existence of preconceived expectations which are frequently explicitly based on perceived class differences between the two men. Grade 6 children generally assume that low class people are likely to get into trouble and high class people are liked and esteemed. Moreover, they have a strong propensity for expecting the father's characteristics to be transmitted to his children. Sometimes this is expressed as an almost fatalistic belief that class and corresponding character traits run in the family. Quite a few children also give sophisticated and sometimes rather realistic reasons for their expectations. The following selection of answers by Grade 6 children shows some of the main trends in the children's arguments. Story 1 (swearing and unprovoked fighting): "Well, Mr. Ellis looks like a bully-type man, and his son would pick a fight. He (E) would probably belt them one in the mouth, and his son would be just like him." "If Mr. Gordon is out with his son, well, if he is as wealthy as he is his son wouldn't hit anybody or swear at a teacher." "He (E) probably drinks a lot, and he wouldn't care about his child, what his child would do, and he would probably let his child swear and that." "I think he is Mr. Ellis' son because he (E) is kind of a drunk, and

mostly drunks swear a lot when they get drunk, and when they fall down and someone tries to help them they get mad at him and swear. Sons, they mostly fall in the same way." "He is the son of Mr. Ellis, because poor people usually have lots of kids. He is bad-tempered, and he always wants the ball." Story 2 (about a boy who receives most valentines on Valentine's Day because he is liked best by the children in his class): "He is Mr. Gordon's son, because everyone seemed to like him because he wasn't a big bully or something, he wasn't lippy or anything, he was a nice guy, and he might not have looked peaceful but he was like his father. He took after his father." "I think he was Mr. Gordon's son because usually when the parents have good manners they share with their friends. And the way he (G) is dressed, and the way he smiles, he looks as if a lot of his friends helped him to get up to where he is now. Their children will follow them and share things back and forth." Mr. Gordon's son would be good, and the other kids liked him more. Maybe Mr. Gordon is more strict and would watch him more often. He would work in an office, and he would not want the other people to think that he has bad children." "Mr. Gordon's because if he is rich you could say that his children will be polite. If you have a father that goes on TV and is popular you would have manners and treat your friends right. Mr. Ellis would treat his friends sometimes meanly, and (only) if they had something that he wanted he would be a nice guy to them. And so Mr. Ellis' son would be real greedy and wouldn't want them to have anything." Story 3 (about a girl who was put into a group of slower readers): "Mr. Gordon's daughter would be in the group that could read best because (she) would have a well-educated father, and Mr. Ellis' daughter would probably be the type who would sit around and fool around all day and wouldn't know anything." "Oh, I think she would be Mr. Ellis' (daughter) because I don't think he would really care whether his daughter could read well or not." "I think she is Mr. Ellis' because they can probably not afford enough books for her to practise reading on. Or she doesn't like reading because her parents don't read a lot, or had to work for the family all the time and did not have time to read." "Mr. Ellis doesn't look that smart. It looks like where he comes from, the house and all that, that he wouldn't have as good an education. Mr. Gordon looks intelligent, and he would probably teach his daughter everything he knew." "Mr. Ellis, he looks poor. Maybe he went to a poor school that did not have as good an education as Mr. Gordon's." "Mr. Ellis, because Mr. Gordon if he found out about it he would probably keep his kids in to work at it. Mr. Ellis might not, or his kids might not tell him about it." Story 4 (of a boy who lies to his mother): "Well, I think this man (G) would look after his children and teach them not to lie or anything, and, you know, would take really good care of his children. But I don't think that Mr. Ellis would really bother. He would think that his children ... that's their own business." "He (E) is the man, if he had kids they would not grow up in a mannerly way, like they would lie and steal and swear at teachers, because he looks like he is a really rough man." "Probably Mr. Ellis' son, because he probably gets very mad and beats his children, and just to get out of that his son would probably lie." "Mr. Ellis' son, because people who don't have jobs seem to lie and say that they are high class. People who don't have jobs seem to lie about their work and say that they have done what they have not done. Mr. Gordon probably taught his son that

lying doesn't pay, and that you get into a lot of trouble by just starting with one lie." "Mr. Ellis looks like a man who would lie a lot. ...."

Not all children in Grade 6 shared the view that high social class goes together with esteemed and successful behaviour, that low class people are trouble- and failure-prone, and that their children usually follow their footsteps. Ten out of 36 Grade 6 children employed standards of evaluation which ran contrary to those used by the majority of the Grade 6 respondents, even though they appeared usually only in connection with one or two of the four stories. The view which these children had of the relationship between social class and behaviour was more differentiated and revealed a more critical view of people like Mr. Gordon. They appeared in particular in connection with the first story. Mr. Gordon's son was seen as more likely to start a fight because he knew about his father's money and thought that he was better: "Since he (G) is so rich his son might think that he is the boss." For the same reason, some of the children also thought that he would not be well-liked in school. Mr. Gordon's son "would be a spoilsport and would have no friends because his dad has a lot of money and he would want everything to be his way." By contrast, Mr. Ellis' son would be popular because he was normal. "If a man is really rich, if you are really rich, he will usually make his son act big too. He (Ellis' son) probably just grew up like he wanted to be and didn't show off and didn't make fun of everybody, and so everybody liked him." Most of the answers reasoned quite rationally, sometimes obviously on the basis of personal experience. Mr. Gordon's social position was not in question. Rather, his importance or his wealth was seen as leading to some unfortunate side-effects with undesirable, but also unavoidable consequences for others. Only in two or three cases did we find an open resentment for people like Mr. Gordon: people who were rich were also likely to be "greedy," and their children tended to be "meaner, because they think they are better." As an afterthought to the last story, one of the Grade 6 boys added: "Mr. Gordon looks like a sneaky little real-estate salesman. Maybe he says a sucker is born every minute, and he started getting all these suckers together and got a lot of money the easy way, just being a little dishonest like a fraud or a con man. . . ."

CONCLUSIONS

The results of our study indicate that by the time the children have reached Grade 6, most of them have not only learned to recognize and classify people and their environment in a context of social inequality, but have also acquired cognitive and affective predispositions which make them expect that lower class persons are more likely to be unsuccessful or to engage in morally disapproved behaviour, and that the behaviour of high class persons is exemplary and esteemed. . . .

One of the most important results of our study is that these views were not affected by the social position of the children's parents. All children seemed to learn to recognize and evaluate social inequality as a dimension of their environment at roughly the same age and in similar ways. . . .

Notes

[1] We were aware that the forced-choice nature of the questions, even if it was moderated by the "don't know" option, led to a number of risks. It did, for instance, not allow us to establish the distance which, in the view of the child, separated Mr. Gordon and Mr. Ellis. Nor did it permit any expressions of additional gradations of social inequality which the children might have been aware of. We felt that these disadvantages were outweighed by the comparability of the three grades which we gained with our design. The taped comments were a further way of registering more differentiated opinions.

References

Hess, R.D. *The Development of Political Attitudes in Children*. Chicago: Aldine, 1967.

Easton, D. and Dennis, J. *Children in the Political System*. New York: McGraw-Hill, 1969.

EIGHT

Socialization of Medical Students

Jack Haas and William Shaffir

JACK HAAS,Professor of Sociology at McMaster University, Hamilton, Ontario, specializes in the study of deviance and control, occupations and
professions, and addiction and recovery. His books, all written or edited with
William Shaffir, include *Decency and Deviance: Studies in Deviant Behaviour* (1974); *Shaping Identity in Canadian Society* (1978); and *Becoming Doctors: The Adoption of a Cloak of Competence* (1987). Professor
Haas has served as reviewer for a wide variety of scholarly journals, and as
review editor for *Symbolic Interaction* and *Sociological Focus*. Recent
articles include "The Process of Apprenticeship" (1988) and "Addiction and
Recovery as Ritual Processes of Transcendence" (1990).

WILLIAM SHAFFIR, Professor of Sociology at McMaster University,
Hamilton, Ontario, specializes in race and ethnic relations and the study of
identity formation. His books include *Fieldwork Experience: Qualitative
Approaches to Social Research*, co-edited with Robert Stebbins and Alan
Turowetz (1980); *The Canadian Jewish Mosaic*, co-edited with Morton
Weinfeld and Irwin Cotler (1981); *An Introduction to Sociology*, co-edited
with Michal Rosenberg, Allan Turowetz and Morton Weinfeld (1983); *Becoming Doctors: The Adoption of a Cloak of Competence*, with Jack Haas
(1987); *The Riot at Christie Pits*, with Cyril Leavitt (1987) and *Experiencing
Fieldwork: An Inside View of Qualitative Research*, co-edited with Robert
Stebbins (1990). Professor Shaffir is a review editor for *Qualitative Sociology* and *Symbolic Interaction*, and reviews articles for a variety of other
scholarly journals.

INTRODUCTION

... This paper[1] describes the adoption of
a cloak of competence as a critical part of
the professionalizing process. We observed medical students in an innovative
three-year program attempting to come
to grips with the problem of meeting exaggerated expectations.[2] The profound
anxiety they feel about learning medicine
and becoming competent is complicated
by the pressing practical demands of the
situation, particularly faculty, staff and
institutional expectations.

As students move through the program
they are converted to the new culture and
gradually adopt those symbols which represent the profession and its generally
accepted truths. These symbols (language, tools, clothing, and demeanor) establish, identify and separate the bearer
from outsiders, particularly client and

paraprofessional audiences. Professionalization, as we observed it, involves the adoption and manipulation of symbols and symbolic behaviour to create an imagery of competence and the separation and elevation of the profession from those they serve. . . .

THE EXPECTATIONS OF COMPETENCE

Medicine is a distinctively powerful and unique profession. Freidson outlines the characteristics of this occupation that set it apart from others. These are:

1. A general public belief in the consulting occupation's competence, in the value of its professed knowledge and skill.

2. The occupational group . . . must be the prime source of the criteria that qualify a man to work in an acceptable fashion.

3. The occupation has gained command of the exclusive competence to determine the proper content and effective method of performing some tasks (1970a: 10–11).

Medicine's position, Freidson notes, is equivalent to that of a state religion: "it has an officially approved monoploy of the right to define health and illness and to treat illness" (1970a: 5). . . .

BECOMING PROFESSIONAL

From the outset, students are impressed by the tremendous responsibility of the physician. During their examination of various "psychosocial" problems, in

Phase I,[3] students recognize that the physician's role is very broad. They learn that the medical professional not only deals with medical problems *per se*, but also with many apparently non-medical problems. The small group tutorial sessions, which form the major vehicle for learning at this stage of medical school, help shape students' enlarging conception of medicine and its practice. While early sessions are intended essentially to introduce students to the school's philosophy — the educational rationale underlying the distinctive structure and organization of the medical curriculum — they also serve to teach students the duties and responsibilities of the medical profession. An excerpt from the Phase I manual for incoming students illustrates this point:

> You are also becoming health professionals — members of an historic community concerned with the alleviation of human illness, the maintenance of health and the understanding of disease. You will begin to realize the special nature of the 'doctor-patient relationship'. Some of you will have initial difficulty with some of the physical things — blood, operations, injury, autopsies. Other experiences are more difficult to incorporate into your growth as a health professional — deformity, chronic illness, death, pain. You will see that physicians and other health professionals are ordinary human beings — with tempers, insensitivities and varied motivations (Phase I Manual, 1974: 25).

The physicians' influence on the way students learn about and define medical situations is critical to the professionalizing process. From the earliest stages of their medical training, and as they advance through the program, students continually watch doctors' working habits, listen to their philosophies of medical practice, take note of their competencies and incompetencies, and reflect upon the nature of their own present and future relationships with patients. . . .

A dramatic shift in the professionalization process occurs when the students are given greater responsibility for patient health care and management. This occurs during the clerkship phase. Students become more integral members of a health care team, are delegated some tasks requiring personal responsibility, and become accountable in ways almost entirely new to them. As they assume increased responsibilities and make medical judgments for which they must account to a variety of professionals, they develop an increasingly sympathetic outlook towards their future profession. . . .

As students observe and experience the problems of medical care and practice, they develop an understanding and identification with the profession and the ways its members confront their problems. Students are less quick to voice criticism of what they see, as they come to take the role, directly or indirectly, of those they will soon follow. . . .

THE SYMBOLS OF PROFESSIONALISM

The professionalization of medical students is facilitated by symbols the neophytes take on which serve to announce to insiders and outsiders how they are to be identified. During the first weeks of their studies students begin wearing white lab jackets with plastic name tags identifying them as medical students. In addition, since clinical skill sessions are included in the curriculum from the beginning, students participate in a variety of settings with the tools of the doctoring trade carried on their person. This attire clearly identifies students to participants and visitors of the hospital/school setting. Along with their newly acquired identity kit, students begin to learn and express themselves in the medical vernacular. . . .

The significance of these symbols to the professionalization process is critical. The symbols serve, on the one hand, to identify and unite the bearers as members of a community of shared interests, purposes and identification (Roth, 1957). Simultaneously, the symbols distinguish and separate their possessors from lay people, making their role seem more mysterious, shrouded, and priestlike (Bramson, 1973). The early possession of these symbols serves to hasten their identification and commitment to the profession, while, at the same time, facilitating their separation from the lay world.

At this point, their very selection of medicine as a career has produced a set of reactions by friends, family and others which reinforce in the students' minds the idea that they are becoming very special people. Immediately upon acceptance into medical school, students perceive themselves being related to, in typified fashion, as medical students and future physicians. This reaction of others intensifies as students enter training and immerse themselves in it. At the same time, students see that they must devote more and more time and energy to their studies, and less time to past relationships and interests. . . .

One of the first difficult tasks that faces students is to begin to learn and communicate in the symbolic system that defines medical work and workers. Immediately in tutorials, readings, demonstrations and rounds, students are inundated with a language they know they are expected to become facile in. Their task is even more difficult because this exotic language is used to describe very complex processes and understandings. Students are taken aback at the difficulty of learning to communicate in their new language. They begin carrying medical dictionaries to help them translate and define terms and phrases. . . .

The separation between "we" and "they" becomes clearer to students as they are absorbed into the medical culture. As they move through the culture, they learn how the symbols are used to communicate and enforce certain definitions of the situation. Students learn how practising physicians use these symbols of the profession to shape and control the definition of the situation. . . .

TURNING OFF YOUR FEELINGS

Previous research on medical students has shown that a major effect of medical education is to make the medical student more cynical and less idealistic (Beale and Kriesberg, 1959; Becker and Geer, 1958; Eron, 1955). Our data also suggest that as students move through school and develop a professional self-image, and thus begin to take on the identity of a doctor, their views on medicine become transformed from what they describe as an idealistic phase to what they believe is a more realistic one. Accounting for this transition, one student claims:

> . . . first of all, the exposure to what really goes on. You sort of keep your eyes open and you really get an idea of the real world of medicine. . . . The other part of it is when you're allowed responsibility . . . and you really become involved with patients.

Students become less vocal in their questioning and criticism of the medical profession. They attribute many of their earlier concerns to naiveté, and argue for a more sympathetic view of doctors and the profession as a whole:

> I think I went through a phase, as I went from knowing very little about medicine to a little bit . . . You go through a sort of stage of disillusion in which you sort of expect doctors to be perfect, and the medical profession and treatment and everything else to be perfect. And you find out that it's not. So you sort of react to that. I think now, after about two years, I'm starting to get to the phase now where I'm quite pleased with it really. Part of it is getting into arguments about other professions and this brings out things that you've thought about but not really verbalized. . . . A particular friend of mine is in law and he was talking about malpractice suits and it really makes you think that knowing doctors the way you do, and I've seen them operate, if other professions were as self-critical as doctors were and had a good sense of responsibility to duty, then I think a lot of the professions would be a lot better off. . . .

Though not entirely pleased by the outcome of this transformation, students know that their views of medicine are being altered. They describe these changes as part of their personal and professional growth. They argue that they are becoming more mature personally and developing a clearer and sharper understanding of the world of medicine. Most importantly, they admit a willingness to accept the situation as a small price for becoming more competent. With only minor exceptions they accept the present sacrifice of their ideals as a necessary condition of medical training, and hope to recapture their idealism at a later time. . . .

The hope and belief that they will be in a more opportune position to express and act upon their initial idealism after graduation is coupled, for many, with a more sombre realization that matters are unlikely to change. On the basis of their observations and deliberations many students become resigned to their behaviour as physicians always coming under close scrutiny and control from their colleagues. Most students do not have high hopes for being able to change medicine

Although they are often initially dismayed by how physicians and other hospital staff treat patients, they come to accept that the objectification of patients is a routine feature of doctor-patient relationships. It is the "professional" way to deal with medical situations.[4] In time they accept the view that patients must be objectified and depersonalized or the doctor will be unable to maintain clinical objectivity (Coombs and Powers, 1975; Emerson, 1970). While initially bothered, even offended, by this detachment, they come to see it as part of the professional situation over which they have little control. . . .

Striving for competence is the primary student rationale to explain avoiding or shutting off emotional reactions. As they progress through the program students come to express the belief that their relationship with the patient should be governed strictly by the patient's medical problem; emotional feelings are a hindrance. They believe that they do not have time for both learning and caring, and learn to stifle their feelings because of the higher value they and others place on competence.

Students also believe that they are being trained for busy lives. Accepting the hectic pace as inevitable, they recognize that it is not temporary, but will continue throughout their medical career. Their work in the hospitals impresses on them the long hours that physicians devote to their work:

> If you look around at people who are teaching you, they often have a pretty rough life as far as time commitment and work. The work doesn't end when you get out of medical school and you can see somebody who is forty-five or fifty and married and has a couple of kids, in on Saturday afternoons working away, and being on call in the evenings.

Students recognize that many physicians work long and irregular hours. As they embark upon the clerkship phase of the program, they discover that the hospital routine they must fit demands that their everyday lives be organized around medicine. . . .

The dominant concern with learning medicine leads students to maintain their learning efficiency and productivity. Students come to believe that they have no time for the frills of emotional involvement and quickly learn to close off feelings that interfere with their work (Lief and Fox, 1963). The following statement by a student emphasizes the idea of productivity:

> You can't function if you think about things like that [death and dying]. Everything you see sort of gets in there and turns about in your mind and you aren't productive. The reason you have to shut it off is because you won't be productive. . . . I think that my prime objective is to learn the pathology and just to know it and then, understanding that, I can go back to these other things and worry about the personal part of it.

During the first ten weeks of the curriculum the students are introduced to, among other things, the psychosocial component of health care. As many students are interested in working with and helping people, and are aware that medical problems have many different causes, the emphasis on the psychosocial issues gives them an opportunity to express their views concerning social, economic, political and moral aspects of medicine.

However, even before Phase I is completed, they are eager to start what they consider to be their "real" medical studies. Reflecting the views of others in the class, a student says:

[In Phase I] you really concentrate on a lot of psychosocial issues. But it becomes really obvious before the ten weeks are up that you are getting tired of talking about that kind of stuff, and you want to get on with it.

The students' concern for the psychosocial aspects of medicine are not entirely ignored when they enter Phase II of their program. As they are gradually introduced to the content and "core" of medicine, they begin to realize that there is too much to know and little time in which to learn it all. Like the religious or political convert who becomes fanatically observant and committed, students devote themselves to the task of learning medicine. Time becomes a commodity that must be spent wisely. They become very concerned about not misusing or wasting their time studying certain topics deemed unproductive. In this context, the psychosocial component becomes less important.

One thing you have to do at medical school is pick up all the pathophysiology and to pick up all of the anatomy and pick up the clinical histories, the presentations, the clinical skills and so on. So psychosocial time is really a luxury, it can't really be afforded sometimes. . . .

Although they put them aside, students continue to recognize that psychosocial matters are important. They believe this area must be neglected, however, in the interests of acquiring as much medical knowledge and competence as possible. They believe that if they feel for their patients and become involved with them

they will not become professionally competent. . . .

Most students move to the view that personal concerns for the patient should not intrude on the physician's professional responsibility. . . .

Student concerns about learning medicine, making the most efficient use of time, and establishing some bases of certainty and security in their work are all reflected in the selected interest they take in patients with unusual pathology (Becker *et al.*, 1961). Discussing the kind of patients that he looked forward to seeing, a student claims:

A patient who has physical findings. Gees, I don't care what the findings are. It's a fantastic experience to see that physical finding. They may only have two or even one. . . . In order to do a physical exam you've got to have something there to feel. Someone can tell you this is the way to feel for a lump in the stomach, but if there is no lump there you are not going to learn how to feel it. . . . I think that's what I get the most out of, getting exposure to the pathology, feeling things that I may not feel.

The high point for students is making a correct diagnosis by sleuthing out relevant material, and knowing with some assurance the diagnosis is valid and the treatment competent. . . .

Students alter their understanding of how medicine should be practised. Unable to feel as deeply concerned about the patient's total condition as they believe they should, they discover an approach that justifies concentrating only on the person's medical problem. As a student remarks:

Somebody will say "Listen to Mrs. Jones' heart. It's just a little thing flubbing on the table." And you forget about the rest of her. Part of that is the objectivity and it helps in learning in the sense that you can go in to a patient, put your stethoscope on the heart, listen to it and walk out. . . . The advantage is that you can go in a short time and see a patient, get the important things out of the patient and leave.

As students learn to objectify patients they lose their sensitivity for them. When they can concentrate on the interesting pathology of the patient's condition, students' feelings for the patient's total situation are eroded. . . . The students do not lose their idealism and assume a professional mask without a struggle. But even when they see and feel the worst, students recognize that they do not have the time to crusade. That would interfere with the learning of medicine and impede their efforts to become competent. . . .

ACTING THE PROFESSIONAL ROLE

Students believe they are expected to act as if they are in the know, not in ways which might put their developing competence into question. The pressure to be seen as competent by faculty, fellow students, hospital personnel and patients narrows the range of alternative roles students can assume. Students recognize their low status in the hospital hierarchy and on hospital rotations. They realize that the extent of their medical knowledge can easily be called into question by fellow students, tutors, interns, residents and faculty. To reduce the possibility of embarrassment and humiliation which, at this stage of their medical career, is easily their fate, students attempt to reduce the unpredictability of their situation by manipulating an impression of themselves as enthusiastic, interested, and eager to learn. At the same time, students seize opportunities which allow them to impress others, particularly faculty and fellow students, with their growing competence and confidence. . . .

Although a basic objective of the school's philosophy is to encourage learning through problem-solving and a questioning attitude throughout the medical career, the philosophy does not help students' overriding problem of appearing competent. A perspective shared by students to manage an appearance of competence is to limit their initiatives to those situations which will be convincing demonstrations of their competence. Some students decide, for example, to ask questions in areas with which they are already familiar, to cultivate an impression of competence.

The best way of impressing others with your competence is asking questions you know the answers to. Because if they ever put it back on you: "Well what do you think?" Then you tell them what you think and you'd give a very intelligent answer because you knew it. You didn't ask it to find out information. You ask it to impress people.

The general strategy that the students adopt is to mask their uncertainty and anxiety with an image of self-confidence. Image making becomes recognized as being as important as technical competence. As one student remarks: "We have to be good actors, put across the image of self-confidence, that you know it all. . . ." The pressure to conform is perhaps even more extreme at this school than at other medical schools because its evaluation system is much more pervasive and a large part of it is generated by students. Students observe each other, seeking to establish a base of comparison. . . .

The students are acutely aware of the relationship between impression management and successful evaluation. While the evaluation ought to consist of an objective assessment of the students'

abilities to conduct a diagnosis and pre-
scribe a course of treatment, the outcome is, in fact, shaped by the students'
abilities to behave as if they are able to
accomplish these tasks. . . .

CONCLUSION

. . . Our findings should be analogous to
other professions and their socialization
processes. The process of making some
expert and more competent separates
professionals from those they are presumed to help and serves to create a situation where the exaggerated expectations of competence are managed by
symbolically defining and controlling the
situation to display the imagery of competence. Impression management is
basic and fundamental in those occupations and professions which profess competence in matters seriously affecting
others.

Edgerton (1967) believes that the central and shared commonality of the mentally retarded released from institutions
was for them to develop themselves in a
cloak of competence to deny the discom-
forting reality of their stigma. The development of a cloak of competence is,
perhaps, most apparent for those who
must meet exaggerated expectations.
The problem of meeting others' enlarged
expectations is magnified for those uncertain about their ability to manage a
convincing performance. Moreover, the
performer faces the personal problem of
reconciling his private self-awareness
and uncertainty with his publicly displayed image. For those required to perform beyond their capacities, in order to
be successful, there is the constant threat
of breakdown or exposure. For both re-
tardates and professionals the problem
and, ironically, the solution, are similar.
Expectations of competence are dealt
with by strategies of impression management, specifically, manipulation and
concealment. Interactional competencies depend on convincing presentations
and much of professionalism requires the
masking of insecurity and incompetence
with the symbolic-interactional cloak of
competence.

Notes

1 This paper is based on data that were collected
largely during the first two years of a three-year
study we are conducting on the socialization of
medical students at a medical school in Ontario,
Canada. The data were collected by means of
participant observation and interviews. We have
observed students during the full range of their
educational and informal activities and to date
have interviewed fifth-five of the eighty students
in the class. We are presently completing the
fieldwork phase of the study as students approach their licensing examination and graduation. We will be writing a monograph, based on
the research, in the coming year.
2 Unlike most medical schools, the school we are
studying has a three-year program where long
summer vacations are eliminated. Admission is
not restrictd to individuals with strong pre-
medical or science backgrounds. The school
deemphasizes lectures and has no formal tests
or grades. Students are introduced to clinical
settings from the very beginning of their studies.
Learning revolves around a "problem-solving"
approach as students meet in six-person tutorial
groups. An analysis of the consequencs of such
innovations will be described in subsequent
writings.
3 The program is divided into five Phases: Phase I
lasts ten weeks; Phase II twelve weeks; Phase III
forty weeks; Phase IV, essentially the last half of

the three-year program, is the clinical clerkship. Student electives, vacations and a review phase — Phase V — make up the remainder of the M.D. program.

4 The core of the professional attitude toward the patient is to be found in what Parsons (1951) has termed "affective neutrality". As Bloom and Wilson have written: "This orientation is the vital distancing mechanism which prevents the practitioner from becoming the patient's colleague in illnesss. . . . Affective neutrality constitutes the physician's prime safeguard against the antitherapeutic dangers of countertransference" (1972: 321). The management of closeness and detachment in professional-client relations is discussed in Joan Emerson (1970), and in Charles Kadushin (1962). For a discussion of the socialization of medical students toward a detached attitude, see Morris J. Daniels (1960). For an insightful analysis of how student-physicians come to manage the clinical role pertaining to death and dying, and learn to retain composure, no matter how tramatic the death scene, see Coombs and Powers (1975).

References

Becker, Ernest, *Escape from Evil.* New York: The Free Press, 1975.

Becker, Howard S. and Geer, Blanche, Hughes, Everett C. and Strauss, Anselm. *Boys in White: Student Culture in Medical School.* Chicago: University of Chicago Press, 1961.

Bloom, Samuel W. and Wilson, Robert N. "Patient-Practitioner Relationships," pp. 315–39 in H.E. Freeman, S. Levine and L.G. Reeder (eds.), *Handbook of Medical Sociology.* Englewood Cliffs, N.J.: Prentice-Hall, 1972.

Bramson, Roy. "The Secularization of American Medicine," *Hastings Center Studies,* (1973), pp. 17–28.

Coombs, Robert H. and Power, Pauline S. "Socialization for Death: The Physician's Role." *Urban Life,* Vol. 4 (1975), pp. 250–71.

Daniels, Morris J. "Affect and Its Control in the Medical Intern." *American Journal of Sociology,* Vol. 66 (1960), pp. 259–67.

Davis, Fred. "Professional Socialization as Subjective Experience: The Process of Doctrinal Conversion among Student Nurses," pp. 235–51 in Howard S. Becker *et al.* (eds.)

Institutions and The Person. Chicago: Aldine Publishing Company, 1968.

Edgerton, Robert B. *The Cloak of Competence: Stigma In The Lives Of the Mentally Retarded.* Berkeley: University of California Press, 1967.

Emerson, Joan P. "Behaviour in Private Places: Sustaining Definitions of Reality in Gynecological Examinations," pp. 73–97 in Hans Peter Dreitzel (ed.), *Recent Sociology.* New York: The Macmillan Company. 1970.

Eron, Leonard D. "Effect of Medical Education on Medical Students." *Journal of Medical Education,* Vol. 10 (1955), pp. 559–66.

Fox, Renée. "Training for Uncertainty," pp. 207–41 in Robert K. Merton, George G. Reader and Patricia L. Kendall (eds.), *The Student Physician.* Cambridge; Mass.: Harvard University Pres, 1957.

Freidson, Eliot. *Profession of Medicine,* New York: Dodd Mead and Co., 1970a.

——. *Professional Dominance.* New York: Atherton, 1970b.

Geer, Blanche (ed.). *Learning to Work.* Beverly Hills: Sage Publications, Inc., 1972.

Goffman, Erving. *The Presentation of Self*

in Everyday Life. New York: Doubleday Anchor Books, 1959.

Haas, Jack. "Binging: Educational Control Among High Steel Ironworkers." *American Behavioral Scientist*, Vol. 16 (1972), pp. 27–34.

_____. "The Stage of the High Steel Iron-worker Apprentice Career." *The Sociological Quarterly*, Vol. 15 (1974), pp. 93–108.

_____. "Learning Real Feelings: A Study of High Steel Ironworkers' Reactions to Fear and Danger." *Sociology of Work and Occupations*, Vol. 4 (1977), pp. 147–70.

Haas, Jack, Marshall, Victor and Shaffir, William. "Anxiety and Changing Conceptions of Self: A Study of First-year Medical Students." Paper presented at the Canadian Sociological and Anthropological Association, May, 1975.

Hughes, Everett C. "The Sociological Study of Work: An Editorial Foreword." *American Journal of Sociology*, Vol. 57 (1952), pp. 423–26.

_____. *Men and Their Work*. Glencoe: The Free Press, 1958.

Kadushin, Charles. "Social Distance between Client and Professional." *American Journal of Sociology*, Vol. 67 (1962), pp. 517–31.

Lief, Harold I. and Fox, Renée. "Training for 'Detached Concern' in Medical Students," pp. 12–35 in Lief, H.I., V. Lief and N.R. Lief (eds.), *The Psychological Basis of Medical Practice*. New York: Harper and Row, 1963.

Mayer, John E. and Rosenblatt, Aaron. "Encounters with Danger: Social Workers in the Ghetto." *Sociology of Work and Occupations*, Vol. 2 (1975), pp. 227–45.

Olsen, Virgina L. and Whittaker, Elvi W. *The Silent Dialogue*. San Francisco: Jossey-Bass Inc., 1968.

Parsons, Talcott. *The Social System*. London: Routledge and Kegan Paul, 1951.

_____. "Research with Human Subjects and the Professional Complex." *Daedalus*, Vol. 98 (1969), pp. 325–60.

Phase 1 Manual, 1974.

Quint, Jeanne C. "Institutionalized Practices of Information Control." *Psychiatry*, Vol. 28 (1956), pp. 119–32.

Ross, Ailen D. *Becoming a Nurse*. Toronto: The Macmillan Company of Canada Ltd., 1961.

Roth, Julius A. "Ritual and Magic in the Control of Contagion." *American Sociological Review*, Vol. 22 (1957), pp. 310–14.

Schanck, Richard L. "A Study of a Community and Its Groups and Institutions Conceived of as Behaviours of Individuals." *Psychological Monographs*, Vol. 43, No. 2 (1932).

Siegler, Miriam and Osmond, Humphry. "Aesculapian Authority." *Hastings Center Studies*, Vol. 1 (1973), pp. 41–52.

Deviance and Control

T his section is about deviance and control. It includes articles on differences in *deviance* and *control* between Canada and the United States, patterns of victimization in the two countries, and the reasons that young people turn to prostitution.

We learned in the previous section that people think, feel, and act as they do largely because they were socialized that way. People continue to behave in certain ways presumably because they have internalized certain values and norms. They feel it is right to act as they do, and wrong to act otherwise. Yet, despite this internalization of controls on behaviour, people everywhere deviate, or break rules. How can sociologists account for this fact? This section explores that question and its implications for society.

Deviance comes in many forms and degrees of severity. Indeed, deviance of minor kinds is quite common. Many studies asking people to admit their own crime, deviance, or delinquency show that much more deviance goes on then ever comes to the attention of public authorities. Further, most people, when deviating, have handy ways of excusing their behaviour. Many deviants do not consider their rule-breaking deviant, let alone harmful. This is surely the case among people who break the speed limits, drink under age, use recreational drugs, or evade full payment of their income taxes. Ordinary people are so willing to break rules and justify their actions that many commentators fear the legal system has lost its "legitimacy" — its ability to gain compliance without naked coercion.

For, if internalized controls on behaviour are not enough, society needs external controls to protect itself from the harm of wrongdoing. For this reason, the topics of deviance and control often go together: one implies the other. It may be as true to say that we have deviance in society because we have controls, as to say that we have controls because we have deviance. To consider this seeming paradox, we return to two founders of sociology, Emile Durkheim and Karl Marx.

Both would have conceded that deviance is universal. Perhaps each would have said that this universal fact results from the existence of social control, which is also universal. However the two theorists would have given different reasons for this strange relationship between deviance and control. This is because the two theorists, Marx and Durkheim, have very different research agendas. Marx's macro-perspective focuses our attention on large social groupings and historical periods. Durkheim's micro-perspective focuses on community standards and individual motivations.

Durkheim (1938) believed social order was very important for individual well-being. Indeed, he thought the social order was, in some sense, separate from and above the individuals making up a community. Being part of a community benefited people, especially if the social order was stable and consistent. Rapid change and cultural confusion harmed people and led in the most extreme cases to suicide. A high (but not too high) degree of social cohesion was best for individual and social well-being.

So, people needed to make and enforce rules, and punish wrongdoers. This would clarify the boundaries of social order and maintain social cohesion. In this context, punishment was a good thing for society: it increased cohesion by reminding everyone of the moral boundary between right and wrong. It drew people together in a tight bond against deviants. This meant society needed deviants, for deviants provided someone to punish. Without deviants, the boundaries separating right from wrong remained unclear, and social cohesion remained weak. Rules and laws helped society find scapegoats to punish.

A strange outlook? Kai Erickson (1966) provides interesting support for this paradoxical theory. His study of witchcraft in seventeenth century New England Puritan communities shows there can never be too much badness. (Or, from a more liberal standpoint, there can easily be too much goodness.) Even people who lived (by our current standards) extremely moral lives could find deviants — in their case, witches — among themselves to punish. From a Durkheimian perspective, they *had* to find witches. Without the "invention" and punishment of witches, Puritan society would have fallen apart.

This tells us there can never be a society without rules, deviants, and punishments. No matter how tolerant or morally lax, no society can accept all behaviours as equally satisfactory. The Durkheimian perspective argues that such indifference would deprive the society of all occasions for social integration. Such a society would break down and disappear, if this theory is correct. It could not survive. That is why we cannot find any society entirely lacking in rules, deviants, and punishment.

Durkheim's theory accounts successfully for the universality of deviance and control, and it is attractive for several other reasons. First, it squares with certain theories of history — for example, Edward Gibbon's theory (1776–1788) of the decline and fall of the Roman Empire — that holds that morally lax civilizations do not survive. Second, the theory squares with observations made at many times and places that, in the face of threats to order, demands for social cohesion increase. So do rule-making and rule enforcement.

On this basis, we would predict that crises in South Africa, Eastern Europe, and the Middle East — due to internal conflict and international pressure — will result in stricter rule enforcement. Authorities will draw the lines between good and bad more sharply and police them more savagely, this theory would argue. The alternatives are societal collapse or a significant change in social organization to reduce conflict.

To judge from his analyses of private property and the state, Karl Marx would have explained the universality of deviance and control quite differently. As already noted, Marx was concerned with the behaviour of large groupings, especially social classes. He would have argued (as he and Engels do, in *The Communist Manifesto*) that states, not societies, make rules. The people who control those states — the ruling classes — use state powers of rule-making and enforcement to protect their own interests. They direct social control against the people who threaten the dominance or interests of the ruling class. Virtually every society has a ruling class with interests to protect, and a state apparatus for making and enforcing rules. Thus, deviance will be "discovered" and punished everywhere. A failure to punish such deviance does not result in the disappearance of society, only the overthrow of the ruling class.

Marx's theory improves on Durkheim's by predicting that certain kinds of deviance are more likely than others to get punished. Specifically, they are offences that menace the ruling class. In our own society, the ruling class is an economic elite. Therefore, the state is most likely to punish economic crimes against the rich. It is least likely to punish economic crimes committed *by* the rich.

The state is only moderately likely to punish non-economic crimes such as crimes against the person (for example, wife battering or rape), especially if the victims are poor. Crimes against humanity in general — for example, promoting war between nations, hatred between groups, or environmental destruction — are also unlikely to get punished.

Marx's theory seems to fit many of the observed facts. However it is not as good as Durkheim's at explaining nonrational (that is, non-instrumental or symbolic) social control. For example, Marx does not help us understand why poor, uneducated people are more likely to support capital punishment (usually carried out against other poor, uneducated people) than rich, educated people. Nor does his theory explain the seemingly irrational, purposeless trait of "punitiveness." Durkheim's theory does, however. It predicts that insecure, isolated people — with the greatest need for clear boundaries and social belonging — will give the strongest support to rule enforcement; and that is what we find.

Nor is Marx's theory as good as Durkheim's in accounting for social control that arises out of non-economic, symbolic, or status-oriented concerns. For example, it does not help us understand why men play so large a role in demands for the criminalization of abortion. (Or why Puritan men were so instrumental in the search for "witches.") Or why small-town Protestants were so adamant about the prohibition of drinking when our grandparents were young.

Consider Joseph Gusfield's (1963) discussion of the laws that, sixty-five years ago, prohibited liquor sales in the United States. Most people resisted "prohibition" from the start. Supporters of the law were rural, Protestant, native-born Americans who felt hostile to, and culturally endangered by urban Catholic immigrants. Leaving aside these few (though influential) supporters, the law quickly proved unpopular and unenforceable; it was also a tremendous boon to organized crime. During its short life, the law did little more than strengthen the cohesion of rural, Protestant, native-born Americans.

We might find similar patterns and motivations if we studied the American "Moral Majority," the pro-capital punishment lobby, REAL Women, the anti-gay lobby, and pro-life groups. Indeed, the membership of these groups seems to overlap. A study by York University sociologist Lorna Erwin (*The Globe and Mail*, Thursday, April 2, 1987, page 1) surveyed over 800 people on the mailing lists of REAL Women, Campaign Life, and other anti-abortion groups. Erwin found that anti-abortionists are frequent church-goers (63 percent go once or more a week) who fear that homosexuals, feminists, and the media are destroying the family. "What has galvanized them," says Erwin, "is their perception that the family is under attack, and they see it everywhere." It is this sense of a danger to tradition, and a belief in absolute right and wrong that makes such a movement to control behaviour possible.

According to Max Weber (see, for example, 1964), membership in a status group is often as important as economic interest for motivating social action. Groups struggle to have their way of thinking prevail because they believe in it. As well, success demonstrates their value and importance to society. Lawmaking and enforcement is, then, a form of unconscious lobbying aimed at increasing a group's social standing. Secondarily, as Durkheim reminds us, it strengthens the allegiance of group members. If so, the sociology of deviance and control turns out to be the study of deviance as produced by control, or the sociology of law.

As Marx has said, laws arise out of class relations and varying ideological conceptions of right and wrong. Thus, we must expect that different societies will make and enforce laws differently. Differences in social integration and cultural punitiveness will add up to national differences in deviance and control. Finally, different social conditions — differences in the attainability of desired rewards by legitimate means, for example — will lead to different rates of deviant behaviour in different countries.

In his article in this section on differences between Canada and the United States, John Hagan attempts to measure and explain national variations in crime and deviance. Before reading this article, it may be wise to reread S.M. Lipset's discussion of Canadian-American value differences in Section Two. Where at least some kinds of crime and deviance are concerned, the United States is a much more deviant, dangerous, or controlling place than Canada: but cultural differences are least important where serious felonies are concerned.

For example, sexual mass murder is a kind of deviance that scarcely arises out of social control or needs for cohesion. Almost everyone everywhere considers rape and murder to be serious deviant acts deserving strong punishment. Indeed, people rarely violate these norms, even if rape and sexual assault are much more common than murder, and more often committed than punished. Most of us consider that people arrested for repeated violence against other persons are deranged. We look for explanations of their behaviour in defects of character, not subcultural or class conflict.

There is a terrible symmetry between the typical patterns of sexual mass murder and their victims. As Rosemary Gartner shows in the article included in this section, women have become more subject to violence as they have entered direct competition with males. This certainly was an underlying theme in the Marc Lepine murders in Montreal in 1989. Gartner's data show that a similar trend in victimization is occurring worldwide. Yet, happily, the data suggest that as women gain higher education, the tie between competition and violence against women begins to weaken.

The victimization of young women is also evident when we study women as lawbreakers — for example, as young prostitutes. John Lowman shows, in the article included in this section, that all of our efforts to help reform deviants will fail until we acknowledge the reasons for their deviation. In the case of young prostitutes, we must take factors like low self-esteem, an abusive home life, and drug addiction into account. Policies that fail to do so will only soothe the conscience of legislators, not solve the problem.

References

Durkheim, Emile. *The Rules of Sociological Method.* New York: Free Press, 1938 (1895).

Erikson, Kai T. *Wayward Puritans.* New York: John Wiley and Sons, 1966.

Gibbon, Edward. *The History of the Decline and Fall of the Roman Empire.* London: J.M. Dent, 1913.

Gusfield, Joseph R. *Symbolic Crusade: Status Politics and the American Temperance Movement.* Urbana: University of Illinois Press, 1963.

Weber, Max. *The Theory of Social and Economic Organization.* Introduced and edited by Talcott Parsons. New York: Free Press, 1964.

NINE

Differences Between Canada and the U.S. in Deviance and Crime

John Hagan

JOHN HAGAN, Professor of Sociology and Professor of Law at the University of Toronto, specializes in the study of crime, deviance and social control. His books include *The Disreputable Pleasures: Crime and Deviance in Canada* (1977); *Deterrence Reconsidered: Methodological Innovations*, (1982); *Quantitative Criminology: Innovations and Applications* (1982); *Victims Before the Law: The Organizational Domination of Criminal Law* (1983); and *Modern Criminology: Crime, Criminal Behavior and its Control* (1985). In addition, numerous papers have been published and presented on related topics. Professor Hagan is currently co-principal investigator in a major research program on legal theory and public policy. He has served as associate editor to many leading sociological journals, including the *American Journal of Sociology; American Sociological Review; Sociological Inquiry; Social Problems; Criminology*; and the *Canadian Journal of Sociology*.

CROSS-NATIONAL DATA ON DEVIANT BEHAVIOUR

By many measures Canada is only a moderately violent nation. Figures 9-1 and 9-2 indicate rates of homicide and violent crime more generally in Canada and the United States. . . . Although some differences exist in the collection and categorization of offences in Canada and the United States, the findings suggest an interesting pattern: with population differences taken into account, violent offences have remained more frequent in the United States than in Canada.

The difference in rates of homicide in Canada and the United States endures despite the fact that our media regularly remind us of the high levels of criminal violence in the United States and of the prospect that the murder and mayhem are spreading to Canada (e.g., Wilson, 1989). . . .

. . . Canadian and U.S. homicide rates diverged most dramatically in the 1970s and the early 1980s, when the post-World War II baby boomers came into violence-prone age groups. Since the early 1980s there is some evidence of decline in both countries, but in the 1980s the difference in rates is still substantially bigger than it was through the early 1960s. . . .

. . . The trends are more pronounced with regard to violent crimes generally. Thus, the index of violent crime graphed

FIGURE 9-1

HOMICIDE RATES IN CANADA AND THE UNITED STATES, 1962–1986

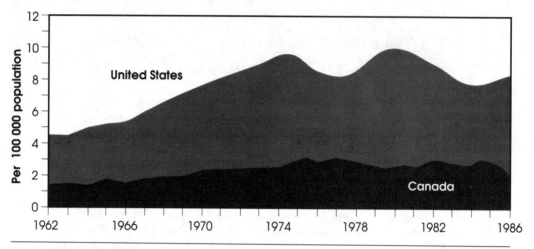

Source: Johnson, Holly, "Homicide in Canada." *Canadian Social Trends*, Winter, 1987, modified to highlight differences in absolute rates.

FIGURE 9-2

SERIOUS VIOLENT CRIME RATES[1], CANADA AND THE UNITED STATES, 1962–1985

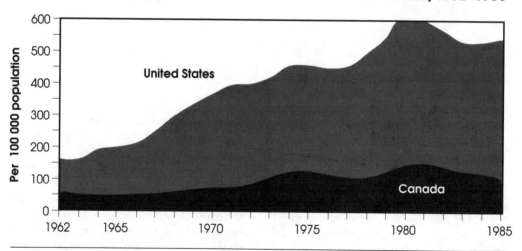

Source: Johnson, Holly. "Violent Crime." *Canadian Social Trends*, Summer, 1987, modified to highlight differences in absolute rates.

[1] The Canadian rate includes homicide, attempted murder, rape, aggravated sexual assault, wounding, and aggravated assault and robbery. The U.S. rate includes murder, rape, robbery, and aggravated assault.

from 1962 to 1985 in Figure 9-2 reveals a widening of the gap between Canada and the United States over the past several decades. Because violent crimes include a variety of more common crimes than homicide, the numbers involved are larger, and they produce ... smoother trends. While there were less than two hundred violent crimes per hundred thousand population in the United States in the early 1960s, and less than fifty in Canada, the respective numbers increased to well over five hundred in the mid 1980s in the United States, compared to just over one hundred in Canada. So the gap in violent crimes seems to have increased ... substantially. ...

... That Canada is a relatively non-violent nation, particularly in comparison with the United States, is echoed in cross-national studies of political violence (Kirkham, Levy and Crotty, 1970). Such studies demonstrate that despite Canada's experiences with groups like the FLQ, the numbers and rates of assassinations, armed attacks, riots, and deaths from political violence have been relatively low. Data reported in the *World Handbook of Political and Social Indicators* demonstrate that Canadians were much less likely than Americans to engage in protest demonstrations or riots between 1948 and 1982 (See Table 9-1). Lipset (1989: Chap. VI) summarizes these data by noting "Although the United States population outnumbers the Canadian by about ten to one, the ratios for political protest activities have been from two to four times as large, i.e., twenty to one to forty to one." In sum, we seem individually and collectively more violent than some, but nonetheless more peaceful than most, and this is particularly apparent in comparison to the United States.

... Michalos (1980: 64) has attempted to summarize ways in which the United States and Canada recently have become similar and dissimilar in matters of crime and justice. His conclusion is that the countries have tended to be or become similar with respect to the following:

1. Clearance of violent crimes

2. Property crime convictions

3. Full-time police department employees

4. Full-time police officers

TABLE 9-1   Political Protest and Violence in Canada and the United States, 1948–1982

Item	Canada			United States		
	1948-67	1968-77	1978-82	1948-67	1968-77	1978-82
Protest Demonstrations	27	33	13	1179	1005	1166
Riots	29	5	0	683	149	93
Deaths from Political Violence	8	4	N/A	320	114	N/A

Source: Seymour Martin Lipset, *Continental Divide: The Values and Institutions of the United States and Canada.*

However, he concluded that the countries have tended to become dissimilar with respect to all of the following:

1. Crime index offences
2. Violent crime
3. Murder
4. Policemen murdered
5. Favouring death penalty
6. Forcible rape
7. At-risk rape
8. Aggravated assault
9. Robbery
10. Property crime
11. Auto theft
12. Larceny $50 and over
13. Burglary
14. Property crime clearance
15. Crime Index violent crime subjects charged
16. Supplemented Crime Index violent crime subjects charged
17. Crime Index property crime subjects charged
18. Supplemented Crime Index property crime subjects charged
19. Violent crime convictions
20. End-of-year prisoners
21. Per capita expenditures on criminal justice.

Clearly, the latter list is substantially longer than the former, again making arguments for convergence unlikely.

Surveys of drug use in the United States and Canada suggest another area of American predominance. Berg (1970) reviewed 69 self-report studies of drug use conducted during 1969 in the United States, while Smart and Fejer (1971) reviewed 22 such studies conducted from 1967 to 1970 in Canada. The conclusions drawn from . . . these reviews were . . .: (1) reported levels of use varied widely within each country; (2) levels of reported use changed substantially in the late 1960s; and (3) the prevalence of non-medical drug use was higher in the United States than in Canada. In this regard Blackwell (1988: 241) echoes the point made earlier about fears of the expansion of U.S. problems into Canada.

> Thus, when we hear from the south of designer or "microchip" drugs or of "crack," the cheaper and smokable version of cocaine, we are understandably concerned that these problems will move north. We can take some comfort from the observation that our use rates for all illicit drugs have been modest in comparison to those of the U.S., even at the peak of epidemic phases.

Student surveys conducted in Canada from 1976 to 1987 (e.g., Addiction Research Foundation, 1982: 116–117) are consistent with this conclusion. For example, a recent study by the Addiction Research Foundation provides for 1986 the first estimates of the student use of "crack" in Ontario. The percentage (1.4 percent) is significantly lower than that reported in the United States (about 4 percent) (see Institute for Social Research, 1988). To the extent that such reports can be taken as valid (for a supportive Canadian test of validity, see Whitehead and Smart, 1972), the prevalence of non-medical drug use in the United States exceeds that in Canada.

Turning to the most frequently abused chemical, alcohol, comparative data are available from a variety of countries.

TABLE 9-2   International Statistics on Liver Cirrhosis Deaths, 1974 to 1985
Per 100,000 Population

Country	1974	1977	1980	1983
Canada	11.6	11.9	11.2	9.4
United States	15.8	14.3	13.5	11.7
Finland	5.5	5.4	6.3	7.0
France	32.8	31.5	28.2	25.7
Germany, Federal Republic	26.9	27.6	26.7	25.1
Italy	31.9	N/A	34.3	N/A
Norway	4.1	4.2	6.1	5.8
Spain	22.5	22.5	22.4	N/A
Sweden	10.5	12.4	12.2	8.2
Switzerland	14.8	12.9	13.3	12.4
United Kingdom	3.6	3.7	4.7	4.1

Source: *Statistics on Alcohol Drug Use in Canada and Other Countries.* Toronto: Addiction Research Foundation, 1989.

Much of this data is built on the . . . fact that alcoholics contribute a disproportionately large share to mortality from cirrhosis of the liver. International statistics on liver cirrhosis deaths are presented in Table 9-2. This information is built into computing formulas used to estimate the prevalence of alcoholism (Popham, 1956). . . . Neither Americans nor Canadians are among the world's heaviest drinkers, but our southern neighbours may once more exceed us. . . .

Generally, . . . the forms of deviance considered most serious by the public (for example, "violent crime" and "hard drug abuse") are found more commonly in the United States than in Canada. . . .

Why is There Less Deviance in Canada than in the United States?

The consensus theories argue that Canadians and Americans differ in their values, particularly in their relative respect for law and order, and that these differences produce a cross-national disparity in the incidence of the more serious forms of deviance. Two factors, one environmental and the other political, are said to explain these differences: (1) the early tradition of strict legal control initiated in the development of Canada's northern and western frontier, and (2) the "Imperial Connection" linking Canada to the elite-based traditions of Great Britain. Together with a more conservative set of national values, these factors are offered in explanation of Canadian-American differences in the incidence of the more serious forms of deviance.

The conflict theories argue that the disparity between Canadian and American rates of deviance are a consequence of "cultural lag." It is then suggested that as the "Imperial Connection" diminishes and the "American Connection" increases, that patterns of deviance in the two countries will become more and more alike. More specifically, as American investment continues and the Canadian economy expands, new resources will become available for increases in police force size and expenditures. These factors are said to result in increasing rates of deviance, both in the United States and Canada. Dislocations in the economy may, of course, modify this picture.

... The consensus theories work best in explaining the most serious forms of deviance, the consensus crimes, while the conflict theories serve best in explaining the societal response to those forms of deviance about which little consensus exists. ... The consensual theories are more interested in explaining *behaviours*, while the conflict theories are particularly concerned with disreputable *status* of those behaviours, as well as the manner in which consensual evaluations of behaviours sometimes emerge. ... Both ... theories can be used to recommend important changes in the Canadian response to deviance.

Studies of the societal response to deviance suggest, on the one hand, that the various agencies of social control fit together in similar ways in Canada and the United States, but that particularly in the area of *crime*, Canadian policies and procedures have been more repressive. Thus, both in Canada and the United States there is evidence that *social resources* have some influence on the application of disreputable labels. When relevant behavioural variables are taken into account, some research on police and court operations indicates that criminal and delinquent labels are applied ... more frequently to the socially disadvantaged, while alcoholic and psychiatric labels are reserved ... more frequently for ... middle- and upper-class persons. ... These observations seem as applicable in Canada as in the United States.

There does, however, seem to be evidence that Canada's system of criminal justice has developed differently than have the criminal justice systems of the United States and other Western nations. Some of these differences are summarized below. ... In the *past* Canada may have used incarceration more than the United States. Procedural safeguards spelled out in the Canadian Bill of Rights and the Charter of Rights and Freedoms were late in coming and of uncertain application, and penal reforms began much later in Canada than in the United States and Great Britain. These findings led us to consider possible changes in the response to crime in Canada. Before we review these findings, consider the following summary comparison of crime and law in Canada and the United States.

Crime and Law in Two Countries

... Two ideal types of societal strategies for maintaining legal order are the "due process" and "crime control" models of law enforcement (Packer, 1964). The due process model has its roots in the Enlightenment and in the notion of John Locke that the law can be used effectively in defence of "natural" and "inalienable rights." Alternatively, the crime-control model receives its philosophical support from the conservative reaction to Enlightenment and from the arguments of Edmund Burke that civil liberties can have meaning only in orderly societies. The distinction between these models is, of course, one of degree. ... It is argued that Canada, more than the United States, tends toward a crime-control model: the "approach which is truest to our experience . . . is that of Edmund Burke, not John Locke. Canadians — neither their judges, nor their politicians — are creatures of the Enlightenment" (Russell 1975: 592). The roots of these differences, are historical. . . .

Historically, the southern part of North America contained resources that could be exploited with relatively minor governmental involvement and control (Clark, 1975: 55). As well, the United States was conceived ideologically as a nation devoted to the rights and responsibilities of individuals (Lipset, 1968). One result was the formation of an ideology of individualism that, when combined with exploitable resources, allowed and encouraged more extensive variations from the norm than was the case in the northern part of the continent (Hagan and Leon, 1978: 1980). Thus, Quinney (1970: 55) notes that on the American frontier local authorities were free to develop their own law enforcement policies or to ignore the problem of crime altogether. Similarly, Inciardi (1975: 88) observes that "The American frontier was Elizabethan in its quality, simple, childlike, and savage. . . . It was a land of riches where swift and easy fortunes were sought by the crude, the lawless, and the aggressive, and where written law lacked form and cohesion." Put simply, the American frontier was also a criminal frontier, a model in some ways for the city life that followed. In Bell's (1953) apt phrase, "crime is an American way of life."

However, as the United States matured, the establishment of a viable legal order also became a priority. On a formal and symbolic level the American commitment to a due process model of law enforcement continued to increase in ideological importance. The antidote to this ideology was an equally significant national commitment and assignment of resources to policing and punishing deviant behaviour. Thus, although an economy of scale might be expected, the United States has

spent more *per capita* on its police than has Canada, substantially more on its courts, and more as well on corrections (Hagan and Leon, 1978: 200). A result is that the United States has produced a legal order that combines high levels of crime with a profuse and coercive police response. Some of the historical irony of this situation is captured in Skolnick's (1975: 246) description of the police as America's "asphalt cowboys."

In contrast the Canadian approach was one of initially more firm, but also necessarily more strategic, control (see McNaught, 1975). In the East problems of law and order were handled by the military . . . (Clark, 1962: 191; see also Clark, 1942). However, more efficient means were required in the West. . . . One means . . . was to assign the North-West Mounted Police a key role in John A. Macdonald's "National Policy," giving the NWMP "power unparalleled by any other police force in a democratic country." Clark (1962: 192) summarizes the situation this way: "In the United States the frontier bred a spirit of liberty which often opposed efforts to maintain order. In Canada order was maintained at the price of weakening that spirit." In more concrete terms the point is that Canada has been able to limit its resource commitment to crime control by re-emphasizing its ideological commitment to the Burkean ideal of social order first and individual rights second. . . .

Important questions remain. For example, how are differences of race and ethnicity between Canada and the United States involved in the crime and law enforcement patterns . . . in the two countries? How was the Canadian emphasis on social order legitimated? What was the process by which the RCMP became a national symbol? And how is the ideology of social order transmitted and instilled?

Regardless of how these . . . questions are answered, . . . there is apparently a very persistent and significant difference in Canadian and American attitudes toward issues of due process and crime control. A contemporary reflection of this difference is that Canadians apparently are more willing than Americans to forgo law reforms in favour of leaving to legal authorities the discretion to decide what accused and convicted persons require and deserve. . . .

Whether the focus is restricted access to probation, discretionary right to counsel, the admissibility of illegally obtained evidence, or a range of other issues, Canadians have demonstrated a considerable willingness to accept laws that give social order precedence over individual rights. . . .

Source: Hagan and Leon (1980).

Past efforts to prevent crime have focused on individual treatment, social reform, and police deployment. None of these approaches brought measurable success. More recent approaches to crime prevention provide an expanded role for the community — through law reform, environmental design, and community corrections programs. Emphasized in many of these programs is the diversion of minor offenders into the community. For example, it was demonstrated that by instituting a more equitable fine system and decriminalizing the public consumption of alcohol as many as half of all Native offenders in Canada could be decarcerated. It was then argued that by diverting minor offenders into the community, new resources could be devoted to a more certain and expeditious response to the serious consensual crimes. Finally, evidence was presented indicating that it is the certainty of punishment, rather than its severity, that deters crime most effectively. In sum it was argued that we can reduce the severity of criminal punishments in Canada without risking a casually significant increase in our crime rates.

. . . The conflict theories . . . suggest that differences in the two nations' rates of crime will be diminished by increases in police force size and expenditures in Canada. In short, the conflict theories argue that the differences in crime rate are largely an artifact of enforcement policies.

. . . Consensus theories . . . insist that the behavioural differences are real, and that they are caused by national differences in attitudes and values. The consensus theories . . . argue that such values are also causally related to repressive legal policies and procedures in Canada. However, the best answers to questions about differences in crime rates in the United States and Canada may require more inventive explanations than either the consensus or conflict approaches can separately provide. These differences in crime rates likely involve both cultural and structural differences in the histories of these countries.

Historically, we have seen that Canada and the United States have followed rather different strategies in dealing with crime. For example, . . . the role of the state in the maintenance of social order has been a central theme in Canadian society, just as individual rights and due process have been central in American society. . . . These themes are historically and culturally entrenched, and they are expressed in alternative structural strategies for dealing with crime.

The consequences of the Canadian and

American strategies of dealing with crime are essentially the same for the socially advantaged. Both nations possess a legal order that allows the safe and stable conduct of social and economic affairs. However, the consequences for the socially disadvantaged in each country can be quite different. The American situation allows a freedom to deviate that is matched for those in subordinate statuses by a heightened likelihood of criminalization. So that in spite of greater attention in the United States to individual rights . . . and due process, we noted . . . the greater propensity of the United States compared to Canada to arrest as well as incarcerate its citizens. By giving symbolic and substantive emphasis to the maintenance of social order, the Canadian approach discourages deviation and at the same time decreases the proportionate likelihood of criminalization of subordinates.

Historical differences between the United States and Canada are particularly apparent and significant as they connect with . . . race relations and gun control. The United States violently suppressed its black and Native minorities within a society that makes a most democratic instrument of violence — handguns — freely available. Canada also socially and economically suppressed its Native People, but with less violence; and Canada made access to instruments of violence, particularly handguns, rather difficult. These . . . distinct structural strategies . . . could be expected to produce . . . different outcomes.

. . .The United States adopted an historical strategy toward crime and deviance that was a blueprint for violence. The results are especially apparent in the relatively higher rates of violent crime and imprisonment in that country. Although links between race and crime are apparent in both Canada and the United States, the results of structural and cultural differences between these countries are most visibly reflected in rates of violent crime and imprisonment among U.S. blacks, accounting for much, but . . . not all, of the difference in violent crime between the two countries. Although differences in violent crime between Canada and the United States may have peaked in the 1970s and early 1980s, the residue of this and earlier periods remains in enduring national differences in violent crime. . . .

References

Addiction Research Foundation. *Statistics on Alcohol and Drug Use in Canada and Other Countries.* Toronto: Addiction Research Foundation, 1982.

Bell, Daniel. "Crime as an American Way of Life." *The Antioch Review* 13 (1953): 131–154.

Berg, D.F. "The Non-Medical Use of Dangerous Drugs in the United States: A Comprehensive View." *International Journal of Addictions* 5(4) (1970): 777–834.

Blackwell, Judith. "An Overview of Illicit Drug Use Epidemiology." In Judith Blackwell and Patricia Erickson (eds.), *Illicit Drugs in Canada.* Scarborough, Ontario: Nelson, 1988.

Clark, S.D. *The Social Development of Canada.* Toronto: The University of Toronto Press, 1942.

————. *The Developing Canadian Community.* Toronto: The University of Toronto Press, 1962.

_____ . "The Post-Second World War Canadian Society." *Canadian Review of Sociology and Anthropology* 12 (1975): 25–32.

_____ . *Canadian Society in Historical Perspective.* Toronto: McGraw-Hill Ryerson, 1976.

Hagan, John and Leon, Jeffrey. "The Philosophy and Sociology of Crime Control: Canadian-American Comparisons." *Sociological Inquiry* 47 (3–4) (1978): 181–208.

_____. "The Rehabilitation of Law." *The Canadian Journal of Sociology* 5(3) (1980): 235–251.

Inciardi, James. *Careers in Crime.* Chicago: Rand McNally, 1975.

Institute for Social Research. "Student Drug Use in Ontario." *Newsletter*, Vol. 3, No. 2 (1988). Toronto: York University.

Kirkham, James, Levy, Sheldon and Crotty, William. *Assassination and Political Violence.* Washington: Government Printing Office, 1970.

Lipset, Seymour Martin. *Revolution and Counterrevolution: Change and Persistence in Social Structures.* New York: Basic Books, 1968.

_____. *Continental Divide: The Values and Institutions of the United States and Canada.* New York: Routledge, 1990.

McNaught, Kenneth. "Political trials and the Canadian political tradition." In M.L. Friedland (ed.), *Courts and Trials: A Multi-Disciplinary Approach.* Toronto: University of Toronto Press, 1975.

Michalos, Alex. North American Social Report. London: D. Reidel Publishing, 1980.

Packer, H. "Two Models of the Criminal Process." *University of Pennsylvania Law Review* 113 (1964): 1–68.

Popham, R.E. "The Jellinek Alcoholism Estimation Formula and Its Application to Canadian Data." *Quarterly Journal of Studies on Alcohol* 17 (1956): 559–593.

Quinney, Richard. *The Social Reality of Crime.* Boston: Little, Brown, 1970.

Russell, Peter. "The Political Role of the Supreme Court of Canada in Its First Century." *Canadian Bar Review* LIII(3) (1975): 576–596.

Skolnick, J.H. *Justice Without Trial: Law Enforcement in a Democratic Society.* New York: John Wiley and Sons, 1966 (1975).

Smart, R.G. and Fejer, D. "The Extent of Illicit Drug Use in Canada: A Review of Current Epidemiology." In Craig Boydell, Carl Grindstaff, and Paul Whitehead (eds.), *Critical Issues in Canadian Society.* Toronto: Holt, Rinehart and Winston, 1971.

Whitehead, Paul and Smart, Reginald. "Validity and Reliability of Self-Reported Drug Use." *Canadian Journal of Criminology and Corrections* 14(1) (1972): 83–89.

Wilson, Deborah. "Racist-Skinhead Violence in U.S. Held Up as Warning to Canada," *The Globe & Mail*, April 5, 1989, A12.

TEN

The Folly of Criminalizing Juvenile Prostitution

John Lowman

JOHN LOWMAN, Associate Professor in the School of Criminology at Simon Fraser University, Burnaby, British Columbia, specializes in the study of crime and deviance. His publications include a research report for the Department of Justice entitled *Street Prostitution: Assessing the Impact of the Law* (1989), and *Transcarceration: Essays in the Sociology of Control*, edited with R. Menzies and T.S. Palys (1987). Professor Lowman's various chapters and research papers include "Police practices and crime rates" (1991), "Prisoner reform: the rhetoric of rehabilitation and the accountability of custodians" (1989) and "The geography of social control: clarifying some themes" (1989). His recent research, all under major grants, has dealt with street prostitution, the history of social control institutions in Canada and the United States, and an evaluation of Bill C-49 in Vancouver.

In the introduction to the 'Juvenile Prostitution Survey' conducted by the Committee on Sexual Offences Against Children and Youths (c.s.o.a.c.y., or the Badgley Committee) we are told:

> Because the unsavoury aspects of juvenile prostitution challenge the roots of Canadian society's moral values, in response to widespread public concern, various instant remedies have been proposed in order to contain or eliminate this problem. Contrasting perspectives alternately portray juvenile prostitutes as exploited deviant victims who need special treatment and services, or they are depicted as potential or actual criminals who should be disciplined and punished (1984: 948).

In trying to resolve the seemingly irreconcilable goals of the 'help' and 'just deserts' perspectives, the committee opts for a pastiche of the two:

> There are no effective means of stopping the demonstrated harms that these children and youths *bring upon themselves* . . . There is no desire on the part of the Committee to affix a criminal label to any juvenile prostitute. The Committee concluded, however, that in order to bring these children and youths into situations where they can receive guidance and assistance, it is first necessary to hold them and the only effective means of doing that is . . . to have a specific criminal sanction prohibiting children and youths engaging in prostitution. (c.s.o.a.c.y., 1984: 1046 emphasis added).[1]

The Badgley Committee's proposal for prostitution law reform strikes a familiar historical chord by proposing a policy . . . to help (i.e., 'rehabilitate') rather than simply punish the offender. But . . . an appraisal of the survey research conducted for the Badgley and Fraser committees[2] suggests the criminalization of young prostitutes, rather than altering their 'life changes,' would result in an institutional system geared mainly to control; in practice 'treatment' would once again become . . . a euphemism for custody.

By focusing almost entirely on the choices made by young prostitutes, rather than on the social milieu in which those choices are made, the Badgley Committee preemptively locates the explanation of youth prostitution at an individualistic level. It pathologizes the prostitute. The question is: How useful is its analysis for informing a theoretical perspective on prostitution?

STRUCTURE/ACTION: THE CONTEXT OF CHOICE

In championing a 'fully social theory of deviance' Taylor, Walton, and Young outline seven components that such theory must incorporate (1973: ch. 9). These include considerations of the origin and nature of behaviour that is defined as deviant, the reasons why it is defined as such, and how the definition influences the character of the behaviour in question. The power of the model, and its improvement on both 'traditional' and 'labelling' perspectives, lies in insisting that a sociology of deviance be based on analyses of both the definition of certain behaviours as deviant, *and* the nature and origins of the behaviours so defined. . . .

My purpose here is to apply Taylor, Walton, and Young's model to contemporary Canadian prostitution by examining the results of the interview surveys conducted for the Badgley (C.S.O.A.C.Y.: ch. 42–46) and Fraser committees (Crook, 1984; Fleischman, 1984; Gemme, Murphy, Bourque, Nemeh, and Payment, 1984; Lautt, 1984; Lowman, 1984; see also Sansfaçon, 1984) in order to reconstruct the Badgley Committee's interpretation of its 'Juvenile Prostitution Survey' and its recommendations for prostitution law reform. . . . Here I am particularly concerned with what Taylor, Walton, and Young refer to as the 'immediate' and 'wider' origins of the act. . . .

There are three main components to the argument presented here, the first constituting the main concern of the paper.

1/   Although the Badgley Committee claims that its methodology allowed youths to tell their own stories, the report is overwhelmed by the . . . constructs of social-scientific discourse. Instead of presenting a 'naturalistic' (see Matza, 1969) or phenomenological perspective on the subjects' self-perceptions, their activity, and motivation, *Sexual Offences Against Children* contains the quantitative dimensions of the aggregated interview data, or case histories of young prostitutes purged of (what the committee considers to be) its subjects' illusions and self-deceptions. But if one claims to express the research subject in order to inform social policy or theory, the fidelity of subjects' accounts must be maintained for an understanding of how they define their situation.[3]

2/   Given the young prostitute's expressed dislike of social programs, particularly the coercive variety, it is difficult to see how more of the same will do anything other than keep them in custody until they reach adulthood. The question becomes one of examining why the Badgley Committee pathologizes the young prostitute so that punishment can be redefined as help. . . .

3/ Having argued for the integrity of a naturalistic perspective to begin a theory of youth prostitution (the 'immediate origins of the act') it must then be connected to . . . the wider origins of prostitution. The committee's . . . focus on the prostitute's social biography (particularly family background and the circumstances of entrance into prostitution) minimizes the structural context of a youth's decision to turn to prostitution. . . .

THE IMMEDIATE ORIGINS OF THE DECISION TO PROSTITUTE

. . . In 1984 and 1985 the results of interviews with 501 prostitutes working in Canada were published. Of these interviews, 229 were conducted for the Badgley Committee (145 with females), and 272 were completed in the regional surveys conducted for the Fraser Committee (225 with females).[4] Most respondents worked the street prostitution trade.

. . . The Badgley Committee's 'Juvenile Prostitution Survey' included as 'juvenile' anyone under the age of twenty-one.[5] This age distinction has no significance either in terms of the current criminal code, or of the committee's recommendations for law reform.[6] This arbitrary cut-off is less a problem when it concerns . . . prostitutes since most 'turned out' as juveniles.[7] . . .

Family Social Class and Standard of Living

From a battery of questions relating to parent occupations, employment, and receipt of government assistance, the Badgley Committee concluded that . . . a large proportion of these youths had grown up in families having a middle class and, in a few cases, an affluent standard of living.' (p. 973).[8] . . . This conclusion issues partly from the observation that 'the great majority of these juvenile prostitutes were raised in homes in which at least one parent had some form of employment and partly from the observation that only one third of the girls, and one in nine boys came from families where one or both parents receive government financial assistance. But too much detail is omitted here. For example, were the subjects describing chronic or occasional unemployment?

Without a careful consideration of the types of occupation in which parents were employed (since occupational type is usually central to a definition of 'class'), the results of the Juvenile Prostitution Survey do not allow the types of conclusion drawn by the Badgley Committee. Unfortunately, the committee never . . . provides the reader with a definition of 'class.' The occupations of the fathers and mothers of the subjects in the Vancouver survey (Lowman, 1984: 733) indicate more of a working-class or blue-collar character (although the group is certainly mixed). Crook concluded that most prostitutes in her east coast survey came from 'low socio-economic backgrounds' (1984: 86) and in Québec, '54% of 81 respondents considered that they were raised in modest circumstances, while 38% described their backgrounds as "very poor" ' (Gemme et al., 1984: 117).[9] . . .

Intrafamilial Sexual Experience

From a comparison of the results of the 'Juvenile Prostitution Survey' and results of their 'National Population Survey' the Badgley Committee concluded, contrary to most American research[10] and the opinions of many Canadian social workers, that . . . juvenile prostitutes were no more likely to have experienced 'unwanted sexual acts' than other Canadian youths. There appear to be several problems associated with this assertion (cf. Badgley, 1984), not the least of which is the apparent discrepancy between definitions of 'unwanted sexual acts' used in the two surveys.

The committee, by extrapolating the results of the National Population Survey, concluded that one in two Canadian females have been the victim of an unwanted sexual act' (C.S.O.A.C.Y., 1984: 193, 977); of these victims, four in five had been victimized prior to their eighteenth birthday, (i.e. 40 per cent of the total sample had been victims of an 'unwantd sexual act' during their childhood). Subsequently, the committee says that 40 per cent of female juvenile prostitutes 'reported that their first unwanted sexual experience had involved the use of threats or force to which they had unwillingly submitted' (C.S.O.A.C.Y., 1984: 978). These figures appear similar only because they compare the first unwanted sexual experiences of respondents to the National Population Survey with the first unwanted sexual acts reported by respondents to the Juvenile Prostitution Survey *involving threats or force to which they had unwillingly submitted.*

An alternative interpretation based on a comparison of tables 6.1 (C.S.O.A.C.Y., 1984: 180) and the figures quoted later in the report (p. 978) indicates that 10.6 per cent of males in the National Population Survey said that their first unwanted sexual experience involved threat or force (if one assumes the category 'attempted/assaulted' in table 6.1 is equivalent to the category 'force or threats/[11]'), while 22.6 per cent of the juvenile male prostitutes reported a similar first experience. The corresponding figures for females are 22.1 per cent and 40 per cent. It appears, then, that prostitutes were *twice as likely* to have experienced a first unwanted intrafamilial sexual act involving force or threats of force as other members of the Canadian population. . . .

. . . In taking the position that 'it cannot be concluded on the basis of the information available that having been sexually abused as a child was, by itself, a significant factor that accounted for their subsequent entry into juvenile prostitution,' it must have been much easier to argue that these juveniles '*bring upon themselves* the demonstrated hardships of street life' (C.S.O.A.C.Y., 1984: 1046). Such views are not only contradicted by the alternative interpretation of survey findings offered above, but also by a number of Québec and British Columbia prostitutes. Of the fourteen Vancouver prostitutes that described sexual interactions with family members,[12] ten claimed the experience was significant in their subsequent entry into prostitution. Similarly, in Québec, Gemme and his colleagues reported that they 'found in many cases that the respondents' sexual histories played an important role in their becoming prostitutes'; of seventy-seven (almost all female) respondents providing the information, '44% indicated having had forced sexual relations with one or more family members' (Gemme et al., 1984: 117). Thirty-five per cent of the women interviewed in Halifax and St. Johns reported sexual interactions with family members.[13] One could interpret these answers as rationalizations, but as one young women quizzically explained to a Vancouver researcher, 'if I was going to stay at home I was going to get screwed, so why not leave home and get paid for it' (author's notes). . . .

Intrafamilial Violence

'The period of transition between home life and street life was generally characterized by the youths as an attempt to sever themselves from parental authority and influence' (C.S.O.A.C.Y., 1984: 980).

One of the clearest findings of the Juvenile Prostitution Survey concerned the frequency with which young prostitutes had run away from home; of the respondents answering this question only 2.4 per cent of the males and 5.5 per cent of the females said that they had never done so. Similarly researchers in the United States find that most juvenile prostitutes were runaways or '*throwaways*' (Weisberg, 1985: 122–3). These findings are not particularly surprising since 'street kids' are likely to be runaways by definition.

What is striking is the Badgley Committee's interpretation of youths' running away as '. . . an immediate means of escaping from some aspect of their home environment with which they found it *impossible* to cope' (C.S.O.A.C.Y., 1984: 983, emphasis added). But the full implications of these comments might have been missed by an interview apparently not asking explicit questions about intrafamilial violence. Nevertheless, some information was obtained tangentially; 45 per cent of the males and 52 per cent of the females reported that their strongest recollection of home life was of 'continual fighting or arguments' (C.S.O.A.C.Y., 1984: 983–4).

Where information was obtained in the regional prostitution surveys about intrafamilial violence we find what are probably relatively high rates. In the Atlantic provinces, for example, more than half of the street prostitutes recalled 'continuous fighting in the family when growing up' (Crook, 1984: 87). In Vancouver 64.6 per cent of the respondents (*n*)46) said that family violence had occurred 'sometimes' or 'often' (Lowman, 1984: 279). Persistent intrafamilial violence was also frequently reported by young American prostitutes (Weisberg, 1985: 88–9, 93–4).

An analysis . . . of these findings would . . . require some knowledge of the level of violence in Canadian families generally. But the fact that family problems were more important at this level of analysis than any other factors combined would seem particularly relevant when it comes to designing policies to address the problems of juvenile prostitutes. For one thing, highly repressive measures may not be appropriate for removing juveniles from the street if the intention (or unintended consequence) is to force them back to a home situation which they define as 'impossible.' And yet, that appears to be the committee's intent when they state that their findings:

> leave no doubt about the emotional and physical harms, the risks and the privations associated with street life. The findings constitute a clear warning to any youth who is considering either running away or turning to prostitution (C.S.O.A.C.Y., 1984: 1047).

Undoubtedly street prostitution in Canada is very dangerous.[14] But the committee, trapped between shock and moral outrage, appeared unable to comprehend or represent its subjects' point of view. If home life is impossible and the street is so dangerous, why are lumpen youth so hesitant to turn to the state for help?

Social Services, Self-Help, and Autonomy

The study of social services reported in the Vancouver survey (Lowman, 1984: ch. 4) strongly supports the Badgley Committee's conclusion that few services are designed specifically for adult and/or juvenile prostitutes. Interviews with prostitutes suggest that those services available are perceived to be of little use (Lowman, 1984: ch. 6). Prostitutes, both adult and juvenile, generally try to minimize their involvement with state 'helping' agencies. Nevertheless, many have used social services extensively . . . And although several Vancouver prostitutes applauded specific social workers . . ., opinions about state help institutions were generally negative (Lowman, 1984: pp. 260–74). Much of this negativity can be traced to the client's perception of social work as a form of control rather than help.

The problems of youth are compounded by their defamilied status — outside the family they are not even eligible to collect welfare. For them in particular, social work often becomes a form of a token-economy or bargain-control. Several prostitutes advocated the establishment of 'safe houses' where runaways could eat and sleep without having to resort to prostitution, but without the . . . control they perceive social workers exercising. In other words, the notion of 'safe' has a number of connotations, not the least of which is that shelters should be safe from the exercise of someone else's authority. Vancouver prostitutes also mentioned the need for 'safe group homes,' an indication of their distrust for

group homes generally (Lowman, 1984: 728).

With these comments in mind it is difficult to envisage the social programs that should be developed for young prostitutes. Since these programs should differ considerably from most of the others developed in Canada to date, they require considerable elaboration.[15]

Having said this much it must also be acknowledged that the runaway-come-prostitute's desire for autonomy, as much as it is a desire for separation from the family or state-home, also represents a yearning for surrogate affiliations, and alternative identities. It is in this respect that street life is magnetic.

THE LURE OF THE STREET: LIFE IN THE FAST LANE

. . . To explain the young prostitute's lack of interest in state helping agencies, and to further individualise the phenomenon of prostitution, the Badgley Committee emphasized the lure of the street. The main reason given by the Badgley study youths (78.6 per cent of the boys and 65.5 per cent of the girls) for entering prostitution was 'rapid financial gain' (c.s.o.a.c.y., 1984: 991).

But the great irony of street life that compelled the Badgley Committee to recommend the coercion of young prostitutes into therapeutic state care, is that it is often more conducive to dependency and danger than to autonomy. The social stigmatization of prostitution creates . . . psychological problems and self-validating stereotypes that . . . entrench the prostitute in street life. This life is often accompanied by increases in drug use. Violence by tricks is widespread. Young female runaways are the most vulnerable to pimps. And even where money is accumulated rapidly, if it is not taken by pimps it quickly disappears in a life-style oriented to conspicuous consumption and the contingencies of the moment. . . . Certainly 'pull' factors play a part in . . . becoming a prostitute; the youngest and most attractive prostitutes make large amounts of money quickly, and this is the image of prostitution that dominates popular conceptions of street life. But . . . street prostitute incomes appear much lower than might be expected.[16] . . .

Alcohol and Illicit Drugs

. . . Although a number of the prostitutes interviewed in the Vancouver survey were heavy users of drugs (with alcohol the most used drug), many were not. . . . The findings of the Juvenile Prostitution Survey reveal a similar pattern in that 'heavy drug and alcohol use may be less prevalent among these youths than might otherwise have been anticipated' (C.S.O.A.C.Y. 1984: 1021). . . . Drug dependency might lead to prostitution in some instances, but . . . other factors are . . . more important.

Nor should we lose sight of the fact that among certain groups of prostitutes there is voracious illicit drug consumption. In Vancouver, for example, the use of a mixture of Ritalin and Talwin (two prescription drugs) is common among street juveniles, particularly in what is termed the skid row area of the East End. Of the prostitutes that did use drugs frequently, several stated they did so to dull the negative consequences of their work, such that they could continue to work at all.[17] It is important to acknowledge that while drug use is important to street culture, this culture can only be understood in terms of a wider culture where certain . . . drugs confer status.

Pimping

While the 'Juvenile Prostitution Survey' and the regional studies provide ample evidence about the role of 'pimps' in turning out female prostitutes[18] and in preventing them from leaving the street,[19] it is debatable if the definition of pimping is as straightforward as the Badgley Committee implies, or if the practice is as ubiquitous as it suggests.

The Committee notes that only fifteen of its subjects at the time they were interviewed admitted working for a pimp, although an additional fifty-five subjects said they had previously worked for one.[20] Apparently the committee did not believe its research subjects, arguing that the Juvenile Prostitution Survey 'indicates that while most young females who engaged in prostitution had initially found their way onto the street by themselves, it was the pimps who kept them there' (C.S.O.A.C.Y., 1984: 1060). Here the issue of evaluating respondent truthfulness, and the accuracy of perceptions, becomes paramount.

The Badgley Committee argues that prostitutes would not admit that they worked for a pimp for fear of his discovery that they had discussed their work. But the committee does not provide much evidence to back this assertion. Researchers in Vancouver found that many women with pimps would not consent to any interview. The Vancouver prostitute sample is geographically biased precisely because women from the exclusively pimped area rarely consented to be interviewed.[21] . . . Unfortunately the differentiation of prostitution within and between cities is generalized away by the Badgley Committee because the geographical dimensions of its survey data are never explored.

Further, if female prostitutes are

duped by pimps so extensively, or are so afraid to talk, how can one account for the wholesale scorn and derision of pimps that many prostitutes express?[22] In Vancouver, the best information about pimps . . . came from women who had previously worked for them. In searching for policies to help to prevent the exploitation of prostitutes by pimps, the ability and desire of many . . . prostitutes to resist such exploitation should not be understated. . . .

In adopting the position that all 'boyfriends' are pimps the Badgley Committee conveys too generalized an image of pimping. Several hustlers interviewed in Vancouver not only prostituted themselves, but lived with prostitute girlfriends who would provide them with money when business was slow or when they were ill. Sometimes the money would flow in the opposite direction. It would be a mistake to believe that all these relationships are based on exploitation as the Badgley Committee appears to argue. . . .

These comments should not be taken as minimizing the consequences of pimping. At least half of the females in the Badgley sample were being pimped or had been pimped. In Halifax . . . Crook found plenty of evidence of pimp violence (1984: 74–85), and Vancouver and Prairie city prostitutes told similar stories (Lowman, 1984: 194–5; Lautt, 1984: 102–3).

The committee notes that women's prostitution careers are longer than those of males,[23] a finding it attributes to pimp influence rather than the structural disadvantage of females in both the legitimate labour force *and in the illicit economy of the street.* Its emphasis on the role of pimps . . . again serves to individualize the problems of prostitutes, casting them as both helpless and deceitful, in a situation they had 'brought upon themselves'.

'HELPING' PROSTITUTES

. . . It is incumbent on the committee to show why correctional programs, which must surely be geared to custodial goals when put into practice, will work when so many others have 'failed'. And although the committee recommended introducing laws prohibiting the purchase of a juvenile's sexual services, and harsher penalties for pimping, it is not likely that such laws would be extensively enforced.[24]

Ultimately, . . . a law making it an offence for juveniles to prostitute themselves would result in a holding operation which would forcefully keep some juveniles off the street until their eighteenth birthday. The youths would then be subject to the added stigma of a criminal label for the act of prostitution itself, a label which may further serve to entrench them in the trade. Instead of 'helping' prostitutes we would succeed in consolidating the perception of prostitution as an illegality without having dealt with the structurally marginal position of women and youths in the labour force.

LUMPEN YOUTH: THE CONTEXT OF CHOICE

. . . The Badgley Committee . . . was asked to 'examine the relationship between the enforcement of law and other mechanisms used by the community to protect children and youths from sexual abuse and exploitation' (C.S.O.A.C.Y., 1984: 3–4). Unfortunately, the discussion of 'other mechanisms' was relegated to a series of amorphous comments about educational and social programs, the logic and operation of which are never articulated. The suggestion that its overall terms of reference did not require analysis of broader structural issues ignores the idea that the substance of law is inevitably founded on a specific vision of social order. . . .

The committee omits a political economy of prostitution . . . and in so doing it decontextualizes prostitution, individualizes the problems of defamilied youth, and proposes strategies aimed at the prostitute as a legal subject (cf. Lowman, 1985). Structural issues languish at the margins of its analysis.

. . . The Badgley Committee's analysis ignores the critical literature on the centrality of the family[25] in the relations of production and reproduction. It does not analyze male power in the family (cf. Clark, 1985a) or the male power to purchase sex. . . . Its analysis ignores arguments about the desirability of creating a series of alternative family structures which are neither patriarchal (cf., Brock and Kinsman, 1986; Clark, 1985a; 1985b), bourgeois, nor necessarily nuclear, and which do not fall under what Brock and Kinsman (1986) refer to as 'heterosexual hegemony.'

In following a doctrine of 'child-centred' reform the committee advocates an elitist or professional centralism in which only the expert can divine the interests of lumpen youth. As a form of 'authoritarian statism' (cf. Hall, 1980; Taylor 1985: 332) – the imposition of benevolence, in this case through the deployment of criminal law – its proposals for prostitution law reform are part of a wider strategy which would radically extend the state's control over sexuality, children, and the family (cf. Sullivan, 1985). By simultaneously (and contradic-

torily) raising the age of sexual consent to sixteen (and for some activities, such as buggery, to eighteen) while lowering the age of criminal responsibility for sexual offending to twelve, the Badgley Committee proposals promise to radically broaden state and professional power.

Discussion of the influence of persistently high unemployment rates on levels of . . . youth prostitution . . . is largely neglected by the Badgley Committee. In British Columbia, for example, while seasonally adjusted unemployment rates have hovered in the 12–14 per cent range during the early 1980s, the 1985 rate for those aged fifteen to twenty-four was 22.4 per cent (Todd, 1985: A10). One wonders how the Badgley Committee would explain the significant increase in newspaper advertisements for escort and other off-street prostitution services in Vancouver after the onset of the economic recession in 1981 (Lowman, 1984: 369–73) . . .

While there is passing reference to the marginal employment status of defamilied youth, the committee's discussion of the family backgrounds of young prostitutes implies that economic factors are not as important in the genesis of prostitution as many suppose. But the fact that young prostitutes do not come from backgrounds of absolute poverty minimizes the idea that it is the *situational poverty* of defamilied youth that is crucial to an aetiology of youth prostitution. With few prospects for rewarding or lucrative employment illicit economies are virtually the only viable means for the runaway to gain independence from the family and the state. For many street prostitutes, irrespective of the age when entering prostitution, *it is the fact that prostitution provides money at all* that is the necessary condition of their turning out and remaining in the business. . . .

CONCLUSIONS

. . . Autonomy and a desire for belonging, are central to a youth's decisions to leave home and to earn money through prostitution.

Once we . . . consider the context of a youth's choice to sell sexual services, it becomes obvious that the choice must be located in the 'wider origins of the deviant act', particularly the marginal position of youth in the labour force, and patriarchal power structures inside and outside the family.

In being told that juvenile prostitutes should be criminalized in order to be saved, we are being asked to recreate a contradiction recurrent over the past 200 years where punishment and treatment are confused. As a result reform is likely to devolve into rhetoric, serving to define, contain, and maintain deviance rather than alter the social structures which limit the young prostitute's life chances.

Ultimately, the solution to juvenile prostitution will require a transformation of male sexual socialization within a diverse system of family forms, and a solution to the marginality of juveniles, particularly females, in the labour force. It is likely that the criminalization of juvenile prostitutes will hinder rather than facilitate these changes. In the interim, laws against the customers of young prostitutes may help to curtail the trade, but the impact will be noticeable only if accompanied by a drastic reduction of youth unemployment and the creation of alternative living arrangements for lumpen youth.

Notes

[1] The committee also recommended criminalizing the customers of juveniles, and increasing the severity of sentences for pimping.

[2] Like the Badgley Committee, the Fraser Committee (Special Committee on Pornography and Prostitution, 1985–S.C.P.P.) also recommended the creation of a law prohibiting the purchase of, or offer to purchase, the sexual services of a juvenile (658–9). But in contrast to the Badgley Committee, the Fraser Committee did not 'believe that there is any justification for penalizing in a young person what is not criminal when done by an adult' (S.C.P.P., 1985: 660).

[3] For first person accounts (as structured by interview schedules), see Lautt (1984) and Lowman (1984).

[4] Because of the small sample sizes and lack of consistency in the presentation of results, the information about male prostitution in the five regional surveys conducted for the Fraser Committee is limited. Because their interview schedules were designed separately, these studies do not always provide matching information.

[5] This leaves the committee in the rather unsatisfactory position of having to refer to eighteen to twenty years of age adults as 'boys and girls'; indeed, only 43 per cent of the prostitutes interviewed in the Badgley Committee Study were juveniles (i.e. 'young persons' in the legal sense) at the time that they were interviewed.

[6] . . . The term 'juvenile prostitute' is problematic in at least two ways.

First, since persons thirteen years of age and under cannot legally consent to sexual intercourse in any circumstances (C.S.O.A.C.Y., 1984: 319), and since the act of prostitution involves a consensual sex act for gain (monetary or otherwise), the term 'juvenile prostitute' is a misnomer if used to describe any person under fourteen years of age. The term 'sexually procured juvenile' is more accurate. None of the Badgley Committee's sample were under the age of fourteen.

Second, while . . . girls between the ages of fourteen and seventeen can consent to sexual intercourse it is not clear that they (or boys) are able to conduct business independently of either their parent or their guardian (Lowman, 1984: 174). Certainly the philosophy of the Young Offenders' Act is guided by the principle that 'young persons' can be held criminally responsible for their actions. But in the realm of civil law children do not have such autonomy. It can be argued that the decision to prostitute themselves is not actually theirs to make. If this argument is correct, the term 'sexually procured juvenile' should replace the term juvenile prostitute.

7 In this paper the term 'juvenile' is used synonymously with 'young person' to denote anyone under the age of eighteen, in accordance with the Young Offenders' Act.

8 The committee also noted that more males than females reported that they had grown up in 'socially and economically privileged backgrounds' (1984: 973).

9 Researchers in the United States have reported, however, that juvenile prostitutes increasingly appear to be coming from middle-class backgrounds (Weisberg, 1985: 153–5).

10 For a review of American research on juvenile prostitution see Weisberg, 1985.

11 In the National Population Survey four categories of unwanted sexual acts were included: touched; attempted/assaulted; exposed; and threatened. Perhaps the second and fourth categories should be added together to make them comparable to the Juvenile Prostitution Survey!

12 Forty-two of the Vancouver Field Study subject group (*n* = 48) answered this question, of whom twenty-seven were female (twelve of the females – 44 per cent – reported sex acts with family members). The six non-respondents were all female. Since it seems reasonable to suppose that someone with a background of sexual contact with family members would be more likely to refuse to answer this question than someone who did not, these proportions could have been greater. Sexual contact was defined as contact involving genital touching of some kind (from fondling to penetration).

13 Rates of intrafamilial childhood sexual abuse among juvenile prostitutes reported in American studies varied between 31 per cent and 66.7 per cent (Weisberg, 1985: chs. 4 and 5).

14 ... One problem posed by tricks is medical. But the much greater problem – the greatest and most frequent danger Canadian prostitutes report that they face – is trick violence. When questioned about problems they had experienced with tricks, prostitutes were quick to describe numerous thefts, robberies and sexual assaults (see Crook, 1984: 28–9; Lautt, 1984: 109–16; Lowman, 1984: 229–34, 249–56). Female prostitutes were victimized much more frequently than their male counterparts.

15 The experience of the Senator Hotel in Vancouver, a project designed to house and provide various programs for street youth, merits a separate study. The hotel closed amidst scandal surrounding various accusations of misconduct involving both social workers and street youths.

16 For estimates of prostitute earnings see Greenstein (1984), Crook (1984: 19); Gemme et al. (1984: 124–6); and c.s.o.a.c.y. (1984: 1018–20). ...

17 For example, 51 per cent of Vancouver prostitutes (*n* = 45) stated they used drugs while working as a way of escaping the realities of the job (Lowman, 1984: 726), and 45 per cent of Québec prostitutes (*n* = 80) stated their intake of alcohol had increased significantly since they started working as prostitutes (Gemme et al. 1984: 121).

18 Males do not appear to be pimped in the traditional sense, although they ... can be exploited, usually by ... older non-prostitute hustlers. ... American research similarly indicates that males are rarely pimped in the traditional sense (Weisberg, 1985: 160).

19 See Lautt, 1984: 47–50 for a description of several pimps' modus operandi.

20 In the Québec study only 29 per cent of the women interviewed admitted to working for or having worked for a pimp (Gemme et al., 1984: 127); in Vancouver eight women acknowledged having worked for pimps although a further fifteen respondents (including several males) said that they shared money with friends and/or lovers/boyfriends.

21 This finding is also supported by Kohlmeyer's study (1982). In the Vancouver Field Study (Lowman, 1984) researchers gained enough familiarity with the street scene ... to find out who was being pimped (in the stereotypical sense) and who was not.

22 See, for example, Gemme et al., 1984: 127.

23 In the case of males, the committee asserts that few of them work as prostitutes after their early twenties, an observation supported by researchers in Vancouver, and generally in the U.S. (Weisberg, 1985: ch. 4).

24 Historically, laws against pimps have been extremely difficult to enforce because prostitutes are unwilling to testify against pimps.

The same hesitancy is likely to occur in the case of young prostitutes testifying against customers, but for different reasons. Given that public pressure to enforce prostitution laws is almost exclusively centred on the visibility of prostitutes, police would probably . . . concentrate their enforcement efforts on young prostitutes rather than their customers.

[25] For an indication of the terrain covered by these debates see: Barrett and McIntosh (1982); Poster (1978); and Thorne and Yalom (1982).

References

Badgley, C. 'Child Sexual Abuse and Juvenile Prostitution: A Comment on the Badgley Report on Sexual Offences Against Children and Youth.' *Canadian Journal of Public Health* 76 (1984): 65–6.

Barrett, M. and McIntosh, M. *The Anti-Social Family.* London: New Left Books and Verso, 1982.

Brock, D. and Kinsman, G. 'Patriarchal Relations Ignored: A Critique of the Badgley Report on Sexual Offences Against Children and Youth.' In J. Lowman, M.A. Jackson, T.S. Palys, and S. Gavigan (eds.) *Regulating Sex: An Anthology of Commentaries on the Badgley and Fraser Reports.* School of Criminology, Simon Fraser University, 1986.

Clark, L. 'Boys Will Be Boys: Beyond the Badgley Report, A Critical Review.' Paper presented at the Symposium on Sexual Offences Against Youth in Canada, co-sponsored by the Centre of Criminology and the Institute of Child Studies, University of Toronto, March, 1985. (An edited version of this paper also appears in J. Lowman, M.A. Jackson, T.S. Palys, and S. Gavigan (eds.), *Regulating Sex: An Anthology of Commentaries on the Badgley and Fraser Reports.* School of Criminology, Simon Fraser University, 1986.)

'Interview with Lorenne Clark.' *Canadian Criminology Forum* 7 (1985): 157–66. Committee on Sexual Offences Against Children and Youth (C.S.O.A.C.Y.)

Crook, N. 'Report on Prostitution in the Atlantic Provinces.' *Working Papers on Pornography and Prostitution Report No. 12.* Ottawa: Department of Justice, 1984.

Fleischman, J. 'A Report on Prostitution in Ontario.' *Working Papers on Pornography and Prostitution Report No. 10.* Ottawa: Department of Justice, 1984.

Gemme, R., Murphy, A., Bourque, M., Nemeh, M.A., and Payment, N. 'A Report on Prostitution in Quebec.' *Working Papers on Pornography and Prostitution Report No. 11.* Ottawa: Department of Justice, 1984.

Greenstein, H. 'Prostitution as a Business.' In J. Lowman, *The Vancouver Field Study of Prostitution.* Ottawa: Department of Justice, 1984.

Hall, S. 'Popular-Democratic versus Authoritarian-Populism: Two Ways of Taking Democracy Seriously.' In A. Hunt (ed.), *Marxism and Democracy.* London: Lawrence and Wisehart, 1980.

Kohlmeyer, K. An Ethnography of Street Prostitution in Vancouver. Unpublished Master's Thesis, Department of Criminology, Simon Fraser University, 1982.

Lautt, M. 'A Report on Prostitution in the Prairie Provinces.' *Working Papers on Pornography and Prostitution Report No. 9.* Ottawa: Department of Justice, 1984.

Lowman, J. 'Vancouver Field Study of Prostitution.' *Working Papers on Pornography and Prostitution Report No. 8.* Ottawa: Department of Justice, 1984.

_____. 'Child Saving, Legal Panaceas, and the Individualization of Family Problems: Some Comments on the Findings and Recommendations of the Badgley Committee.' *Canadian Journal of Family Law* 4(4) (1985): 508–14

_____. 'Prostitution in Vancouver: Some Notes on the Genesis of a Social Problem.' *Canadian Journal of Criminology* 28(1) (1986): 1–16

_____. 'Street Prostitution.' In V. Sacco, *Deviance, Conformity and Control.* Toronto: Prentice-Hall, 1988.

Matza, D. *Becoming Deviant.* New Jersey: Prentice Hall, 1969.

Poster, M. *Critical Theory of the Family.* New York: Seabury, 1978.

Sansfaçon. D. *Prostitution in Canada: A Research Review Report.* Ottawa: Department of Justice Special Committee on Pornography and Prostitution (S.C.P.P.), 1984.

Sullivan, T. 'The Politics of Juvenile Prostitution.' Paper presented at the International Conference on the Status of Girls, Montreal, October 1985.

Taylor, I. 'Criminology, the Unemployment Crisis, and the Liberal Tradition in Canada: The Need for Social Analysis and Policy.' In T. Fleming, *The New Criminologies in Canada: State, Crime, and Control.* Toronto: Oxford University Press, 1985.

Taylor, I., Walton, P. and Young, J. *The New Criminology: For a Social Theory of Deviance.* London: Routledge and Kegan Paul, 1973.

Thorne, B. and Yalom, M. *Rethinking the Family: Some Feminist Questions.* New York: Longman, 1982.

Todd, D. 'School Aid Officers Assail B.C. Program.' *Vancouver Sun* 16 November, 1985, pp. A1, A10.

Weisberg, D.K. *Children of the Night: A Study of Adolescent Prostitution.* Lexington: D.C. Heath, 1985.

ELEVEN

Patterns of Victimization

Rosemary Gartner

ROSEMARY GARTNER, formerly Associate Professor in the Department of Sociology and the Faculty of Law at the University of Toronto, specializes in studies of crime, deviance, and victimization. Her publications include *Violence and Crime in Cross-National Perspective*, co-authored with D. Archer (1984). This book was the winner of the 1985 Award for Outstanding Scholarship from the Society for the Sociological Study of Social Problems and the 1986 Distinguished Scholarship Award from the American Sociological Association's Criminology Section. Professor Gartner also has published numerous book chapters and research articles, including "Peacetime casualties: the effects of war on the violent behaviours of non-combatants," with D. Archer (1981), and "The victims of homicide: a temporal and cross-national comparison" (1990). She is currently on the Editorial Boards of three research journals: *Journal of Criminal Law and Criminology*, *Social Problems*, and *American Sociological Review*.

People born in different times and places face very different chances of being victims of homocide,[1] and societies and eras differ in how much they promote or inhibit criminal violence. The chances of becoming a homicide victim depend not only on when and where one lives, but also on certain personal characteristics. For instance, males, young adults, and the economically disadvantaged face higher risks of homicide victimization[2] than do females, children and the elderly, and the economically advantaged. These gender and age differences in homocide victimization appear with remarkable consistency in different places and times. In Canada, for example, males' chances of being killed have been about twice as high as females' for as long as records have been kept; and Canadians over the age of 14 are three times as likely to be killed as those between the ages of one and 13.[3]

The fact that criminal violence tends to be a male-dominated activity has strongly shaped sociological research and theorizing about homicide. The explanations that have traditionally characterized the field are based on studies of male offenders and victims, or on total homicide rates, in which the majority of cases involve young adult males. While this work is extremely informative, it leaves unanswered many questions about homicides involving females and children. My research has been concerned with these less studied groups, and with explaining variations in rates of female and child homicide victimization in different societies and over time. In par-

TABLE 11-1   Mean Sex-and Age-Specific Homicide Victimization Rates[a] for 18
Nations, 1965–1984

Country	Males over age 14	Females over age 14	Children aged 5–14	Children 1–4	Infants under 1 year
United States	14.92	4.18	.99	2.11	5.40
Finland	4.89	1.51	.55	.89	6.92
Canada	3.28	1.55	.58	1.04	3.17
Italy	2.45	.69	.24	.22	.80
Australia	2.30	1.41	.51	1.06	3.00
Austria	1.67	1.20	.48	.89	6.81
Belgium	1.53	1.13	.33	.73	.98
West Germany	1.48	1.03	.56	1.03	5.59
New Zealand	1.46	.83	.38	1.71	4.49
Sweden	1.41	.83	.44	.84	1.36
France	1.39	.79	.26	.48	1.92
Japan	1.34	.74	.80	2.26	7.64
Norway	1.20	.59	.23	.35	1.80
Ireland	1.09	.43	.10	.18	2.05
Switzerland	1.04	.81	.51	.75	4.57
Netherlands	1.00	.51	.21	.43	1.63
England & Wales	.88	.71	.28	.99	4.30
Denmark	.75	.78	.65	.83	2.21
Mean, all 18 nations	2.45	1.10	.45	.93	3.65

[a] All rates are calculated per 100,000 persons in the appropriate sex or age group, except rates for infants,
which are calculated per 100,000 live births.

Source: World Health Organization, World Health Statistics Annual

ticular, I have been interested in how long-term social changes, and social and cultural factors affect women's and children's risks of becoming victims of homicide.

I began investigating these issues by comparing homicide victimization rates of adult females, adult males, and children in 18 developed democracies over the last three decades (Gartner, 1990a). These rates are shown in Table 11-1. In that study, I found a number of factors were associated with higher rates of homicide for all three groups. Nations with higher levels of economic ine-

quality, lower levels of government spending on welfare, and more family dissolution had higher rates of female, male, and child victimization. As well, nations with greater cultural and ethnic diversity, and greater exposure to official violence (such as the death penalty or involvement in wars) had higher rates of all types of victimization. However, I also found some factors were important for some types of homicides but not others. To explore these further, I went on to study homicides of females and children separately and in more depth.

FEMALE HOMICIDES AND GENDER INEQUALITY

The mass slaying of 14 women at the University of Montreal in December 1989 shocked all Canadians deeply, but had especially profound effects on women. After the tragedy, many expressed concern about whether it signaled a trend in violence against females — a sort of 'backlash' in response to the movement of women into arenas traditionally dominated by males. Those reacting against this fear have noted the Montreal killings were unprecedented and atypical. After all, mass killings are rare, especially in Canada; and rarer still are those targeted at specific groups, including women. But, while the likelihood of more massacres of women is extremely remote, is it not possible that such backlash violence could be increasingly directed against individual women in less spectacular, but no less deadly incidents?

This question prompted me to look at the relationship between changing gender roles and women's vulnerability to violence (Gartner 1990b). While females are the victims of homicide less often than males, the size of this female protective advantage varies considerably. For example, in Italy and the United States since 1950, males have faced risks of homicide three times greater than females' risks. In other societies, this female advantage has been negligible: in the 1980s in Denmark and England, for instance, women were killed almost as often as were men.[4] There is much less variation across societies in who kills women. Males are the perpetrators in over 80% of the killings of females, and in about 90% of the killings of adult females.

What accounts for females' lower risks of homicide, relative to males' risks? Biological determinist arguments were favoured among criminologists for several decades. A Finnish criminologist named Veli Verkko explained the gender gap in homicide by referring to "innately different biological qualities of men and women" such that "the woman naturally lives in a somewhat different and more peaceful atmosphere than the man: (Verkko 1951: 54). On this basis, he formulated his "universal laws of homicide" that stated that women's risks of homicide vary little over time or place, and are always less than men's risks, because — according to Verkko — women's biologies are essentially immutable and different from men's.

Obviously, such biological arguments cannot explain why females' risks of homicide vary widely even among relatively similar societies; or why the gender gap in homicide is almost non-existent in some societies and not others. To explain these patterns, we need to look at women's social and economic environments, including the contexts within which women raise their families, participate in the labour force, and carry out myriad other roles.

Anthropological and historical evidence shows that the killing of women is relatively infrequent, and the gender gap in homicide is relatively large, in many societies that are sharply gender-stratified (Curtis, 1974). In these societies, family arrangements are especially patriarchal, women are not allowed to participate in economically productive activities (or their economic activities are devalued), and females are socialized to be extremely passive and subservient. Yet despite these disadvantages, women appear to be at much less risk of homicide than are men. On the other hand, in many societies where gender inequality is less pronounced, women's risks of being killed are closer to men's risks. This suggests women in contemporary western societies might come to face risks of being killed similar to men's as various forms of gender inequality and discrimination diminish.

To explore this issue, I collected homicide victimization rates of females and males in 18 developed nations for the years 1950 to 1980.[5] I also gathered information on the roles and status of women, and on gender inequality in each nation. This included women's participation in the labour force and in higher education; gender segregation in occupations; and the rate at which women had children outside of marriage, got divorced, and delayed marriage past their early twenties.

Two perspectives on the relationship between greater gender equality and female homicide can be distinguished. One, the "criminal opportunity" approach, deals largely with homicides in the public domain. According to this approach, criminal victimization, such as murder, occurs when a motivated offender encounters a suitable target (victim) in the absence of capable guardians (Hindelang et al., 1978; Cohen and Felson, 1979). How people move through the routine daily activities of life — where they spend time, how many and what types of people they spend time with — all influence their opportunities for being homicide victims. It follows that where women's and men's activities are more alike, their chances of being killed ought to be more alike.

A second perspective on the gender gap in homicide is suggested by feminist discussions of changing gender relations. According to this view, with reductions in gender inequality, women should be freer to avoid or to challenge male domination in a number of spheres of social life. Violent victimization is obviously only the most extreme form of this domination. Thus, where women have more alternatives to violent relationships with men, or more resources to protect themselves from victimization, their risks of being killed should be lower than where their choices and opportunities are more limited, if this view is correct.

This approach is more general than the criminal opportunity perspective, in that it can be applied to homicides in both the public and private domains. Women with more resources can leave abusive relationships more easily. They can also protect themselves more adequately in their public lives, for example, by choosing to live in safer neighbourhoods or taking taxis rather than walking late at night. Moreover, women with more resources can direct them toward collective advantages. For instance, they can lobby for more public protection of women, through changes in the substance and enforcement of laws against violence toward women.

The criminal opportunity perspective and the feminist approach seem to predict different outcomes for changes in gender stratification. The former suggests that gender equality *increases* the likelihood of women being killed; whereas the latter predicts that gender equality *reduces* the likelihood of women being killed.

Both may be right, however. Gender stratification is a complex phenomenon. It is composed of both differences in the *roles and activities* women and men perform, as well as differences in the *status and power* women and men hold. With greater gender equality in *roles*, women's daily activities could expose them to more dangerous situations, as they spend more time out at night, on their own, and in places that provide little protection. This could increase the opportunities for female victimization. However, with greater gender equality in *status*, women could individually and collectively claim more control over their lives and their environments. This could decrease the opportunities for female victimization.

In other words, changes in gender stratification could operate to increase or decrease homicides of females, depending on which process had the strongest effects.

These processes may operate within different time frames and unfold at different speeds. Over the last few decades, the greatest changes in women's lives have been in their day-to-day activities, as they have moved into the labour force in unprecedented numbers, taken on a wider array of non-domestic responsibilities, and moved away from lives circumscribed largely by family ties. So gender inequality in roles has declined at a fairly steady pace.

Gender inequality in status, however, has been more obdurate. More women are working outside the home and heading households. But gains in status have not kept pace with changes in women's roles. For example, women's economic status has improved little in the last few decades, either in an absolute sense or relative to males. There are many disturbing examples of this, from the continued gender gap in wages to the growing proportion of poor households headed by females.

These differences suggest that recent changes in women's roles and changes in women's status may have had countervailing effects on women's risks of being killed. Moreover, improvements in women's status, however gradual, may have slowed any increase in women's risks of victimization by counteracting the risk-enhancing effects of women's less traditional roles.

To explore these issues, I combined and analyzed the time-series data on women's roles, status, and homicide for all 18 nations. The patterns I found, then, are general, applicable across these nations. I discovered:

- where women are less embedded in *traditional family and reproductive roles* — that is, where they had children out of wedlock more often, divorced more often, and delayed marriage longer — their risks of being killed were higher, and the gender gap in homicide was less pronounced.

- where women competed with men for *economically productive roles* — that is, where women made up a larger proportion of the paid labour force, and where occupations were less gender-stratified — their risks of being killed were also higher, and the gender gap in homicide was less pronounced.

- however, where women had *greater access to higher education* (and, I would argue, to the status, resources, and power that higher education confers) their risks of being killed eventually declined, and the gender gap in homicide did not narrow.

So, changes in women's roles and changes in women's status appeared to have counterbalancing effects on their risks of being killed. However, as anticipated, gains in women's status seemed to take time to translate into protection against violence. In the short run, as women assumed a greater range of roles and responsibilities, they also became more vulnerable to violence.

I decided to explore a bit further. Did women's less traditional roles always lead to greater risks, or did this depend on how much status women had? Perhaps where gender differences in status were less pronounced, women did not face increased risks of homicide when they moved into non-traditional roles; whereas where gender differences in status remained large, women were vulnerable when they took on more non-traditional roles.

I divided the 18 nations into two groups, depending on the level of female status in the nations (measured by female college enrollments). Some nations in the 'high status' group were Canada, Sweden, Finland, and the United States; 'low status' nations included Ireland, Japan, Italy, and the Netherlands. I found it was only in the low status group that women's less traditional roles substantially raised their risks of being killed. In the high status group of nations, the rate at which women were killed did not rise as gender differences in roles diminished.

It appears, then, that in societies that allowed fuller participation of women in higher education — a major avenue to higher status — women were not as likely to lose their protective advantage as they competed with men in the labour force or as they moved out of traditional domestic arrangements. Thus, this cost of women's fuller participation in society appears to be neither inevitable nor long-term. The context within which women participate seems to determine their vulnerability to violence.

What do these findings about female homicides in 18 nations over thirty years have to tell us about Marc Lepine's murder of 14 women at the University of Montreal? At first glance, the Montreal killings do not seem to fit the general pattern I found. They occurred in Canada, a nation with relatively high female status. The setting was a university, a source of advances in women's status. On the other hand, most of the women killed were engineering students; they had entered a traditionally male-dominated field. And the verbal and written comments Lepine left behind indicated he was resentful and infuriated by "feminists" and other women who sought opportunities in less traditionally female ways. For him, such women had prevented his success professionally and personally.

Thus, I think the Montreal massacre can be seen both as part of a more general phenomenon of male backlash violence against women, and as a particularly aberrant expression of that pattern. In other words, Lepine's hostility toward successful women cannot be dismissed as merely the attitude of one isolated and psychotic individual. At the same time, it would be a mistake to conclude that seeking gender equality through higher education or professional advancement is a risky strategy for Canadian women.

CHILD HOMICIDES, FAMILY STRUCTURE, AND WELFARE SPENDING

The analysis of homicides of females was based on the knowledge that their killers are usually men. That is why it was important to focus on gender relations in explaining changes in women's risks of victimization. Similarly, studying the homicides of children requires some knowledge of who presents the greatest risks to children's lives, and under what circumstances.

Children, like women, face the greatest risks from people they are related to or living with. For infants, the most likely killer is a parent; as children grow older, the risks from their parents decrease, while the risks from other family members or other persons who know them well grow. This suggests it is important to explore family relations and structures in studying child homicide.

Certain types of family structures are known to increase children's vulnerability to violent victimization, including homicide. For example, children with young parents, single parents, step- or foster-parents, or many young siblings face elevated risks of being physically abused or killed (Daly and Wilson, 1988). Where such families are also exposed to economic stresses, children's risks are especially high.

These well-known patterns have been explained in different ways. The "systems" or ecological approach proposes that a group's balance of resources for coping with stressors determines the level of violence in the group. From this approach, the family is a microsystem that is sometimes structured to limit the extent to which resources can be marshaled to cope with stressors (Garbarino, 1981). Where parents have fewer personal and social resources to draw on, where they are isolated from support systems, and where family size exceeds resource capacity, child abuse and homicide should be greater.

According to a systems approach, this relationship between family risk factors and violence against children operates at two levels. Not only will individual families that are isolated and resource-poor be particularly prone to child abuse. In addition, large numbers of such families in a social system (for example, a neighbourhood, city, or nation) can raise the risks of violence for all families in the system. This occurs because networks of informal control and support become weakened in the system as a whole.

A second explanation of the higher risks of homicide for children in certain family settings is provided by evolutionary psychology (Daly and Wilson, 1988). According to this perspective, through natural selection, individual decision making is oriented toward promoting one's genetic posterity or reproductive fitness. Consequently, the likelihood of infanticide is greater where a child is

> of dubious quality, . . . where there is some doubt that the offspring in question is indeed the putative parent's own [and where there are] extrinsic circumstances that might bode ill for a particular childrearing effort: food scarcities, a lack of social support, overburdening from the demands of older offspring, and so forth. (Daly and Wilson, 1988: 44)

According to an evolutionary perspective, certain family structures or parental characteristics may increase the likelihood of child homicide, even when they are not accompanied by resource constraints. For example, teenage mothers should be more likely than older mothers to kill their children, in part because the potential future reproduction of teenage mothers is greater. Children raised by step-parents and unrelated caregivers should be at greater risk of violence, in part because these children do not enhance the reproductive fitness of their caregivers. Furthermore, maternal characteristics that are associated with premature, underweight, and less healthy babies should also be associated with elevated risks of child homicide.

Although the systems approach and the evolutionary perspective differ in important ways, they identify similar types of risk factors for children. According to both, where there are more single and very young mothers, non-intact families, and families with many young children, child homicide rates should be higher. Furthermore, where systems of social and economic support for families are less developed and less generous, child homicide rates should also be higher. I examined these predictions using child homicide data from the same set of nations described earlier for the years 1965 to 1984 (Gartner, 1991). I also collected data on family structures and welfare spending in these nations, including information on births to teenage and single mothers, divorce rates, and the ratio of young children to adult women in the population. A number of these high-risk characteristics of families increased between the late 1960s and the late 1970s in these nations. For example, divorce rates more than doubled, and rates of births to teenage and single mothers also grew. I asked if these changes in family structure were associated with changes in the homicide rates of infants and young children and found:

- infants under the age of one were more likely to be killed where rates of births to teenage mothers were higher, and where government spending on welfare programs was more limited;

- children aged one to four were more likely to be killed where rates of births to teenage mothers and to single mothers were higher, where divorce rates were higher, and where government spending on welfare programs was more limited.

These findings show that particular family structures as well as government welfare policies can influence the vulnerability of children to violence. Both the systems and the evolutionary ap-

proaches predicted this would be the case. However, both approaches also suggest that the risks associated with certain family structures can be lessened by providing families with resources to deal with the stresses they face. One way to do this is through government programs designed to alleviate economic deprivation.

To look at this issue, I divided the nations into two groups: one had higher than average government spending on welfare programs, while the other had lower than average spending. I then analyzed family structures and child homicide in these two groups. This analysis revealed that

- in nations where welfare programs were less generous, the risks associated with certain family structures were much greater than in nations where welfare programs were more generous.

In other words, higher government spending on social welfare was associated with lower risks of violence against children that resulted from the prevalence of particular family structures.

CONCLUSION

There are two important implications of these studies of female and child homicides. First, they show that social processes and structures can raise the risks of being killed for all members in society, regardless of gender or age. Second, they show that some social processes and structures pose particular risks for females and children. Therefore, theories of homicide based solely on studies of males are likely to be inadequate or even misleading when applied to females and children. Homicide, like other social behaviours, is a complex and diverse phenomenon. Understanding and explaining homicide requires knowledge of the full variety of people and relationships involved in it, and the social contexts within which it occurs.

Notes

[1] By "homicide," I mean the purposeful killing of a person by another person or persons (not in the context of warfare). Not all homicides are crimes; some are considered "justifiable" acts, as when a police officer shoots a person who is threatening others with violence. Homicides include the legally punishable acts of murder and manslaughter, but the definition of these criminal acts often varies among societies and historical periods.

[2] These same groups are also over-represented among homicide offenders. In other words, the demographic profiles of homicide victims and offenders are very similar.

[3] Unlike other young people, infants under a year old have quite high risks of homicide. Between 1965 and 1985, for example, the average homicide rate was 3.17 for Canadian infants, and 3.28 for Canadian males over the age of 14.

[4] In fact, between 1950 and 1980 the homicide rate for Danish women (.85 female homicides per 100,000 population) was slightly higher than for Danish men (.76 male homicides per 100,000 population). Cross-national comparisons should be interpreted with care. While Danish or English women and men face similar risks of homicide, they are much less likely to be murdered than Italian or American women and men, as is shown in Table 11-1.

[5] These homicide rates were compiled by the World Health Organization. Information on the victim's sex and age group is reported; unfortunately, no information about the identity of the offender is available. From other sources, we know that the vast majority of female victims of homicide are killed by intimate partners (current and former spouses and boyfriends) or family members.

References

Cohen, Lawrence E. and Felson, Marcus. "Social change and crime rate trends: A routine activity approach." *American Sociological Review* 44 (1979): 588–607.

Curtis, Lynn. *Criminal Violence: National Patterns and Behavior.* Lexington, MA: D.C. Heath, 1974.

Daly, Martin and Wilson, Margo. *Homicide.* New York: Aldine de Gruyter, 1988.

Garbarino, James. "An ecological approach to child maltreatment." Pp. 228–267 in L.H. Pelton (ed.), *The Social Context of Child Abuse and Neglect.* New York: Human Sciences Press, 1981.

Gartner, Rosemary. "The victims of homicide: A temporal and cross-national comparison." *American Sociological Review* 54 (1990a): 92–106.

_____. "Gender stratification and the gender gap in homicide victimization." *Social Problems* 37 (1990b): 593–612.

_____. "Family structure, welfare spending, and child homicide in developed democracies." *Journal of Marriage and the Family* 53 (1991).

Hindelang, Michael J., Gottfredson, Michael R., and Garofalo, James. *Victims of Personal Crime: An Empirical Foundation for a Theory of Personal Victimization.* Cambridge, MA: Ballinger, 1978.

Verkko, Veli. "Are there regular sequences in crimes against life which can be formulated as laws?" *Homicides and Suicides in Finland and Their Dependence on National Character.* Scandinavian Studies in Sociology #3. Copenhagen: C.E.S. Gads Forlag, 1951.

Social Inequality

This section is about social inequality, and it includes readings on how groups exercise their power, why social class matters to people, and how inequality in Quebec has changed in recent years.

Social inequality is any inequality that has social consequences. Often, it is an inequality with roots in social values or practices, not biology. Usually, it affects people's lives through the operation of social processes.

Some inequalities interest sociologists more than others. For example, people who are beautiful or tall receive more respect and a somewhat higher income, on the average, than people who are ugly and short. However, inequalities due to physical appearance have not concerned sociologists very much. Typically, they pay more attention to inequalities that are particularly marked; also, inequalities most people would perceive as illegitimate. As well, it may prove easier — and more important — to reduce gender or racial discrimination, for example, than discrimination against the ugly or short.

The study of social inequality includes such topics as unequal access to wealth, power, and respect. Sociologists study inequalities between groups, regions, and even countries. We want to learn the processes by which some groups dominate others: upper classes over lower classes, richer regions over poorer regions, and industrial nations over pre-industrial nations, for example. Only by a historical study of political and economic relations between groups can we hope to understand societal inequality as it exists today.

We shall explore various types of inequality in the remaining sections of this book. The next section examines race and ethnic relations; these are partly understandable as social inequality. A later section on gender relations explores inequalities between males and females. Finally, the section on social movements and social change examines the ways Canadians have reacted to social inequality.

Thus, the present section does little more than set out some of the general issues of research in this area. Later sections consider these issues at greater length.

A place to start is with the notion of "life chances." These are the chances we have to get things we need for a happy, healthy life. Whatever affects the chances to acquire what we need and value most affects our lives significantly. Sociologists have found that people's life chances are unequal in all known societies. Always, some people have a greater chance of getting what they need and want than others do. True, this inequality of life chances varies from one society to another, and over time. However, within a given society at a given moment, some people have a much better chance of fulfilment than others.

People have needs for food, shelter, and physical security that must be satisfied. If these needs are not satisfied, people will live fewer years, in worse health. Rich people are known to live longer, healthier lives than poor people. Reasons for this include better opportunities for good nutrition, medical care, housing, and rest; less risk of injury on the job; and healthier lifestyles.

Some developmental psychologists (e.g., Maslow, 1954) have argued that people also have needs for belonging, sharing, creativity, and self-determination. Without satisfying these, people will lead much less happy and fulfilling lives. Some of these needs are socially or culturally specific. We learn them through childhood socialization at home, school, church, and in the mass media. This learning creates "relative deprivation": a sense of being without what one needs. Relative deprivation causes pain because the unequal opportunity for a needed good or status implies less personal worth, limits social acceptance, and invites labelling as a deviant.

For example, people manage to survive even if they cannot afford to own a shiny new car or fashionable clothes. However, their lives are much less happy. In a consumer-oriented society like ours, other people "read" our material belongings for signs of our human worth. (Recall that Baldus and Tribe found this in their study of schoolchildren; see Section Three.) Then, we judge our own worth from what we "read" about ourselves in other people's eyes.

Just because a deprivation is relative, not absolute, does not make it trivial. How others view us, and we view ourselves, is often more important than absolute deprivation. The willingness of patriots, saints, and martyrs to risk their lives for God and country shows this is so. The willingness of ordinary students to skimp on sleep and lunches in order to buy fancy new clothing shows it too.

The first article in this section, by Paul Bernard and Jean Renaud, makes this very point. It sets out a general picture of changing inequality in

Quebec since World War II. What happened in Quebec is special in some respects. In other respects, it duplicates the experience of all Canadians since World War II. Economic growth of the 1950s and 1960s benefited large numbers of people. This general improvement reduced the pressure on government to redistribute wealth and opportunity. However, growth slowed down in the 1970s, creating a "zero-sum society." The poor and economically vulnerable were hardest hit. Lines of cleavage sharpened, conflict intensified, and inequality became both more severe and more obvious. A redistribution of wealth, the classic concern of radical thinkers, became more obviously necessary than ever.

Today, in a new recession, we do not know how and when governments will succeed in rekindling economic growth. Nor do we know whether success in this venture will quiet the demands for a redistribution of wealth. This article shows that people's perception of an inequality problem depends on comparison. People judge their present lives against past and expected lives, and their own well-being against that of others.

The other articles in this section theorize about the strategies different groups use to gain advantages in a zero-sum situation. These theories start from different premises and study different conflicts, but they reach similar conclusions. The place to begin our examination is with a general formulation of the problem.

In his article, Raymond Murphy attempts to combine the insights of Weber, Collins, and Parkin in a general theory of *closure*. To understand the unequal distribution of resources for a good life, we must understand the processes that capture and dole out needed resources. According to Murphy, this means understanding power as an exclusionary code. Powerful groups are able to specify how resources will be shared.

For example, access to high paying jobs in industrial societies increasingly requires a "credential." This testimonial, often in the form of an educational degree, shows that the possessor has completed certain courses. In this sense, he or she is qualified for selection. Degrees from medical and dental schools are particularly valuable, since almost no doctors or dentists are unemployed or poorly paid. Who, then, determines how these scarce resources, these degrees, will be handed out — to whom given, how many, and in return for what? Whoever controls this resource has an important power.

By "professionalizing," an occupational group becomes able to restrict entrance into its ranks; in this way, it gains closure. For example, doctors and dentists have succeeded in limiting the numbers of incoming graduates and defining the conditions of service (including the fees charged). Non-professional workers have greater difficulty doing this. Some, like the teachers Murphy discusses, unionize to achieve closure. Still, their efforts to achieve power through closure are less successful, for a variety of reasons. The public is less sympathetic to unions than to professional associations, and an eligible, appropriately skilled work force is more readily available for these jobs.

Closure is hardest to achieve in what some have called the "marginal" labour force. Workers such as clerks, waitresses, and taxi drivers can exercise little control over entry into jobs or the remuneration they bring. Hence they cannot limit competition for their own jobs: this means a lack of job security and low pay.

Professionalization is only one way of achieving closure. Ethnic group cohesion is another. We can find many workplaces where employers recruit people with identical ethnic backgrounds and reject all other candidates. As a result, certain ethnic groups control entire industries. When an ethnic group monopolizes an economic activity, allowing access to that activity only or primarily on the basis of ethnic affiliation, it is a practising closure. (Those excluded in the process would call it "discrimination.")

Ethnic closure is greatest under conditions of what Breton (1981) calls "parallelism" (also, "institutional completeness"). A high degree of parallelism threatens other ethnic communities, increasing the likelihood of conflict between them. When this threat becomes intense and visible, group leaders bargain for power with one another, often at the federal governmental level.

How serious the conflict becomes depends on the degree of overlapping of domains within which this conflict is going on. Ethnic closure on a field of activity that does not interest other groups will incite little conflict. To reduce threats to societal integration will demand regulating the conflict, incorporating communal activities in larger societal activities, and directly assimilating community members into the larger society.

Ethnic closure poses a danger to the whole society, because it threatens national unity. Therefore, in the long run, closure may hurt the ethnic community member. In the short run, ethnic closure provides a definite advantage for the member of a large, prosperous or highly mobilized ethnic group.

Do social classes practise closure? A *social class* is a group of people with similar life chances. Members may or may not be aware of their common characteristics and shared interests. If unaware, they may not be taking conscious action on their own behalf. Is "closure," as Weber defines it, the general principle that sorts people into classes? Is it the way the ruling class rules and the reason why people find it so hard to enter the ruling class from below? And if so, are class relations simply a sub-category of all relations of inequality and not, as Marx argued, the uniquely determining form of social inequality?

Max Weber holds that social classes function more or less like ethnic groups and occupational groups, in seeking to gain advantages for their members. In this sense, social inequality has many roots. Not all inequality traces back to relations of production and class exploitation, as Marx asserted. Whether Weber (and Murphy) are right on this point is extremely important to our general understanding of inequality.

Closure proves to be important not only between classes but also within classes. Understanding whether, how, and why class fragments cooperate will necessarily be part of a general theory of inequality. It helps us understand how ruling classes gain power, exercise power, and lose power. What remains puzzling is John Porter's (1965) finding that Canada's ruling class contains people with varied economic and political interests, despite similar class backgrounds and a common commitment to capitalism.

Wallace Clement's article on social classes gives us a richer sense of the theoretical debate between Marxists and non-Marxists. It also reminds us — if we needed reminding — that social classes matter to all of us, not merely to theorists about inequality.

References

Maslow, Abraham. "Hierarchy of human needs." In *Motivation and Personality.* New York: Harper and Row, 1954.

Porter, John. *The Vertical Mosaic: An Analysis of Social Class and Power in Canada.* Toronto: University of Toronto Press, 1965.

TWELVE

The New Shape of Inequality

Paul Bernard and Jean Renaud

PAUL BERNARD, Professor of Sociology at the Université de Montréal, specializes in the study of inequality and social classes, careers and labour markets. He has recently published studies on the relationship between education and career outcomes, on ethnic and gendered division of labour, and on a comparison of social mobility and socio-economic achievement in Québec and Poland. He is currently involved in studies about economic and labour market segmentation, about changes in the middle classes, and about job instability. He heads an inter-disciplinary network of researchers who want to establish a long-term panel study of Canadian households. He also has an interest in the epistemology of the social sciences.

JEAN RENAUD, Professor agrégé at the Université de Montréal, has collaborated with Paul Bernard on a number of papers about work, careers, and social mobility. He is currently studying the socio-economic and socio-linguistic settlement of a cohort of new immigrants in Quebec. Other interests include quantitative methods and urban poverty.

"There are limits to growth; what some appropriate, others must surrender."

There is no such thing as a purely economic crisis. Society enters crisis when established ways of doing things become incompatible with new circumstances, economic or otherwise; when the old "social contract" no longer holds. Society enters crisis when changes and gaps appear in traditional relationships between segments: economic powers, middle classes, union and nonunion workers; public and private sectors; old and new elites; sexual or ethnic groups; etc. Society enters crisis when fundamental shifts in the production and control of wealth threaten patterns of income distribution. It enters crisis when social inequality sharpens or assumes new forms; when palliative measures no longer cushion social injustice; when its plans come to be set in an uncertain future.

The social, political, and ideological — as well as economic — dimensions of the current crisis can only be grasped by putting it in historical perspective.

Since the 1940s the Québec labour market has gone through three major phases. A model for the distribution of education, employment, and income typifies each period. These models specify the conditions under which agreement and compromise are possible between social groups.

THREE PHASES SINCE THE 1940s

Phase 1 — An Asymmetric Society

During the forties and fifties education, professional status, and income were distributed on the same strongly asymmetric basis. Most workers were poorly educated, held blue-collar jobs which were often unskilled, and earned little; opposite this mass stood the privileged few, those at the top of their particular sector; between these two extremes there was scarcely a middle layer. This was the Québec of the Plouffes and of local solidarities, of the working class's defensive pride in French-Canadian tradition; while it had the advantage of demographic strength and homogeneity, it lacked economic weight and control.

Phase II — Sharing the Surplus

A completely different society appeared with the late fifties and the sixties. Growth in capitalist economies increased differences of education, employment, and income in the work force. Significant intermediate social strata emerged, running from highly skilled workers through different levels of white-collar workers to technicians and semi-professionals. The asymmetric society's polarization gave way to the fine-grained professional and economic stratification of a work force increasingly ranked and differentiated by education.

Was this the American Dream come true, an egalitarian middle-class society with the wealthy and those left behind by progress perched on its periphery? Not at all. Although middle classes now existed, social inequality had not disappeared. Growth in general prosperity, as reflected in increased buying power, certainly reduced the relative number of workers at the bottom of the pay scale. But at the same time social differentiation intensified because those who were already privileged profited further when surplus was shared. If, in the Québec of the Quiet Revolution, there was something for everyone, everyone did not benefit equally: heightened relative disparities hid behind absolute over-all gains.

Phase III — Zero-sum Redistribution

Today's labour market has been changing in directions which were already partly visible during the mid-seventies. While growth has not stopped, it is now very limited. As a consequence, surplus-sharing has increasingly been replaced by the reallocation of available income: a zero-sum game in which some must surrender what others appropriate. Whether jobs or income are involved, there is currently less room for manoeuvre. Confrontations have sharpened, while alliances are more fragile; austerity measures coexist with the highest standard of living ever seen in Québec. Inequalities which were present but hidden during Phase II now stand out clearly, accompanied by new and contradictory words: rationalization, restraint, cuts.

TWO TRANSITIONS

Change from one type of society to another, or from one phase to another, cannot happen overnight. Since the various components of a situation change at different speeds, and readjustment takes time, there are periods of transition.

Shifts in the relationship between education and work predominated during the transition from Phases I to II. The educational system underwent extensive reforms; it had to adjust to a jump in school attendance, following early signs of growth during the previous decade. Starting in 1960, cohorts entering the job market were markedly better-educated than in the past, and education increasingly determined their career prospects. The young were therefore the first to reflect the emerging model of social organization, while older, less educated cohorts experienced severe competition.

Alongside these developments, job qualifications diversified, while Québec's public sector, a bastion for Francophones excluded from large private enterprises expanded far more quickly than the rest of the labour market. Little seemed to contradict the familiar belief that education and income went hand in hand.

While the transition from Phases I to II was accompanied by high spirits, the gradual descent into stagnation between Phases II to III translated into crisis. The first sign that things had changed came when inflation hit education. Education certainly remained the prime determinant of career opportunities, but more and more of it became necessary to attain given occupational or income levels. In other words, those who had completed any given educational program (apart from the few with university degrees) found themselves headed for jobs with increasingly lower status. According to these modified rules of the game, new arrivals had to run faster and faster just to keep up.

However, this was only one among many dimensions of a crisis which gradually spread until it pervaded society at the beginning of the eighties.

FEATURES OF THE CURRENT CRISIS

Three important phenomena prevailed during this second transition, and became established during Phase III. In the first place, economic uncertainty resulting from the energy crisis was so disabling that normal methods of macro-economic planning and management became useless. Growth was nil, if not negative, in areas such as job creation.

In the second place, during the seventies the labour force ballooned with the entry of baby boomers and increasing numbers of women into the job market. In the third place, the financial crisis affecting nearly all the Western world hit Québec particularly hard. The rapid growth of the State, which had sought to fulfill Francophones' desire for public service as well as collective social change, became especially costly under the economic and demographic circumstances mentioned above.

These phenomena had numerous effects on the labour force. More importantly, they affected various sub-groups at different times. In the early seventies the youth unemployment rate was already growing faster than that for over-25 year olds, and was well beyond increases in the proportion of youths within the working population. The same was true of women relative to men. Nevertheless, average real income (for those who still held a job) only dropped in the last years of the decade. Recently, the number of jobs has also tended to shrink.

In other words, some sub-groups, such as youth and women, were hit earlier and harder, while others have until recently remained relatively immune. For this reason, much more than because of fluctuations in energy prices or interest rates, the onset of crisis is difficult to pinpoint. Its date varies according to the sub-group's perspective, while the crisis' effects follow from a conjuncture of slowly unfolding economic, demographic, and political trends peculiar to Québec. As a consequence no one, especially in the public sector, can still guarantee or even promise that success lies just around the corner. This is the economic as well as social source of the current crisis: modes of distribution from the surplus-sharing phase meet the realities of slowing growth; expectations nurtured by relative affluence run into the new austerity; the second phase's source of social stability throws the third phase off balance.

In early 1982, this crisis has now spread throughout the work force, touching even the most privileged workers, and sectors which are usually safest. As La Fontaine wrote, "though it did not kill all, all were afflicted." Cuts in primary and secondary education over the past few years have been followed by others in the State's activities, particularly social programmes and higher education. The crisis has not spared Québec's traditionally weak private sector. Today no one in the labour force can avoid the prospect of scarcity, or even the end of growth.

UPHEAVAL IN THE WORKPLACE

Although entry into the workplace is becoming increasingly impossible for members of "minority" groups (women, youth, nonunionized, and unskilled workers), they no longer bear the repercussions of crisis alone. All workers have been affected to varying degrees, whether through layoffs, the qualitative underemployment of the overqualified, or the quantitative underemployment of those wanting more than part-time work. More generally, the scarcity of jobs makes switching them difficult. This has had many consequences. Without new personnel, institutions become increasingly bureaucratized. Workers' often limited hopes for social mobility through promotion are jeopardized. Francophones find that they can no longer use the labour market to make up lost ground. On this count, Francophones' access to high-level positions hardly improved during the last decade; their higher work force participation merely created the illusion of catching up. Language legislation pertaining to the workplace has aimed at opening up the private sector to Francophones.

In a climate that exacerbates social cleavage, many groups' demands not surprisingly include requests for positive discrimination, such as affirmative action for women or the handicapped. Problems created by preferential quotas are worsened because the number of available jobs either stagnates or drops instead of growing. Similarly, unions are singled out for neo-conservative attack under the pretext that the traditionally legitimate defence of workers' rights is the cause of crisis. On the contrary, we have tried to show that this crisis is due to structural problems of an economic, demographic, and social nature, and that one should therefore question established ways of doing things rather than the strategies of particular subgroups such as unionized workers, welfare recipients, the unemployed, youth, the elderly, women, etc.

In today's society, where one person's gain is another's loss, Québec's neo-nationalistic social-democratic ideological compromise is crumbling. Are we headed towards a deep political polarization? The handling of social and employment inequalities will answer this question.

THIRTEEN

Social Closure Among Quebec Teachers

Raymond Murphy

RAYMOND MURPHY, Professor of Sociology at the University of Ottawa, specializes in the sociology of education, the sociology of the environment, Weberian social theory, and the study of stratification. His books include *Sociological Theories of Education* (1979) and *Social Closure: The Theory of Monopolization and Exclusion* (1988). His most recent article is entitled "Proletarianization or Bureaucratization: The Fall of the Professional?" Since 1980, Professor Murphy has served as an associate editor of the *Canadian Journal of Sociology*. He is presently writing in the area of the sociology of the environment.

This paper will contribute to the ongoing debate concerning the relationship between ethnicity and social class by suggesting a theory of the role of power, interests, language, and attitudes in that relationship. An attempt will be made to specify the articulation of changes in macro-level economic structures, micro-level attitudinal changes, and collective aspirations for changes in large-scale political structures. . . .

A STRUCTURAL THEORY OF EXCLUSION

The basic elements for a theory which avoids the difficulties inherent in a cultural values theory or a theory of ethnic class have been sketched by Collins (1971), Bourdieu and Passeron (1970), and Parkin (1974).[1] Collins argues that job requirements in organizations are not technically fixed and technically detemined; rather status groups which control jobs impose their cultural standards on the selection process. These cultural standards are arbitrary as far as organizational performance is concerned but they serve the interests of the dominant group and constitute barriers to the advancement of other status groups. Hence they are a form of symbolic violence (Bourdieu and Passeron, 1970). Parkin (1974) views stratification in terms of two related modes of social closure. The first includes practices of exclusion in which one group attempts to maintain its privileges by creating another group of ineligibles beneath it. Group advantages are enhanced by defining a subordinate group as inferior.

A structural theory of exclusion implies that the dominant position of a group in the social structure enables it to impose its linguistic and cultural standards on the advancement process and these tend to exclude members of other groups from advancement. For example, even when English work settings and the market are characterized by formal equality, their linguistic and cultural requirements transform the language and culture of anglophones into important resources in the career contest and in business expansion and constitute barriers to francophones. Not only do these requirements amount to a frontier that interferes with the advancement of francophones (Guindon, 1978), but they are also the means by which anglophones are sponsored.

Exclusion, as used here, necessarily involves inclusion, but on the terms set by the dominant group. It involves imposing criteria according to which the dominant group can include members of other groups in a way that leads the latter to be treated as inferior and members of the dominant group as superior. Individual members of the subordinate group are not directly and completely excluded. It is a particular characteristic, such as their language, that is excluded. The principle behind exclusion is that of imposing criteria which are applied equally to all, thereby legitimating inequalities, but which are more suitable to the dominant group, thereby reproducing inequalities. Thus struggles among status groups overtly involve conflict over the criteria of inclusion, such as the language of work, but it is exclusion which underlies these struggles.

I will attempt to demonstrate that a structural theory of exclusion can also contribute important elements which help to explain differences in work attitudes between francophones and anglophones as well as the recent desire among

many francophones for a collective political change.

A structural theory of exclusion would lead us to believe that the context of economic power, with the mechanisms which facilitated English advancement and constituted barriers to the French, was central in forming different work attitudes among the members of these two linguistic communities. Rocher (1976) argues that the environment contains obstacles which can be so great that, on the one hand, they inhibit or destroy motivation or, on the other hand, are surmountable enough to constitute a challenge which stimulates motivation. Individuals internalize these attitudes either through their own experience with the facilitators or barriers or by being socialized by other members of their linguistic community who have had such experiences.

A structural theory of exclusion also suggests another consequence. Collins (1971) argues that since power, prestige, and wealth are scarce goods, the desire of some individuals for more than their equal share sets in motion the counterstruggle of others to escape subjection, disesteem, and dispossession. This struggle is primarily between rather than within status groups and internal cohesiveness is an important resource in the struggle. The second mode of social closure in Parkin's (1974) theory, solidarism, is the response of excluded groups to resist the state of dominance by exclusion practices. Solidarism is a form of social closure which implies different standards of distributive justice from those inherent in exclusion practices. It challenges the present stratified order by threatening to reduce the share of resources monopolized by the dominant group.

It should be noted that a structural theory of exclusion is not so much based on the assumption that individual identity is determined by status group membership as it is on the observation that common feelings of identity can be fostered and used to combat practices of exclusion. Corresponding to the two levels suggested by a structural theory of exclusion, this paper will examine attitudes in terms of the individual work ethic and the desire for a counter-struggle by the subordinate ethnic collectivity. . . .

It is also necessary to consider the evolution of the structures of exclusion. According to Sales (1974) and Eccles (1972), the dominant position of the English community in Quebec originated with the British conquest. This cut off French Canadians from their commercial and banking connections with France while permitting English traders to support their economic activity with a network in Great Britain which was much less accessible to French Canadians. Until the early nineteen fifties French Canadians tended to be structurally excluded from the career contest in the private sector and from expanding the market for their businesses, resulting in their strong under-representation in these areas as reported in Hughes (1943), Rocher and de Jocas (1957), and Niosi (1978). The environmental obstacles were so great that they most likely inhibited the motivation for individual and collective advancement in these areas. Taylor's (1964) description of attitudes may have been applicable during this period.

The massive American investment in Canada in the nineteen fifties (Levitt, 1970) and the subsequent demand for qualified personnel resulted in a profound transformation of the division of labour. A large-scale movement occurred out of the rural and "unskilled" working classes and the middle class was broadened enormously (Clark, 1976).[2] In Quebec, this resulted in an increase in incomes, an expansion of the local market (Niosi, 1978), and a tendency toward convergence in the occupational structures of the French and English communities (Dofny and Garon-Audy, 1969; McRoberts et al., 1976; and Boulet, 1979). What Clark (1976) calls the first stage of the quiet revolution was marked by the development of opportunities for advancement which were not in conflict with the establishment.

I would suggest that the opportunities created by the massive direct foreign investment stimulated aspirations among both the French and the English. In order to seize these opportunities, however, the French had to make a greater investment of effort than the English: for example, they had to learn a second language. This was because the economic sector was dominated by the English who imposed their linguistic and cultural requirements on jobs they controlled. The need for qualified personnel resulted in the inclusion of the French at the middle levels of the private sector, but on the terms dictated by the controlling English group. During this period of expanded opportunity the presence of these surmountable obstacles conditioned the French much more than the English into norms emphasizing individual striving for occupational success. Francophones internalized such norms as they grew up in this first stage of the quiet revolution. This is why Bélanger and Pedersen and others referred to earlier detected a stronger work ethic among French students than English students in 1965. French and English attitudes in 1965 were the result of processes of internalization during the first stage of the quiet revolution based on the structure of obstacles and opportunities faced by the two linguistic groups in the Quebec labour market during that period.[3] The "forced mobility" (Dofny and Garon-Audy, 1969), resulting from changes in the division of labour and in the opportunity structure subsequent to the massive foreign investment of the nineteen fifties, stimulated a work ethic among francophones in search of further upward mobility.[4]

The branch-plant, peripheral, Canadian economy dependent on the American metropolis was, however, incapable of absorbing, especially at higher levels in the labour market, the next generation which had swelled with the high birth rate after the war. This new generation could be absorbed in the late nineteen sixties and seventies only if the establishment was pushed out. What Clark (1976) refers to as the second stage of the quiet revolution involved a zero-sum game in which rewards could be acquired by the newcomers only if there were diminished rewards for the establishment. Norms held by francophones which emphasized individual striving and sacrifice in order to surmount barriers of exclusion tended to be replaced in the Quebec of the late sixties and seventies by a desire for a collective political effort to eliminate the barriers and with them the English establishment.[5]

It was precisely the increased opportunities for upward mobility resulting from the need for qualified personnel during the economic expansion provoked by American investment that stimulated the aspiration in the first stage to surmount barriers of exclusion. The limited possiblities for further mobility in an externally dependent economy transformed this aspiration in the second stage into a desire for a collective politi-cal effort to eliminate those barriers. This argument suggests that the massive investment in Quebec by an external bourgeoisie triggered changes in the structures of opportunity and exclusion, in orientations at the individual and collective levels, and a potential change of political structures in Canada. This investment expanded opportunities at the middle levels, raising aspirations, but not eliminating barriers of exclusion faced by francophones especially at the upper levels. The result was a collective political reaction in Quebec. This argument specifies the consequences of the internationalization of capital for the internal structure of one dependent society — in this case, Quebec. An externally provoked development inherently limited by the interests of the external centres of decision making gave rise to an autonomous internal source of development as an emergent property.[6]

By increasing aspirations as well as the demand for qualified personnel, the investment also resulted in the rapid expansion of institutions for training personnel. It resulted, for example, in the widespread desire for a reform of the educational system. These institutions were linguistically segmented and mostly provided positions for persons working with cultural goods, for instance, in teaching. . . .

Fournier (1977) argues that structural changes in the economy of Quebec have created and expanded a new petite bourgeoisie (which includes teachers) who specialize in the production and diffusion of cultural goods. Since their skills can be readily appreciated only in the Quebec market, they have a vested interest in consolidating the national identity. The defence of language and culture cannot be dissociated from the defence of profession and market. He claims that only a change in the political relationship between French and English Canadians can assure the conditions necessary to maintain and improve the social position of those who produce and diffuse knowledge and culture in the French language. The new petite bourgeoisie therefore looks to the state to accomplish this change. Fournier argues that there has been a conversion of cultural nationalism into the political nationalism of the petite bourgeoisie. He contends that this new petite bourgeoisie has supported and worked for the Parti Québécois.

One fraction of the new petite bourgeoisie, teachers, acts as principal agents of the socialization of the young, a position of particular importance for the conservation or change of Quebec society. The fact that teachers were collectively affected by the barriers of exclusion and the indissolubility of teachers' defence of their language and culture from the defence of their market was evident in the school enrolment crisis of the early and midnineteen seventies and the reaction of teachers to it. The English domination of the Quebec economy, especially at the upper levels, and the resulting imposition of English linguistic and cultural requirements on jobs led immigrants and even francophones to choose to send their children to English schools to improve their chances for upward mobility. Hence, until the adoption of law 101, the drop in the birth rate seriously affected attendance at French schools (and therefore teachers' jobs) but not attendance at English schools which was compensated by the children of immigrants. Teachers in the French school system were collectively affected by the English domination of the Quebec economy. Their collective aspirations and their individual interests are intimately bound together in their desire to make French the language of work

at all levels of Quebec society as well as the language of schooling. The converse is true of teachers in the English school system. They have come out strongly against the Charter on the French Language (Morisette, 1977c and 1977d) and in favour of freedom of choice of schooling for all, including the children of immigrants, in order to conserve the market for their services. Teachers are well aware that, in the absence of legal constraints, parental choice of the school for their children will be determined by language constraints imposed on jobs by those who control the economic sector. . . .

Moreover, the effort by teachers in the French school system to remove the linguistic barriers faced by francophones in Quebec does not bring with it the threat of job loss, as is the case for francophones who work in federal institutions or in English companies (Laporte, 1974: 118). Upward collective mobility does not carry the threat of downward individual mobility.

It was precisely in this linguistically segmented sector dealing with cultural goods, where francophones were collectively rather than individually affected by the barriers of exclusion, that there developed an awareness that collective political efforts to eliminate the barriers were more appropriate than individual effort and sacrifice to surmount the barriers. I would suggest, therefore, that the desire for a collective political response to remove the linguistic and cultural barriers of exclusion is especially strong among the new petite bourgeoisie in general and among teachers in the French secondary school system in particular.

TEACHERS

It is within and with respect to this structural context of exclusion that the economic and political attitudes of teachers in Quebec must be examined and explained. These attitudes will be investigated at the two levels which correspond to those suggested by a structural theory of exclusion — the individual level and the level of a collective counter-struggle.[7]

The Individual Level

Teachers in the French and English school systems in 1965 had different work orientations even after their individual occupational origins were controlled.[8] . . . Teachers in the French system ranked security, advancement, and pay higher than did teachers in the English system. The latter ranked the intrinsic enjoyment of the work and friendly fellow workers at a higher level than did their counterparts in the French system.

. . . Teachers in the French system gave higher priority to the security of steady work because members of the French community were subject to more risks in a labour market that placed before them special linguistic and cultural barriers not faced by the English.

One might be tempted to conclude that the higher value teachers in the English system attached to "the enjoyment of the work itself" indicated that they had a stronger work ethic than their counterparts in the French system. . . . But teachers in the French system attached more importance to the job and to an occupational career, were more willing to make sacrifices for their job, and viewed the roles of parents and the school more in terms of individual advancement and preparation for an occupational career than teachers in the English system, this being true of those from blue- and white-collar origins.[9] A work ethic in this sense

was more characteristic of teachers in the French system than of those in the English system. The surmountable linguistic and cultural obstacles (not faced by anglophones) in the job market during a period of expanded economic opportunity conditioned francophones into such a work ethic ideology, into norms emphasizing the necessity of laborious striving and sacrifice to get ahead, with the role of parent and the school being to provide the means.[10]

I would suggest that these attitudinal differences were characteristic not just of teachers but of all upwardly mobile segments of the population and perhaps even of the French and English communities in general during the economic expansion in the first stage of the quiet revolution in Quebec society. Bélanger and Pedersen and other investigators referred to previously have shown that similar attitudinal differences held true for the secondary school students. I would submit that francophones growing up during this period learned norms emphasizing a work ethic from other members of their linguistic community (parents, relatives, friends) who had experienced or observed the surmountable linguistic and cultural barriers. . . . I would suggest that during this first stage of the quiet revolution the ideology of a work ethic, after having been internalized early in life, remained particularly strong among francophones sheltered from the direct effects of the barriers, such as those who worked in linguistically segmented institutions (for example, schools) or who had not yet entered the labour market (students).

Teachers in the French school system were more satisfied with the recognition given to their work by their community than were teachers in the English system. This was because the position reached was higher relative to their comparatively low reference group. French teachers were at a higher place in the stratification system of their linguistic community than were English teachers because there was a stratification of the two linguistic communities. . . .

These differences between the work attitudes of teachers . . . in the French and English school systems need to be explained in terms of the position of the French and English communities in the social structure of Quebec and the resulting context of exclusion. The dominance of one status group enables it to impose its cultural standards on the selection process in the job market. The conquest of the French by the English enabled the latter to impose their language and culture on economic activity in Quebec. These transformed the language and culture of members of the English community into valued resources for career and business success and constituted barriers to members of the French community, whose cultural resources were ignored. These facilitators or obstacles respectively faced by the two status groups led their members to internalize different attitudes. Barriers which, without being insurmountable, decrease the probability of advancement or hiring of members of a status group explain the under-representation of the group at higher levels, the cultivation of a work ethic by its members during periods of economic expansion, and their search for job security.

By 1972, the work attitudes of teachers in the French school system had approached (but were not identical to) those of teachers in the English school system. This was after the upward mobility of the French collectivity had enabled it to approach (but not equal) the English collectivity in the stratification system of

Quebec (Dofny and Garon-Audy, 1969; McRoberts et al., 1976; and Boulet, 1979) and after the linguistic and cultural barriers faced by the French community had become proportionately fewer because of expansion in the francophone-dominated public sector and in the local market which francophone businesses could penetrate. The work ethic necessary to surmount the barriers diminished as proportionately fewer positions in the job market contained those linguistic and cultural barriers to francophones.

However, the limit to the rate of expansion of the public sector in general and in particular of the French side of linguistically segmented cultural institutions within a predominantly English private enterprise context was reached in the late sixties. For French teachers, the downturn in the birth rate posed a threat to their jobs in this English-dominated private enterprise context where most immigrants and many French parents chose to send their children to English schools. As the expansion of the public sector slowed down in this second stage of the quiet revolution, the intellectual petite bourgeoisie who worked with French cultural goods in linguistically segmented institutions, particularly teachers in the French school system, became collectively affected by the barriers of exclusion in the private sector. They therefore returned from an individualistic work ethic to a desire for a collective political struggle to change the English-dominated private enterprise context itself.

The Collective Counter-Struggle

A structural theory of exclusion suggests a reaction at the collective level, in the sense of a desire for a solidaristic counter-struggle by the excluded group. Reasons have already been given to support the hypothesis that in the second stage of the quiet revolution this desire is particularly strong among the intellectual petite bourgeoisie in Quebec, which includes teachers, and that it is directed toward a parliamentary struggle. My evidence confirms this line of argument.

Table 13-1 shows that the proportion who had the intention to vote for the Parti Québécois (the political party which had the strongest program for the removal of linguistic and cultural barriers to francophones) in 1972 was much higher among teachers (41.0 per cent) in the French secondary school system than in the overall population (15 per cent). In 1972 76 per cent of teachers in the French secondary school system who had decided which party to vote for decided in favour of the Parti Québécois. The corresponding percentage in the overall population in 1972 was 28 per cent. Although the latter figure and the last column of Table 13-1 are not broken down by linguistic affiliation, they are so different from the voting intentions of teachers in the French school system that one can safely conclude that more teachers in the French school system favoured the Parti Québécois than did members of other occupational groups and social classes within the French community.

There are other indications of French teacher support for the Parti Québécois. Shortly after the latter was elected in 1976 the critical socialist ideology of the leaders of the French Quebec teachers union (C.E.Q.) during the Liberal regime was attacked by its members as having been rendered inappropriate by the results of the election and the union was urged to adopt a "prejudice in favour" of the Parti Québécois because "it is the party of the members of the C.E.Q." (Sacy, 1977). A large number (14) of Parti Québécois members elected to the

TABLE 13-1   Voting Intentions, Secondary School Teachers and the Overall Population of Quebec, 1972 (in Percentages)

If there were provincial elections today, for what party would you vote?[a]	Secondary School Teachers		Overall Population[b]
	French system	English system	
Liberal Party	10.5	45.6	42
Union Nationale	2.6	1.8	4
Parti Québécois	41.0	9.7	15
Social Credit	1.5	1.8	8
I would be very undecided	34.2	31.8	31
I would abstain from voting	3.7	5.6	
I am not at all interested in politics	6.6	3.8	

[a] Bélanger and Rocher (1976: 109). The survey was carried out in the spring of 1972. I have already described the sample on which it was based.

[b] *Le Devoir* (22 avril 1976: p. 2). This survey based on a random sample of the Quebec population was carried out by the survey institute CROP in October 1972. The results were not broken down by English and French populations.

Quebec parliament were elementary or secondary school teachers.

Still another indication of the desire of teachers in the French school system for collective political effort to dismantle the linguistic barriers faced by the French community was the reaction of their union to the Charter on the French language in Quebec (1977) proposed by the Parti Québécois government. The French teachers' union (C.E.Q.) completely supported and was generally satisfied with the Charter because they saw in it the reflection of the union's own orientation. As far as the language of schooling was concerned, the union wanted to go further than the proposals of the Parti Québécois Government by progressively eliminating English educational institutions within the next decade and by requiring immigrant and French children now in English school to attend French schools (Morissette, 1977a and 1977b). The union later became more flexible with respect to the education of anglophones coming from other provinces but remained firm in regard to other groups (Morissette, 1977e).

Thus in the second stage of the quiet revolution in Quebec society teachers in the French school system, who are one fraction of the intellectual petite bourgeoisie, have become deeply involved in the political counter-struggle to remove the barriers of exclusion faced by the French community. This is indicated by their particularly high frequency of intention to vote for the Parti Québécois (the political party which has the strongest program for the removal of the linguistic and cultural barriers to the advancement of francophones) as early as 1972, by their high rate of participation in the party in 1976, and by the reaction of their union to proposed legislation on the language of work and schooling in

Quebec. Teachers in the French school system are seeking to impose their language, values, and cultural standards on the selection process in organizations within their territorial base, thereby extending the institutional completeness (Breton, 1964) of their status group. The separation of their workplace along linguistic lines is the model they propose for the parts which presently form the Canadian nation.

The support among teachers in the French system for a party whose goal is political independence marks a change from the past. Bélanger and Juneau (1975) found that in 1960 their sample of teachers in the French system showed them as optimistic or conciliatory with respect to Canadian unity. At that time the teachers felt that the diversity of religions, languages, educational systems, laws, customs, and traditions was compatible with the realization of Canadian unity.

The change, I suggest, is due to the upward mobility in an absolute sense and the resulting heightened aspirations of the French community, together with its continuing inferior position in a relative sense and the existence of barriers at the upper levels which have a collective effect on the intellectual petite bourgeoisie in general and on teachers in particular. This has promoted the development of a consciousness among these subgroups that the solution to the barriers faced by members of the French collectivity is less that of individual striving and sacrifice to surmount barriers and more that of a collective political response to eliminate them. . . .

The work ethic of the intellectual petite bourgeoisie may have declined but it has not disappeared. Fournier (1977) has observed that the political ethics and public image of the Parti Québécois during the 1976 election campaign were principally inspired by a petite bourgeois morality, emphasizing individual responsibility, a high value attached to work and workmanship, and a serious outlook. The work ethic discussed in my paper has been projected by the intellectual petite bourgeoisie from the individual to the collective level.

The Parti Québécois government is merely the most recent and militant agent of the collective political reaction. Even prior to the victory of that party in 1976, francophones turned more and more to the political state apparatus to increase their representation in the bourgeoisie (Niosi, 1978) and to remove the barriers in the private sector. The overall result has been a transformation of those barriers even at the upper levels. Formerly the English language and culture were imposed at the upper levels of the private sector and the French language and culture were ignored. Now it is bilingualism that is imposed at the upper levels of the private sector in Quebec.[11] Furthermore, there is reason to believe that many highly paid unilingual anglophones have left Quebec and that their jobs have gone with them.[12] That is the "last resort" practice by which francophones are excluded from top positions in English companies.

The existence of barriers which tend to exclude francophones in the private sector of the market economy has provoked in the second stage of the quiet revolution a collective political effort for their elimination by francophones in the French side of linguistically segmented cultural institutions. The existence of these barriers of exclusion also has promoted a radical questioning of the capitalist market economy by the leaders of unions (C.E.Q. and C.S.N.) representing francophones in linguistically segmented

institutions. Such barriers of exclusion also stimulated from an earlier date a collective search for alternative organizational forms, best exemplified by the cooperative movement, which has been much stronger among Quebec francophones than among anglophones in North America. . . .

CONCLUSION

. . . A structural theory of exclusion focuses on the power of status groups to impose their cultural standards on positions and institutions they control. It also focuses on barriers to the advancement of members of other status groups embodied in those in order to explain the existence of a vertical mosaic — the over- or under-representation of status groups in the various strata of the stratification system. These standards and barriers are the structural points of articulation between the inequality of collectivities per se and the inequality of opportunity for individuals who make up those different collectivities.

A structural theory of exclusion sees the barriers as having an important formative influence on the orientation of the members of these groups. It looks to changes in the structures of opportunity and exclusion as an important source of change in orientation, including the priority given to resignation, to individual striving to surmount the barriers, or to collective struggle to eliminate them.[13] This paper's empirical investigation of teachers shows that their economic and political attitudes can best be understood in terms of the evolving structural context of exclusion in Quebec society. . . .

Notes

1 The threefold division of theoretical approaches given in this paper toward explaining the subordinate position of francophones in Quebec is similar to that in the literature on the sociology of national development. Portes (1976) distinguishes three different approaches in the sociology of national development: the "social differentiation" approach; the "enactment of values" approach; and the "liberation from dependency" approach. The first two are very similar to one another, both being based on value orientations. The third, dependency theory, has several versions. The economic imperialism version claims that dependency is "the conditioning structure" of poverty and implies that a higher standard of living for the masses in Third World countries will automatically come about with the elimination of economic imperialism. Portes (1976: 79) argues that "we must look elsewhere for studies of development-oriented elites, conditions under which they come to control the state, and circumstances which permit them to mobilize the masses into a national development effort." Thus the theoretical approach based on value orientations, the economic imperialism version of dependency theory (one nation seen as a more or less homogeneous entity exploited by another), and Portes' less rhetorical, less crude version of dependency theory parallel the three-fold division of approaches to the subordinate position of francophones in Quebec suggested in my paper.

2 Although investment by American companies in Quebec began before the nineteen-fifties and was but one source of the overall processes of industrialization and modernization, it reached such important proportions at that time that it became the key source of the structural and attitudinal changes which followed.

3 Differences in work attitudes can also be influenced by differences in the structure of barriers between regions and between particular organizations. Thus one can expect some variation in attitudes from one locality to another and from one organization to another. However, today's workers are not serfs. They are not completely restricted to one locality or to one organization. I am suggesting a theory at the level of the overall Quebec labour market because it is the most appropriate level for analyzing the attitudes of francophones in Quebec.

4 According to a French proverb quoted by Quebec Prime Minister Levesque during a visit to Washington, "it is in eating that one acquires the appetite to eat more."

5 I would suggest that the recent decreased interest among French Quebec students in learning English is one indication of the shift in emphasis from advancement as an individual effort to surmount the barriers to advancement as a collective effort to eliminate such barriers.

6 There are undoubtedly both parallel processes and structural differences to be found by comparing Quebec with other societies. See Laczko (1978) for an interesting suggestion along these lines. It would be a fascinating theoretical challenge to explain why the penetration of the economies of Canada, Australia, and New Zealand by foreign-owned multinational corporations and accompanying dependency resulted in a higher per capita income in these countries whereas it resulted in massive misery in most economically dependent Third World countries. Although the answer to such a question lies well beyond the scope of this article, I would suggest that a structural theory of exclusion could contribute important elements to the explanation.

7 The data for 1965 analyzed in this study were taken from the Quebec portion of Breton's (1972) survey of Canadian secondary schools. His data were based on a probability sample of secondary schools. His survey included 106 (5.4 percent) secondary schools in Quebec. All teachers within the school selected were asked to complete the questionnaire. Thus the sample included 1930 secondary school teachers (1922 when weighted): 1594 in the French educational system and 328 in the English systems. I have combined English Protestant and English Catholic schools to form what I refer to as the English system. The data for 1972 were taken from Bélanger and Rocher's (1976) survey (ASOPE) of Quebec secondary schools. Schools were first sampled as in Breton's study, but in contrast to the latter teachers were then sampled within the schools selected. One hundred and thirty-three secondary schools were chosen and of the 2296 teachers selected in these schools, 1586 (73 per cent) completed the questionnaire. This included 1309 teachers in the French secondary school system and 376 in the English system, where French and English

refer to the language of instruction in the school. The similarity of the populations investigated and the data gathering procedures used in the two surveys justifies the comparison of their findings. More detailed information on the sampling and on the data gathering procedures used has already been published by Breton (1972) and Bélanger and Rocher (1976) and will not be repeated here.

8 Since they are members of the same profession, their present occupation and intergenerational mobility are also controlled.

9 These four items were found to be strongly interrelated, thereby showing that they indicate the same underlying dimension.

10 My evidence does not support the idea that the differences in the work attitudes of teachers in the French and English systems were the result of differences in their immediate work settings. Controlling the social origins of teachers indirectly controls work setting variables which are associated with differences in recruitment. More direct evidence is provided by the fact that when school size was controlled the attitudinal differences between teachers in the French and English systems remained. This important work setting variable cannot explain such differences.

11 Boulet (1979) found among males in Montreal that, whereas unilingual and bilingual anglophones were the two top income earning groups in 1961, and 1971, by 1977 bilingual anglophones, bilingual francophones, and bilingual allophones (those having other mother tongues) were the top income earners in that order. Unilingual anglophones have dropped to the fourth rank by 1977. Unilingual francophones remained in the sixth rank, their position being unchanged from 1961 through 1977. The anglophone community has quickly adjusted to the bilingualism barrier. Boulet (1979) found that 74 per cent of anglophones and 64 per cent of allophones were bilingual at the beginning of 1978 compared to 48 per cent of each in 1971. A higher proportion of anglophones than francophones (64 per cent) in the male Montreal labour force are now bilingual. This is a striking change from the past, for example, when as late as 1971 62 per cent of francophones as opposed to 48 per cent of anglophones were bilingual. The bilingualism requirement itself demonstrates the power which remains in the hands of the English in the Quebec private sector in that it is imposed in a province where eight of every ten individuals are of French origin and only one of ten is of English origin.

12 This is suggested by the following data (Boulet, 1979): the proportion of unilingual anglophones in the Montreal male labour force fell from 13 per cent in 1961 to 5 per cent in 1978; the proportion of bilingual anglophones grew more slowly — from 10 per cent in 1961 to 13 per cent in 1978; the relative earnings of the category "unilingual anglophones" decreased significantly during this period; and the proportion of the total mass of earnings monopolized by the 15 per cent most highly paid decreased from 36 per cent in 1961 to 30 per cent in 1978.

13 This paper has been limited to the analysis of the French and English in Quebec. If other status groups were to be analyzed additional factors would have to be taken into consideration. Barriers of exclusion have differential effects on different status groups. These effects depend on the relative distance between the cultural requirements imposed on work positions by the status group controlling those positions and the cultural capital of the remaining status groups. Moreover, the latter groups have different resources. For example, francophones in Quebec can control a provincial government apparatus and use it to increase the power of their group even in the private sector, a possibility which does not exist for other status groups, such as Italians or Inuits in Canada or francophones outside of Quebec. Therefore the priority given to resignation, to individual striving to surmount barriers, or to a collective effort to eliminate them and the form that such a collective effort takes vary among subordinate status groups.

References

Archibald, Kathleen. *Les deux sexes dans la fonction publique.* Ottawa: Information Canada, 1973.

Beattie, Christopher. *Minority Men in a Majority Setting: Middle-level Francophones in the Canadian Public Service.* Toronto: McClelland and Stewart, 1975.

Bélanger, Pierre et Juneau, A. "Les Maîtres de l'enseignement primaire: étude socio-culturelle." Pp. 91–193 dans Pierre W. Bélanger et Guy Rocher, *Ecole et Société au Québec,* Nouvelle édition. Montréal: Editions Hurtubise HMH, 1975.

Bélanger, Pierre W. et Pedersen, Eigil. "Projets des étudiants québécois." *Sociologie et Sociétés* (1) (1973) 1.91–110.

Bélanger, Pierre W. et Rocher, Guy. *A.S.O.P.E. Aspirations scolaires et orientations professionnelles des étudiants: analyse descriptive des données de la première cueillette (1972), Les enseignants.* Vol. III 2e édition corrigée. Montreal: Université de Montréal, 1976.

Bernard, Paul et Renaud, Jean. *Le Devoir,* Montréal, vendredi 9 mars, 1979: 3.

Boulet, Jac-André. "L'évolution des disparités linguistiques de revenus de travail dans la zone métropolitaine de Montréal de 1961 à 1977." Document No. 127. Conseil économique du Canada, Ottawa, 1979.

Bourdieu, Pierre et Passeron, Jean-Claude. *La reproduction.* Paris: Editions de minuit, 1970.

Breton, Raymond. "Institutional Completeness of Ethnic Communities and the Personal Relations of Immigrants." *American Journal of Sociology* LXX (September, 1964): 193–293.

_____. *Social and Academic Factors in the Career Decisions of Canadian Youth.* Ottawa: Manpower and Immigration, 1972.

Breton, Raymond and McDonald, John C. *Career Decisions of Canadian Youth.* Ottawa: Department of Manpower and Immigration and Queen's Printer, 1967.

Cardinal, Pierre. "Regard critique sur la traduction au Canada." *Meta* 23(2) (1978): 141–7.

Carlos, Serge. *L'Utilisation du français dans le monde du travail du Québec. Etudes réalisées pour le compte de la commission d'enquête sur la situation de la langue française et sur les droits linguistiques au Québec.* Québec: l'éditeur officiel du Québec, 1973.

Clark, S.D. *Canadian Society in Historical Perspective.* Toronto: McGraw-Hill Ryerson, 1976.

Collins, Randall. "Functional and conflict theories of educational stratification." *American Sociological Review* 36 (December, 1971): 1002–19.

Crysdale, S. and Beattie, C. *Sociology Canada.* Toronto: Butterworths, 1973.

Dofny, Jacques. "Les stratifications de la société québécoise," *Sociologie et Sociétés* x(2)(1978): 87–102.

Dofny, Jacques et Garon-Audy, Muriel. "Mobilités professionnelles au Québec." *Sociologie et Sociétés* 1(2)(1969): 207–301.

Dofny, Jacques and Rioux, Marcel. "Social Class in French Canada." P. 307–18 in Marcel Rioux and Yves Martin (eds.), *French-Canadian Society,* Vol. 1. Toronto: McClelland and Stewart, 1964.

Eccles, W.J. *France in America.* New York: Harper and Row, 1972.

Fournier, Marcel. "La question nationale: les enjeux." *Possibles* 1 (2)(1977): 7–18.

Guindon, Hubert. "The modernization of

Quebec and legitimacy of the Canadian state." *The Canadian Review of Sociology and Anthropology* 15(2)(1978): 227–45.

Hughes, E.C. *French Canada in Transition.* Chicago: University of Chicago Press, 1943.

Jain, Harish C., Normand, Jacques, and Kanungo, Rabindra N. "Job motivation of Canadian Anglophone and Francophone employees." *Canadian Journal of Behavioural Science* 11(2)(1979): 160–4.

Laczko, Leslie. "English Canadians and Québécois nationalism." *The Canadian Review of Sociology and Anthropology* 15(2)(1978): 206–17.

Laporte, Pierre E. *L'usage des langues dans la vie économique au Québec: situation actuelle et possibilités de changement. Synthèses réalisées pour le compte de la commission d'enquête sur la situation de la langue française et sur les droits linguistiques au Québec.* Québec: L'éditeur officiel du Québec, 1974.

Levitt, Kari. *Silent Surrender.* Toronto: Macmillan, 1970.

McRoberts, Hugh, Porter, John, Boyd, Monica, Goyder, John, Jones, Frank, et Pineo, Peter. "Différences dans la mobilité professionnelle des francophones et des anglophones." *Sociologie et Sociétés* 8(2)(1976): 61–79.

Morissette, Rodolphe. "La CEQ propose un plan de 12 ans." *Le Devoir*, 25 mars, 1977a: 7.

_____ "Les minorités s'élèvent contre le livre blanc." *Le Devoir*, 5 avril, 1977b: 3.

_____ "Le vrai problème est d'ordre économique, souligne la PAPT." *Le Devoir*, 15 avril, 1977c: 3.

_____ "Les anglo-catholiques se doteront d'un fonds de défense." *Le Devoir*, 16 avril, 1977d: 7.

_____ "Tout Québécois 'qui se respecte'

appuiera le projet no. 1." *Le Devoir*, 30 avril, 1977e: 2.

Murphy, Raymond and Denis, Ann B. "Schools and the Conservation of the Vertical Mosaic." Pp. 75–90 in Danielle Juteau Lee (ed.), *Frontières Ethniques en Devenir/Changing Ethnic Boundaries.* Ottawa: University of Ottawa Press, 1979.

Murphy, Raymond with the collaboration of Ann B. Denis. *Sociological Theories of Education.* Toronto: McGraw-Hill Ryerson, 1979.

Niosi, Jorge. "La Nouvelle Bourgeoisie Canadienne Française." Pp. 174–222 dans *Actes du Colloque annuel de l'Association canadienne des sociologues et anthropologues de langue française*, 1978.

Nolle, David and Greenwood, Donna. "Adolescent Values and Outcomes: A Canadian Test." Reported on pages 110–11 of S. Crysdale and C. Beattie, *Sociology Canada.* Toronto: Butterworths, 1973.

Parkin, Frank. "Strategies of social closure in the maintenance of inequality." Unpublished paper presented to the Eighth World Congress of Sociology. Toronto, Canada, 1974.

Porter, John. *The Vertical Mosaic.* Toronto: University of Toronto Press, 1965.

Porter, Marion, Porter, John, and Blishen, Bernard. *Does Money Matter?* Toronto: Institute for Behavioural Research, York University, 1973.

Portes, Alejandro. "On the Sociology of National Development: Theories and Issues." *American Journal of Sociology* 82(1)(1976): 55–85.

Raynauld, André. *La propriété des entreprises au Québec: les années 60.* Montréal: Les presses de L'Université de Montréal, 1974.

Rocher, Guy. "Research on occupations and social stratification." Pp. 328–41 in Marcel Rioux and Yves Martin (eds.), *French-Cana-*

dian Society Vol. 1. Toronto: McClelland and Stewart, 1964.

———— "Toward a psychosociological theory of aspirations." Pp. 391–406 in Jan Loubser, Rainer Baum, Andrew Effrat, and Victor Lidz (eds.), *Explorations in General Theory in Social Science* Vol. 1. New York: The Free Press, 1976.

Rocher, G. and De Jocas, Y. "Inter-Generation Occupational Mobility in the Province of Quebec." *The Canadian Journal of Economics and Political Science* 23(1)(1957).

Sacy, Hubert. "Le PW. parti des members de la CEO." *La Presse*, 11 janvier, 1977: A5.

Sales, Arnaud. "Différenciation ethnique des directions industrielles." *Sociologie et sociétés* VI(2)(1974): 101–13.

———— "La question linguistique et les directions d'entreprises." *Le Devoir*, 27 avril, 1977: 6; 28 avril: 17; 29 avril: 9.

Taylor, Norman W. "The French-Canadian industrial entrepreneur and his social environment." Pp. 271–95 in Marcel Rioux and Yves Martin (eds.), *French-Canadian Society* Vol. 1. Toronto: McClelland and Stewart, 1964.

FOURTEEN

Does Class Matter?

Wallace Clement

WALLACE CLEMENT, Professor of Sociology at Carleton University, Ottawa, specializes in the study of comparative class structure, power, and the labour process. His books include *The Canadian Corporate Elite: An Analysis of Economic Power* (1975); *Continental Corporate Power: Economic Linkages Between Canada and the United States* (1977); *Hardrock Mining: Industrial Relations and Technological Change in Inco* (1981); *Class, Power and Property: Essays on Canadian Society* (1983); *The Struggle to Organize: Resistance in Canada's Fishery* (1986); *The Challenge of Class Analysis* (1988); and *Relations of Ruling: Class, Gender and Postindustrialism in Comparative Perspective* with John Myles (forthcoming). He has conducted research in Germany, Sweden, and Australia, and is currently engaged, with John Myles, in collecting and analyzing data as part of the Comparative Class Structure Project, funded by the Social Sciences and Humanities Research Council of Canada on class power and the nature of the state. Professor Clement has lectured widely in Canada and abroad.

. . . For the purposes of this discussion, I will adopt the convention of defining classes in terms of property rights to the means of production and control over the labour power of others. The key in the following definition is that the classes are not merely categories, but relationships that are undergoing processes of change. The capitalist class controls property rights and commands the labour power of others. The working class is excluded from control over property and is obliged to sell its labour power. Estrangement from the *means* of labour and the *rights* of property are the key criteria for identifying the working class. This distinguishes them from the traditional petite bourgeoisie who control their own property (that is, access to the ability to

labour). The modern petite bourgeoisie (or new middle class) performs the tasks of capital (which include surveillance and discipline along with co-ordination and direction) and the tasks of labour, thus exercising both the rights of property and the obligations of labour, even though, like the working class, it must sell its labour power (Clement, 1983).

The fundamental direct *contradiction* in this formulation is between the capitalist class and the working class, yet there are key *tensions* involving especially the trajectories of the new middle class and the traditional petite bourgeoisie. Relationally defined classes are always in tension: they are only in contradiction at particular historical moments. Tensions can promote social changes, whereas contradictions can transform entire epochs. Both are antagonisms, but of a different order.

The tradition of class studies in Canada has been influenced by both the Weberian and Marxist formulations (Clement, 1983). Currently class analysis is at a crossroads. It is under attack for being too limited and narrow, particularly with respect to gender, ethnicity and region, and overly rigid with respect to economic determination. I wish to make an argument for coaxing class analysis along a more nuanced, powerful path.

The academic exercise is not to *simplify*, but to *clarify* — to provide conceptual tools for richer understanding. Class, I contend, is one such clarifying concept, but one which has suffered greatly from simplification. I undertake to resurrect class from its contemporary abuse as a simplifying concept and attempt to raise it again to a clarifying one.

Part of the complexity of class is the fact that its analysis proceeds at several levels of abstraction. Mino Carchedi, for example, has identified four such levels: the "pure capitalist economic structure," which primarily involves the logic of surplus value production; the "capitalist socio-economic system," which includes political and ideological dimensions along with the economic; the "concrete society," which is composed of several co-existing modes of production; and the "conjunctural level," which is a specific junction of a concrete society and the level at which political action occurs (1977: 18–23). A similar, yet less complex, set of levels has been identified by Ira Katznelson in his insightful book *City Trenches*. Most abstract is the level of capital accumulation and the mode of production. This is followed by the level of the labour market and workplace patterns. Finally, there is class as "a happening" rather than "a thing" whereby classes act as an historical collective (1981: 202–5). Analysis can proceed at any of these levels of abstraction and should be able, at least theoretically, to move between levels while retaining its integrity.

Increasingly there have been demands, particularly led by social historians, that class be understood and analyzed at the most concrete level of class action. In part this is a response to the limitations of abstractions that tend to be economistic, thus failing to capture the political, cultural and ideological richness of the totality of class not only as a structure but as an experience. Moreover, the dimensions of class as economic/reproductive, political/legal and cultural/ideological are, at the most, moments of one another. Class cannot be only any one of these; class can only exist in their combination. To quote Michael Burawoy's most recent formulation of this issue in *The Politics of Production*, "Any work context involves an economic dimension (production of things), a political dimension (production of social relations), and an ideological dimension (production of an experience of those relations) (1985: 39). (See also Przeworski, 1977). Class in this sense is the combined "effect" of all these dimensions. At the conjunctural level of analysis, class is manifest through each of these dimensions, as my recent research on the emergence of resistance among Canadian fishers attests (Clement, 1986). Such "effects" are transparent among unionized fishers who sell to capitalist enterprises or even the state, but it is also the case for the more translucent co-operatives. Co-ops are class-based institutions. During their formative periods of struggle they were typically directed against large capital, yet as they began to operate, their principal struggle became against labour. Anti-capitalist ideologies and practices were transformed into anti-labour ideologies and practices, both of which were comprehensible given the material conditions of co-op members and the market situation of co-ops as institutions. The Prince Rupert Fishermen's Co-operative, for example, has had its most bitterly fought struggles with unionized labour on the West Coast, including both the shore workers who process the fish and the crew on co-op member boats catching the fish. Labour has been the Achilles heel of the co-op movement and has dramatically affected the ideology and politics of class experience within that movement.

As I will argue in some detail, class relations are everywhere, but they never exist in "pure" form; that is, they always combine with other social relations (except at the very highest level of abstraction). These other social relations include gender, ethnicity, age and region. These combined social relations have significant effects on one another. Class-blind analysts, like gender-blind ones, fail to grasp essential facts of social life. A social scientist without a refined class tool is one ill-prepared to comprehend social relations. But class is more than an analytical tool. It is also an ideology and a practice. It involves not simply categories, but dynamic relationships.

THE "CHEMISTRY" OF CLASS

Classes, I contend, never enter the political arena in "pure" economic form; that is, the political expression of class is always in combination with other forces whether they be over issues of nation, ethnicity, gender, region or even political party. Parties are not classes. Even in Sweden, where class has its clearest political expression, the Social Democratic Party is not identical with labour centrals, nor are either identical with the working class. Political parties, by their very nature, combine popular forces with class forces. To put the point even more forcefully, class forces can never exist alone in pure form at the concrete level; they must express themselves in other than strictly economic forms.

The primary contention of this discussion is that if one wishes to gain an understanding of Canadian society, class in isolation is not sufficient. Analysis requires gender, region, ethnicity, etc. Having said that, however, in order to grasp the essence of Canadian society, class is essential. Most enriching is the "chemistry" of class and other factors. The processes of class formation may be universal, but worthy of note are the specific configurations. While class "conditions" non-class cleavages (gender, region, ethnicity, etc.), it is also conditioned by them. I am not arguing that class is an independent variable and all others are dependent variables. Instead, these factors are relational and interactive, not determined but dialectic.

The most significant challenge to traditional class analysis in recent times has come from the women's movement. Transformations in the household and the labour force, broadly speaking the social division of labour, were the material bases for the women's movement. That movement, it has often been observed, has an internal class character in a similar sense that class is also "gendered." The challenge is to bridge the gap between the workplace, home and community. This connection has been brought to the fore by women's greater labour force participation and the ensuing demands that have been articulated by the women's movement. Analytically these include issues of domestic labour and its impact on both paid labour and gender relations; politically it has involved struggles for day care, community services and family law reforms. Class issues have been affected in significant ways.

Ironically, the domestic labour debate has been overly economistic (Fox, 1980) focusing upon the production of value and productive/unproductive labour, exchange in the context of the reproduction of labourers, and labour power — all of which are class issues, but at the highest level of abstraction. Patriarchy, for example, is a concept germane to gender relations, yet it does not operate at that purely abstract level. Patriarchy is a power relationship between genders wherein men dominate women; men expand their freedom at the expense of women, including the economic, political and ideological manifestations of that domination. What I find most important is the "chemistry" of class and patriarchy. Patriarchy is *not* confined to the family or domestic labour, but is practised in the "public" work world as well; that is, there are gendered patterns of labour force segmentation and patterns of workplace domination (Armstrong, 1984). There are no separate public and private worlds since each strongly shapes the other; each affects what is possible in the other through wages brought into the family or the availability for wage labour, depending upon the domestic situation. These issues are ignored at our peril, as Jane Barker and Hazel Downing's study of gender and the office illustrates. They call for "a recognition that where, when and under what conditions women's work is governed by the mechanisms of the family

and patriarchy ... patiarchal relations [are] increasingly firmly rooted in and defined by the relations and needs of capital" (Barker and Downing, 1980: 65).

A further challenge has come from race and ethnicity. Some of the most exciting recent work in this field has placed class at the centre of such discussions. An excellent example is Ron Bourgeault's work on class and native people, particularly noteworthy since gender is so integral to his analysis (Bourgeault, 1983a, 1983b).

Calling upon my own research in the fisheries, the Native Brotherhood of British Columbia is a solid example of the intersection of class and race. Historically racial conflicts in the B.C. fishery included Japanese, native and white fishers in bitter rivalries where class was the terrain of struggle. The Native Brotherhood incorporates within itself class relations that bring it at times in alliance with the United Fishermen and Allied Workers Union and at times in conflict. Within the Native Brotherhood there are both seine captains who employ crew and the crew members themselves, whereas the union excludes seine captains who own their boats. This rivalry is also gendered since Native women tend to work in the fish processing plants, where the union is strongest, whereas the Native Brotherhood represents Native men on the fishing vessels. It is impossible to comprehend adequately the West Coast fisheries without a firm grasp of gender, race *and* class.

CLASS AND RESERVE LABOUR POOLS

A further feature too seldom examined with respect to class is age. Particularly noteworthy is the high unemployment among young people, but also the nature of the work they do experience. Increasingly they are being marginalized into part-time, non-union, low-skilled jobs. These jobs are expanding rapidly with the increasing use of franchises in areas of fast-food, retail stores, gas stations, etc. The responsibility of franchise holders is to supervise labour and direct operations according to the specified (and contractual) rules set by large-scale capital. This reduces large-scale capital's risk and its need to spend on the supervision and recruitment of labour. The class experience of young people who are the bulk of the labour force in franchise operations is being moulded. These jobs are uniform in every sense: clothing, procedures and practices. There is no room for innovation or initiative, and it is dead-end work. They do not even have to add — only be able to identify a "Big Mac."

This type of work is not developing talents, initiative or solid class traditions. In today's labour market, many young people find that when they are out of school this type of work is all that is available, often stringing together several part-time jobs to make ends meet. Recently Ester Reiter published her study of "Life in a Fast-Food Factory" (1986). She shows that Canadians now spend a third of their food dollar outside the home and much of that in franchise establishments that maximize the use of minimum-wage, part-time labour. She identifies "the emerging market importance of the young worker" as fast-food franchises reach industrial proportions wherein "young workers become ideal commodities; they are cheap, energetic, and in plentiful supply." It is worth quoting her findings:

Making up about 75 per cent of the Burger King workforce, the youngsters who worked after school, on weekends, and on holidays were called "part-timers" ... The daytime workers — the remaining 25 per cent of the workforce were primarily married women of mixed economic backgrounds. ...
The women and teenagers at Burger King are under the sway of a labour process that eliminates almost completely the possibility of forming a workplace culture independent of, and in opposition to, management — there are indications that the teenagers and women who work in this type of job represent not an anomalous but an increasingly typical kind of work, in the one area of the economy that continues to grow — the service sector (Reiter, 1986: 321, 324).

The character of the working class is being transformed by such developments and is impacting disproportionately on young people and women who are structured out of the traditional industrial working class, which is unionized and male (not to mention central Canadian). Marginalization is not confined to franchises. Increasingly the central firms and employers (such as municipalities) are using subcontracting of non-union firms for cleaners, garbage collection and a multitude of services (airlines, for example, contract out as much work as possible). Alongside these practices is the increasing use of part-time workers in clerical and sales jobs. Again these disproportionately affect women and young people.

The drawing upon reserve labour pools is an issue that involves women and young people, but in Canada it is also a regional issue. Region itself is a relationship; that is, regions can only be a region in relation to something else. Regions are not simply areas of unequal power. They are areas in relation to one another and connected in such a way that one is enhanced at the expense of the other. I would argue that regionalism is a consequence (rather than cause) of uneven economic development. Uneven development is historical, spatial and, most crucially, relational; that is, it represents the unfolding of unequal power relations with regional manifestations. The basis of these unequal power relations is class. Class in this case is manifest both at the level of control over capital accumulation and making pools of surplus labour available.

Class and region are bound together in numerous ways. A rather bold example is the so-called resettlement program in Newfoundland. It involved the transformation of the outport household as both a production and consumption unit. Families were relocated from outports to "centres" such as Arnold's Cove. Once moved, there was a commodification of their consumption patterns, involving food preparation, child care, clothing and shelter, which forced families to seek greater wage income. The Arnold's Cove resettlement was tied, not coincidentally, to the Come by Chance oil refinery project. Its failure left the people detached from their new jobs and from their previous means of realizing their labour power. Eventually they readopted fishing in Placentia Bay (although many had moved on to Ontario in search of jobs). To practise fishing, the men must return to their old berths in the abandoned outports during the week while the women work for wages in the new National Sea fish plant. The plant is supplied by two collector boats that make daily rounds to the fish camps. An available labour force was created by detaching people from their subsistence and means of realizing their labour power and drawing them into a situation where wages were required. These workers are "free" to remain unemployed should the fish plant follow the path of Come by Chance. Once

again, it is evident that the class relations of this situation are not only regional, but gendered: men become *dependent* commodity producers and women industrial workers, both detached from earlier domestic commodity production which they shared. The major actors in this drama are the large-scale capitalists who control the oil refineries and the fish plants.

Not all social relations are class relations, but class affects all social relations; that is, gender, region, ethnicity, and so on are all *relational* concepts that are affected by class (although class does not *determine* these relations). This does not mean that gender, regional or ethnic groups are "classes." A key corollary of this argument is that classes *never* exist in isolation — "pure" classes only exist in abstraction. Conversely, classes are *always* conditioned by other social relations.

What needs to be stressed are relations and processes. At its highest level of abstraction, class struggle hinges on the contradiction between the development of the forces of production in capitalism and the limitations imposed by the relations of production inherent in that system. It is this contradiction that provides class with its dynamic, its motor force. At the socio-economic level the politics of class struggle include a history, culture and ideology that give life to basic economic situations. As Marx noted in the *Grundrisse* (1973 [1939]), "Society does not consist of individuals, but expresses the sum of interrelations, the relations within which those individuals stand." Classes are not "things." They are relations and processes. Since these relations and processes are experienced through people, they never manifest themselves in "pure" form, but take on and are affected by the characteristics of people — that is, their gender, race, region, etc., all of which are themselves social characteristics. Similarly, objective positions in the labour process are not *identical* with class, nor is class reducible to such positions; yet these positions have social, political and ideological effects that contribute to the experience of class.

Having discussed some factors that interact with and impact on class, I will now briefly turn to some of the processes under way within class relations in order to reflect upon current changes.

PROCESSES OF CHANGE IN CLASS RELATIONS

A key process in the transformation of class relations is that of proletarianization. People enter the labour market because they are separated from the means to realize their labour power and must provide for their basic needs. The means of production are also their means of realizing their labour; that is, these are opposite sides of the same process whereby capital accumulates. Just as it is necessary for capital to accumulate or die, so is it equally necessary for labour to seek a place to utilize its labour power or perish. In the terms introduced earlier, when the traditional petite bourgeoisie experiences the effects of proletarianization, they increasingly come to resemble the working class or, if the process is completed, actually become members of the working class. There is also another side to the proletarianization process, which involves the differentiation of aspects of capitalist rights into the new middle class. As that new middle class declines in performance of the rights of capital and increases in performing the obligations of labour, it too experiences pro-

letarianization (Clement, 1983). Proletarianization is a *process*; to be proletarian is a condition. They are part of a relationship between the rights of capital and the obligations of labour, on one side expressed in processes involving the traditional petite bourgeoisie and labour, while on the other side, the relation between capital and labour.

The new middle class arises out of the division of capitalist rights concerning surveillance and discipline, but also out of productive activities necessary for the working class which involve co-ordination and direction of the labour process. Surveillance and discipline involve the realization of surplus value (unproductive labour), while co-ordination and direction involve creation of surplus value (productive labour), to use a language appropriate to the highest level of abstraction (Poulantzas, 1977: 118). Whereas the traditional middle class was "independent" in the sense of not employing the labour power of others (aside from its family where patriarchy acts as a key relationship), the new middle class truly stands between capital and labour exercising both co-ordination and surveillance aspects of the labour process.

A central feature of the new middle class is its supervisory activity. I will take one piece of evidence from the International Class Structure Project concerning supervisors and work through some implications for types of control structures. In Sweden 8 per cent of the men and 6 per cent of the women are supervisors, while in Finland 5 per cent of each are supervisors. In the United States these proportions rise to 15 per cent for men and 12 per cent for women, while in Canada a similar 11 per cent of men and 9 per cent of women are supervisors (Finnish Class Project, 1985: 62). Don Black and John Myles have done some detailed analysis of similar patterns. Notable are the significant differences in the proportions of supervisors, but also in their types of activities. They report that "virtually all Canadian and American supervisors have sanctioning authority," which I have been calling surveillance and discipline, while "only a majority of the Swedish supervisors, have such authority. For the most part, Swedish supervisors merely co-ordinate the labour of others." This is what I have been calling co-ordination and direction (Black and Myles, 1985: 20). Black and Myles make an interesting observation: "What is most remarkable is the enormous amount of "administrative overhead" that goes into the work of control and surveillance in Canada and the United States. In the United States, almost 29 per cent of all employees are engaged in disciplining other employees as compared to less than 12 per cent in Sweden. For Canada as a whole the figure is 23 per cent but rises to 28 per cent in the extractive/transformative industries (Black and Myles, 1985: 22). The Swedes and Finns have much lower expenditure on supervision and adhere much more to administrative or bureaucratic forms of control. They also have a fearless approach to technology (which is made possible by labour market policies that ensure employment at decent minimum standards).

The introduction of technology is often a key point of struggle in relations between capital and labour in North America. Labour often resists because of the way technology is implemented (that is, to maximize capital accumulation rather than to improve the quality of work life), which in turn is determined by the industrial relations context of its implementation. Although both operate within capitalist economies, it is evident the Scandinavians have created a much more productive and less conflict-ridden system of industrial relations than in North America, where unproductive supervision flourishes. The Scandinavians have a system that provides much more autonomy for workers and has less need to spend on coercive control structures.

Bureaucratic control structures that operate in place of direct supervision are not without their problems. It is through bureaucratic structures that unions are often drawn into management's system of control. In order to protect the interests of present members, unions have often neglected part-time workers, who are often excluded from the advantages of concessions gained through bureaucratic arrangements such as grievance procedures, bidding for jobs, pensions, etc. Such arrangements often operate to the disadvantage of women and young people, as does the way technology is introduced into the office through automation (Morgall and Vedel, 1985: 93).

Automation is not uniform in its impact on the working class because the working class itself is not homogeneous by skill, industrial sector or gender, as will be argued in the following chapter. The point is that class and automation are not simple processes. They are uneven within the working class and have different effects on various fractions of the working class which correspond to variously skilled and gendered jobs. Assessing the impact of automation requires a textured understanding of class and class fractions.

THE SUBJECTIVE SIDE OF CLASS

Another aspect of class demanding careful attention is its so-called "subjective" side. This means more than "class consciousness" as traditionally understood by that term. It means class *experiences* and class *struggle*, which are actual manifestations of class. More important than "consciousness" per se is ideology, which provides an account or explanation for people's practices. The leading voice in this tradition has been E.P. Thompson who, in his classic *The Making of the English Working Class*, tells us that "class experience is largely determined by the productive relations into which men [and we should add women] are born — or enter involuntarily. Class-consciousness is the way in which these experiences are handled in cultural terms; embodied in traditions, value systems, ideas, and institutional forms. If the experience appears as determined, class-consciousness does not (Thompson, 1963: 9–10).

I have tried to apply some of these principles in two case studies of class formation and experience. In *Hardrock Mining* I focused on managerial strategies and workers' resistance as manifestations of class struggle. In the fisheries study, *The Struggle to Organize*, the focus was on differences in the politics and organization of capitalist, petty bourgeois and proletarian "characters" of unions, co-operatives and associations. The purpose was not only to distinguish organizational types, but to explain the behaviour between the two largest unions, the United Fishermen and Allied Workers Union, which excludes skippers who regularly employ three or more crew, and

the Newfoundland Fishermen, Food and Allied Workers Union, which includes skippers. The class content within these unions explains their tendencies and concrete practices (Clement, 1981; 1986).

To this point attention has been focused on the working and middle classes, but some brief comments on the upper class are appropriate. . . .

It would be difficult to exaggerate the disparities of power between the ruling class and working class. The Canadian state is most accommodating to capital and both are highly integrated. The implications of this highly concentrated power are enormous for Canadians as consumers and as employees. The actions of the ruling class have consequences for everyone.

Why should one care about class theories? Theories are intended to lend insight into building explanations, which in turn guide the way individuals think about and act toward their society. It is the contention of this discussion that class can and should be an integral part of such an understanding. Class, however, cannot be narrowly understood if it is to fulfil its analytical promise. Class does matter, but not isolated from gender, region, politics, ideology, culture and classes in relation to one another. Indeed, without these various social relations class is a static, economistic category. With them it is a dynamic explanatory concept central to the social sciences and fundamental to everyday life.

References

Armstrong, Pat. *Labour Pains: Women's Work in Crisis*. Toronto: The Women's Press, 1984.

Barker, Jane and Downing, Hazel. "Word processing and the transformation of the patriarchal relations of control in the office," *Capital and Class*, 10, (Spring) 1980.

Black, Don and Myles, John, "Dependent industrialization and the Canadian class structure: a Comparative analysis of Canada, the United States and Sweden." *Canadian Review of Sociology and Anthropology*, 23: 3, (May) 1986.

Bourgeault, Ron. "The Indians, the Metis and the fur trade: Class, sexism and racism in the transition from 'communism' to 'capitalism'," *Studies in Political Economy*, 12 (Fall), 1983a.

_____. "The development of capitalism and the subjugation of native women in Northern Canada," *Alternate Routes*, 6, 1983b.

Burawoy, Michael. *The Politics of Production*. London: Verso, 1985.

Carchedi, Mino. *On the Economic Identification of Social Classes*. London: Routledge and Kegan Paul, 1977.

Clement, Wallace. *Hardrock Mining: Industrial Relations and Technological Change at Inco*. Toronto: McClelland and Stewart, 1981.

_____. *Class, Power and Property: Essays on Canadian Society*. Toronto: Methuen, 1983.

_____. *The Struggle to Organize: Resist-*

ance in Canada's Fishery. Toronto: McClelland and Stewart, 1986.

Finnish Class Project. *Reality of Social Classes in Finland*. Tampere: University of Tampere, 1985.

Fox, Bonnie (ed.) *Hidden in the Household: Women's Domestic Labour Under Capitalism*. Toronto: The Women's Press, 1980.

Katznelson, Ira. *City Trenches: Urban Politics and the Patterning of Class in the United States*. Chicago: University of Chicago Press, 1981.

Marx, Karl. *Grundrisse: Introduction to the Critique of Political Economy*. London: Pelican, 1973 [1939].

Morgal, Janine and Vedel, Gitte. "Office automation: the case of gender and power," *Economic and Industrial Democracy*, 6, 1985.

Poulantzas, Nicos. "The new middle class," in Alan Hunt (ed.) *Class and Class Structure*. London: Lawrence and Wishart, 1977.

Przeworski, Adam. "Proletariat into a class," *Politics and Society*, 7 (4): 365–367, 1977.

Reiter, Ester. "Life in a fast-food factory," in Craig Heron and Robert Storey, (eds.) *On the Job: Confronting the Labour Process in Canada*. Montreal: McGill-Queen's University Press, 1986.

Thompson, E.P. *The Making of the English Working Class*. Harmondsworth: Penguin, 1963.

Race and Ethnic Relations

T his section is about the relations between Canada's ethnic and racial groups, and it focuses on discrimination. The section includes readings on job discrimination against people of colour today, discrimination against Chinese immigrants two generations ago, and the historic disadvantage of Canada's Native people.

In the previous section on social inequality, we claimed that racial and ethnic groups sometimes practise closure and exclude "outsiders" from scarce positions and rewards. But sociologists have far more to say about race and ethnic relations in Canada. This section will provide a broader picture of ethnicity and racism as important subjects for sociological analysis. Sociologists have viewed ethnicity from at least three perspectives: as a cultural system, an institutional system, and an economic system.

As most people use the term, *ethnicity* is a form of personal identity. It leads people to identify themselves with a birthplace, and a cultural or ancestral origin. Ethnicity exists because people feel it does. A number of factors make people feel strongly enough about their ethnic origins to want to associate with others of the same origin and keep up traditional customs. Reitz (1980) shows that language retention is one means by which ethnic groups hold on to their culture and identity. Anthropologists have shown that language is not only a way of describing the world; it is a way of thinking about it.

Still, it remains difficult to make blanket statements about ethnicity and ethnic groups. Ethnic communities differ as much one from another as they do from the dominant Anglo-Saxon community. Breton (1968) found large variations in what he called *institutional completeness*. This is the degree to which an ethnic group creates enough social, cultural, and economic institutions to allow the group to isolate itself from the rest of society.

What causes institutional completeness to vary from one group to another, and does it matter how institutionally complete an ethnic group may be? Well, first, institutional completeness affects immigrants' willingness to assimilate into the larger, non-ethnic society. Breton finds that the degree of institutional completeness in an ethnic group determines the proportion of people who conduct most of their social life within the ethnic group. Ethnic organizations discourage group members from looking outside the community. Instead, they provide a context within which community members can meet and interact with other community members. Ethnic organizations also raise the salience of ethnic membership and press for group interests. Organization leaders act to maintain or increase participation in these ethnic organizations.

Thus, the politics of ethnic communities are enormously important in shaping communal organizations. Through them, ethnic leaders affect the personal lives of immigrants and their children. As well, institutional completeness has a great importance for the inter-ethnic conflict over scarce resources.

As Breton points out "ethnic communities are formed, grow and disappear; they go through a life-cycle." Institutional completeness and its effects change over time, after the first waves of immigration and community building. Factors affecting institutional completeness include group distinctiveness (language, colour, and religion among others) and the resources (including wealth and job skills) immigrants bring to Canada.

Ethnic communities and sentiments may survive long after discrimination, an inability to speak English, or the need for economic cooperation have disappeared. Two cases particularly come to mind: the Jews and the Chinese. Members of these groups tend to be highly educated, largely middle class, fluent in English, born in Canada, and well protected (in law, if not always in fact) against discrimination. Both groups possess strong institutional completeness, despite the disappearance of many conditions that might have once called for communal action.

Peter Li (1986; also, Bolaria and Li, 1985) argues that discrimination against the Chinese in Canada remains a serious problem today. And even perceived discrimination increases the ethnic identification and solidarity of Chinese Canadians. An article by Peter Li in this section shows that Chinese institutional completeness first grew out of the conditions Chinese Canadians faced as immigrants. Between 1923 and 1947, the Chinese were even barred from immigrating to Canada and subjected to numerous legal restrictions if already in the country. To survive economically, this victimized ethnic minority had to maintain strong kinship and communal ties.

One successful strategy was the establishment of business partnerships based on kinship. These partnerships were fluid and subject to changing opportunities in a hostile environment. However, they were usually reliable and always available when needed. In this way, kinship and friendship helped Chinese immigrants survive in a hostile environment.

Discrimination against Jewish-Canadians is less evident today than discrimination against Chinese-Canadians. Indeed, Canadian Jews are doing better economically than any other Canadians with the same amount of education. Perhaps Jews remain ethnically cohesive because of perceived, anticipated, or feared discrimination.

All we can say with certainty is that Jews and Chinese Canadians, like other ethnic Canadians, tend to maintain their communities because they are institutionally complete. Their community structure helps them in the inter-ethnic struggle for scarce resources. And they like to be a part of their community: ethnicity is a positive sentiment, as well as a response to hostile forces.

"Institutional completeness" protects insiders from more powerful outsiders. By contrast, racism is an action directed by the powerful against a visibly different racial or ethnic group. Typically it protects insiders from less powerful outsiders. Like ethnicity, racism has complex origins. Racist behaviour may be consciously or unconsciously motivated, and may (or may not) have roots in economic or political self-interest. Like ethnicity, racism is a form of *ethnocentrism* — the belief that one's own group is the best of all. Just as racism strengthens ethnic identity, so ethnic sentiment, taken to an extreme, produces racism.

People have offered many explanations of racism. One, typically put forward by racists, is that minorities bring racism on themselves by behaviour that is clannish, exclusive, or disrespectful of the dominant society. Andorno's (1969) study of the "authoritarian personality" showed that this way of thinking is part of a world view that values submission and uniformity, at whatever social cost.

Another explanation of racism is primarily economic. Some, like Peter Li (1991), argue that constructing racial categories is economically advantageous. It justifies giving some groups, defined as less deserving, lower wages and fewer legal rights. Accordingly, racism often surfaces in times of economic turmoil (e.g., post-World War I Germany). It typically denies the essential similarity of the oppressed and oppressor. Political turmoil is equally likely to excite racist sentiments. Like the control of deviance, racism is a way of defining and enforcing a group's moral boundaries. It strengthens group solidarity by finding scapegoats — people to punish. Racist theories provide justifications for this behaviour.

Exploitive economic thinking must somehow underly the continued practice of job discrimination against people of colour, especially those of African origins, in Canada today. An article by Frances Henry and Effie Ginzberg in this section reports on an experiment to measure the true extent of discrimination in hiring. It finds a level of discrimination that will shock anyone who believed that Canadians were fair and just in their dealings with people of other racial origins.

One must reach similar conclusions from the evidence of Canada's treatment of its Native peoples. In their article in this section, Jean Elliot and Augie Fleras review the historical treatment of Native peoples in Canada. White governments have given Canada's Native peoples the same status as colonized racial minorities in other parts of the world. In its first instance, this form of racism takes the form of theft and murder. The conquerors — often styling themselve "discoverers" — take valuable land away from people who already inhabit it. But once force has established the new order, racism takes other forms: demeaning paternalism, neglect, and occupational discrimination.

In Canada, no social group has suffered as extreme racism as the Native peoples. This problem continues today, but changes are in the making. Tougher anti-discrimination laws make racism harder to practise openly. As well, Canada's Native peoples are organizing more effectively to claim their treaty land rights. Some governments are paying somewhat more attention to these claims than they did in the past. However, violent incidents like those at Oka, Quebec in the summer of 1990 remind us that justice for Native peoples is not yet at hand.

A century ago, evolutionary theories justified racism on the grounds that Anglo-Saxons had achieved a higher stage of civilization than non-European peoples. Such theories no longer command much respect today. Few Canadians really believe that Natives lack the competence to govern themselves. However, serious economic and political issues remain unresolved around the question of native self-government. Thus, the most extreme case of racism in our history, the treatment of Native peoples, has not been laid to rest.

Typically, racism is somewhat subtler today than it once was. For example, the last two decades have seen an encouraging increase in the percentage of adult Canadians who approve of marriage between Roman Catholics and Protestants, Jews and non-Jews, and whites and blacks (Lambert and

Curtis, 1985). Least approving are "ethnic" Canadians of neither French nor English ancestry who have, themselves, historically experienced discrimination and prejudice. Not only are they less accepting today, but their rate of change towards acceptance has been slowest of all groups.

Lambert and Curtis (1985) note that "It is precisely in minority groups where intergroup marriages are most likely to occur and where consequently there is most threat from them" that we find the strongest opposition to intergroup marriage. Such a group faces a real challenge to survival. If this theory is valid, we should be seeing a reduced acceptance of intergroup marriage among francophones. This group has grown increasingly concerned about group survival over the past decade.

Where is Canadian ethnicity headed? John Porter (1965) named his classic work about Canadian society *The Vertical Mosaic* because he viewed Canadian society as a hierarchy (hence, "vertical") made up of numerous, differently coloured and unmixing elements (hence, "mosaic"). Porter feared that ethnic groups were assimilating too slowly for Canada's good. Faster assimilation required more social mobility, which in turn required more educational opportunity. Porter held that minorities still occupied positions for which they had been imported (sometimes) generations earlier, when Canadians had been unwilling or unable to do a required job. Because of their limited mobility, ethnic minorities continued holding down the worst positions, getting too little education, and having too little importance in the society.

Today, much of this has changed. Ethnic minorities (other than the Jews) are still largely absent from the ruling elite, but they are doing well economically. Many statistics suggest that immigrants and their children do better economically than native-born Canadians. Thus, people are not locked into what Porter called their "entrance statuses." In truth, Porter's classic work, published in 1965, reflects a Canadian society that has largely passed away.

This is not to deny Porter's grand vision — unquestionably a compelling metaphor of Canadian society. Nevertheless, we must acknowledge the rapid and profound changes that have taken place in the last two decades. Today Canadian society is less of a vertical mosaic than it used to be. It remains vertical (that is, stratified), but members of every ethnic and racial group can be found at every level of the structure. Discrimination remains a problem, especially for recent immigrants and Native Canadians. As for the rest, class position is (primarily) a result of class origin, and (secondarily) education. We must hope that Canada will be even less of a vertical mosaic in the next century than it is today.

References

Adorno, Theodor et al. *The Authoritarian Personality*. New York: W.W. Norton, 1969.

Bolaria, B. Singh and Li, Peter S. *Racial Oppression in Canada*. Toronto: Garamond Press, 1985.

Breton, Raymond. "Institutional completeness of ethnic communities." *American Journal of Sociology*, 20, 2, (September 1964), pp. 193–205.

Lambert, Ronald D. and Curtis, James. "Racial attitudes of Canadians," *Past and Present*, February 1985, pp. 2–4.

Li, Peter. "Race and ethnic relations." In L. Tepperman and R.J. Richardson (eds.) *The Social World*. Second edition. Toronto: McGraw-Hill Ryerson, 1991.

Porter, John. *The Vertical Mosaic*. Toronto: University of Toronto Press, 1965.

Reitz, Jeffrey G. *The Survival of Ethnic Groups*. Toronto: McGraw-Hill Ryerson, 1980.

FIFTEEN

Chinese Immigrants on the Canadian Prairie, 1910–47

Peter S. Li

PETER LI, Professor of Sociology at the University of Saskatchewan, specializes in the study of race relations and methods of social research. His books include *Occupational Mobility and Kinship Assistance: A Study of Chinese Immigrants in Chicago* (1978); *Social Research Methods* (1981); *Racial Minorities in Multicultural Canada* co-edited with B. Singh Bolaria (1983); *Racial Oppression in Canada* with B. Singh Bolaria (1985); *The Chinese in Canada* (1988); *Ethnic Inequality in a Class Society* (1988); and *Race and Ethnic Relations in Canada*, ed. (1990). Professor Li has served as Associate Editor of the *Canadian Review of Sociology and Anthropology* and in several executive capacities for the Western Association of Sociology and Anthropology. He has travelled in China three times to lecture on sociology by invitation of the Chinese Academy of Social Sciences and several universities.

. . . The materials of this paper are based mainly on a 1979–80 study of the oral history of the Chinese in Saskatchewan. The aim was to collect detailed life histories of elderly Chinese in the province, with particular reference to their work experiences in Canada. A total of fifty-five completed interviews were conducted. The subjects were selected from a snow-ball sample in which respondents were asked to refer interviewers to other elderly Chinese immigrants living in Canada for a long period of time. About half of the subjects were living in Saskatoon at the time of the interview. Other subjects wer selected from Regina, Yorkton, Swift Current, and six other communities in Saskatchewan. Most of the respondents had worked and lived in other

parts of Canada before settling in Saskatchewan. . . .

The Chinese immigration to Canada began around 1858 after gold was discovered in the Fraser Valley, British Columbia. The initial wave of Chinese immigrants consisted of miners from the west coast of the United States, and immigrants from Kwantung province in China. Subsequently, large numbers of Chinese labourers were recruited to Canada to fill a labour shortage, especially between 1881 and 1885 when the Canadian Pacific Railway was constructed. Between 1881 and 1883, for example, the number of Chinese arriving by ship at Victoria was 13,245 (Li, 1979). The wave of Chinese immigration continued after the CPR was completed, albeit at a slower rate. Between 1886 and 1894, the number of Chinese entering Canada and paying a special head tax was 12,197. This number was increased to 32,457 for the period 1895–1904 (Li, 1979).

As early as 1875, the provincial government of British Columbia passed anti-Chinese bills to disenfranchise the Chinese, and to restrict their civil rights. The Dominion Government of Canada had resisted passing a federal bill to control the flow of Chinese immigration before 1885, for fear that it would create a shortage of labourers, and impede the construction of the CPR. The first federal anti-Chinese bill was passed in 1885, in the form of a head tax of $50 imposed upon every Chinese person entering Canada (Statutes of Canada, 1885, c. 71). The tax was raised to $100 in 1900 (Statutes of Canada, 1900, c. 32), and $500 in 1903 (Statutes of Canada, 1903, c. 8). In 1923, the federal government passed the most restrictive Chinese Immigration Act, essentially excluding all Chinese from entering Canada (Statutes of Canada, 1923, c. 38). The act was in effect until 1947 (Statutes of Canada, 1947, c. 19).

Prior to 1900, close to 98 percent of the Chinese were concentrated in British Columbia. The intensification of the anti-Chinese movement on the west coast, and the changing occupational demand for the Chinese had the effect of dispersing some to the interior of Canada. By 1911, for example, 13 per cent of the Chinese in Canada were located in the three prairie provinces. This figure was increased to 19 per cent in 1921, and 20 per cent in 1931 (Li, 1979).

Initially, the Chinese were recruited to the west coast as labourers in various pioneering industries such as mining, railroad construction, and later canning and other manufacturing. They were attractive to employers because of low labour cost and large supply. As white workers increased in number in British Columbia, the Chinese were perceived as competitors who were willing to undercut wages, and to serve as scabs in labour disputes. As organized labour began to grow, the Chinese became increasingly the target of labour exclusion. Organized labour demanded the exclusion of the Chinese from trades, and eventually their total exclusion from the country. The anti-Chinese sentiments received political support as politicians saw the advantage of adopting a platform to exclude the Chinese. By 1880, for example, all political parties found it necessary to take on such a platform to gain popular support.

As a result of the anti-Chinese movement and subsequent legislative control, the Chinese found it difficult to compete with white labourers in the core labour market. Many were forced to take up employment in the marginal sector. The hostile labour market also accelerated the growth of ethnic business among the Chinese, first concentrating in laundry operations, later in restaurants. The marginal sector and the ethnic business provided an occupational refuge for many Chinese when opportunities were restricted in the core labour market.

Census statistics indicate that in 1921, 24 per cent of the Chinese were labourers and unskilled workers, and 35 per cent were employed as store employees, servants, cooks, laundry workers, and waiters. These percentages reflect the concentration of the Chinese in the marginal and ethnic business sectors. The figures for 1931 show an increase in such a concentration. Labourers and unskilled workers constituted 21 percent of the employed Chinese, while store employees, servants, cooks, laundry workers, and waiters made up another 42 per cent. These figures illustrate in part the restrictive employment opportunities open to the Chinese.

BACKGROUND OF CHINESE RESPONDENTS

The case histories of the thirty-one respondents who came between 1910 and 1923 show a striking similarity in background. All of them, for example, came to Canada in their late teens or early twenties. They originated from Kwangtung province in regions neighbouring the city of Canton. Toishan (T'aishan), in particular, seems to be the predominant county of origin. The respondents came from rural families in which many male members went overseas. Major financial support for these families consisted of remittances from relatives abroad, in addition to some limited farming activities.

Since the respondents immigrated at an early age in their careers, many had no working experience prior to immigration, aside from working in agricultural fields. All of them had limited formal schooling, and spoke practically no English before coming to Canada.

Like many of their predecessors who went overseas, the Chinese immigrants who migrated to Canada in the early part of the twentieth century left home to escape economic hardship in the search for better employment opportunities. In many cases, the Chinese immigrants borrowed from relatives in Canada to finance the trip and paid them back after they had a chance to work and save up in Canada. As one immigrant described it: "We were poor and starving, and we needed money at home. We had to borrow money to come over here, and when we came over here, we had to work hard to pay back the money that we owed."

Most of the respondents came to Canada with the assistance of a relative who had immigrated to Canada at an earlier date. The relative, usually the father, a brother, or an uncle, paid for the passage expense and the head tax for the respondents, in addition to making other legal arrangements of immigration, and receiving them upon arrival. The following case illustrates the way in which many Chinese came to Canada prior to 1923: "I came here in 1918. I was 18 years old. We were very poor at home. People came here to look for money. My uncle was here then, and he applied for me to come. He paid the $500 head tax for me. . . . So I came and went to wash dishes."

Kinship assistance frequently was extended beyond the initial stage of immigration. Some respondents worked for their relatives for a period of time after arrival, and others learned of employment opportunities through their relatives. Here is one example: "My brother gave me the money to come over. Afterward, I paid him back by working in his laundry. It took me 2 or 3 years. . . . It was $30 a month. . . . I worked there for several years, maybe 8 or 10 years, and then I went to wash dishes for an Englishman." Other studies (Li, 1977; MacDonald and MacDonald, 1964) have shown that the pattern of kinship assistance is common among immigrants who have little marketable resources, and have to rely on kinship help in overcoming some of the legal and social obstacles of immigration.

OPPORTUNITIES AND CONSTRAINTS IN THE LABOUR MARKET

The job histories of the thirty-one prewar immigrants have a number of characteristics in common. For example, all the jobs were menial in nature and poorly paid. They often worked as domestic servants, laundry workers, and restaurant workers. As Chinese laundries declined in the thirties, the restaurants, both Chinese and non-Chinese owned, provided the main source of employment for many Chinese. All the respondents had a working history of high turnover from job to job. The mobility was frequently from one prairie town to another, but the line of work remained the same. The following case illustrates well the typical job history among the Chinese.

> I came to Moose Jaw in 1913. . . . First I washed dishes, making $35 a month. I worked for 14 to 16 hours a day. I knelt down on the floor and washed the floor and washed the dining room every morning. I had a potato bag to make it easier for my knees. Then after that, I went to work for a Japanese owner of a restaurant. That was 1914. . . . After a while, I went to Simpson, at harvest time, up north, it was the CPR line. I worked in a farm. I got up 6 o'clock in the morning, milked the cow, and came back to the house to cook breakfast for my boss. . . . He was not a very friendly person. . . . It was no good, so I quit. I came back to Moose Jaw to work for my brother for $50 a month for 12 hours a day. At night I scrubbed the floor and waited on tables. Then in 1918 I went back to China to get married. . . .

Jobs among the Chinese have all the features typical of employment in the marginal labour market. These features include long hours of work, little security, low pay, and low skill. The employment opportunity open to the Chinese was limited mainly to laundries and restaurants in the service sector. One respondent described the job situation for the Chinese in Moose Jaw around 1913 as follows: "At that time there were about 450 (Chinese) men and two women. . . . In Moose Jaw, there were about 35 to 38 Chinese laundries and three cafés. . . . All the Chinese worked there."

On the surface, it would seem that lack of occupational and language skills would explain why so many Chinese had low-status jobs in the service sector. Although skills in general enhance the market value of employees, jobs open to the Chinese required little skill. As long as employment in other sectors was not available to the Chinese, improvement in language and other skills would help little in enabling the Chinese to gain higher paying jobs.

There is strong evidence to indicate that the Chinese faced a discriminatory job market even in cases where Chinese employees had the necessary skill to perform the task. . . .

. . . Apart from the unfriendly social atmosphere, the Chinese were also victims of legal exclusions.[1] One respondent explained the following to us: "If you run a café, you are not supposed to hire a female. If you run a grocery store, you are not supposed to hire a female. You got no vote at all. The election has nothing to do with you because you are Chinese. . . . You got nothing to say about it anyway. If you don't like it, you go." One of the effects of social discrimination and legal exclusion was to reduce the market value of the Chinese as employees. Since employment opportunities outside of the service sector were virtually unavailable to the Chinese, they remained highly vulnerable in the labour market.

ETHNIC BUSINESS

Since employment opportunities in the labour sector were highly restrictive, many Chinese immigrants ventured into an ethnic business to preserve a job and to maintain a living. The Chinese first entered into the laundry business, and later into the restaurant business. The Chinese restaurants in the prairie towns in the twenties and thirties, however, were very different from the post-war Chinese restaurants in metropolitan centres. These earlier restaurants were small in scale, poorly decorated, and labour intensive. The hours of operation were long, and the profit margin was small. The restaurants simply provided a business venture for many Chinese whereby they could put up a small amount of capital to secure a guaranteed place to work and live. The case histories clearly indicate that in those cases where the respondents became part owners of a restaurant, they were doing the same kinds of work in their own restaurant as they did when working for somebody else. The restaurants provided an economic refuge for the Chinese in a restrictive labour market.

Twenty-two of the respondents had the experience of holding a partnership in a restaurant sometime in their career. In many cases, the respondents, reported a history of moving back and forth between employment and self-employment in restaurants. There was little doubt in the minds of the respondents that self-employment in one's restaurant was just as much a job as employment in another restaurant.

Partnership was a viable means for many Chinese to start a restaurant because it allowed meagre capital and labour to be pooled. Given the kinds of jobs most Chinese had, the capacity to save a large amount of capital for investment was limited. Partnership provided a means of joint venture with little capital. The business partners also worked as a team in running the restaurant to reduce the cost of hiring other workers. The following is an example of how partnership business was formed and conducted:

> ... the partners get a few relatives together and just chip in some money each. ... If there is no business and you have to leave, then you sell it and split the money, that's all. ... Everyday ... fixed meals, cooked the meat, made a few pies, and made some soup. Whatever you needed we made them. ... There's no boss. Everyone did it right. That was the way we did it. Just worked for ourselves. In the end, whoever had a share had a share of the profit ... if you really don't like it and can't get along, then you can buy me out, or I can buy you out. ...

In some cases the respondents had no capital, but they could still enter into a partnership by working with some Chinese, and use their salary to repay their share of the capital. Here is one example: "Someone asked me to be a cook in Kinistino. Then he gave me a share because he didn't want me to leave. I didn't have anything. I just made the money from the salary until I paid up the share, and then I owned the share. I worked a couple of years for it."

Aside from the small capital needed, the partnership restaurant business had low risk, and it provided a refuge in economic hard times. One respondent explained what life was like in a small town restaurant during the winter months.

> In the small towns you don't have to know too much English. Just use your eyes to see what they want. ... You don't have to do too much because the menu is the same from year to year. ... The business was cheap. ... Save all the money, and then you can buy a business. Before in Goven, I bought a business for $350. ... As long as you had a place to sleep and some work, then it didn't matter. In the winter time it was cold and there were no people there. Some days we had only a few people, just sold a few loaves of bread and a few cups of coffee, that's all. No, it didn't matter as long as you had a place to stay. ...

During the Depression, the restaurants provided a means of survival for many

Chinese. As one respondent described the situation of a restaurant during the early thirties: ". . . there were 4 partners and 10 others who just stayed there because there was nowhere else to go. . . . There was no work to do elsewhere, and they looked after the restaurant."

Movement in and out of partnerships was as frequent as changing jobs in other employment. A person would sell his partnership when he took a trip to China, only to join the partnership on his return. The following case is an example: "I sold it and went to China. There were about 7 or 8 of us there. They were my cousins, and so I sold my part of the business to them. So then when I came back, the restaurant was busy, and they asked me to stay and work for them. I worked for 3 or 4 months, and they asked me to become a partner."

A number of factors probably facilitated the formation of business partnership among the Chinese immigrants. The fact that many respondents came to Canada by way of relative sponsorship means that they had certain kinship ties that could be used as a basis for business partners. Indeed, partnerships were frequently formed between fathers and sons, uncles and nephews, and brothers. In some cases, the partnership may be extended to more distant relatives and friends. Since the Chinese immigrants emigrated from predominantly the same region, common lineage and clanship ties provided the Chinese immigrants with a web of both close and distant relatives from which partners could be drawn. The prevalence of business partnership was confirmed by all the respondents. As one of them described it: "In the old days, it was partnerhip . . . we all worked partnerships. . . . In my case, I worked together with my brothers."

Partly because of the kinship ties, but also because of the nature of the business, the financial arrangements of partnership were usually made on an informal basis. One respondent explained the partnership arrangements as follows: ". . . get a few relatives together, and each just chip in together. You don't need a lawyer, and you don't have to sign, just take each other's words. . . . If he is a good man or if he is your cousin then you would be his partner."

Business partners were not only co-investors, but also co-workers in the same cafe or restaurant. It was just as necessary for the partners to pool their labour as to pool their capital. Since most partnership businesses did not employ outside help, the partners in essence were creating jobs for themselves in their investment venture. From the point of view of the Chinese immigrants then, partnerships reduced the capital cost as well as the operating cost in running a restaurant.

Since the meagre return in operating a Chinese restaurant required using unpaid labour to reduce the operating cost, most Chinese immigrants needed to rely on business partners in the absence of their immediate family. Ironically, the separation of the Chinese men from their families in China facilitated the formation of business partnerships because these men could not rely on wives and young children for labour.

The partnership business among the Chinese declined after the war as more Chinese were allowed to bring their families to Canada. The family members provided additional labour power to operate the restaurant. Many partnership businesses broke up as the post-war immigration altered the demographic pattern among the Chinese community.

MOBILITY DREAM

To many Chinese immigrants before the war, the only hope of success was to work hard in Canada, and save enough money to retire in China. Meanwhile, during their stay in Canada, they aspired to visit China periodically, where they could unite with their families for a short period of time. This mentality is sometimes described as a "sojourner's orientation" (Siu, 1953) or a "marginal personality" (Park, 1928; Stonequist, 1937) which basically results from a clash of two cultures, leading to the immigrants' inability to identify with the host community. In the case of the Chinese in Canada, there is every indication to suggest that their mobility aspiration to return to China was greatly influenced by a number of structural factors.

For example, the restrictive immigration laws against the Chinese meant that most Chinese men in Canada before the war were unable to bring their families (Li, 1980). Before 1923, the law stipulated a head tax of $500 for practically every Chinese person entering Canada. After 1923, the Chinese Immigration Act precluded the Chinese from admission to the country. Aside from the restrictive immigration laws, the social atmosphere was very unfriendly to the Chinese as a group. They were excluded from many aspects of life in Canadian society. Their ties to the host community were maintained in a symbiotic relationship in which the Chinese provided cheap labour and service in the marginal and ethnic business sectors in exchange for meager pay to support themselves and their families in China. The position of the Chinese in the economy was similar to that of many migrant workers in industrial societies.

Many respondents described a strong desire to return to China, since separation from their families and discrimination forced them to remain as aliens in Canadian society. "Before, the Chinese came to work in Canada, but the person's mind was in China. Your relatives, uncles, mother, children and wife were in China. So you saved all the money and you could go home to visit them. Over here . . . the white people didn't mix with you and you yourself didn't know the language, there was nothing to enjoy."

Although many of the Chinese wanted to visit their families in China, not all were able to do so. In some cases, the husband in Canada never saw wife or children until decades after separation. As one immigrant said: "Everybody was like that. You came here and if you behaved, worked for a few years, then you could go home. Sometimes a person came here for 30 or 40 years, and never went back to see his family. I know of one guy here. When he came here, he was just married for a couple of months. . . . He never saw his wife for 40 years, never saw his boy either."

It is difficult to estimate how many Chinese immigrants actually retired in China, and how many stayed in Canada. For those who stayed, their way of thinking changed radically after the war as the treatment of the Chinese improved, and their families were allowed to immigrate to Canada. The 1949 socialist revolution in China also may have discouraged overseas immigrants from returning. The difference of the pre-war and post-war mentality was clearly explained by one respondent: "After the war, they allowed us Chinese to bring the wife, and then the children here. . . . Now you are ambitious to teach the children to go to school so others wouldn't look down on you. . . . Before, it was not the same . . . even if you were educated, even if you knew how to do the job, the government wouldn't hire you because nobody wanted orientals."

SUMMARY AND CONCLUSION

The oral history of the Chinese shows that immigrants before the war found a limited number of jobs in the service industry. These jobs had many of the features common to marginal labour, such as long hours of work, menial labour, low pay and lack of promotion opportunity. The Chinese also reported a history of changing from one menial job to another, including a movement between employment and self-employment in the ethnic business.

The predominant Chinese business was the restaurant which provided a viable employment opportunity for many in a restrictive labour market. Limited by capital and manpower, the Chinese made use of partnership investment to build their restaurant business. The organization of partnership enabled a maximum use of labour power among partners to reduce labour cost, at the same time providing enough flexibility to cushion business risks and uncertainties. The popularity of the restaurant business among the Chinese before the war represents a successful attempt on their part to adapt to the structural constraints of the labour market.

Aside from the general restrictive employment opportunity which encouraged many Chinese to seek alternative avenues in the ethnic business sector, a number of other factors also facilitated the formation of business partnership among the Chinese. Partnerships were largely formed on the basis of kinship ties. Since most of the Chinese immigrants came to Canada through the sponsorship of relatives, the kinship ties which were instrumental in their immigration remained important for the subsequent stage when partnerships were struck. The web of kinship ties was also enriched by the fact that most of the immigrants came from the same place of origin. The absence of Chinese wives and young children as a result of the restrictive immigration law compelled Chinese men to rely on business partners for additional labour in their business operation. The success of Chinese restaurants as survival vehicles was related to Chinese immigrants' ability to mobilize kinship assistance.

This study suggests the importance of studying the conditions of the labour market as well as the adaptive responses of an ethnic group for an understanding of its structural position in the economy. The development of ethnic business among the Chinese calls for further attention to the enclave economy in theories of a dual labour market.

Note

[1] For example, a Saskatchewan act of 1912 (Saskatchewan Statute, 1912, c. 17) prevented a white woman from working in any restaurant or laundry owned or managed by the Chinese. The Saskatchewan Election Act of 1908 (Saskatchewan Statute, 1908, c. 2) disfranchised persons of the Chinese race. The Chinese did not gain voting rights in Saskatchewan until 1951.

References

Averitt, Robert T. *The Dual Economy: The Dynamics of American Industry Structure*. New York: W.W. Norton, 1968.

Bach, Robert L. "Mexican Immigration and the American State." *International Migration Review* 12 (1978): 536–58.

Baron, Harold M. and Hymer, Bennet. "The negro worker in the Chicago labour movement." Pp. 232–85 in J. Jacobson (ed.), The Negro and the American Labour Movement. New York: Doubleday, 1968.

Blau, Peter and Duncan, Otis D. *The American Occupational Structure*. New York: John Wiley and Sons, 1967.

Bonacich, Edna. "A theory of ethnic antagonism: the split labour market." *American Sociological Review* 37 (1972): 547–59.

_____. "Advanced capitalism and black/white race relations in the United States: a split labour market interpretation." *American Sociological Review* 41 (1976): 34–51.

Breton, Raymond. "Ethnic stratification viewed from three theoretical perspectives." Pp. 270–94 in J. Curtis and W. Scott (eds.), *Social Stratification: Canada*. Scarborough, Ontario: Prentice-Hall of Canada, 1979.

Burawoy, Michael. "The functions and reproduction of migrant labour: comparative materials from southern Africa and the United States." *American Journal of Sociology* 81 (1976): 1050–87.

Davis, K. and Moore, Wilbert E. "Some principles of stratification." *American Sociological Review* 10 (1945): 242–9.

Duncan, Beverly and Duncan, Otis D. "Minorities and the process of stratification." *American Sociological Review* 33 (1968): 356–64.

Duncan, Otis, D., Featherman, David L., and

Duncan, Beverly. *Socioeconomic Background and Achievement*. New York: Seminar Press, 1972.

Edwards, M. Reich and Gordon, David M. *Labour Market Segmentation*. Lexington Mass.: D.C. Heath, 1975.

Featherman, David L. "The Socioeconomic achievement of white religio-ethnic subgroups: social and psychological explanations." *American Sociological Review* 36 (1971): 207–22.

Featherman, David L. and Hauser, Robert M. *Opportunity and Change*. New York: Academic Press, 1978.

Gordon, David M. *Theories of Poverty and Underdevelopment*. Lexington, Mass.: D.C. Heath, 1972.

Horan, Patrick M. "Is status attainment research atheoretical? *American Sociological Review* 43 (1978): 343–541.

Li, Peter S. "Ethnic businesses among Chinese in the U.S." *Journal of Ethnic Studies* 4 (1976): 35–41.

_____. "Occupational achievement and kinship assistance among Chinese immigrants in Chicago." *Sociological Quarterly* 18 (1977): 478–89.

_____. "A historical approach to ethnic stratification: the case of the Chinese in Canada, 1858–1930." *Canadian Review of Sociology and Anthropology* 16 (1979): 320–32.

_____. "Immigration laws and family patterns: some demographic changes among Chinese families in Canada, 1885–1971." *Canadian Ethnic Studies* 12 (1980): 58–72.

Light, Ivan H. *Ethnic Enterprise in America*. Berkeley, California: University of California Press, 1973.

MacDonald, John S. and MacDonald, Leatrice D. "Chain migration: ethnic neighbourhood formation and social networks." *Milbank Memorial Fund Quarterly* 42 (1964): 82–96.

Park, Robert E. "Human migration and the marginal man." *American Journal of Sociology* 32 (1928): 881–93.

Siu, Paul. "The Chinese laundryman: a study of social isolation." Unpublished PH.D. dissertation, University of Chicago, 1953.

Statutes of Canada 1885. An Act to restrict and regulate Chinese immigration into Canada. Chapter 71.

_____ 1900. An Act respecting and restricting Chinese Immigration. Chapter 32.

_____ 1903. An Act respecting and restricting Chinese Immigration. Chapter 8.

_____ 1923. An Act respecting Chinese Immigration. Chapter 38.

_____ 1947. An Act to amend the Immigration Act and to repeal the Chinese Immigration Act. Chapter 19.

Statutes of Saskatchewan 1908. An Act respecting Election of Members of the Legislative Assembly. Chapter 2.

_____ 1912. An Act to Prevent the Employment of Female Labour in Certain Capacities. Chapter 17.

Stonequist, Everett V. *The Marginal Man.* New York: Scribner, 1973.

Wilson, Kenneth L. and Portes, Alejandro. "Immigrants enclaves: an analysis of the labour market experience of Cubans in Miami." *American Journal of Sociology* 86 (1980): 295–319.

Yancey, William L., Eriksen, E.P. and Julian, R.N. "Emergent Ethnicity: a review of reformulation." *American Sociological Review* 41 (1976): 391–403.

SIXTEEN

Racial Discrimination in Employment

Frances Henry and Effie Ginzberg

FRANCES HENRY, Professor of Anthropology at York University, specializes in Race and Ethnic Relations. Her books and publications include *Who Gets the Work: A Test of Racial Discrimination in Employment* (with E. Ginzberg), published in 1984 and recently replicated in 1989; *Research in Race Relations in Canada: A State of the Art Review*, 1986 and revised in 1989. She has also published *Victims and Neighbors: A Small Town in Nazi Germany Remembered*.

Professor Henry is currently editing *Race Relations in the United Kingdom and Canada: Policy, Practice and Research* (with M. Thompson, Centre for Race and Ethnic Relations, University of Warwick, U.K.). Her other research includes a study of Caribbean Communities in Toronto in collaboration with A.H. Richmond and A. Simmons. She is currently part of a research consortium comparing racial tension and conflict in Canada, the U.K., and the U.S., on behalf of the Race Relations Directorate of the Ontario Ministry of Citizenship.

EFFIE GINZBERG, Manager of Human Resources and Employment Equity Planning, Municipality of Metropolitan Toronto, specializes in research on prejudice and discrimination in employment and the media. Recent publications include *Who Gets the Work: A Test of Racial Discrimination in Employment*, with Frances Henry (1985) and *Power Without Responsibility: A Content Analysis of the Toronto Sun* (1986). She is currently involved in the development of a handbook for employment equity practitioners and has presented numerous seminars on conducting workforce audits and goals and timetables planning.

Until the publication of our report *Who Gets the Work?* (1985) efforts to demonstrate that there is racial discrimination in the Canadian employment arena have been limited to census data analysis, personal reports of victims of discrimination, and attitude studies. Each of these three types of research is limited in its capacity to prove that discrimination based on race is actually the cause of discrepancies in income and access to employment. Critics, sceptics, and racists have easily been able to doubt the presence of racial discrimination in view of weaknesses inherent in these indirect measures of discrimination. *Who Gets the Work?* sought to test directly for the presence or absence of discrimination in the Toronto labour market through the process of field testing — a quasi-experimental research technique.

For the first time in Canada, a study tested racial discrimination in employment by actually sending individuals, White and Black, to apply for advertised positions in order to find out if employers discriminate by preferring White to non-White employees. We believe we were successful in proving definitively that racial discrimination in Canada affects the employment opportunities of non-White Canadians. Whites have greater access to jobs than do equally qualified non-Whites.

Our study was guided by two questions. One, is there a difference in the number of job offers that White and Black applicants of similar experience and qualifications receive when they apply to the same jobs? And two, are there differences in the ways in which White and Black job applicants are treated when they apply for work? Both questions were tested by two procedures: *person testing* and *telephone testing*.

DEFINING DISCRIMINATION

Discrimination can take place at any point in the employment process. It may exist in such areas as recruitment, screening, selection, promotion, and termination. At the level of employee selection, for example, discimination against non-Whites can take place when job applicants are called to the initial interview. To the extent that the employer's staff or the other employees themselves practise discrimination, either as a result of racial attitudes of the interviewer or because of instructions to screen out non-Whites as a matter of company pol-

icy, non-Whites will not get beyond the initial screening of job applicants. Similarly, in terms of promotion policies, non-Whites may be hired at lower levels, but their promotion to the upper ranks is effectively stopped by discriminatory barriers to mobility. For example, the employer may believe that the other employees will not accept a non-White as their supervisor.

Discrimination in employment can be intentional as well as inadvertent. Employers may not realize that their practices and policies have the effect of excluding non-Whites. The use of standard tests of personality or intelligence to select employees places certain minority groups at a disadvantage since they come from cultures other than the one for which the tests were designed. Recruiting through in-house word-of-mouth techniques often excludes minority applicants since they do not hear about available positions. Requiring Canadian experience and education can effectively eliminate non-Whites, many of whom are immigrants, from job opportunities even though such experience is not necessary to successful job performance.

Thus, there are numerous types of discrimination and numerous ways in which discrimination can be carried out. Our study concentrated essentially on the entry point and/or the selection procedure. In this study, the dynamics of discrimination are studied as discriminatory practices occur, that is, when a job seeker either makes an inquiry on the phone or comes in person to be interviewed. It is at this point that the applicant can run into a prejudiced employer or "gatekeeper" who either presumes that non-Whites are not desired or merely acts according to company policy. The telephone inquiry is particularly crucial at this stage since it is often the first approach made by the job applicant. An individual can be screened out, that is, told quickly and efficiently either that the job has already been filled or that the applicant's qualifications are not suitable. In all likelihood, the applicant will not know that he or she has been the victim of discrimination.

For the purposes of this study, we defined discrimination in employment as those practices or attitudes, willful or unintentional, that have the effect of limiting an individual's or a group's right to economic opportunities on the basis of irrelevant traits such as skin colour rather than an evaluation of true abilities or potential.

IN-PERSON TESTING

In the in-person testing, two job applicants, matched with respect to age, sex, education, experience, physical appearance (dress), and personality, were sent to apply for the same advertised job. The only major difference between our applicants was their race — *one was White and the other, Black.* We created four such teams: one junior male, one junior female, one senior male, and one senior female. The younger teams applied for semiskilled and unskilled jobs such as gas station attendant, bus boy, waitress and clerk and sales help in youth-oriented stores. The senior teams applied for positions in retail management, sales positions in prestigious stores, and waiting and hosting positions in expensive restaurants. The senior team members were, in fact, professional actors. Applying for middle-class type jobs meant that they would be required not only to present a sophisticated image but also to participate in a fairly demanding job interview. Professional actors, we believed, would be more convincing in playing the many roles required for this project. The résumés of the team members were carefully constructed to be as alike as possible. In order to further control possible biases, the staff of testers was changed several times so that no individual personality could account for the results.

The younger teams were composed of high-school and university students who would normally be applying for the same types of job that they applied for in the testing situation. Since we were not testing for sex discrimination and did not want this type of discrimination to account for any of our results, the male teams were sent to traditionally male jobs and the women went to jobs traditionally associated with women's work. In some types of jobs, for example waiter/waitress, both men and women were acceptable. Men and women were sent to such jobs but never to the same job. Each tester had a different résumé for the various types of positions that he or she was applying for, so each member of the senior female team, for example, carried several résumés, one for a secretary, another for a retail sales assistant, a third for a dental technician, etc. Each résumé contained the names of references supplied by business people and friends who had agreed to support our research. Our applicants could thus be checked out by a potential employer who could obtain a reference for the applicant. In actuality, only two employers ever called for references.

RESEARCH PROCEDURE

Each evening, a listing of jobs would be selected for the next day from among the classified advertisements. Some types of jobs were excluded such as those involving driving, where licences could be checked. Jobs which required highly technical skills were also excluded.

The testers were instructed either to go to a certain address or to phone for an appointment. They used standard Canadian accents when phoning since we did not want them to be screened out over the phone. The testers would arrive within approximately one half-hour of each other so that there was little chance that a job had been legitimately filled. In most cases the Black applicant went first. After their interviews the testers completed a summary data sheet especially designed for this project in which they wrote down the details of their treatment and the kinds of information they had been given. Their résumés listed telephone numbers which were in actuality lines connected to the research office. Call-backs for second interviews or with offers of employment were received and recorded by the researchers. On-the-spot offers to the field testers were accepted by them. In the case of call-backs and on-the-spot offers, employers were phoned back, usually within an hour and informed that another position had been accepted, in order to make sure that employer could fill the vacancy as soon as possible.

RESEARCH RESULTS: THE IN-PERSON TEST

In three-and-one-half months of field testing, the testers were able to apply for 201 jobs for a total of 402 individual applications.

For our purposes, racial discrimination in employment was tested in two ways. First, was an offer of employment made to one of the applicants, both applicants, or neither applicant? Second, during the interview, were there any differences in the treatment of the two applicants? The tables below present the numerical results.

Blacks received fewer job offers than Whites. Of a total of 37 valid job offers, 27 went to Whites, 9 to Blacks, and in one

TABLE 16-1   Offer of a job versus no offer

	Number	%
Both offered job	10	5.2
White offered job; Black not	27	13.4
Black offered job; White not	9	4.5
No offer to either	155	77.1
Totals	201	100

TABLE 16-2   Treatment of applicants

	Number of cases
Treated the same	165
Treated differently	36

case both were offered the job (Table 16-1). There were an additional 10 cases where both were offered jobs, but these were for commission sales which involved no cost to the employer. Our overall results therefore show that *offers to Whites outweigh offers to Blacks by a ratio of 3 to 1.*

We had thought that the nature of the job might influence whether Blacks or Whites would be hired. Only Whites received offers for managerial positions or jobs as waiters and waitresses or hosts and hostesses in the restaurant trade. A Black was offered a job in the kitchen when he applied for a waiter's job!

As noted above, the second measure of discrimination was whether differential treatment had occurred during the interview. Table 16-2 presents the results.

Blacks and Whites were treated differently 36 times and in all cases but one the White applicant was preferred to the Black. The ways in which differential treatment took place provide a great deal of insight into the nature of discrimination and its subtleties. Differences in treatment were sometimes very blatant, as the following examples show.

1. Mary, the young Black tester, applied for a sales position in a retail clothing store and was told that the job had already been taken. Sylvia, our White tester, arrived a half-hour later and was given an application form to fill in and told that she would be contacted if they were interested in her.

2. In a coffee shop Mary was told that the job of cashier was taken. Sylvia walked in five minutes later and was offered the job on the spot.

This pattern occurred five times. Another form of differential treatment was

as follows: the Black was treated rudely or with hostility, whereas the White was treated politely. This occurred 15 times.

3. Paul, our White tester, applied for a job as a waiter. He was given an application form to fill out and an interview. He was told that he might be contacted in a week or so. Larry, the Black tester, was also given an application form and an interview. But as the Manager looked over Larry's résumé, he asked Larry if he "wouldn't rather work in the kitchen."

4. Applying for a gas station job, the White tester was told that there were no jobs at present but that he could leave a résumé. The Black tester was told that there were no jobs, but when he asked if he could leave a résumé, he was sworn at: "Shit, I said no didn't I?"

Another form of differential treatment occurred when the wage offers to Blacks and Whites were different. There were two occasions where the Black tester was offered less money than the White tester for the same job. On a few occasions, derogatory comments were made about Blacks in the presence of our White testers. The Blacks being referred to were our own testers!

These results indicate that Black job seekers face not only discrimination in the sense of receiving fewer job offers than Whites but also a considerable amount of negative and abusive treatment while job hunting. The psychological effects of such experiences became evident in the feelings expressed by the research staff. The Black staff felt rejected and some doubted their own ability: "I was beginning to wonder what was wrong with me and why Jean [the White tester] was so much better than me."

In sum, the findings of the in-person test reveal that in 48 job contacts, or 23.8 per cent of the cases, some form of discrimination against Blacks took place. These findings indicate that Blacks and Whites do not have the same access to employment. *Racial discrimination in employment, either in the form of clearly favouring a White over a Black, even though their résumés were equivalent, or in the form of treating a White applicant better than a Black, took place in almost one-quarter of all job contacts tested in this study.* When we examine the results of telephone testing, we will see that this pattern of discrimination occurs again and, if anything, more clearly and strongly.

RESEARCH RESULTS: THE TELEPHONE TEST

We have all had the experience of calling for a job and being told that the job has been filled. We experienced a twinge of disappointment but we rarely felt the need to ask ourselves seriously if we have been told the truth. Members of minority groups have good reason to question whether they have indeed been told the truth. Our study tested this by having callers phone numbers listed in the classified employment section of the newspaper to present themselves as job applicants.

In total, 237 job numbers were phoned. Each job was called four times, once by someone with no discernible accent (apparently a White-majority Canadian), once by someone who had a Slavic or Italian accent, once by a Jamaican-accented caller and finally by a person with a Pakistani accent. Many different jobs

were called ranging from unskilled labour, secretarial, and service, to skilled trade, to managerial. To exclude sex discrimination, callers did not cross traditional sex-role categories. Men were of the same age, education, number of years of job experience, and so on for each type of job. Callers were "older" for jobs requiring more experience and maturity. A profile was provided for each of the callers for each type of job so that they had a secretarial profile, a managerial one, one for waitressing and so on. Jobs to be called were selected from among those that had not appeared in the newspaper the previous day; they were all new jobs. Callers within each sex were given identical lists of jobs to call on the next day and were instructed to begin their calls from the top of the list and proceed in order down the list. All callers were to begin the calling at the same time so that the time span between callers would be minimized. All callers were instructed to use standard English, full sentences, and correct grammar so that the lack of language would not be a discriminating factor against them.

In the telephone testing, discrimination was said to occur when one caller was told that the job had been filled while another caller was told that the job was still available. Discrimination was also said to take place when one caller-applicant with a certain set of qualifications was screened out and told that he or she did not qualify although other callers with the same qualifications were told that they did qualify and were invited to apply. Another form of discrimination was identified as occuring when callers were treated differently from one another in that some and not others were screened to see if they had the experience the employer sought. It has been argued that screening some applicants and not others is not necessarily discriminatory. However, if there is not systematic discrimination present, then we would expect all racial or immigrant groups to be subject to the same proportion of screening.

Results of this procedure were that in 52 per cent of all jobs called there was some form of discrimination present. Either one of our testers was told that the job was filled when another tester was told that the job was open, or one of our testers was treated differently in that he or she was screened while another was not.

There were nine instances where our accented callers were told that they did not qualify for the job even though they presented the same experience and qualifications as the White-majority callers. Needless to say, the White callers were told by these same nine employers that they qualified and were invited to apply. In addition, the employers did not perceive the need to screen all of the four minority-accented callers to the same degree. Employers who treated callers differently, that is, the 123 employers who discriminated in some way, never screened non-accented callers. Italian- or Slavic-accented callers were screened 5 per cent of the time and the two non-White minority callers received three times as much screening as the Whites, on between 15 per cent and 20 per cent of all their calls.

Minority-accented callers did not receive the same information about the status of the job as did Whites. Forty-eight per cent of the jobs were closed to Blacks and 62 per cent were closed to Pakistanis in that the employers told them that the job was filled when the non-accented caller was told that the job was available. Statistical analysis revealed that there were significant differences in the treatment and the type of information that Whites and non-Whites received about work. The Toronto employers discriminated against immigrants in general but to a significantly greater degree against non-White immigrants.

The results of our telephone testing demonstrate that to secure 10 potential job interviews a White Canadian has to make about 11 or 12 calls. White immigrants have to make about 13 calls. Racial minorities must work harder and longer since they must make 18 calls to get 10 potential job interviews. Clearly there are differences in what Whites and non-Whites are being told over the phone about the availability of work in Toronto. And, as noted in the in-person testing, discrimination does not end when a job interview has been obtained.

A RATIO OF DISCRIMINATION

An Index of Discrimination was developed by combining the results of the in-person test and the telephone testing to demonstrate the degree of discrimination experienced by equally qualified persons prior to actual employment. On the phone, Blacks were told that the job was closed to them 20 per cent of the time, whereas the job was closed to Whites only 5.5 per cent of the time. In the in-person test, Blacks experienced discrimination in some form in 18.3 per cent of their job contacts. If these figures are translated into the actual chances of having success in the job search, the figures become even more revealing. Blacks have a 64 per cent chance of getting through a telephone screening, which means that they can secure 13 interviews out of 20 calls. But their chances of actually getting a job *after* an interview are only about 1 in 20. White applicants, on the other hand, are able to pass through screening very successfully, 87 per cent of the time. They can achieve an interview in 17 out of 20 calls. Out of these 17 interviews they manage to receive three offers of employment. *The overall Index of Discrimination is therefore 3 to 1.* Whites have three job prospects to every one that Blacks have.

CONCLUSION

The results of this study clearly indicate that there is very substantial racial discrimination affecting the ability of members of racial minorities to find employment even when they are well qualified and eager to find work. This study examined discrimination only at the very early stages, or entry level, of the employment process. Once an applicant is employed, discrimination can still affect opportunities for advancement, job retention, and level of earnings, to say nothing of the quality of work and the relationships with co-workers.

The findings also support the results of other types of studies done in Canada. We know that indirect measures of discrimination, such as those which reveal income disparities between Whites and non-Whites, all come to similar conclusions: non-Whites in this country are discriminated against. Our studies suggest that discrimination is more widespread than has been thought. Employment discrimination appears not to be the result of a few bigoted employers; there is a system-wide bias against hiring non-Whites. The systemic nature of the discrimination implies that attempting to change the behaviour or the attitudes of individual discriminators will not address the problem. What is required is redress at the system level in order to remove the barriers to the employment of non-Whites so that all Canadians, regardless of colour, can achieve their full potential.

SEVENTEEN

Historical Perspective on Native Peoples

Augie Fleras and Jean Leonard Elliott

AUGIE FLERAS, Associate Professor of Sociology at the University of Waterloo, Waterloo, Ontario, specializes in the field of race and ethnic relations in Canada. He is co-author with Jean Leonard Elliott of *Unequal Relations: An Introduction to Race and Ethnic Dynamics in Canada* (1991) and *Multiculturalism in Canada: Principles, Policies, and Practices* (1991). He also has edited, with Chris O'Toole and Brian Cryderman, *Police, Race and Ethnicity: A Guide for Law Enforcement Officers* (1991). Professor Fleras is currently involved in studies of policing and minorities including programs for culturally-sensitive policing and race relations education for police officials.

JEAN LEONARD ELLIOTT, Associate Professor of Sociology and Social Anthropology at Dalhousie University, Halifax, specializes in the study of indigenous peoples in settler societies. Her books include *Two Nations, Many Cultures: Ethnic Groups in Canada* (1983) and, more recently with Augie Fleras, *Racial and Ethnic Dynamics in Canada* (1991). She has conducted research on Polynesian peoples in Oceania funded by the Social Sciences and Humanities Research Council of Canada.

INTRODUCTION

Canada's treatment of the First Nations people has been called a 'national tragedy' and a 'disgrace,' with ominous parallels to the white supremacist regime in South Africa. There is ample evidence to back up this assertion if only on the grounds of reported federal neglect, longstanding bureaucratic oppression, rejection of meaningful dialogue, and disempowerment of First Nation communities. The First Nations continue to lag far behind non-Native Canadians in terms of socioeconomic status and attainment (Frideres, 1988). Levels of unemployment, undereducation, violent deaths, imprisonment, and ill health outstrip those of other Canadians in virtually all age brackets. Negative stereotypes prevail, in spite of nationally recognized accomplishments on the part of aboriginal individuals in fields as diverse as art, literature, and architecture. Instead of sympathetic portrayals, the First Nations are subjected to intense media publicity — much of it reflecting a popular view of aboriginal peoples as (a) "social problem," (b) "having problems" which cost the Canadian taxpayers, and (c) "creating problems" of concern to Canadian society as a whole. The circulation of this misinformation is unfortunate. Considerable public sympathy and good will toward aboriginal peoples is dissipated as Canadians remain abysmally unaware of what aboriginal peoples want, why they want it, and how they propose to get it (Ponting, 1988). Even the widely publicized incidents at Oka and Akwesasne do not appear to have affected either public or political perception of the first peoples as the "nations within."

This paper will examine the changing fortunes of First Nations-government relations by looking at historical developments in aboriginal policy in its evolution from dependency to limited autonomy. . . . Central to our review is a discussion on the collective restructuring of aboriginal status, from that of dependency and underdevelopment to one that nominally is commensurate with First Nations aspirations for "nations within" status (Fleras, 1990). The next section explores contemporary policy dimensions with respect to First Nation perspectives on aboriginal and treaty rights, land claims settlements, and self-determination through self-government. Finally, government initiatives and responses to aboriginal demands are discussed in light of efforts by federal authorities to "manage change" without losing control of the national agenda.

ABORIGINAL FIRST NATIONS: AN OVERVIEW

Aboriginal peoples comprise an extremely diverse constituency, with numerous tribes (Ojibwa, Cree, Dogrib,

Mohawk, and so on) and varying legal divisions. The term 'aboriginal' encompasses status Indians, non-status Indians, Métis, and Inuit. Status Indians total in excess of 512,000 (about 2 percent of Canada's population) peoples. Membership is defined by (a) admittance to a general registry, (b) affiliation with one of 592 bands (although membership is not automatic) and (c) jurisdiction under the Indian Act. Status Indians reside on one of 2,272 reserves whose populations range in size from about ten to 16,000 at the Six Nations Reserve in Brantford, Ontario. . . .

The population of non-status Indians stands at approximately 75,000. In legal terms, non-status Indians and their descendants have opted out of the Indian Act and are no longer governed by its provisions or privileges. In the past, Native persons relinquished their official status for the right to vote, drink alcohol off the reserve, or (in the case of women) marry a non-Indian. Despite this formal estrangement from their roots, many non-status Indians continue to identify themselves as aboriginal peoples because of shared affinities. Inclusion of non-status Indians as aboriginal peoples by the Canadian Constitution of 1981 has legitimized the identity and concerns of non-status Indians. Nevertheless, relationships between non-status and status Indians have been fraught with difficulties because of competition over limited federal resources.

The third class, the Métis, constitute a rather amorphous category comprising the offspring (and descendants) of mixed unions between Native Indians and early European occupants. Numbering between 100,000 and 400,000 persons, they often dwell in relatively remote communities (in some cases, settlements, such as in Alberta) throughout the Prairie provinces. Although ignored by the Indian Act (like non-status Indians), Métis are officially regarded as aboriginal peoples with a corresponding right to make certain claims upon the Canadian state. Recent government land transfers involving Métis and non-status Indians have given these groups full or partial control of much of Canada's northern land mass. The Alberta government has also recognized Métis' self-governing rights along with the right to limited institutional autonomy.

The Inuit or Eskimo constitute the final category. The 25,000 Inuit enjoy a special status and relationship with the federal government despite never having signed treaty arrangements. The Inuit are currently in negotiations with Ottawa for control over their homeland — Nunavut — in the Eastern Arctic. . . .

COLONIZING THE NATIONS WITHIN: ASSIMILATION AS GOVERNMENT POLICY

> The great aim of our civilization has been to do away with the tribal system and assimilate the Indian people in all respects with the inhabitants of the Dominion, as speedily as they are fit for the change.
>
> Sir John A. Macdonald (1887)
> quoted in Miller (1989).

Federal policy toward aboriginal peoples has evolved over the last century. An initial period of cooperation and accommodation was succeeded by a longstanding objective to eradicate the Indian problem through assimilation and directed culture change. A commitment to assimilationist goals resulted in policy directives focused around (a) Segregation (1867–1945); (b) Integration (1945–1973), and (c) Limited Autonomy (1973–

present). Segregation involved the concentration of Native groups onto reserves for protection from unsavoury white influences, followed by exposure to positive influences for assimilation into the mainstream as independent and hardworking Christian farmers (Miller, 1989). By the late 1940s, there was evidence of a shift from segregation to a move toward integration and ordinary citizenship. In rejecting an agenda of wardship and control, government policies and programs sought to 'normalize' relations with aboriginal peoples by doing away with special and separate status (Boldt and Long, 1988). But aboriginal reaction to the White Paper proved to be strong. By the early 1970s, policy discourse shifted toward a greater tolerance of aboriginal languages and culture as well as proposed institutional control over health and education. At present, the government-federal relations have continued to explore the logical consequences of a commitment to limited autonomy and power-sharing. Nevertheless, a fundamental adherence to assimilation can be detected despite bold talk about self-government, aboriginal and treaty rights, and land claims settlement. In this sense it might be argued the changes in aboriginal-government policy during the past 150 years have been more apparent than real, with major developments restricted to strategies and symbols rather than objectives and content (Boldt and Long, 1988).

[1] Symbiosis and Cooperation (Pre-Confederation)

The ancestors of Canada's Native Indians first appeared as far back as 50,000 years ago by way of the land bridge across the Bering Sea. Prior to the arrival of the first

Europeans, aboriginal nations were firmly established as hunters and foragers throughout much of Canada. Initial contacts with French and British explorers, missionaries, and traders were reasonably cooperative and mutually beneficial. Relationships were based on a principle of co-existence involving reciprocal trade, commercial partnerships, and practical accommodation. The forging of military alliances created a situation where the First Nations were treated diplomatically as powerful nations whose favour had to be curried in pursuit of national goals (Miller, 1989).

[2] Segregation, Wardship, and Protection (1867–1945)

This symbiotic relationship began to unravel by the turn of the 19th century following military transfer of Indian control to civilian forces (Purich, 1986). Reciprocity and accommodation were replaced by a system of internal colonialism and conquest-oriented acculturation, reflecting the need for (a) political control of native populations, (b) protection of British and French interests, and (c) removal of competition for scarce resources. After the 1812 War with the United States, British colonizers no longer required Native Indians as allies. Native lands were increasingly viewed by land-hungry settlers as open spaces for settlement and agriculture.... The First Nations were dismissed as irrelevant to colonial needs. Policy directives revolved about a perception of Natives as an impediment for removal in the march toward progress and settlement (Miller, 1989).

A policy of assimilation evolved as part of this resolve to subdue and control Native Indians. From the early 19th century onwards, the elimination of the Native problem occupied the colony's — later the Dominion's — concerns. Their value as allies, explorers, or traders diminished, with the result that indigenous tribes became irrelevant ... obstacles to the progressive settlement of Canadian society. Authorities rejected extermination as a means to solve the problem, but focused instead on ... assimilation (Miller, 1989). Under assimilation, the dominant sector sought to undermine the cultural distinctiveness of aboriginal tribal society; to subject the indigenes to the rules, values, and sanctions of Euro-Canadian society; and to absorb the deculturated minority into the mainstream through a process of "anglo-conformity" (Frideres, 1988). Strategies to achieve this outward compliance with Euro-Canadian society ("anglo-conformity") lay in the hands of missionaries, teachers, bureaucrats, and law makers (for example the Gradual Enfranchisement Act of 1869 to strip worthy Native individuals of status).

To hasten the assimilation process, Native Indians were placed on reserves for protection from lawless elements interested only in profit or amusement. Reserves offered protection from the ravages brought about by alcohol, trade, and even indigenous practices such as the Sun Dance. Reserves also served as "holding pens" to facilitate the resocialization of these "misguided heathen" or "pestiferous vermin" (depending on one's point of view). Here, the "industrious and peaceful habits" of civilization and Christianity were to be inculcated not only to wean Natives from barbarism but to transform these "wards" of the state into productive, reliant, and God-fearing citizens of the Dominion. ... Federal trusteeship of the First Nations remains intact at present.

The 1985 Supreme Court ruling ('the Musqueam case') confirmed Ottawa's obligation to discharge its trust responsibilities in a manner that protected and advanced aboriginal interests (Miller, 1989).

The reserve system failed to bring about anticipated changes. Even legislation ostensibly aimed at improving the lot of Native communities did not achieve much. The Indian Act of 1876 stripped the indigenes of their political sovereignty, while imposing a system of indirect (elected band council) rule and pervasive segregation. Imposition of internal colonialism resulted in the denial of self-governing rights, foreclosure of social and economic opportunities, and restriction of language and cultural values. These actions proved detrimental to Native Indian communities, despite the protective measures inherent within the Indian Act. Treatment of Native Indians left much to be desired in light of racist and evolutionary philosophies which disparaged them as inferior and helpless (Weaver, 1984). Treaty agreements signed with the federal government resulted in sometimes fraudulent arrangements and illegal land transfers. The concept of guardianship reinforced the stereotype of Native Indians as childlike wards of the state in need of protection by civilizing powers (Davies,1985a; Ponting and Gibbins, 1980; Ponting, 1986). Still, efforts to solve the Indian 'problem' by imposing an assimilationist framework upon Native-government relations prevailed well into the twentieth century.

[3] Integration and Formal Equality (1945–1973)

Canada's treatment of aboriginal people came under scrutiny after the Second World War. Policy reconsiderations came about as a result of the slow pace of directed culture change and economic development, coupled with increases in the Native population and intellectual fashions following wartime experiences (Miller, 1989). A commitment to assimilation gave way to the principles of integration and formal equality as successive governments sought to redefine their responsibilities to aboriginal peoples. In 1947, the government's decision to abolish separate status and administrative structures was formally announced before a Parliamentary Joint Committee (Boldt and Long, 1988). Strategies to desegregate Native Indians and to integrate them into the mainstream gathered momentum during the 1960s. By 1969, the Liberal government under Pierre Elliot Trudeau had proposed legislation for restructuring First Nations-government relations (Weaver, 1981).

The 'White Paper' recommended the eventual elimination of privileges for Native Indians by "normalizing" their entry into Canadian society as 'equals.' Reflecting a belief that the separate and special status of Native Indians kept them from attainment of socioeconomic equality, the White Paper sought to abolish Indian status, terminate federal obligations, allocate reserve resources to individual ownership, and phase out the Department of Indian Affairs (Miller, 1989). The reaction of the Native community caught federal policy-makers off guard. Aboriginal groups were galvanized into protest. ... Foremost among their concerns was the attainment of justice and equality on aboriginal terms, not on those imposed by the central policy structures. Chastened by this collective show of strength, both political and public sectors have displayed growing awareness of and sensitivity to aboriginal issues.

[4] Limited Autonomy (1973–present)

A commitment to the principle of limited autonomy has characterized recent federal initiatives. Since a crucial Supreme Court ruling in 1973, the Canadian government has formally acknowledged the legitimacy of Indian land claims and aboriginal and treaty rights. Even more noticeable have been initiatives by Native Indians to transform the federal policy agenda along lines that recognize the principle of aboriginality. This focus on self-determination through self-government has become more politicized, assertive, and geared toward the constitutional entrenchment of collective aboriginal rights.

In recent years, aboriginal-government relations have continued to explore the potential of a limited autonomy model. The federal government has exhibited a willingness to renegotiate its contractual obligations with the First Nations. Political authorities have reconsidered the principle of aboriginality as a practical alternative, given that moderate reforms no longer strike a responsive chord among aboriginal leaders and activists. This represents a significant reversal from the previous decade when aboriginal and treaty rights were derogated as contrary to liberal-democratic values (Morse, 1985). As we shall see, however, subsequent efforts to specify the nature of these rights have stumbled. The reality gap between original expectations and government actions suggests the so-called 'Indian problem' is indeed a complex and tenacious one.

CONTEMPORARY POLICY DIMENSIONS

Contemporary First Nation policies are focused around several key dimensions related to self-government, aboriginal and treaty rights, and land claims settlement.

(a) Self-Determination Through Self-Government

A major platform revolves about the promotion of First Nation self-determination through implementation of aboriginal self-governing structures. Aboriginal peoples are determined to exercise control over political, cultural, economic, and social issues of concern to them. Constitutionally entrenched provisions for recognition of aboriginal self-governing rights are perceived as an essential step toward resumption of their rightful place as the original occupants of Canada. Ironclad guarantees will allow them to define who they are, who they want to be in the future, and who they were in the past.

The rationale for this argument is based on several lines of reasoning. Arguments for self-government encompass the principle that (a) all aboriginal peoples have the right to control their destiny; (b) international law (to which Canada was a signatory in 1967) stipulates the right to aboriginal self-determination; and (c) such a measure is necessary to avert the further loss of traditional social and cultural patterns. Aboriginal leaders have endorsed self-determination as essential to break the cycle of deprivation, dependency, and underachievement. Some degree of Native control is imperative to achieve meaningful decision-making powers over issues of relevance to them. While acknowledging various models of self-determination (for example, guaranteed Parliamentary representation), current appeals are focused around the concept of Indian self-government powers — a proposal of such elusiveness that most calls for clarification have generated more heat than light.

Attainment of political self-determination through Indian self-government is touted as a key aboriginal plank (Penner, 1983; Little Bear et al., 1984). Even federal and provincial authorities have joined in the growing chorus for support of self-government (Weaver, 1990). To the dismay of policy officials, the concept of self-government is not self-explanatory. Nor do aboriginal groups want to agree on a common definition in keeping with the spirit of local self-determination. Precise definitions are virtually

non-existent outside of a commitment to reduce political and economic dependency in a revised relationship with central authorities. Consensus regarding an ideal self-governing model is nearly absent, although major differences can be discerned between aboriginal and government perceptions as Table 17-1 indicates.

Reflecting the unique historical, demographic, and social circumstances of each reserve, self-governing structures are expected to evolve over time in accordance with local needs and regional aspirations. Yet general patterns can be detected: First, self-governing structures are envisaged as genuine political units that encompass a *distinct order of government* at federal and provincial (occasionally at municipal) levels. Self-govern-

TABLE 17-1　Models of Self-Government

Aboriginal Demands	Federal/Provincial Position
1) Distinct order of government with provincial-like powers	A municipal-type level of government
2) Powers defined by constitution, specifics worked out later	Powers specifically defined by legislation, then constitutionally entrenched
3) Charter individual rights + collective aboriginal rights	Strict application of Charter rights
4) Total ownership of resources + institutional autonomy	Limited ownership and decision-making input
5) Content and style of self-government accountable to Native communities	Self-governing structures accountable to Parliament or constitutional law
6) Powers inherent within aboriginal status and conferred by the Creator for "time immemorial"	Powers to be delegated from central authorities as a 'privilege' that must conform to Canadian laws

ing structures are not delegated by federal authority or Canadian law, but rooted in the reality of aboriginal nationhood, which has never been extinguished.

Jurisdictional matters are expected to vary from band to band, but are likely to include (a) control over the delivery of social services such as policing, education, and health and welfare ('institutional autonomy'); (b) control over resources and use of land for economic regeneration; (c) control over the means to protect and promote the distinct cultural values and language systems; (d) control over band membership and entitlements; and (e) control over federal expenditures according to aboriginal priorities rather than those of the government or bureaucracy. Also anticipated are political structures that reflect local decision-making ('consensual') styles as well as a workable division of labour between the different levels of government. Lastly, strategies to sustain the legitimacy of self-governing doctrines will need to be devised.

The concept of self-government can also be discussed in terms of what it is *not*. Contrary to popular belief, most aboriginal sectors are not interested in seceding from Canadian society. Sovereignty is not identical to political independence or territorial autonomy except perhaps at the level of rhetoric. Native Indians do not want to incur the costs and obligations associated with complete and sovereign status. What is promoted instead is the concept of 'sovereign-association' (first popularized by the Québécois during the 1970s) with relatively autonomous powers over political, economic, cultural, and social domains.

Increasingly apparent in this adjustment process is aboriginal endorsement of a 'nations within' status. Aboriginal leaders categorically reject the view of the First Nations as a collection of Canadian citizens who happen to live on reserves. They see themselves as sovereign and self-governing nations who occupy distinct political status within the Canadian nation-state. Certain inalienable rights and claims follow upon that fundamental recognition. As a 'nation within,' they are anxious to deal with federal authorities on a government-to-government basis. Nor are they pleased with modified models of self-government such as the largely municipal level of government negotiated by the Sechelt in British Columbia in 1986. This version is viewed as dangerous and inadequate (Miller, 1989). Inadequate because the jurisdiction is seen as limiting comprehensive social reform and economic development. Dangerous because municipalities are legal entities that fall squarely under the control and jurisdiction of provincial governments. In other words aboriginal leaders are likely to reject any colonialist model that undermines an inherent right to self-rule and control over their political destiny. But failure to achieve these self-governing rights — despite constitutional guarantees to this effect — indicates further struggles are in store in collectively redefining the 'nations within.'

(b) Aboriginal and Treaty Rights

The second component of aboriginal aspirations revolves about the recognition, definition, and constitutional entrenchment of aboriginal and treaty rights. The First Nations have refused to be labelled as another ethnic or immigrant minority. They ... define themselves as a 'sovereign' entity whose collective rights are guaranteed by virtue of their ancestral occupation. They question an exclusive commitment to individual rights as insufficient for their historically-defined collective aspirations (Boldt and Long, 1984). Nor are they anxious to be integrated as an ethnic component into a Canadian multicultural mosaic — with a corresponding diminishment of their claims. What has been proposed instead is recognition of their sovereign status as the aboriginal inhabitants of Canada, not unlike that of the French in Quebec. Claims to sovereignty are defended either by appeal to natural law or by reference to spiritual grounds (Ahenakew, 1985). As the original occupants whose inalienable rights have never been extinguished by treaty or conquest, aboriginal claims against the state are defended as intrinsic and basic rather than contingent on government largesse or political decree.

Underlying this notion of aboriginal rights are fundamental assumptions that strike at the core of aboriginal-government relations. First and foremost is the notion of aboriginality. Put bluntly, the concept of aboriginality encapsulates a politicized set of claims and entitlements against the state for a fundamental redistribution of power and resources. It rejects the validity of non-native legal, political, cultural, and social values as relevant for aboriginal needs and aspirations. This commitment is particularly evident with moves to attain self-governing control over agendas of pertinence to aboriginal realities. This rejection of non-native priorities is also manifest through attempts to establish institutional autonomy over native education and criminal justice procedures. In light of their unique historical and legal status, programs and policies that apply to other Canadian minority groups are dismissed as inapplicable — even counterproductive — to aboriginal ambitions.

Equally important is the enforcement of federal treaty obligations in renewing aboriginal-government relations. Treaties are regarded as ongoing and organic agreements that specify the special legal status of aboriginal nations. By formally establishing aboriginality as a legal status, the treaties also serve as a basis for meaningful political dialogue at government-aboriginal levels (Hall, 1989). Aboriginal spokespersons have long upheld treaties as semi-sacred and binding documents. Land and resources were exchanged in the past for treaty rights and access to goods and services in perpetuity. As far as these leaders are concerned, the government remains bound to honour the contractual obligations of these treaties. Access to benefits and services (such as free education and tax exemptions) is not a charitable handout. Nor should it be regarded as a benevolent gesture on the part of an enlightened authority. Rather, treaty benefits derive from a legally binding exchange which the Native Indians have paid for over and over again, not only by the expropriation of land and resources, but also through the loss of their lives and lifestyle.

(c) Land Claim Settlements

Recognition of land claims settlements is of upmost importance. Aboriginal ownership and control over land and resources is imperative if Native communities are to secure a solid economic base as a basis for further prosperity and development. Economic benefits can be derived by renting out lands and resources at rates that are favourable to Native interests. They also can be achieved through local development (in tandem with public or private interests) at a pace that reflects community priorities and developmental levels. Recourse to a solid economic base is central. Indeed, any fundamental changes in the status of aboriginal people can only be achieved when negotiating from a position of economic strength and the political power that sustains it.

To recapitulate, aboriginal demands are consistent with their image as a unique nation within a federalist framework. Aboriginal peoples are not seeking to separate from Canada. They do not want to impose their vanishing lifestyles on the non-native component. Instead, they are looking to find a *middle* way.... A commitment to self-governing status is endorsed as a compromise between the extremes of separatism and absorption. Second, they don't want to preserve their cultural lifestyle in amber for the edification of purists or tourists. But they also refuse to abandon their language and culture in exchange for an alien and incompatible set of non-native values and beliefs. As a compromise, they want to take select and relevant elements of the past and to apply them to the realities of the present. They want to be modern in other words, but not at the expense of what makes them unique. Third, aboriginal peoples are pragmatists who wish to achieve a working balance between the cultural and spiritual values of the past on the one hand, with the technological benefits of modern society on the other. Fourth, achievement of political and economic power is viewed as critical in order to rebuild their communities into flourishing centres of meaningful activity. Yet these goals are unacceptable if attained at the cost of undermining their social obligations, collective and community rights, and cultural/spiritual val-

ues. Whether aboriginal peoples can utilize the resources available to forge a 'golden mean' between seemingly unworkable extremes cannot be answered as yet.

FEDERAL RESPONSE — SUBSTANCE OR SMOKESCREEN?

Both federal and provincial reaction to aboriginal demands is shaped by a fundamental duality. On the one hand, political authorities appear receptive to aboriginal claims. A revised social-political contract based on the principle of self-determination through Indian self-government has achieved moderate success (Mulroney, 1985). Certain bands have exerted some level of control over the design and delivery of service programs, in addition to some say in spending priorities through "alternative funding agreements" and "community-based negotiations" (Frideres, 1990; Weaver, 1990). Implementation of self-governing apparatus has taken place among the Naskapi-Cree of James Bay in 1975, the Nishnawbe-Aski Nation of Northern Ontario, and the Sechelt in British Columbia, with negotiations currently underway elsewhere.

The settlement of outstanding land claims has also shown promise. In 1988, for example, the federal government transferred almost 180,000 square kilometres plus $500 million to the 13,000 Dene and Métis of the MacKenzie River Valley — making it the largest North American land transfer since the United States purchased Alaska from Russia in 1867 (*Toronto Globe and Mail*, 3 September 1988). Two additional agreements in principle proposed for ratification in the 1990s will transfer ownership of another 550,000 square kilometres, as well as a say in the development of another 2.5 million square kilometres. When coupled with earlier arrangements, northern aboriginal peoples will possess full or partial control of over 40 percent of Canada's land mass.

Yet federal authorities have been slow to respond to aboriginal demands. In spite of lofty promises and reassuring speeches, there remains a noticeable lack of political will for implementing much of this rhetoric (Weaver, 1990). Government foot-dragging in this area appears guided by perceptions of the general public as ignorant of, disinterested in, or opposed to, key aboriginal issues (Ponting, 1988). It is also undermined by a pervasive commitment to assimilate the First Nations into Canada's institutional framework by transfering federal responsibility to provincial spheres (Boldt and Long, 1988). Instead of the cultural assimilationist ethos that prevailed prior to the 1970s, assimilation is now couched in efforts to (a) phase out separate institutional structures, (b) formally rationalize First Nation-government relations through land corporations and municipal governing structures, and (c) incorporate the First Nations into the legal, administrative, and political structures of Canadian society. Moves to operationalize the principle of aboriginality as well as to clarify its meaning and nature, have thus proceded slowly. This is hardly surprising in view of the risks involved in defining a new order of government. There are numerous pitfalls in trying to politically accommodate the principle of aboriginality into the overall polity of a sovereign state (Asch, 1984). None more so than a fundamental paradox that inheres in formulating government policy and administration.

Ambiguity and Paralysis

Much of the resistance and reluctance in redefining aboriginal-government relations reflects inherent limitations in the policy design and implementation process. Put bluntly, federal policy and administration is not necessarily aimed at assisting those it was designed for. Instead of dealing with a problem and solution, both policy and administration decisions reflect a response to values, priorities, and constraints of those often remote from constituents and administered by others who are not answerable to clients for their actions (Miller, 1989).

Reflecting this fundamental ambivalence in the decision-making process, policy officials are understandably less than enthused about dissolving once habitual patterns of domination in place of radically-defined concepts for aboriginal rights and self-determination (Boldt and Long, 1985). They prefer to accept Indian self-government as an accountable political concession, rather than an aboriginal right derived from natural or spiritual law (Tennant, 1985). Self-governing structures are limited to those that are consistent with Canada's legal and constitutional makeup such as the Charter of Rights and Freedoms. Devolutionary powers are delegated and answerable to central authorities, not inherent and expansive as proposed by the First Nations (see also Fleras, 1991 for comparable analysis in New Zealand). Not surprisingly, even concessions by the government are scrutinized carefully by aboriginal leaders. In the case of the Sechelt of British Columbia, the attainment of municipal-type level of self-government has been attacked as extending provincial jurisdiction over aboriginal affairs (Hall, 1986).

Equally evident has been the absence of political unanimity over aboriginal issues. Dualistic viewpoints exist regarding the nature of the 'Indian problem' and how best to resolve it. As Ponting notes (1988):

> This ambivalence might reflect the tension between two Canadian conceptions of equality — equality of status (no special privilege) and equality of opportunity, where the latter sometimes requires remedial action that contradicts the former by virtue of the fact that it is intended to benefit only some people.

This ambiguity is expressed on the one hand by those who favour federal spending cuts, abolition of the Department of Indian Affairs, and curtailment of federal services (*Toronto Globe and Mail*, 12–13 March 1986; also, 11 May 1988). Such a position would appear consistent with current political moves toward fiscal restraint, political rationality, and debureaucratization of the social policy agenda (see Prince, 1987). On the other hand are those who have endorsed self-government and aboriginal rights as a basic human right (Penner, 1983; *Toronto Globe and Mail* 20 May 1986). Failure to establish a coherent and enlightened policy framework has been detrimental in forging an acceptable formula for aboriginal-government relations.

THE DEPARTMENT OF INDIAN AFFAIRS: FROM RESISTANCE TO RESIGNATION

Nowhere are the ambiguities in restructuring First Nation-government relations more visible than at the level of policy administration. For the past 125 years, government policy and administration by the Department has remained remarkably steadfast (Ponting and Gibbins, 1980). Reflecting a commitment to assimilate and civilize, Departmental policy has labelled Natives as a problem whose cultural and social idiosyncracies preclude a smooth absorption into society. After World War II, political awareness of the problem shifted from cultural assimilation to the eradication of poverty at physical, social, cultural, and psychological levels (Shkilnyk, 1985). In an effort to do away with the Indian problem, there appeared a commitment to "modernization" under the guise of economic development of Native communities.

Removal of obstructions to development and growth entailed a variety of strategies. Native Indians were encouraged to move off the reserves (which were dismissed as nothing more than breeding grounds for violence, apathy, and alienation). Exposure to modern values and institutional involvement was extolled as crucial for facilitating this transition. Alternatively, the government became anxious to modernize reserves by upgrading facilities and infrastructures with federal funding and expertise. While benefits appeared from . . . this largely economic solution, the continued inpoverishment and alienation of Native communities suggests errors in the analysis and assessment of the problem, followed by misguided (if well intentioned) solutions (Shkilnyk, 1985).

The Department of Indian Affairs has provided questionable leadership for furthering aboriginal concerns. This is hardly unexpected in light of its prevailing mandate and constraints under which it must operate. Firmly rooted in the antiquated 1951 Indian Act, the Department remains a largely administrative organ, rather than a developmental agency to enhance First Nations concerns (Weaver, 1990; also Fleras, 1985). For example,

Ponting (1986) has referred to the Department as a 'money-moving' agency whose primary role is to allocate funds on the basis of compliance to organizational directives. Others have also described such government bodies as systems of containment with bureaucratic imperatives at odds with aboriginal needs (Fleras, 1989). Rather than promoting change from within, attention instead is focused on control, predictability, and reliability — primarily by (a) reinforcing rules, (b) proper communication ('going through the channels'), (c) primacy of conformity ('go by the book'), and (d) pervasive hierarchy (see Weber, 1947). To no one's surprise, the potential for meaningful interaction is diminished when aboriginal-government interaction is conducted along the grounds of impersonal and hierarchical authority formal rationality, a complex division of labour, and specificity of procedures and rules.

OKA AND BEYOND: ONE STEP FORWARD ...

If nothing else ... incidents at Akwesasne and Oka during the summer of 1990 have drawn public and political attention to inadequacies in government policy and administration of First Nations affairs. While it was easy to be blinded by the dazzling array of armaments and blockades, the underlying issue in each case revolved about the more fundamental issue of restructuring aboriginal-government relations in a manner that reflected First Nations interests rather than those of federal or provincial authorities. However, despite the seeming novelty of the stakes at hand, government assessment and reponse (a "law and order" issue) was not altogether unex-

pected given the political economy of Canadian society.

Governments have sought by varying means to defuse, perhaps even circumvent, aboriginal challenges to the prevailing social order. They have attempted to address aboriginal concerns, but not outside the framework of central policy structures or the liberal-democratic state (Fleras, 1989). Policy responses to aboriginal demands have been ambiguous to say the least. Conflicts and contradictions continue to pervade the interaction between political and aboriginal sectors. Some are confused or frustrated by the highly unorthodox nature of aboriginal demands. Others are against aboriginal claims preferring, instead, the . . . status quo. Still others are in general agreement with aboriginal aspirations, but seek refuge in conventional solutions.

At one level, political authorities appear willing in theory to acknowledge the plausibility of aboriginal demands as a policy item, if only to avert a crisis of legitimacy and restore some semblance of political tranquility. Such an endorsement can be attributed in part by a desire to maintain credibility in the face of potential embarrassment and ridicule (Dyck, 1985). In part it also stems from fear of international censure and the threat of sanctions. Few politicians can afford to dismiss the existence of aboriginal rights or ignore the validity of special status and preferential treatment. What they have debated instead are answers over defining their limits, and how best to concede these rights without destroying the social fabric in the process. Also evident is political resignation to negotiate over issues related to self-determination, even self-government if necessary, although not to the extent of condoning territorial secession and dismemberment of the state (Boldt and Long, 1985).

At another level, however, are widespread misgivings about the concept of aboriginal status and the corresponding assumptions underlying the distribution of power and resources in society. The principle of aboriginality and aboriginal rights are often vague and amorphous, and beyond the comprehension of central authorities. The grounds for miscommunication are readily discerned. Aboriginal claims — with their focus on charter status and non-negotiable collective rights — are often in conflict with the individualistic and universal values embedded within liberal-democratic contexts (Weaver, 1984; Boldt and Long, 1984). Not unexpectedly, acceptance has been slow in acknowledging aboriginality as a guiding principle for redefining abo-riginal-government relationships. . . . Recent changes in aboriginal-government relations are more symbolic than real.

With the exception of the Constitution Act of 1982 (that entrenched aboriginal and treaty rights) there has been little appreciable gain with respect to First Nation empowerment. What we have instead is bitterness and acts of retribution following a breakdown in negotiations. The omens for the future of Canada are foreboding in light of the precedent-smashing initiatives of Elijah Harper and the Warrior Societies. How many more Okas will Canada endure before First Nation-government relations achieve a level of cooperation and power-sharing that is acceptable to both parties?

References

Ahenakew, David. "Aboriginal Title and Aboriginal Rights: The Impossible and Unnecessary Task of Identification and Definition" in *The Quest for Justice. Aboriginal Peoples and Aboriginal Title*, Menno Boldt and J. Anthony Long, (eds.). Pp. 24–30. Toronto: University of Toronto Press, 1985.

Asch, Michael. *Home and Native Land: Aboriginal Rights and Canadian Constitution.* Toronto: Methuen, 1984.

Boldt, Menno and J. Anthony Long. "Tribal Traditions and European-Western Political Ideology: The Dilemma of Canadian Native Indians." *Canadian Journal of Political Science* 17 (1984): 537–554.

———. "Native Self-Government: Instrument of Autonomy or Assimilation? In *Governments in Conflict? Provinces and Indian Nations in Canada.* J. Anthony Long and Menno Boldt, (eds.). Pp. 38–56.

Toronto: University of Toronto Press, 1988.

Davies, Maureen. "Aspects of Aboriginal Rights in International Law." In *Aboriginal Peoples and the Law.* Bradford W. Morse, (ed.), pp. 16–47. Ottawa: Carleton University Press, 1985a.

Dyck, Noel, ed. *Indigenous People and the Nation-State. Fourth World Politics in Canada, Australia, and Norway.* St. John's, Nfld: Memorial University, 1985.

Fleras, Augie. "Towards 'Tu Tangata': Historical Developments and Current Trends in Maori Policy and Administration." *Political Science* (NZ) 37 (1985): 18–39.

———. "Inverting the Bureaucratic Pyramid: Debureaucratizing the Maori Affairs Bureaucracy in New Zealand." *Human Organization* 48(3) (1989): 214–225.

———. "Race Relations as Collective Definition: Aboriginal-Government Relationships in Canada." *Symbolic Interaction* 13(1) (1990): 19–34.

_____. "Aboriginality as a Language Issue: the Politicization of 'te Reo Maori' in New Zealand." *Plural Societies* 17(2) (1991): 25–51.

Frideres, James. *Native Peoples in Canada. Contemporary Conflicts.* 3rd Edition. Scarborough, Ont: Prentice-Hall, 1988.

_____ "Policies on Native Peoples in Canada" in *Race and Ethnic Relations in Canada.* Peter S. Li (ed.). Toronto: Oxford University Press, 1990.

Hall, Anthony J. "Self-Government or Self-Delusion? Brian Mulroney and Aboriginal Rights." *Journal of Native Studies* VI (1986): 77–89.

Little Bear, L., Boldt, Menno, and Long, J. Anthony, eds. *Pathways to Self-Determination. Canadian Indians and the Canadian State.* Toronto: University of Toronto Press, 1984.

Miller, J.R. *Skyscrapers Hide the Heavens. A History of Indian-White Relations in Canada.* Toronto: University of Toronto Press, 1989.

Morse, Bradford, W., ed. *Aboriginal Peoples and the Law.* Ottawa: Carleton University Press, 1985.

Mulroney, Brian. "Statement by the Prime Minister of Canada to the Conference of First Ministers on the Rights of Aboriginal Peoples." In *The Quest for Justice. Aboriginal Peoples and Aboriginal Rights.* Menno Boldt and J. Anthony Long, (eds.). Pp. 148–156, Toronto: University of Toronto Press, 1985.

Penner, Keith. *Indian Self-Government in Canada.* Report of the Special Committee chaired by Keith Penner. Ottawa: Queens Printer for Canada, 1983.

Ponting, J. Rick. *Arduous Journey. Cana-dian Indians and Decolonization.* Toronto: McClelland and Stewart, 1986.

_____. "Public Opinion on Aboriginal Rights and Land Issues in Canada and Australia." Paper Presented to the 1988 Biennial Conference of the Association of Canadian Studies in Australia and New Zealand." Canberra, Australia, 1988.

Ponting, J. Rick and Gibbins, Roger. *Out of Irrelevance: A Socio-Political Introduction to Indian Affairs in Canada.* Toronto: Butterworths, 1980.

Prince, Michael J. "How Ottawa Decides Social Policy: Recent Changes in Philosophy, Structure, and Process." In *The Canadian Welfare State: Evolution and Transition*, Jacqueline S. Ismael, (ed.). Pp. 247–273. Edmonton: University of Alberta, 1987.

Purich, Donald. *Our Land: Native Peoples in Canada.* Toronto: James Lorimer, 1986.

Shkilnyk, Anastasia. *A Poison Stronger Than Love.* New Haven, Conn: Yale University Press, 1985.

Tennant, Paul. "Aboriginal Rights and the Penner Report on Indian Self-Government." In *The Quest for Justice. Aboriginal Peoples and Aboriginal Rights.* Menno Boldt and J. Anthony Long, (eds.). Pp. 321–332. Toronto: University of Toronto Press, 1985.

Weaver, Sally M. *Making Canadian Indian Policy: The Hidden Agenda, 1968-1970.* Toronto: University of Toronto Press, 1981.

_____. "Struggles of the Nation-State To Define Aboriginal Ethnicity: Canada and Australia." Pp. 182–210 in *Minorities & Mother Country Imagery*, edited by G. Gold. Institute of Social and Economic Research Number 13. St John Nfld: Memorial University Press, 1984.

Weber, Max. *The Theory of Social and Economic Organisation.* New York: Oxford University Press, 1947.

Gender Relations

This section is about the unequal relations between males and females — *gender relations* — in Canada today. It includes articles on work-sharing in the home, changed patterns of thinking in the (male-dominated) steel factory, and the reasons why women became segregated into office work.

North Americans seem to be more involved in the battle of the sexes than they are in the class struggle. Gender relations in Canada really are a battle; and, like the class struggle, they are a battle about inequality. Canadians are generally aware of the gender struggle, and they have sympathy for the underdog too. In fact, most women are fully aware of being underdogs.

The materials in this section on gender relations run the ideological gamut. Some are traditionally liberal: mainly concerned about equal treatment for women at home and in the workplace. Others illustrate the radical feminists; they are concerned with locating gender inequality within a broader historical pattern of domination and exploitation.

A problem for radical feminists is reconciling Marxist theories of class domination with theories of "patriarchy" or male domination. In a very general way, the two inequalities are similar. Marx emphasized that control over the means of production is the basis of all inequality. In western societies, which followed the Roman legal practice of *patria potestas* (literally, the "powerful father"), the male family head exercises supreme legal authority over his family. The family head historically controlled means of production within the household.

In a society based on this patriarchal tradition, wives, like children, servants and pets, have no legal authority over the family or its property. Women exercise some actual control over household functioning and child rearing. However it is the all-powerful father/husband who bestows his managerial right. A wife's authority cannot stand up against her husband's in a conflict of wills.

Thus, there is male domination of the means of household production, just as class exploitation is typically male domination of the means of paid production. What is not clear is why biological (i.e., sexual) characteristics should influence domination at all. Why is sex an important dividing line between dominator and dominated, while other biological traits like hair colour, shoe size, and IQ are not? Nor is it clear how and why gender inequality continues, despite a reduction of class inequality. If private property or capitalism are to blame, why does gender inequality remain a serious problem in many socialist and communist countries?

For whatever reason, *patriarchy* — the domination of women by men — is part of our cultural heritage (Fox, 1988). Patriarchy has a very long history. Some part of the male domination that persists today is simply a holdover from earlier, agricultural times. Then, a sexual division of labour may have been more necessary; in any event, men could impose it more easily.

If we search beyond this "cultural lag" explanation, we realize that discrimination against women often benefits men economically. When discrimination is widely accepted, male employers can pay female workers less than they would have to pay male workers. Discrimination in hiring and promotion also reduces, by half, the number of people with whom male workers have to compete.

With the growth of dual earner families, this problem begins to solve itself. After all, the discriminated-against women are consumers as well as producers, wives and daughters as well as competitors. Perhaps, as more women enter the labour market, this contradiction itself will help to eliminate gender discrimination.

However domestic duties also impede women's economic progress. Married women who work for pay customarily work a "double day": one day's work for their employer and another day's work for their family. A great deal of evidence from around Canada and elsewhere shows that when married women go out to work for pay, their husbands do *not* significantly increase the time they spend on domestic duties. Moreover, there is little sign that husbands are improving from one decade to another: domestic work remains very unequal.

There are only so many solutions to this problem. Wives can try to force their spouses and children to cooperate more; but so far, such attempts have met with little success. Wives can simply work harder and risk their mental and physical health. They can opt for part-time rather than full-time paid work — especially while their children are very young — and there is evidence that many women are doing this. They can rely more on paid domestic and child-care services (daycare, fast food, house cleaners, and so on). Or they can set their aspirations and expectations low and think of the paid work they are doing as a job, not a career.

In traditionally male-dominated careers, women have the greatest difficulty lowering their aspirations and expectations; and here, women's domestic lives are at the greatest risk. Compared with women in traditionally female careers or mere jobs, women in traditionally male careers are less likely to marry; if married, less likely to remain married; or, if remaining married, less likely to bear children (Marshall, 1987). Women find it virtually impossible to have a serious career *and* a serious marriage, since they are expected to carry their full weight in both activities. Our culture forgives husbands for a lack of domestic involvement, but it does not forgive wives.

By assigning women a double day, our culture is saying that housework is worth little in comparison with other kinds of work. Women are worth little, since they earn less than men at paid work; therefore, they should do the housework. In conclusion, women's time is worth less than men's. As Margrit Eichler (1990) has written, "when we cease to define people as dependents, or when the power position of a group of people changes, the value of their time will change." And only then.

When women accept a heavy domestic responsibility, they find it hard to compete effectively with men at work. Employers consider female employees less valuable, since they are less available. Continued gender inequality at home almost ensures continued gender inequality in the workplace.

This aside, many young women are continuing to train for occupations that have limited potential for employment, promotion, or pay. Educational streaming starts well before a person reaches post-secondary education. In fact, it has begun by the time a student enters adolescence and selects his/her high school courses.

Research shows girls are less likely than boys to select academic, university-bound programs of study. If they aim at post-secondary education at all, they are likely to head for community colleges. And if they aim at university, they are more likely than males to head for a university program that females have traditionally dominated — arts, nursing, social work. Typically, graduates of these programs receive lower pay than graduates of male-dominated university programs.

Finally, cultural incapacitation plays a part in gender inequality. Our culture teaches women that they cannot do many kinds of activity: they are sexual objects and delicate pets, not thinkers, decision-makers, political actors. Women are made to feel dependent, and this dependency justifies their subordination. Ever fewer women are accepting such "second class citizenship," but many still feel guilty about straying outside their prescribed "ladylike" roles.

A paper in this section, by Martin Meissner, studies the "domestic economy" and attempts to measure what women do at home. Males have traditionally believed that (females) homemakers contribute little of value to the family's well-being or the economy as a whole. Homemakers receive no wages or pension for the work they do, and since our society values most what is paid most, homeworkers appear valueless.

Today, we are gaining a new appreciation for homemakers. As more women go out to work, husbands increasingly have to pay cash for homemaking services that wives once provided "free of charge." This payment of cash for daycare, food preparation, house cleaning, laundry, and otherwise, helps husbands appreciate what they have lost. And, as more marriages dissolve, more men have to master the traditionally female skills of child care and housekeeping. This acquaints them firsthand with the effort and skill that homemaking has always required.

Still, wives continue to inhabit the worst of all possible worlds. They have to perform household duties that consume their time and skill and, therefore, are tiring. Yet no one pays for these efforts in cash or respect. Wives with careers spend slightly less time on housekeeping than other wives, but get little more help from their husbands. They are expected to contribute significantly to the family income and prove themselves "equal to men" in the workplace. In short, the widespread entry of women into the workforce has created a cadre of overworked, underappreciated women.

The result was predictable. Increased tension feeds marital conflict and leads women to make excessive use of tranquilizers. Many women also feel guilt and anxiety about the jobs they have done inadequately.

In his classic work *The Sociological Imagination* (1959), C. Wright Mills argued that a main purpose of the sociological enterprise is to show the connection between personal troubles and major trends in society. Important social changes produce personal problems. To mobilize for social change, people need to see the connection between their troubles and social or political issues.

Consider, then, women's double day as a personal trouble and public issue. Women do much more than their share of family work. Because they do so much, they are always short of time. Even little things like getting the kids out of bed, dressed, and off to school create a lot of tension. After taking care of everyone else, mother must ready herself for work, board the public transit (typically, father has taken the family car), and get to work on time.

Can we solve this personal trouble by treating it as a public issue? Michelson (1985) suggests we ought to increase flexibility in work timing, public transportation, and the location of shopping and workplaces. This would make it easier for working women to meet all their obligations. But should this really be a public issue, to be handled by public debate, legislation, and the spending of tax dollars?

Some might argue that women can solve the problem within their own home, as a personal trouble: for example, by taking a more assertive approach towards their husbands and children. Then, women would not try to do everything; they would force their husbands to share the load (and the family car). Either both spouses would share the load equally, or they would learn to live with lower standards of family caretaking. In either case, the pressure on women would lessen.

Such a change does not seem to be in the cards, largely because of the cultural tradition of female service and subservience. Most people view too much assertiveness and too little nurturance as "unfeminine" behaviour. Perhaps the problem will be remedied in a few generations, by women who have been socialized differently. But many women may not want to wait that long for a change. For the sake of adult participants and their innocent children, the battle of the sexes needs a quick and fundamental resolution.

The workplace is also in crisis. Here, people fight the battle of the sexes in terms of economic and organizational issues. The article below by David Livingstone and Meg Luxton shows that the fight is particularly acute in workplaces — such as steel factories — that have historically been dominated by men. There, a traditional masculine culture makes it very difficult for male workers to accept female workers as colleagues. As in the home, people's thinking about gender relations and women's problems vary widely. One approach supports equal opportunity and opposes discrimination against women. Another wants to change women's aspirations and encourage non-traditional ambitions.

Gender inequality in the workplace is, at least in part, a result of differential career selection. In turn this traces back to educational streaming and childhood socialization. Rooting out job discrimination against women will be easier when women regularly equip themselves with the skills and aspirations male-dominated occupations often demand. (As Jane Gaskell's article in Section Ten shows, it will also require a change in our thinking about what skills really matter in the work world, and a reassessment of the skills women possess.)

The parental division of labour significantly affects girls' own job and family expectations. However we can do little about what goes on in people's homes. That's why we need to concentrate our efforts elsewhere — for example, in the schools — to achieve gender equality. School is one place to teach egalitarian social values and show the possibility of gender equality. Schools can go much farther than they have towards achieving this goal.

With the rapid increase in office automation, women also need new work skills. That is because employers need fewer women to do clerical work than in the past, for example. Except for robotics, which displaces the unskilled and semi-skilled manual worker, automation has had little impact on males. Automation is likely to affect a large portion of the female labour force far more profoundly.

Work has already become very bureaucratic — that is, more rule-oriented — and more dependent on high technology. The effects of bureaucratization (in particular) are captured in an article by Graham Lowe. His historical perspective helps us understand some of the current peculiarities of modern office work: why, typically, it is not unionized, is done by women, and is subject to major technological change. Office work will undoubtedly see a lot of turbulent change in the next few decades, as technological and organizational innovations make themselves felt.

The new technology may throw many women out of work. Other women will be stuck with less varied and responsible jobs than they had before. Men may be the first, if not only, beneficiaries of technological advance. For this reason, unemployment is increasingly a women's issue. Other things being equal, women are more often unemployed than men; but other things are not equal. Women generally work in jobs where unemployment is more likely and the consequences more severe than in other sectors. Women are less likely to be unionized, hence more vulnerable. Women get paid less, hence can save less to prepare themselves for the effects of unemployment.

As already noted, women are more likely to suffer discrimination in hiring and promotion. Unmarried women with children to raise are more likely to work part-time, and are therefore less protected by benefits and pensions. They are more likely to fall into poverty and, without good inexpensive daycare, less likely to get a job that would pull them out of it. Taken together, all these factors, and others are producing what people are calling the "feminization of poverty."

References

Eichler, Margrit. "Gender and the value of time." Pp. 396–405 in James Curtis and Lorne Tepperman, (eds.) *Images of Canada: The Sociological Tradition*. Scarborough: Prentice-Hall Canada, 1990.

Fox, Bonnie. "Conceptualizing patriarchy." *Canadian Review of Sociology and Anthropology*, 25: 2 (May, 1988) 163–182.

Marshall. Katherine. "Women in male-dominated professions." *Canadian Social Trends*, Winter, 1987.

Michelson, William. "The daily routin employed spouses as a public affairs

agenda." *Public Affairs Report*, Vol. 26, August, 1985, No. 4.

Mills, C.W. *The Sociological Imagination*. New York: Oxford, 1959.

EIGHTEEN

The Domestic Economy

Martin Meissner

MARTIN MEISSNER is Professor of Sociology at the University of British Columbia. Since he published the book, *Technology and the Worker*, he has studied the difference that technology makes in communication between industrial workers ("The language of work"), and described "The sign language of sawmill workers in British Columbia" (together with the anthropologist, Stuart Philpott). He has examined the sexual division of labour in households, analyzing time budgets of married couples in Vancouver ("No exit for wives," "Sexual division of labour and inequality." "The domestic economy — half of Canada's work"); and the way in which sexual inequality is perpetuated in daily communication practices ("The reproduction of women's domination in organizational communication"). Professor Meissner is now studying the effect of changing technology on the knowledge and skill requirement of work in offices and households. As part of his research work, Professor Meissner spent a year at the International Institute for Labour Studies in Geneva, and some time in Paris, on invitation from the Laboratoire de Sociologie du Travail and the Organization for Economic Cooperation and Development.

THE CASE OF MRS. GRIFFITHS

Not far from Hope, British Columbia, in 1973, a Canadian Pacific locomotive collided with an automobile at a level crossing. Mrs. Griffiths, a passenger in the car, died a week later. . . .

David Griffiths sued Canadian Pacific Railways. . . .

The lawyer asked me to be an expert witness at the trial in the Supreme Court of British Columbia and to prepare an estimate of the number of housework hours that a women in Mrs. Griffiths' circumstances would do for the remainder of her life with Mr. Griffiths; an actuary was asked to translate these hours into a monetary claim. At age 30, with a husband aged 35, and five children between 4 and 11 years old at the time of her death, Mrs. Griffiths would have done over 84,000 hours of housework until her husband reached the life expectancy for men of his age.

In his decision, Justice Mackoff reduced the amount claimed under the Families Compensation Act for the loss of household services accustomed to be performed by the wife, which will have to be replaced by hired services" (Mackoff, 1974: 11) from $157,410 to $40,000. His reasons went as follows:

The actuarial evidence . . . only places a dollar value on services but it does not subtract therefrom . . . the dollar cost to obtain those services. It fails to take into consideration the cost to the husband in providing for the wife's food, clothing, shelter, etc., for the period of time for which damages for the loss of her services is claimed. It also fails to take into account the contingencies of life.

The prospects of remarriage of the husband require consideration. At the present time, realistically, the prospects are poor indeed. The plaintiff stated, "I don't think I would want to remarry." But even if he had affirmatively expressed his wish to remarry, it is most unlikely that any reasonable women would marry this man and assume the burden of raising five children in the circumstances therein described. However, with the passage of time as the children grow up and leave home, his prospects for remarriage, should he wish to remarry, will brighten. He is 39 years of age and his youngest child is 7. Ten years from now he will still be a relatively young man, the children will have grown up and the prospects of his remarriage will be totally changed from what they are at present. As well to be taken into consideration in such cases was the possibility of the loss of the wife's services by reason of her being incapacitated, either temporarily or permanently, because of illness or accident. Nor can it be assumed in today's society that a marriage will not terminate by separation or divorce. None of the foregoing were taken into account by the actuary and that being so, the figure arrived at is obviously not the answer to the question before me (Mackoff, 1974: 12–13).

A double irony seemed at work. A man received money for the missed personal services of his dead wife, while she was paid nothing for it when alive. (Note the exclusion of conceivable money transfers to the wife from the judge's list of the costs of household services.) The improbable future wife was also not worth the money from Canadian Pacific that would have been meant for that part of Nellie Griffiths' unlived housekeeping life which she, the unlikely second Mrs. Griffiths, would perform.

The case was a "first." It introduced into Canadian courts the recognition of the full value (in hours at least, though not in money) of a women's lifetime of domestic labour. At the same time it confirmed its worthlessness for a *living* wife, while granting its value for the benefit of the husband.

In one breath, almost, housework is first noticed and valued and then disappears again. It suffers that peculiar fate — now you see it, now you don't — from all sides. The magazine for women, *Ms.*, put the phrase "working women" prominently on its cover of May 1980, and specified inside (p. 2) who they are: decidedly not housewives. Over the full spectrum of opinion, the pervasive usage of "working" "productive" and "active" (as in "the active population") turns the domestic *work* of women into nonwork, the daily, year-long and lifetime effort into inactivity.

ECONOMIC ACCOUNTS

Housework has not figured much in economic work, in theory or in economic accounting. On the accounting side, seven U.S. estimates from 1919 to 1970, and a British and a Swedish estimate were reviewed and made comparable by Hawrylshyn (1976: 108–11). These estimates were expressed as a ratio of the value of housework relative to the value of the GNP exclusive of housework, and averaged 34 percent. Hawrylshyn also made three assessments for Canada with the census of 1971. The opportunity cost, the cost of replacing individual functions, and the cost of replacement by a housekeeper came to a dollar value of housework "equivalent to 39, 40, and 33 percent of GNP," respectively (Hawrylshyn, 1978: 29).

When I take my estimate of labor-force hours as the time equivalent of the GNP, and domestic work hours as equivalent to the dollar value of housework, the result is a figure of 95.7 percent, a ratio of domestic to market activity two-and-a-half times that of the average money estimates. Each of the three methods of estimating the money value of housework has built into it the social prejudices that make for different incomes of women and men. At the same time that this rare instance of economic accounting seems to give housework its proper place, it takes much of it away again in the undervaluation of women's work which underlies the wage rates used for these calculations. A similar "now you see it, now you don't" has occurred in the Marxist-feminist debate (summarized in Fox, 1980; Kaluzynska, 1980; and Molyneux, 1979), on the question of whether housework is "productive labor."

How Much Housework Does a Woman Do?

How much housework has there been, relative to other work, and how has that relation changed in the 65 years from 1911 to 1976 in Canada? In answer to the question of how much, I start with hours of work in three different ways. One of these tells of average hours spent in a week, for samples of people with different characteristics. I then go back to the court case, in order to estimate the lifetime hours that one (artificially constructed) married woman would devote to domestic work. The third answer is an assembly of contemporary averages applied to the population figures for an estimate of the collective magnitude of the domestic work, in comparison to nondomestic work hours, in the entire econ-

omy, and changes in that relation in past decades. These factual accounts signify that much is omitted in the "non-work," "unproductive," "inactive" accounts of domestic work.

The first kind of account, the contemporary averages, is shown in Table 18-1. The table reports research results from data gathered in 1971, for 340 married couples in Vancouver. It tells us the difference that employment and young children make, and how much less husbands contribute. When excluding necessary transportation, a full-time housewife works a full-time working week of over 40 hours. In comparison, the domestic work week of employed women drops drastically, while their workload goes up, combining job and domestic work.

A Lifetime of Housework

For an account of how much time a women might spend doing housework during her life as a wife, I have put together the life of a "typical" woman, Molly, and her family, as a repository of population distributions. The account takes Molly through the 50 years of her married life, from the average age of first-time brides and bridegrooms (Canada, 1977: 209–10) to the time when her husband reaches the age of his life expectancy (Canada, 1979: 14 and 16). These 50 years contain 19 of the 22 years in the labor force which correspond proportionately to the labor-force participation rate of married women. She will have two children, for the average family size, and return to a job in the labor force after the youngest has started going to school.

Molly can expect in her married life 106,032 hours of domestic work, an average of 2,121 hours a year, a quantity similar to the 2,000 hours that a man's 50 40-

TABLE 18-1   Domestic Work Hours, by Employment Status and Children Under Ten (Estimated Weekly Hours, 340 Married Couples in Vancouver, B.C., in 1971

| | Housewives | | Employed wives | | |
Activities	No child under 10	Child under 10	No child under 10	Child under 10	Employed husbands
Cooking and meal preparation	8.5	9.7	5.3	7.2	0.7
Dish washing and kitchen	1.9	2.1	0.9	1.3	0.3
House cleaning	9.1	8.6	5.1	6.9	1.1
Laundry	3.4	3.9	1.3	1.9	0.1
Shopping	4.9	5.1	2.8	3.0	1.2
Care of children	0.7	8.7	0.2	4.2	0.7
Gardening and animals	3.5	2.6	0.8	0.0	2.5
Irregular food preparation and clothes	5.0	2.4	1.6	2.0	0.1
Repairs and sundry services	3.3	1.6	0.7	1.5	3.8
Total domestic work per week	40.3	44.7	18.7	28.0	10.5
Necessary transportation	6.4	6.4	8.7	6.9	8.8
Total including transportation					
per week	46.7	51.1	27.4	34.9	19.3
per day	6.7	7.3	3.9	5.0	2.8
(Number of cases)	(131)	(106)	(85)	(18)	(340)

hour weeks would come to. Making these calculations with the U.S. data from Walker and Woods (1976: 52–53), the total comes to 102,382 and the annual average to 2,048 hours.

We can build up a comparison of Molly's and her husband's lifetime workloads which include their estimated housework hours during the marriage and the job hours in the labor force for the years from 15 to 65, reduced according to the proportion of women and men in the labor force. I take the job week of men to be 40 hours and of married women 35 hours. (The Vancouver time budgets have about one hour a weekday of job time less for women than for men, the result of a greater proportion of married women in part-time jobs, and in office jobs where the hours are shorter). With two weeks vacation, the job year comes

to 50 weeks. Molly's job year would be 1,750 hours and her husband's 2,000. The labor-force participation rate of men 15 years and older in 1976 was 75.5 percent. Applying that percentage to the 50 years from 15 to 65 makes for a 38-year job life of Molly's husband, or 76,000 life-time job hours. A married man's domestic workday in the Vancouver study is 2.8 hours, including 1.3 hours necessary transportation (mostly journey to and from work), or 1,022 hours a year. For 50 married years, that comes to 51,000 hours. The life-time workload of Molly's husband adds up to 121,100 hours.

Molly's 22 years employment in the labor force amount to 38,500 hours and her 50 years of housework are 106,032 hours. Her total life-time workload is 144,532 hours, or 114 percent of her husband's. (I have ignored housework that Molly and her husband might have done before marriage, and that Molly would do for herself after her husband's death, for lack of comparable data.)

We have so far the daily domestic work hours derived from contemporary time-budget studies, and the life-time working hours of one typical woman compared with her husband's. Both accounts tell us that housework is substantial in relation to labor-force job time, and that married women's share in overall working hours is large. We now turn to the working hours of the population and a history of working hours at home and on the job.

THE CONTEXT OF LABOR AND LEISURE IN CANADA 1911–76

The context of changes in working hours is defined critically by three developments in men's contribution to work. (1) The labor-force *participation* rate of men has dropped by 14 points from 89.6 percent in 1911 to 75.5 percent in 1976. (2) The percent of the male labor force in *agriculture* has declined 45 points from 51.3 percent to 6.5 percent from 1911 to 1971. (3) Weekly *job hours* in the non-agricultural labor force have gone down nearly 14 hours from 49.6 hours in 1926 to 35.8 hours in 1976. (These and subsequent labor-force participation data are from the Labour Force (Industries) sections of successive censuses for Canada; nonagricultural labor-force hours from Ostry and Zaidi, 1979–80; and the agricultural hours from Urquhart and Buckley, 1965: 105.) All these tendencies add up to a decline in men's contribution to work. There have been proportionately fewer men at work. The agricultural labor force has shrunk (with its longer work hours of about one-third more than the

nonagricultural labor force). Job hours themselves have been reduced. These facts correspond with the rosy picture of "the leisure society," characterized by fewer and fewer men (meant literally) spending fewer and fewer hours "at work," the result of automation. However, these facts are countered by other facts.

The labor-force participation rate of married women has risen dramatically from 4.5 to 43.7 percent between 1941 and 1976. According to several comparisons of earlier and more recent time budgets, the hours of housework have remained stable for wives with and without labor-force employment (Robinson, 1980). When taking housework hours to have been nearly stable, the labor-force participation of married women to have increased, and the housework contribution of husbands to remain small and unchanged regardless of different household demands, we would expect a collective increase in the overall workload of women. . . .

THE COLLECTIVE WORKLOAD OF CANADIANS

In order to estimate labor-force job hours and the hours of domestic work for each census year 1911-71, and the mid-census of 1976, we need the number of men, and of married and not married women, in the agricultural and nonagricultural labor force, that is, six categories of persons. These numbers have to be reduced by those not at work in the labor force and multiplied by the estimated weekly work hours in labor-force jobs.

No Canadian time-budget studies were made before 1965. Results of comparisons of older and more recent time budgets in the United States (Robinson,

1980: 54) suggest generally unchanged average housework hours. A long series of eight time-budget studies in the Soviet Union allows an assessment of changes in housework time between 1923 and 1968. Housework hours have remained more or less the same (Zuzanek, 1979: 208–09). The seemingly best approach to estimating collective hours of domestic work for the 1911–76 period was to multiply the *same* time-budget average each census year by the number of married women in and out of the labor force, not married women, and married and not married men. ("Not married" includes single, divorced, and widowed, while "married" includes separated.)

The data sources and composition of the time-budget averages for domestic work hours are described in Table 18-2. (The Vancouver figures for married women are weighted averages of the two categories, with or without children under ten, of Table 18-1. Necessary transportation was excluded from these estimates, in order to avoid distortions in the comparison of job and domestic hours.) The average weekly hours were multiplied by the number of persons in each of the five categories. Similarly, the weekly labor-force job hours were multiplied by the number of persons in the six categories developed for that purpose. For each census year, I calculated the sum of all work hours, including domestic work hours and labor-force job hours of women and men, calling it the "collective workload."

. . . The proportionate contribution of men's job hours has been shrinking during the period 1911–76. The major interruption to the trend was introduced through the depression and the war-time experience. The collective domestic work hours of men, and all work hours of not married women, have remained the same as a proportion of the collective workload. The proportionate contribution of married women has risen steadily, except for wartime 1941. Since then the increase has been produced by the greater contribution of job hours and domestic work hours of married women. As a result of the dramatic growth in married women's labor-force participation, the housework hours (in percent) of married women working at home full time has shown a noticeable decline since 1961.

Domestic work hours as a percent of the collective workload have increased throughout the period (always with the

TABLE 18-2   Domestic Work Hours per Week: Port Alberni, Vancouver, Halifax

Sex, work type, and marital status	Port Alberni 1965	Vancouver 1971	Halifax 1971–72	Average
Married women				
not in labor force	no data	42.3	48.8	45.5
in labor force	22.0	20.3	24.5	22.3
Married men	13.0	10.5	9.8	11.1
Nonmarried women	13.1	No data	16.1	14.6
Nonmarried men	9.0	No data	7.7	8.3

Sources: Port Alberni time budgets (Meissner, 1971, pp. 255 and 257); Vancouver time budgets (Meissner et al., 1975, pp. 434–35); Halifax time budgets (Harvey and Clarke, 1975, pp. 12 and 15).

FIGURE 18-1

WEEKLY WORKLOAD HOURS PER PERSON 15 YEARS AND OVER, BY SEX, 1911–1976

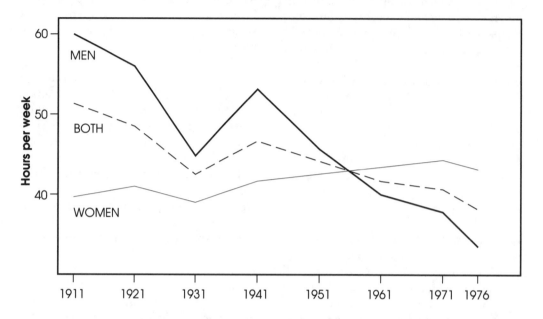

1931–41 dip), by 12 percentage points from 1911 to 1961. They had reached 50 percent in 1961 and leveled off to within one or two percentage points since then. If one were to assess the value of economic activity in working hours (as, for example, Marx suggested one should) the domestic economy *equals* the value of the nondomestic economy.

. . . Women's proportion of the collective workload passed the 50 percent mark between 1951 and 1961, and reached 55 percent in 1976. When expressing the relation in proportions, the spare-time gain of men *had* to be women's loss. To what extent the shift in burden was "real" can be seen in Figure 18-1, for which the collective workload hours were divided by the population 15 years and older. The central, broken line describes the experience of women and men combined, and it suggests that the working population has

profited from an 11.9-hour drop in workload hours per person from 1911 to 1976. When such a per capita workload is separated for women and men, it becomes apparent that it was only men who gained (34.7 hours less work), while women's workload increased slightly by 2.6 hours per person. . . .

CONCLUSIONS

The estimates of working hours developed in this chapter draw attention to some important facets of the relation of housework and labor-force work, and of the work of women and the work of men. Since 1961 Canadians have been putting half of their collective working hours into the unpaid labor of the domestic economy, and half into the monied labor force. In 1971, Canada's domestic work hours were 49 percent of all working hours. In the life-time economic contributions of a typical wife and husband, a married woman's workload comes to 53 percent of the life-time work hours of both combined. From 1911 to 1976 the contributions of men in their job hours have declined, and the contributions of married women in their overall working hours have increased. Domestic working time as a proportion of all work hours has increased to 1961 and then leveled off. The working time of women as a proportion of all work hours had increased to 55 percent by 1976. Women carry more than "half of the sky," and half of the work of Canadians is not in the market economy, but in the household. . . .

References

Canada, Statistics Canada. Canada Year Book 1976–77. Ottawa: Publications Distribution, Statistics Canada, 1977.

Canada, Statistics Canada. Life Tables, Canada and Provinces 1975–1977. Ottawa: Minister of Supply and Services, 1979.

Fox, Bonnie. "Introduction." In *Hidden in the Household: Domestic Labour Under Capitalism.* Edited by B. Fox, pp. 9–23. Toronto: Women's Educational Press, 1980.

Harvey, Andrew S., and Clarke, Susan. *Descriptive Analysis of Halifax Time-Budget Data.* Halifax: Institute of Public Affairs, Dalhousie University, 1975.

Hawrylshyn, Oli. "The Value of Household Services: A Survey of Empirical Estimates." *Review of Income and Wealth*, No. 2 (June, 1976): 101–31.

_____. *Estimating the Value of Household Work in Canada 1971.* Ottawa: Statistics Canada, 1978.

Kaluzynska, Eva. "Wiping the Floor with Theory: A Survey of Writings on Housework." *Feminist Review*, 6 (1980): 27–54.

Mackoff, A.A. Griffiths et al. versus Canadian Pacific et al.: Reasons for Judgment. Vancouver: Supreme Court of British Columbia. No. 29830/74, 1974.

Meissner, Martin. "The Long Arm of the Job: A Study of Work and Leisure." *Industrial Relations*, 10 (1971): 239–60.

Meissner, Martin, Humphreys, E.W., Meis, S.M., and Scheu, W.J. "No Exit for Wives: Sexual Division of Labour and the Cumulation of Household Demands." *Canadian Review of Sociology and Anthropology*, 12 (1975): 424–439.

Molyneux, Maxine. "Beyond the Domestic Labour Debate." *New Left Review*, 116 (1979): 3–27.

Ostry, Sylvia and Zaidi, Mahmood A. *Labour Economics in Canada.* 3rd ed. Toronto: Macmillan, 1979.

Robinson, John. "Housework Technology and Household Work." In *Women and Household Labor*, edited by Sarah Fenstermaker Berk, pp. 53–68. Beverly Hills: Sage, 1980.

Urquhart, M.C. and Buckley, K.A.H., editors. *Historical Statistics of Canada.* Toronto: Macmillan, 1965.

Walker, Kathryn E. and Woods, Margaret E. *Time Use: A Measure of Household Production of Family Goods and Services.* Washington: American Home Economics Association, 1976.

Zuzanek, Jiri. "Time-Budget Trends in the USSR: 1922–1970." *Soviet Studies*, 31 (1979): 188–213.

NINETEEN

Gender Consciousness at Work

David W. Livingstone and Meg Luxton

D.W. LIVINGSTONE, Professor of Sociology at the Ontario Institute for Studies in Education, Toronto, specializes in comparative political economy and education, ideologies and political consciousness, and alternative social and educational futures. His publications include *Class, Ideologies and Educational Futures* (1982); *Social Crisis and Schooling* (1985); *Critical Pedagogy and Cultural Power* (1987); *Working People and Hard Times* (1991), co-edited with R. Argue and C. Gannage; and *Public Attitudes Toward Education in Ontario: Eighth OISE Survey* (1991), co-authored with D. Hart and L.E. Davie. Professor Livingstone is currently completing a book on *Class and Class Consciousness in Advanced Capitalism*.

MEG LUXTON is Professor in the Department of Social Sciences and the Women's Studies Program, Atkinson College, York University, Toronto. She specializes in the study of gender, work, and family. Her publications include *More Than a Labour of Love: Three Generations of Women's Work in the Home* (1980); *Feminism & Political Economy: Women's Work, Women's Struggles*, edited with H.J. Maroney (1987); *Through the Kitchen Window: The Politics of Home and Family*, with H. Rosenberg and S. Arat-Koc (1990); and several influential chapters and journal articles. Professor Luxton is a member of the Editorial Boards of *The Canadian Review of Sociology and Anthropology* and *Canadian Woman Studies*, and has been on the Editorial Board of *Labour*.

INTRODUCTION

... this paper focusses on particular aspects of gender consciousness by investigating the reproduction and modification of the male breadwinner norm in a factory in the steel industry — which is widely regarded to be one of the strongest preserves of traditional white working class masculine identity and opposition to women trying to do a 'man's job'.[1] By examining the shop floor cultural practices and expressed attitudes of married white working class men employed in the steel industry, the perceptions of their spouses and the experiences of a small number of women who were hired in the steel plant, the paper documents the articulation of the male breadwinner norm and assesses the various experiences which either lead to a modification of or actually challenge that norm.

Views on the gendered division of labor, as expressed most explicitly through acceptance or rejection of the male breadwinner norm, are among the most basic ingredients of oppositional gender consciousness. Whether one is inclined to a feminist, male chauvinist or more ambivalent sense of oppositional gender consciousness is likely to be intimately related to both dispositions on fundamental dimensions of gender identity, and predispositions to act to maintain or create alternative forms of gender relations.

The Hilton Works of the Steel Company of Canada (Stelco), in Hamilton, Ontario, is one of the largest manufacturing plants in Canada. With a labor force of between 8,000 and 14,000, it has been the major employer in the city of Hamilton since the early 20th century. Unionized in the late 1940s by the United Steelworkers of America (Local 1005), its relatively high wages and benefits have made it one of the most desirable industrial workplaces in the city. The production labor force has been almost entirely white and male.

Until recently, because of the relatively high wages and the relative job security, the vast majority of men at Stelco were economically able to support dependent wives and children, thus realizing the male breadwinner ideal. Indeed, from 1945 to 1981 when there was a world decline in steel manufacturing, Hamilton consistently had among the lowest rates of women's employment in Canada, a fact made possible by the wages from the heavy industry which dominates the city and of course supported by the discriminatory hiring practices by those same industries (Webber, 1986). During World War II, women were employed to replace male workers who had joined the army and after the war almost all those women were let go. Between 1946 and 1961, a few women were hired occasionally, but by 1961 they were all employed in one particular work site — the tin mill. Between 1961 and 1978, no women were hired although approximately 30,000 women applied for jobs during those 19 years (Luxton, forthcoming). By 1978, there were 28 women working in the tin mill; the rest of the production workers were men. In 1979–80, a union-supported committee, The Women Back Into Stelco Committee, launched a highly public campaign, which included a discrimination complaint with the Ontario Human Rights Commission, to force Stelco to hire women for production jobs in the Hilton Works. As a result, Stelco hired approximately 200 women. The highly publicized campaign and the subsequent hiring of a number of women focussed attention on the question of gender and paid employment and for the women and men involved posed sharply the issue of gender identity (Eason, Field and Santucci, 1983).

We examined patterns of gender consciousness among white married male steelworkers and their spouses, and among white female steelworkers who entered Stelco as a result of their political campaign. Our study was conducted in 1983–84 in the wake of massive layoffs by Stelco, including most of the women hired in this campaign. We interviewed a random sample of 184 married steelworkers (182 were men), drawn from the Local 1005 membership list, who were living with their spouses and employed at Stelco. We also interviewed their spouses (76 of the women spouses were full-time housewives and 106 were in paid employment; the 2 male spouses were employed). In-depth follow-up interviews were also conducted selectively. For comparative purposes, a representative sample of individuals living with partners in the Greater Hamilton

Area was given a similar interview ($N = 795$). We also interviewed the leaders of the Women Back Into Stelco Campaign and 25 women who, though not part of the original campaign, were hired as a result of it. This paper investigates patterns of gender consciousness among men and women who, for the most part, are living in nuclear families where the man's income forms the greater part of the household income. It also looks at the impact on that consciousness of the women who got jobs at Stelco. We consider what factors foster support for a sharply differentiated sex/gender division of paid labor and, particularly, the ideal of the male breadwinner, and conversely what leads to a recognition that women and men can and ought to do the same paid work for the same remuneration. Most specifically, we attempt to investigate the links of masculine shop floor culture with ideologies of work and the male breadwinner norm in this core of the Hamilton working class.

Masculine Shop Floor Culture

In occupational settings where the large majority of workers are male, there is often an equation of paid work with masculinity. It is assumed that workers in that field are, and should be, male. Such ideas are part of a larger ideology which accepts the existence of a decisive sex/gender division of labor, fundamental to which is the belief that women should be first and foremost wives and mothers and that men are primarily breadwinners. . . . As Paul Willis (1979) and Cynthia Cockburn (1983) have demonstrated, the equation of paid work with masculinity is frequently characteristic of large scale industrial settings where much of the work involves manual labor or where the

work environment is particularly noisy, dirty and noxious. Existing studies of masculine shop floor culture also describe the meaning and pleasure that men extract in the midst of boring and alienating work situations. The assertion of masculinity is partially a defence, a way of insisting on the exclusion of women to protect specific jobs and more general job skills from increased competition (Cockburn, 1985). It is also an integral part of the ideology of the male breadwinner. Such studies show why male camaraderie, based on masculinity, is important and why the men are often threatened if their culture is challenged (for example by the presence of women).

In workplaces such as Stelco where many parts of the plant have involved dangerous or heavy work, and where — with the exception of the cafeteria, the cleaning and office staff and the tin mill — all workers were men from 1945 until the challenge in 1979, manual labor, dangerous work or even work with large machinery is often identified as men's work. This may militate against individuals recognizing the class nature of this work and therefore retard their sense of class identity. A male steelworker described the qualities needed to work at Stelco: 'You got to be tough and you got to be willing to take risks. You got to be strong. It takes a real man to work here.'

The shared experience of work, the camaraderie of co-workers, is shaped by their shared masculinity (Stewart, 1981). As John Lippert (1977: 208) observed of his experience as an auto worker:

> Each member of the group seems concerned mainly with exhibiting sexual experience and competency through the competition . . . None of what happens between men in the plant is considered 'sexuality'. That remains as what we do with (or to) our women when we get home . . . But even through this competition, it

is easy to see that many, many men enjoy their physical interaction and that they receive a kind of physical satisfaction from it that they just don't get [from the work itself or] when they go home.

The unpleasantness and the brutality of the working situation is sometimes re-interpreted into a heroic exercise of manly confrontation with the task. In this way, a potential for developing opposi-tional class consciousness may be modi-fied or even deflected by a gender con-sciousness that validates certain stereotypic notions of masculinity. Diffi-cult, uncomfortable or dangerous work-ing conditions are not seen directly as employer-imposed hazards for the work-ers, but as challenges to masculine pro-wess: A male steelworker noted: 'The coke oven, where I am, is really rough. The men who work there, they got to be really tough you know, just to keep at it, day after day.'

Discontent with work in male-domi-nated factory environments is often not articulated as political discontent di-rected against the bosses but rather is mediated through forms of language and interplay among workers that express sexual competition and antagonism (Gray, 1984; Meissner, 1986). Sexually antagonistic language pervades the steel mill. Work itself — especially difficult work — is characterized as feminine and to be conquered: 'it's a real bitch,' 'give her hell'. Similarly, malfunctioning ma-chinery is called by derogatory terms for women — bitch, slut — which often have explicit sexual connotations. Disliked bosses are similarly described by terms which cast aspersion either on their mas-culinity and sexual ability — wimp, cream puff, dick — or identify them with negative female terms — bitch. Specific anger is expressed using terms for sexual intercourse and workers' descriptions of

their exploitation by management are usually articulated using rape terms — 'we're getting fucked' or 'we're getting screwed around'.

Gender codes are central to the ways in which male workers approach other as-pects of their work. One of the few ways workers can influence the design of the work sites is in their choice of pictures on the walls. Frequently lunch rooms are wallpapered with pinups of apparently sexually available women — imagery which both continues the theme of sexual symbolism and suggests a potential alter-native activity which sharply contrasts with the workplace. This alternative for men involves both fantasized sexual ac-tivity which is deemed to be physically and emotionally pleasurable in ways that the reality of work is not, and sexual dom-ination where the male (at least as viewer) is in a position of power over (at least the image of) the woman in ways that the worker never has power at work.

Even when discontent at work is ex-pressed as direct political opposition to management, it is filtered through a lan-guage of masculinity. Male workers de-scribe standing up to management in masculine terms. One male Stelco worker described another approvingly: 'He never takes any shit from the foreman and when they give him a hard time, he fights back hard — he's a real man.' In plant floor confrontations, and in con-tract negotiations, masculine charac-teristics and behaviors are commonly mobilized. As Paul Willis has noted (1979: 198), the spectacle, especially of the potential fist fight, and the bluff, or strong and combative language, register real expressions of anger and opposition. These may be very effective in the short run and certainly represent a strong force. But this 'masculine style of con-frontation demands an appropriate and

honourable resolution: visible and immediate concessions' (Willis, 1979: 198). As
a consequence, contract negotiations
often result in cash settlements, gains
which are immediately visible but which
may 'actually conceal longer-term de-
feats over the less visible issues of control and ownership' (Willis, 1979: 198;
Winter and Robert, 1980). . . .

The Challenge from Women and the Modification of the Male Breadwinner Norm

. . . There were about 14,000 men employed at Stelco when the first women
walked through the doors after the success of the campaign. Their responses to
women's employment at Stelco varied.
One of the women noted:

> Some of them feel if you can do your job you
> got a right to be there. And others feel you got
> a right to be there if you are the only
> breadwinner. And then others . . . you
> shouldn't be there. And then there are others,
> that you should be there.

Male steelworkers, their spouses, and
women steelworkers almost unan-
imously supported, in the abstract, the
general principle of equal opportunities
for women in the labor market. . . . In our
interview survey, male steelworkers and
their spouses both expressed strong consensus (>70%) on the general statement:
'If given the chance, women could and
should do the same work as men now do,
and men could and should do the same
work as women now do (except for pregnancy)'. They also demonstrated support
for the principles of equal pay for equal
work when they strongly disagreed
(>85%) with the proposition that
'women should not be paid the same as
men'. . . .

However, despite this general support
in principle for women's right to paid
employment and equal pay for equal
work, attitudes toward more specific aspects of full sex/gender equality are
much more mixed. . . .

The most pertinent questions asked in
both our Hamilton-wide and steelworker household surveys dealt with priority for jobs in hard times, and affirmative action in traditionally male jobs
(see Tables 19-1 and 19-2). Overall, the
pattern of responses indicated that
Hamilton couples also remained quite divided on these more specific issues of
gender equality, that male Stelco workers
were somewhat less supportive than
Hamilton men in general, and that employed women were more supportive
than homemakers.[2]

As Table 19-1 shows, small majorities
of women and men in Hamilton couples
rejected men's priority for jobs in hard
times. A bare majority of Stelco wives did
as well. Only among male Stelco workers
was there a small majority in favor of
giving men priority for jobs. As one male
steelworker insisted: 'Between a single
mother with kids and a guy supporting a
family, I would take the guy first'.

Women's employment typically had a
significant effect on the views of both
spouses. Among Hamilton couples generally, over 60 per cent of employed women
and of men with employed spouses supported women's equal right to paid employment in times of high unemployment. Both Hamilton women presently
working exclusively as homemakers and
men with homemaker spouses were
about equally divided on the issue. Male
Stelco workers and their spouses exhibited fairly similar differences by employment status of the woman. The employed wives of Stelco workers showed a
virtually identical pattern of majority

TABLE 19-1   'In Times of High Unemployment, Men Should Have Priority for Jobs'

| | **Hamilton Households** | | | | | |
	Men with Employed Spouses	**Men with Homemaker Spouses**	**All Men**	**Employed Women**	**Homemaker Women**	**All Women**
% disagree	69	41	58	63	48	54
% agree	24	47	33	34	45	40
% can't say	7	12	9	3	7	6
N	238	153	390	164	238	403

| | **Steelworker Households** | | | | | |
	Men with Employed Spouses	**Men with Homemaker Spouses**	**All Men**	**Employed Women**	**Homemaker Women**	**All Women**
% disagree	50	35	43	60	37	50
% agree	45	60	52	37	56	45
% can't say	5	5	5	3	7	5
N	106	76	182	106	76	182

support to Hamilton working women in general. Conversely, definite majorities of both male steelworkers with homemaker wives and their wives themselves expressed agreement with men's priority for jobs. Perhaps most notably, male Stelco workers with employed wives remained about equally divided, and therefore less moved by their wives' employment than Hamilton men in general to support women's equal rights to jobs. However, the general pattern in Table 19-1 supports the not surprising conclusion of several prior studies that people in both middle class and working class households with wives in paid employment are more likely to reject the male breadwinner norm (cf. Huber and Spitze, 1983; Ferree, 1983; Anderson and Cook, 1985; Smith, 1985; Black and Creese, 1986). Also, as in prior studies, significant correlations of youthfulness and higher educational attainment with more

egalitarian views on women's employment rights have been found both for men and women, whether the wife is employed or not.

On the issue of affirmative action in traditionally male jobs, the overall pattern of responses was again similar, as Table 19-2 indicates. Most notably, the majority of women in all categories — including Stelco homemaker wives — were likely to support such affirmative action practices, while men in general remained more divided and a small majority of male Stelco workers expressed opposition.

Our in-depth interviews with Stelco workers and their spouses offer further insight into the complexities and dynamics of the current renegotiation of these features of breadwinner power and, by implication, of gender identities in general. The other side of the argument that certain occupations, such as steelmak-

TABLE 19-2   "The Proportion of Women in Traditionally Male Occupations Should Be Increased Through Special Training and Hiring Initiatives'

	Hamilton Households					
	Men with Employed Spouses	**Men with Homemaker Spouses**	**All Men**	**Employed Women**	**Homemaker Women**	**All Women**
% agree	47	49	48	65	52	58
% disagree	41	41	41	26	35	31
% can't say	13	10	12	9	13	11
N	238	153	390	164	238	403

	Steelworker Households					
	Men with Employed Spouses	**Men with Homemaker Spouses**	**All Men**	**Employed Women**	**Homemaker Women**	**All Women**
% agree	42	47	44	60	53	57
% disagree	56	48	53	37	39	38
% can't say	2	5	3	3	8	5
N	106	76	182	106	76	182

ing, are only for men is the insistence that men must be breadwinners.So, while there is rarely any overt denial of women's right to paid work, an underlying identification of breadwinner status with men's work remains strong among many male steelworkers. While some men actively supported the efforts of the women to get hired at Stelco and welcomed them when they succeeded (and the union formally and practically gave full support to the campaign), many men insisted that steelmaking, especially given the dirty, dangerous and heavy work at Stelco, must be men's work:

> It's not for women. There's a lot of heavy work . . . I feel that Stelco should be for men . . . I feel the steel industry is just for men.

The notion of steelmaking as essentially men's work is not merely a simplistic assertion of male chauvinism, but is typically bound to a deeper sense of responsibility to provide for their families. Both the wages earned and the very sacrifice and strength required to do the work offer a basic self-esteem and self-worth. The wage packet is seen as conferring breadwinner power and status and confirming that the man has fulfilled his obligation as family provider. The male breadwinner ideal may have been expressed baldly:

> Like I believe a man is the breadwinner, you know. He supports his wife and kids. That's just the way it is. And that's the way it should be. Men earn the money.

Or with some qualifications:

> People have their rights. But I also believe that a man is the breadwinner and that the woman should stay home . . . My wife went out to work for six weeks one time in a restaurant, 'cuz she wanted to get out of the house. And I said

okay, but that was therapy, it was not to make money or anything like that. She went out and done her thing, and then she came back. And I don't need my wife to work. If I can't support her, there's something wrong.

But in virtually every case, the steelworker's male identity appeared to be integrally tied to his perceived capacity to bring home a 'decent' or 'living' wage.

Homemaker wives of steelworkers most frequently expressed the conmitant belief that women's place is in the home: 'I think a mother should be home with her children. It's better for them, isn't it?' But some homemaker wives' comments reflected both an awareness of the centrality of their own domestic work to the reproduction of their husband's labor power and also asserted their own continuing right to seek paid work:

> I make sure he goes to work happy and in a good mood every day. So he is going into his workplace not thinking about things. He can go and put his mind into his job, not worry about what is worrying at home . . . I gave up my job when we got married, but that was a mutual agreement. I didn't do it for him. He didn't make me quit my job, you know. I could probably go back to work somehow.

Homemaker wives of steelworkers frequently reiterated versions of the male breadwinner norm, but those who supported women working in steel typically did so on the same basis as they supported their husbands working there, the wage packet:

> It's the best money that women can earn. My husband heard stories from the guys in the plant before the women came in about the women during the war and they were really something. I think women should get those jobs if they can. The pay is really good. My girlfriend is working at Dofasco and she really likes it.

Employed wives frequently showed both a deeper appreciation of the negative side of male breadwinners' responsibility and a determination to maintain their own employment, albeit generally in low paid or part-time jobs:

> The man might think it's terrible because he has to go to work every day. He can't afford to take a day off. The way society has put it, the man is the breadwinner in the family. And that must be a lot of stress on you, like thinking — 'I have to go to work, I have no choice, I have to work full-time. If I don't work full-time, then we don't get our money and we don't survive' . . . I never thought of staying home for long. I really enjoy getting out. And I think as soon as you lose your workplace friends, you become all your husband's friends kind of thing. And you don't have that other outlet who understand how you think. . . .

Steelworkers' wives, whether employed or full-time homemakers, tended to be quite pragmatic about the possibility of women's employment at Stelco, not articulating any notion that the work is too much for women. . . .

The employed wives of steelworkers in general expressed support for women steelworkers, and some also saw benefits to male entry into female job ghettos. . . .

Women steelworkers noted the extensive resistance to their presence and explained it in terms of masculine ideologies:

> I think a lot of the men were threatened . . . here was a woman coming along who said she could do it just as well as they could.

Despite the common tendency for male steelworkers to construe their gender identities through their perceptions of their jobs as tough and dangerous, the presence of committed, full-time women steelworkers through the divisions of the Hilton Works began to seriously erode the basis of the masculinist ideology of steelwork.

The women recognized the masculine shop floor culture and argued that men felt very threatened when women entered those previously all-male terrains. In particular, they suggested that men were embarrassed to have their shop floor cultural practices made public to women. . . .

> For them it's like having two personalities. Like Jekyl and Hyde sort of thing . . . At work they swear, they throw their garbage on the floor. I'm sure they don't do that at home . . . They're like kids at work . . . and I could just see them go home and be you know, straight and narrow, very serious with their wives, and as soon as they get to work it's crazy. . . .

They also noted that the presence of women challenged and undermined the basic premises of the male breadwinner ideology and the sex/gender division of labor itself:

> The man goes out and does the job, it doesn't matter how he does it, he's got to make a lot of money and the women stay home and take care of the children . . . It's a very nice, well-ordered life and we were changing that order. Not only were we working with them, many of us were also going home and doing what their wives were doing as well and it was very difficult for some of them.

In fact, the challenge to the masculine ideology of work potentially reveals the actual oppressive character of that work. Occasionally the words of the men themselves offered a glimmer of insight into the way in which concepts of masculinity at the workplace hinder a clear critique of the work itself. . . .

> It's dirty, heavy, it's no climate for a woman. The men's world is a little rougher than the women's. Physically a man is in better shape. Men are more mechanically minded . . . There

is nothing wrong with women, it's just that sometimes with heavy work . . . Everywhere you find place for some women, could be as strong as men, you know. But if you take the overall picture, muscularity has always been the man's. It doesn't mean that he has more brains because that is not true, but muscularity. I think that women should be outside. It is no place for women. I hate it.

Women steelworkers have most clearly perceived the limits of the masculinist ideology of steel work: 'I've never seen a job that I couldn't do or any other women couldn't do. Men will say this is no place for a woman, but it's not really good for men either.'

Some men who defended women's general employment rights displayed ambivalence about them as steelworkers. . . .

> . . . In an environment like Stelco, I agree she has the right to be there, but in a life threatening situation I wouldn't want my life being dependent on how she is going to react to that situation at that time, and we do get into some precarious positions. . . .

Other men expressed more direct antagonism to women steelworkers, arguing that they posed a direct threat to men's breadwinner power. . . .

Some of the women steelworkers noted that men were opposed to hiring women because so many men were unemployed: 'They figured it was a man's job, a man's world, and there a lot of unemployed men still out there.'

Steelworkers and their spouses were very aware of actual or threatened unemployment. At the time of the study, about 5,000 Stelco production workers had been let go and many more had received layoff notices. As many other workplaces in Hamilton were also laying off, most Hamilton residents had close contact with someone unemployed (Webber,

1986). . . . A male steelworker reacted:

> What really bothers me is where there are two breadwinners. That's not fair. I don't care who the breadwinner is, the man or the woman, but there shouldn't be two breadwinners in some families when some people have no jobs. I know everyone wants to get ahead, but it's not fair when some have no jobs.

While the vast majority were unable to think about this in class terms, not able to make the leap to criticizing the existence of the real inequalities of wealth (Livingstone and Mangan, forthcoming), they found it hard to break with the notion of one primary breadwinner. Most acknowledged circumstances in which the woman might well be the breadwinner but still felt that ideally the man should be. They could also accept circumstances in which both men and women were employed but the women had a conventional (lower paid) 'woman's job'. . . .

For many women and men who accepted the idea of the male breadwinner norm, the employment of women at Stelco could only be tolerated if those women were required by necessity to take on that breadwinner role themselves. . . . Other men were more ambivalent about the issue. . . .

Because so many male steelworkers were outright antagonistic to or at best ambivalent about the employment of women in the plant, the women who started at Stelco were at least initially greeted with considerable resistance. As a result of the campaign and because there were so few women, each was highly noticeable in her work site. Most of them described being tested by male co-workers. Several, especially those who had led the campaign, were harassed both by fellow workers and by foremen (Gray, 1984; 1986). . . . Despite this, most

expressed satisfaction with their jobs and said that after a few months they ceased to be perceived merely as women intruders and became Stelco workers like everyone else (Luxton, forthcoming). . . .

The actual experience of working closely with women was the most effective antidote to male skepticism about women's capacity to do the work. . . .

> One woman that worked in our department was good and better than some of the young fellows. She had the right personality and the right character to fit into our department . . . She knew her job. It took her a while but she knew her job. I have no qualms about working with a woman like that.

The recognition that women can actually do most of the work (cf. Deaux and Ullman, 1983) has encouraged some male steelworkers, particularly those with employed wives and more secure jobs, to express explicit support for the principle of gender equality even in Stelco. . . .

CONCLUDING REMARKS

Our findings show that male steelworkers, who are widely regarded as occupying one of the strongest bastions of working class masculinist ideology, strongly supported a general rhetoric of gender equality, as well as giving formal support through their union to the campaign to hire women. Some of these men were fully committed to women's equality. However, many men continued to believe that steelmaking should be men's work and that men should be primary breadwinners. Those male steelworkers who were more ambivalent about asserting the validity of the male breadwinner norm, and those who, despite massive layoffs in Stelco, expressed support for women's equal right to scarce jobs, tended to be men who had had direct experiences of women's employment. Either their wives had significant employment experience or they themselves had worked with women. Among the wives of steelworkers, their own employment experiences obviously sharply affected their adherence to male breadwinner ideologies, but even a majority of full-time housewives expressed general support for women working in traditional male jobs like steel. Clearly, the male breadwinner norm as a basis of gender identity is undergoing modifications in steelworker families, as well as in Canadian society generally. Such changes in gender consciousness are occurring primarily in response to the growing importance of married women as essential wage earners, but are also stimulated by the women's movement (in this case the explicitly feminist Women Back into Stelco campaign) . . .

Note

[1] The findings reported here are part of the Steelworker Families Research Project funded by the SSHRC (Grant number: 410-83-0391). We are grateful to our co-investigators, Wally Secombe and June Corman, for their general assistance. . . .

References

Anderson, Kristi, and Cook, Elizabeth A. 'Women, work and political attitudes.' *American Journal of Political Science* (August, 1985) 29(3): 606–25.

Black, D., and Creese, G. 'Class, gender and politics in Canada.' Unpublished paper, Department of Sociology, Carleton University, Ottawa, 1986.

Cockburn, Cynthia. *Brothers; Male Dominance and Technological Change*. London: Pluto Press, 1983.

———. *Machinery of Dominance: Women, Men and Technical Know-How*. London: Pluto Press, 1985.

Deaux, K., and Ullman, J. *Women of Steel: Female Blue-Collar Workers in the Basic Steel Industry*. New York: Praeger, 1983.

Ferree, Myra Marx. 'The women's movement in the working class.' *Sex Roles* 9(4) (1983): 493–505.

Gray, Stan. 'Sharing the shop floor.' *Canadian Dimension* (June, 1984) 18(2): 17–32.

———. 'Fight to survive — the case of Bonita Clark.' *Canadian Dimension* (May, 1986) 20(3): 15–20.

Huber, Joan, and Spitze, Glenna. *Sex Stratification: Children, Housework and Jobs*. New York: Academic Press, 1983.

Lippert, J. 'Sexuality as consumption.' Pp. 207–13 in J. Snodgrass (ed.), *For Men Against Sexism*. Albion, CA: Times Change Press, 1977.

Livingstone, D.W., and Mangan, J.M. 'Class, gender and expanded class consciousness in

Steeltown.' In M. Dobkowski and I. Wallimann (eds.), Research in Inequality and Social Conflict. Greenwich: JAI Press, forthcoming.

Luxton, Meg. 'Getting to work: The challenge of the women back into Stelco campaign.' Forthcoming.

Meissner, Martin. 'The Reproduction of Women's Domination in Organizational Communication.' In L. Thayer (ed.), *Organisation-Communication: Emerging Perspectives* I. Norwood: Ablex, 1986.

Smith, Tom. 'Working wives and women's rights: the connection between the employment status of wives and the feminist attitudes of husbands.' *Sex Roles* (March, 1985) 12 (5–6): 501–8.

Stewart, Katie. 'The Marriage of Capitalist

and Patriarchal Ideologies: Meanings of Male Bonding and Male Ranking in U.S. Culture.' In L. Sargent (ed.), *Women and Revolution*. Montreal: Black Rose, 1981.

Webber, M.J. 'Regional Production and the Production of Regions: The Case of Steeltown.' Pp. 197–224 in A.J. Scott and M. Storper (eds.), *Production Work, Territory: The Geographical Anatomy of Industrial Capitalism*. Boston: Allen and Unwin, 1986.

Willis, P. 'Shop-floor culture, masculinity and the wage form.' Pp. 185–98 in J. Clarke et al. (eds.), *Working Class Culture: Studies in History and Theory*. London: Hutchinson, 1979.

Winter, M.F., and Robert, E.F. 'Male dominance, late capitalism, and the growth of instrumental reason.' *Berkeley Journal of Sociology* 24–25 (1980): 249–280.

TWENTY

Administrative Revolution in Canadian Offices

Graham Lowe

GRAHAM LOWE, a Professor of Sociology at the University of Alberta, specializes in the study of work. During the 1989–90 academic year, he was Social Sciences Visiting Professor at Carleton University. He has also been a visiting researcher at Cambridge University, the University of Warwick, and the Swedish Centre for Working Life. A fuller account of this article can be found in Graham's book, *Women in the Administrative Revolution: The Feminization of Clerical Work* (University of Toronto Press, 1987). He is also the co-author (with Harvey Krahn) of a widely used textbook entitled *Work, Industry and Canadian Society* (Nelson, 1988). His latest book (co-edited with David Ashton) is *Making Their Way: Education, Training and the Labour Market in Canada and Britain* (University of Toronto Press, 1990). His current research examines the transition from school to work. Graham is the Editor of the *Canadian Journal of Sociology*.

THE ADMINISTRATIVE REVOLUTION: MAJOR OCCUPATIONAL AND ORGANIZATIONAL DIMENSIONS

Not all offices, even within large organizations, experienced the full impact of the administrative revolution. We can nonetheless assert that by the Depression, five characteristics could be found in central offices of leading firms and major government departments across the country. Here, then, is what gave shape to the administrative revolution between 1911 and 1931: (a) a huge increase in the clerical sector of the labour force; (b) a dramatic shift in the clerical sex ratio toward female employees; (c) a concentration of new clerical jobs in the leading industries of corporate capitalism; (d) a relative decline in the socio-economic position of the clerk; and (e) the rationalization of office work by an emergent group of "scientifically oriented," efficiency-conscious office managers.

The Growth of Clerical Occupations

The proportion of clerical workers in a country's labour force is a good index of both the internal bureaucratization of enterprises and the general level of industrialization (Bendix, 1974: 211). It is thus not surprising to find that rapid clerical growth paralleled the ascendancy of corporate capitalism in Canada after 1900. Table 20-1 shows that the number of clerks increased from 33,017 in 1891 to 1,310,910 in 1971. In other words, the proportion of the total labour force engaged in clerical occupations shot from 2 per cent to 15.2 per cent. Now the largest single occupational group in Canada, clerks have been at the forefront of the expansion of the white-collar labour force throughout the century.

The clerical growth rate peaked between 1911 and 1921. While this was followed by another decade of intensified

expansion between 1941 and 1951, the earlier period is most significant because it demarcates the administrative revolution. The 1911 to 1921 boom in clerical jobs cannot be attributed to either population or labour force growth, both of which were much more pronounced during the preceding decade. The lag in clerical growth during the 1920s does not mean that the administrative revolution was losing its force. Rather, it was in this decade that the growing army of clerks was moulded into an efficient corps of administrative functionaries. Clerical procedures were increasingly rationalized and mechanized to consolidate and control the burgeoning office staffs. By the 1930s, the foundations of the modern office had thus been laid.

TABLE 20-1   Total Labour Force, Clerical Workers and Female Clerical Workers, Canada, 1891–1971*

	Total Labour Force	Total Clerical	Clerical Workers as a Percentage of Total Labour Force	Females as a Percentage of Total Clerical	Female Clerks as a Percentage of Total Female Labour Force
1891	1,659,335	33,017	2.0%	14.3%	2.3%
1901	1,782,832	57,231	3.2	22.1	5.3
1911	2,723,634	103,543	3.8	32.6	9.1
1921	3,164,348	216,691	6.8	41.8	18.5
1931	3,917,612	260,674	6.7	45.1	17.7
1941	4,195,951	303,655	7.2	50.1	18.3
1951	5,214,913	563,083	10.8	56.7	27.4
1961	6,342,289	818,912	12.9	61.5	28.6
1971	8,626,930	1,310,910	15.2	68.9	30.5

* Data ajusted to 1951 Census occupation classification.

Sources: Canada D.B.S., Census Branch, *Occupational Trends in Canada, 1891–1931* (Ottawa, 1939), Table 5.
Meltz, *Manpower in Canada* (Ottawa: Queen's Printer, 1969), Section I, Tables A-1, A-2 and A-3.
1971 Census of Canada, Volume 3, Part 2, Table 2.

The Feminization of Clerical Work

Nowhere has the feminization trend in the labour force been more pronounced during this century than in clerical occupations. Strictly male-dominated at the turn of the century, by 1941 the majority of clerical jobs were held by women (see Table 20-1). The rate of feminization in the office was highest from 1891 to 1921. Increases exceeded 166 per cent in each decade, almost ten times that for the total female labour force (Lowe, 1980). There was an absolute increase in the number of female clerks over this period from 4,710 to 90,577, with the female share of clerical jobs reaching 22.1 per cent by 1921 (Table 20-1). This signals the emergence of a trend which resulted in the concentration of 30.5 per cent of all female workers in clerical occupations by 1971.

The segregation of women into a small number of relatively unrewarding occupations has remained fairly stable since 1900 (Armstrong and Armstrong, 1978: 20). This is especially true of clerical work, where the share of clerical jobs held by females steadily increased over this century. Segregation characterized certain key office jobs even in the early stages of the administrative revolution. In stenography and typing, for example, the "female" label became firmly affixed as the proportion of jobs held by women rose from 80 per cent to 95 per cent between 1901 and 1931 (Lowe, 1980). ...

The Changing Industrial Distribution of Clerical Workers

There is a direct connection between shifts in the industrial employment patterns of clerks and the advance of corporate capitalism. In brief, clerks became concentrated in manufacturing and in major service industries. The most rapid expansion of clerical jobs between 1911 and 1931 occurred in manufacturing, the sector most directly connected with the entrenchment of corporate capitalism. Facilitating the creation of a manufacturing base in the economy was the development of a wide range of services, especially in trade, finance and transportation and communication. By combining these four sectors — manufacturing, transportation and communication, trade and finance — we can account for over 85 per cent of total clerical growth between 1911 and 1931. It was during this period that the most dramatic shifts in the industrial distribution of clerical employment occurred.

Most of the new clerical jobs created in manufacturing and service industries between 1911 and 1931 were fundamentally different from the craft-like bookkeeping jobs typical of the nineteenth-century office. Traditional clerical tasks were fragmented and routinized. Employers thus offered lower salaries, expecting less job commitment from workers. Women were considered more suitable for this new stratum of clerical jobs than men. Lower female wage rates, the higher career aspirations of male clerks and stereotypes of women as better able to perform monotonous, routine work underlay this shift in clerical labour demand. Consequently, we find that by 1931 manufacturing, trade and finance each accounted for over 20 per cent of all female clerical employment (Lowe, 1980). These three sectors had over 40 per cent of their positions occupied by women by 1931 (Lowe, 1979: 190). The most dramatic shift in sex composition occurred in the finance industry. Women were a rarity in banks, insurance companies and other financial institutions in 1900, yet within years they came to occupy almost 50 per cent of the clerical posts in such firms (Lowe, 1979: 184).

The Relative Decline of Clerical Earnings

Accompanying the rapid growth of clerical jobs was the erosion of the clerk's socio-economic position. This is to be expected, given the de-skilling of the clerical labour process and the influx of lower paid females into offices.... Wages entered into a steady decline after 1921, cutting below the labour force average wage by 1951.[1] Influencing this general trend was the rise in blue-collar wages over the century, and the expansion of the potential clerical supply through the spread of public education.

The feminization process created two fairly distinct clerical labour pools, one male and the other female. It is noteworthy then that the wages for both groups have declined relative to the total labour force since 1901. Male clerical wages dropped from 25 per cent above the labour force average in 1931 to 11 per cent below the average by 1971. Likewise, female clerks, while better off than women in other job ghettos, have been rapidly losing ground. From a wage advantage of between 48 per cent and 49 per cent from 1931 to 1941, female clerical salaries fell to only 6 per cent above the female labour force average by 1971. In making the comparisons between male and female clerical wage trends, we must bear in mind that female clerks earned 53 per cent of their male counterparts in 1901, inching up slightly to 58 per cent by 1971 (Lowe, 1980).[2] ...

... The advance of office rationalization, when combined with the general clerical wage trends, provides evidence of gradual clerical proletarianization. Indeed, the women who now operate modern office machines are considered the most proletarianized sector of the white-collar work force (*Work in America*, 1973: 38; Rinehart, 1975: 92; Glen and Feldberg, 1977). Clearly, the roots of proletarianization can be traced back to the administrative revolution in the early decades of the twentieth century.

The Rationalization of the Office

The transition from nineteenth-century small scale entrepreneurial capitalism to twentieth-century corporate capitalism involved a number of fundamental organizational changes. Foremost among these was the growing predominance of bureaucracy, for it was the form of work organization best suited to capitalism (see Weber, 1958: 1964). As Bendix (1974: 2) argues, industrialization is "the process by which large numbers of employees are concentrated in a single enterprise and become dependent upon the directing and co-ordinating activities of entrepreneurs and managers." Accompanying the rise of bureaucracy was the emergence of a new occupational group, the expert salaried manager. The growing size and complexity of enterprises compelled owners to delegate daily operating responsibility to hired managers. Administration thus became a specialized activity after 1900, as managers sought the most efficient ways to achieve organizational goals (see Chandler, 1978; Nelson, 1975). The major strategy utilized by managers was organizational rationalization. Consequently, rigid hierarchies with clear lines of authority were developed, new accounting procedures were implemented to control production and labour costs, traditional labour skills were broken down as the division of labour became more specialized, and workers' control over the productive process passed to management with increasing standardization and mechanization of tasks. Braverman (1974: 107) claims that the key to all modern management is "the control over work through the control over decisions that are made in the course of work." This principle applied equally to office and factory.

When William H. Leffingwell (1917) published the first book on scientific office management in 1917, he found a receptive audience among many American and Canadian office managers. By the early 1920s, there is evidence that large offices were being rationalized according to the dictates of scientific management in order to increase administrative efficiency.[3] In fact, after 1910 major business publications such as the *Monetary Times*, *Industrial Canada* and the *Journal of the Canadian Bankers' Association* devoted increasing coverage to a variety of managerial reforms designed to rationalize work procedures. Even as early as 1905, Canadian manufacturers were cautioned to control rising office overhead (*Industrial Canada*, July 1905: 843). In the finance sector, the Bank of Nova Scotia pioneered a system for measuring the efficiency of branch staff (Bank of Nova Scotia Archives, n.d.). Not until 1910, however, did the new science of management really catch hold in Canadian industry. Canadian businessmen, as well as senior government administrators, were attracted to the ideology of efficiency inspired by F.W. Taylor's program of scientific factory management. . . .

Mechanized clerical procedures were perhaps the most visible feature of office rationalization. As we have indicated above, tasks such as typing and operating other office machines were defined as "women's work" from their inception. The close interconnection between feminization and the mechanization of office work clearly demonstrates how the rationalization of the clerical labour process was fundamental to the administrative revolution. Interestingly, early stenographers performed craft-like jobs — evidenced by their consequently attained considerable socio-economic status (Lowe, 1980). However, by World War I, dictation and typing, the two core elements of the job, were being separated. Dictation machines facilitated the organization of central typing pools. Combining technical innovation with organizational rationalization, these pools gave rise to the "office machine age" (Mills, 1956: 195). . . .

ADMINISTRATIVE CONTROL AND THE TRANSFORMATION OF THE OFFICE

. . . We have argued that the modern office is the administrative centre of corporate capitalism. Through the office, managers attempt to exercise greater control and co-ordination over internal operations and employees as well as larger environmental factors affecting the organization. However, in order for the office to function effectively in this role, increasing control had to be exercised over office administration. The notion of administrative control thus has a dual meaning. In the first sense, control can help us explain the growth of clerical occupations. The second can account for the rationalization of the office and the clerical labour process. In short, we are suggesting that in order for administrative control to be exercised *through* the office, managers also had to apply the same principles of control *over* the office.

Let us set this argument out in more detail before exploring its theoretical underpinnings. The concept of administrative control encompasses the organizational, occupational and economic dimensions of the adminstrative revolution. But exactly how did these variables interact to transform the means of administration? On the economic plane, the rise of corporate capitalism after 1900 brought rapid expansion to Canada's manufacturing and service industries. It was in these industries, we have noted, that the escalating demands for the processing, analysis and storage of information created a boom in clerical employment. The central organizational feature of the administrative revolution was the rise of the office bureaucracy. Driven by the competitive forces of the marketplace, capitalists carried out mergers and consolidations. The resulting corporate entities had their equivalent in the public sector in the form of large government bureaucracies. Whether the organizations were public or private, or engaged in services or manufacturing, the office became the nerve centre of management. For it was through the office that the daily operations of large-scale organizations were run. This brings us to the main occupational dynamic underlying the administrative revolution. The modern corporation — and in a similar fashion, the public bureaucracy — delegates operating authority to expert salaried managers. This new semi-professional group became increasingly concerned over aspects of organizational design, the work process and other nontechnical factors which may have hindered the achievement of overall goals, be they profit maximization or efficient public service.

As the role of the office became enlarged to include co-ordination of internal activities and regulation of environmental factors impinging upon the organization's future, strains and inefficiencies resulted. In short, the office itself became stricken with bureaucratic maladies. Soaring clerical costs threatened to undermine profits or, in the case of public bureaucracies, cost efficiency. By the First World War, office managers were beginning to recognize the advantages of office rationalization. It was the managerial drive for higher efficiency in clerical operations and greater regimentation of the office labour force which underlay the rationalization of the clerk's job.

Two trends thus converged, precipitating a transformation in office work. First, more clerks were required to process the flood of information. Second, managers increasingly came to rely upon the office as the support system for their power and authority. The office was the key instrument in all managerial decision making. Together, these factors magnified the scope of office procedures. Inefficiencies in clerical routines — resulting from organizational weaknesses as well as from the underlying tensions of worker resistance to their subordination — were exacerbated. This launched a managerial drive for control over the clerical labour process. The result was a highly rationalized office in which deskilled jobs were defined as suitable women's work. What this suggests is that three factors, linked by the concept of administrative control, underlay the administrative revolution: (a) the rapid growth of manufacturing and service industries; (b) the growing predominance of large-scale bureaucratic work organizations; and (c) the operation of these organizations by a cadre of salaried managers concerned with the efficient co-ordination of work activities and the regulation of workers. It is now useful for us to analyse how each of these factors contributed to the administrative revolution.

The Dynamics of Corporate Capitalism

There can be little doubt that the rise of corporate capitalism paralleled the changes we have already documented in administration between 1911 and 1931. Manufacturing, the cornerstone of an industrial economy, underwent tremendous expansion after 1900. Between 1880 and 1929, the number of manufacturing establishments was reduced from 50,000 to 22,000 through mergers and acquisitions (Firestone, 1953: 160). At the same time, the gross value of production soared from 700 million to 3,116 million (constant) dollars (Firestone, 1953: 160). The wheat boom in western Canada during the first decade of the twentieth century provided the primary stimulus for this rapid industrialization (Buckley, 1974: 4; Brown and Cook, 1976: 83–84). The First World War also was crucial, precipitating faster, more far-reaching expansion of industry than would have occurred under normal conditions. Much of the new industry established was accounted for by U.S. direct investment. The number of U.S. manufacturing branch plants increased from 100 in 1900 to 1,350 by the end of 1934 (Marshall, et al., 1976: 18). By 1918, we find that "the foundation for a modern industrial economy had been laid" (Firestone, 1953: 1952). . . .

A direct measure of the growing demand for clerical workers in manufacturing is the changing ratio of administrative to production workers. As the economy expanded and factories grew,

more office staff was required to administer the rising production. We thus find that the number of administrative employees (mainly clerical, but also including supervisory workers) for every one hundred workers in manufacturing increased from 8.6 in 1911 to 16.9 by 1931 (International Labour Office, 1937: 513). What this demonstrates is the direct connection between the advance of industrialization and the development of large central offices.

Service industries also underwent remarkable growth in response to the demands of an emerging industrial economy. Similarly, this sparked an enlargement of office staff. The development of white-collar bureaucracies was, in fact, most apparent in the service sector. For example, the insurance business grew by 850 per cent between 1909 and 1929, yet the number of companies only increased by one, to 41 (Poapst, 1950: 14). Sun Life Assurance began acquiring other insurance firms in 1890, when its head office staff numbered 20. Between 1910 and 1930, a total of 13 acquisitions was made, bringing the number of head office staff to 2,856 employees (see Neufeld, 1972; Sun Life Archives, Personnel File no. 2). . . .

In sum, the rise of manufacturing and service industries established a modern capitalist economy in Canada by the 1930s. Fundamental to this economic development was the concentration of employment into large bureaucracies. It is indeed significant that, during the period we are studying, there were two major waves of corporate mergers and acquisitions, one from 1909 to 1913 and another more pronounced wave from 1925 to 1929 (Weldon, 1966: 233). This combination of industrialization and bureaucratization set the stage for the rise of modern administration.

BUREAUCRACY AND THE MODERN OFFICE

. . . Neither the Marxian nor the Weberian view alone can fully address the question of how and why the administrative revolution took place. It is therefore useful to combine aspects of both. The Marxian perspective helps us to see how modern management largely entails the transfer of control over the productive process from workers to managers. The results, plainly evident in the twentieth-century office and factory, are devastating: job fragmentation, rigid hierarchies, and the coercive discipline and surveillance of workers — what Braverman (1974) refers to as the degradation of labour. But it is also reasonable to assert that inefficiency stemming from organizational problems often has sparked rationalization. How else would one explain the dramatic transformations in government offices, executed by foremost American scientific management experts, during the 1920s? The issue of organizational inefficiency suggests, then, that a modified Weberian view is also useful. The problems of large-scale organization reflect the tendency for co-ordination and integration to break down with increased division of labour and structural differentiation. These are organizational problems although one could argue that the rise of modern bureaucracy was itself fundamentally a by-product of capitalist development. What this misses, however, is that against the background of capitalist development, managerial initiatives were also directed against problems resulting directly from the expansion of bureaucracy.

By combining the economic and class perspectives of Marxism with the organizational emphasis of the Weberian tradition, we can thus account for the growth of clerical jobs and the transformation of office procedures in both public and private bureaucracies. This is achieved by defining administrative control as encompassing strategies to deal with the economic forces of competition and capital accumulation, means of regulating labour and diminishing class conflict, and systems to improve the co-ordination and integration of organizational operations. To more fully understand how administrative control was exercised through the office, and its impact on clerical workers, we must consider the origins and functions of modern management.

Modern Management and the Office

The rise of modern management was a crucial aspect of the administrative revolution, for only through the actions of this new semi-professional group were changes brought about in the office. The office began to assume its contemporary functions in the closing decades of the nineteenth century. Litterer (1963) documents how specialized staff functions originated with the advent of cost clerks and production control clerks in factories (see Nelson, 1975). Cost accounting — toward which Canadian manufacturers turned their attention after the turn of the century — and other scientific approaches to factory management were the administrative sequel to mechanized production (Landes, 1969). The office thus began to dominate the factory, becoming the "visible hand" of management. . . .

The most prominent managerial strategy for dealing with organizational problems and regulating workers' activities was Taylorism. Frederick W. Taylor's science of management widely disseminated by the start of the First World War, involved three basic axioms: (a) the dissociation of the labour process from the skills of the workers; (b) the separation of the conception and execution of a task; and (c) the application of management's resulting knowledge of the labour process to control each step in production (see Braverman, 1974; Copley, 1923; Urwick, 1957; Nelson, 1975). The cumulative effect of these initiatives leads Rinehart (1978: 6) to observe that "today, most workers are locked into jobs that require little knowledge and skill and that are defined and controlled from the upper echelons of complex organizations."

Two points can be made regarding the impact of the managerial thrust for control of the office. First, especially in manufacturing we find a direct link between the extension of managerial control and clerical growth. ... And second, as the scope of office operations expanded, managers in both manufacturing and service industries found it necessary to apply principles of rationalization, which originated in the factory, to clerical work.

"Management, the brain of the organization," to use a physiological analogy, "conveys its impulses through the clerical systems which constitute the nervous mechanism of the company" (Murdoch and Dale, 1961: 2). This underlines how clerical work furnished the means of integrating the components of an organization. Even in white-collar industries, such as insurance or banking, special departments were established to facilitate managerial control over administrative practices. As one insurance executive asserts, "office administration is not a job by itself. We are in the insurance business, and office administration, scientific office administration, is merely one

of the tools to help us carry on the insurance business more efficiently" (Life Office Management Association, 1927: 188). By the First World War, office managers in both Canada and the U.S., already aware of the importance of systematic administration, were being told that Taylorism and other scientific factory management schemes could be easily adapted to the office (Hagedorn, 1955: 167; Leffingwell, 1917: 5). The logic of office rationalization is clearly expressed by the father of scientific management, W.H. Leffingwell (1917: 35, 111, 109):

> Effective management implies control. The terms are in a sense interchangeable, as management without control is inconceivable, and both terms imply the exercise of a directing influence. ... The clerical function may then be correctly regarded as the linking or connecting function, which alone makes possible the efficient performance of hundreds of individual operations involved in the "subassembly" cycles of the business machine as a whole. ...

This statement encapsulates the essential nature of the modern office. Without clerical procedures as efficient, predictable and regimented as the factory assembly line, managerial control over external and internal factors affecting organizational goals would be diminished.

CONCLUSIONS

The purpose of this paper has been to analyse the administrative revolution which occurred in major Canadian offices between 1911 and 1931. By the onset of the Depression, the central features of the contemporary office were well in place. Increasingly, the typical clerk was a woman who performed a specialized job, often machine-paced, in a highly regimented bureaucratic setting. As in any kind of large-scale social change, the transition from the old nineteenth-century counting house to the modern twentieth-century office was not a smooth, all-encompassing process. The changes described above in the nature of clerical work as well as in office organization and management took place in a more or less halting, uneven fashion. Evidence suggests, though, that alterations in the means of administration were sufficiently sweeping and well rooted by the 1930s to characterize them as a "revolution."

Theoretically, our task has been to unite into a comprehensive explanation the broad occupational, economic and organizational forces associated with the rise of modern administration. This has been achieved by using the concept of administrative control. We have shown that control was the central feature in both the growth of the office and its rationalization by management. . . .

Notes

[1] This wage pattern seems to be standard in advanced capitalist societies. Research in the U.S. by Braverman (1974) and Burns (1954) and in Britain by Lockwood (1966) documents how the growth of the white-collar sector of the labour force has been marked by a relative decline in clerical wages.

[2] This is consistent with broad labour force trends. In 1971, the average income of women doing paid work was about half that of men (Armstrong and Armstrong, 1975: 371).

[3] While Taylorism was undoubtedly the label most commonly attached to attempts to rationalize the labour process, it was only one strategy in the broad "thrust for efficiency" which took root after 1900 (see Palmer, 1975). The term scientific management includes, then, a variety of systematic programs initiated by management to inject order and efficiency into the organization and execution of work.

References

Albrow, Martin. *Bureaucracy.* London: Macmillan, 1970.

Armstrong, Hugh and Armstrong, Pat. "The Segregated Participation of Women in the Canadian Labour Force, 1941–71," *Canadian Review of Sociology and Anthropology* 12 (1975): 370–84.

_____. *The Double Ghetto: Canadian Women and Their Segregated Work.* Toronto: McClelland and Stewart, 1978.

Bank of Montreal (1956) *The Service Industries.* Study No. 17, Royal Commission on Canada's Economic Prospects.

Bank of Nova Scotia Archives n.d. "The Bank of Nova Scotia, 1832–1932, One Hundredth Anniversary." Toronto.

Bendix, Reinhart. *Work and Authority in Industry.* Berkeley: University of California Press, 1974.

Blau, Peter M. *The Dynamics of Bu-*

reaucracy, revised ed. Chicago: University of Chicago Press, 1963.

Braverman, Harry. *Labour and Monopoly Capital: the Degradation of Work in the Twentieth Century.* New York: Monthly Review Press, 1974.

Brown, Robert Craig and Cook, Ramsay. *Canada 1896–1921: A Nation Transformed.* Toronto: McClelland and Stewart, 1976.

Buckley, Kenneth. *Capital Formation in Canada, 1896–1930.* Toronto: McClelland and Stewart, 1974.

Burns, Robert K. "The Comparative Economic Position of Manual and White-Collar Employees," in *Journal of Business* 27 (1954): 257–67.

Canada Censuses, 1891–1971 (published and unpublished data).

———. Wage-Earners by Occupations. 1901 Census, Bulletin 1. Ottawa: King's Printer, 1907.

———. Occupational Trends in Canada, 1891–1931. Special Bulletin, D.B.S. Census Branch, Ottawa: King's Printer, 1939.

———. *Manufacturing Industries of Canada.* Ottawa: D.B.S., 1961.

———. *1971 Annual Census of Manufacturers, Summary Statistics, Preliminary.* Ottawa: Statistics Canada, 1973.

———. *Canada Year Book.* Ottawa: Information Canada, 1974.

Chandler, Alfred D., Jr. *The Visible Hand: The Managerial Revolution in American Business.* Cambridge, Mass.: Harvard University Press, 1977.

Clement, Wallace. *The Canadian Corporate Elite.* Toronto: McClelland and Stewart, 1975.

Copley, F.B. *Frederick W. Taylor, Father of Scientific Management,* 2 Vols. New York: Harper and Row, 1923.

Dreyfuss, Carl. *Occupation and Ideology of the Salaried Employee,* 2 Vols. trans. Eva Abramovitch. New York: Works Progress Administration and the Department of Social Science, Columbia University, 1938.

Firestone, O.J. "Canada's Economic Development, 1867–1952," paper prepared for the Third Conference of the International Association for Research in Income and Wealth, Castelgandolfo, Italy, 1953.

Glen, Evelyn Nakano and Feldberg, Roslyn L. "Degraded and Deskilled: The Proletarianization of Clerical Work," in *Social Problems* 25 (1977): 52–64.

Gulick, Luther. "Notes on the Theory of Organization," in *Papers on the Science of Administration.* Luther Gulick and L. Urwick (eds.) New York: Institute of Public Administration, 1937.

Haber, Samuel. *Efficiency and Uplift: Scientific Management in the Progressive Era, 1890–1920.* Chicago: University of Chicago Press, 1964.

Hagedorn, Homer J. "The Management Consultant as Transmitter of Business Techniques," in *Explorations in Entrepreneurial History* 7 (1955): 164–173.

Hoos, Ida R. *Automation in the Office.* Washington: Public Affairs Press, 1961.

Industrial Canada

International Labour Office. "The Use of Office Machinery and Its Influence on Conditions of Work for Staff," in *International Labour Review* 36 (1937): 486–516.

Journal of The Canadian Bankers' Association

Kaufman, Herbert. "The Administrative Function," in *International Encyclopedia of the Social Sciences* Vol. 1, David Sills (ed.) New York: Macmillan Co. and the Free Press, 1968.

Landes, David. *The Unbound Prometheus: Technological Change and Industrial De-*

velopment in Western Europe from 1750 to the Present. Cambridge: Cambridge University Press, 1969.

Lederer, Emil. *The Problem of the Modern Salaried Employee: Its Theoretical and Statistical Basis.* Trans. E.E. Warburg. New York: State Department of Social Welfare and the Department of Social Science, Columbia University, 1937.

Leffingwell, William Henry. *Scientific Office Management.* Chicago: A.W. Shaw, 1917.

Life Office Management Association: Proceedings of Annual Conferences.

Litterer, Joseph A. "Systematic Management: Design for Organizational Recoupling in American Manufacturing Firms," in *Business History Review* 37 (1963): 369–391.

Lockwood, David. *The Blackcoated Workers.* London: Allen and Unwin, 1966.

Lowe, Graham S. "The Administrative Revolution: The Growth of Clerical Occupations and the Development of the Modern Office in Canada, 1911–1931." Unpublished Ph.D. thesis, University of Toronto, Toronto, 1979.

———. "Women, Work and the Office: The Feminization of Clerical Occupations in Canada", 1901–1931, in *Canadian Journal of Sociology* 5 (1980): 361–381.

Marglin, Stephen A. "What Do Bosses Do?: The Origins and Functions of Hierarchy in Capitalist Production." Harvard Institute of Economic Research, Discussion Paper No. 222, 1971.

Marshall, Herbert, Southard, F.A., and Taylor, K.W. *Canadian-American Industry.* Toronto: McClelland and Stewart, 1976.

Melman, Stewart. "The Rise of Administrative Overhead in the Manufacturing Industries of the United States, 1899–1947," in *Oxford Economic Papers*, New Series 3 (1951): 62–112.

Meltz, Noah M. *Manpower in Canada, 1931–1961.* Ottawa: Queen's Printer, 1969.

Merton, Robert K. "Bureaucratic Structure and Personality," in *Reader in Bureaucracy.* R.K. Merton et al. (eds.) New York: Free Press, 1952.

Mills, C. Wright. *White Collar: The American Middle Classes.* New York: Oxford University Press, 1956.

Monetary Times

Murdoch, Allan A. and Dale, J. Rodney. *The Clerical Function: A Survey of Modern Clerical Systems and Methods.* London: Sir Isaac Pitman and Sons, 1961.

Nelson, Daniel. *Managers and Workers: Origins of the New Factory System in the United States, 1880–1920.* Madison: University of Wisconsin Press, 1975.

Neufeld, E.P. *The Financial System of Canada.* Toronto: Macmillan, 1972.

Palmer, Bryan. "Class, Conception and Conflict: The Thrust for Efficiency, Managerial Views of Labour and the Working Class Rebellion, 1903–22," in *Radical Review of Political Economics* 7 (1975): 31–49.

Poapst, James. "The Growth of the Life Insurance Industry in Canada, 1909–47." Unpublished M.Comm. thesis, McGill University, Montreal, 1950.

Rinehart, James W. *The Tyranny of Work.* Don Mills: Longman Canada, 1975.

———. "Contradictions of Work-Related Attitudes and Behaviour: An Interpretation," in *Canadian Review of Sociology and Anthropology* 15 (1978): 1–15.

Rountree, Meredith G. *The Railway Worker: A Study of the Employment and Unemployment Problems of the Canadian Railways.* Toronto: Oxford University Press, 1936.

Rushing, William A. "The Effects of Industry Size and Division of Labour on Administration," in *Administrative Science Quarterly* 12 (1967): 273–295.

Shepard, Jon M. *Automation and Alienation: A Study of Office and Factory Workers.* Cambridge, Mass.: M.I.T. Press, 1971.

Simon, Herbert A. "Decision-Making and Administrative Organization," in *Reader in Bureaucracy.* R.K. Merton et al. (eds.) New York: Free Press, 1952.

———. *Administrative Behaviour*, 3rd ed. New York: Free Press, 1976.

Sun Life Assurance Co. Archives, Montreal.

Urquhart, M.C. and Buckley, K.A.H. *Historical Statistics of Canada.* Toronto: Macmillan, 1965.

Weber, Max. *From Max Weber: Essays in Sociology.* Trans. and ed. H.H. Gerth and C.W. Mills. New York: Oxford University Press, 1958.

———. *The Theory of Social and Economic Organization.* New York: Free Press, 1964.

Weldon, J.C. "Consolidation in Canadian Industry, 1900–1948," in *Restrictive Trade Practices in Canada*, L.A. Skeoch. (ed.) Toronto: McClelland and Stewart, 1966.

Work in America. Report of a Special Task Force to the U.S. Secretary of Health, Education and Welfare prepared by the W.E. Upjohn Institute for Employment Research. Cambridge, Mass.: M.I.T. Press, 1973.

Theodorson, George A. and Theodorson, Achilles G. *A Modern Dictionary of Sociology.* New York: Thomas Y. Crowell, 1969.

Urwick, Lyndall P. *The Life and Work of Frederick Winslow Taylor.* London: Urwick, Orr and Partners, 1957.

The Family

The last section showed that gender relations are in a serious state today, with important effects on family life. This section will examine the current state of family life in Canada. It includes articles on female lone parenting, domestic violence, and the growing variety of family structures.

Research from around the world shows that nuclear families are becoming more common and laterally extended families less so. People have fewer kin available to them than in the past and more people live alone or outside conventional families; generally, the variation in household forms is increasing. However, domestic form seems to make less difference to people's lives than in the past. Many family functions are even being performed by non-families today. Yet, perhaps as a result of these changes, people continue to sentimentalize the traditional family.

In relations between husbands and wives, most wives work a "double day" and husbands persist in their traditional behaviour, though people are inclined to exaggerate the change in spousal roles. Women continue to suffer from a discontinuity between the socialization they received in childhood and the work they must do as adults. Indeed, modern spousal roles continue to puzzle married people throughout the world. Some societies have even made special efforts to bring about changes in spousal behaviour as part of modernization. All of this rapid change has increased uncertainty about the performance of familial roles.

People seem to have less need of marriage than in the past. True, traditional forms of marriage persist amid more choice and variety; but traditionalism is waning. When people do marry, they typically enjoy more independence in selecting their mates than ever before, and they choose across what used to be fairly rigid boundaries of religion, ethnicity, and social class. As a result, more people are marrying for love, not for the potential spouse's ability to provide an income, keep house, or bear sons.

As legal marriage declines in popularity, cohabitation increases as a form of trial marriage, or substitute for it. And fewer people want to marry after dissolving a previous union.

With more variety and freedom in intimate unions, wives — not their spouses or kin — are making the decisions about childbearing. In turn, women's education and work aspirations play an ever greater part in fertility decisions. Facilitating decisions to avoid or delay childbearing is a lower cost of contraception: preventing parenthood is easier than ever in human history. Another factor reducing fertility is a lower preference for sons over daughters in many parts of the world. Some states (such as China) have succeeded in enforcing a birth limitation program. However no such program is needed in the developed world. There, individualistic values push fertility well below replacement levels.

This lowering of reproduction, in turn, contributes to higher rates of divorce. So do easier divorce laws and better work opportunities for women. More women are divorcing their spouses when they are able to earn an income, since they do not have to remain in an unsatisfactory relationship. Cohabitation also increases the rates of dissolution of both informal and (later) formal unions. As a consequence, more people around the world are feeling the health and income consequences of divorce.

These dramatic changes are recent and enormously important. To see the magnitude of this change, consider what existed a mere generation or two ago in Canada. Then, whatever kept women in the home performing unpaid work for the working man kept them, indirectly, in the (unpaid) employment of the husband's boss. Today, even working class wives are getting jobs and many are unionizing. In general, economic dependency on a husband has become less common. This means that women enjoy more economic and personal freedom than ever before. This fact has transformed modern family life.

Of course, it may no longer be realistic to speak about a "typical" modern family. Certainly, evidence suggests that the traditional family — made up of a mother staying home, a father going out to work, and a few dependent children biologically related to mother and father — is not typical any more. Nor has a single form of family life replaced it; rather, variety, fluidity, and idiosyncrasy are the norm.

Increasingly, mothers are going out to work. Increasingly, marriages are dissolving: the divorce rate has grown dramatically since the late 1960s. Second batches of children often follow divorce and remarriage, and ever fewer Canadian households contain people related by blood alone.

Because of these changes, family members have increasingly unpredictable relations with one another. We are far from knowing what kinds of social and economic responsibilities ought to accompany these family roles, but we can no longer assume they are being performed as they were in the past.

We cannot assume, for example, that Johnny's mother's new husband will take on a responsibility — economic, social, and psychological — toward Johnny that is anything like the responsibility Johnny's father assumed by the mere fact of biological fatherhood. Once Johnny's biological father remarries and fathers some new children, he may even ignore his own legal (and emotional) obligations to Johnny. For example, the payment of child support by biological fathers, a minimal obligation, is very far from certain at present. A great many fathers pay nothing at all, or pay sporadically; and otherwise give their children little time or attention. Many Canadian children go without adequate fathering today.

No one quite knows how family life is supposed to operate today. The traditional norms of "love, honour, and obey," whether between spouses or between parents and children, are so commonly violated that we cannot assume they are in effect. New family forms — more varied, changeable, and complex than before — have not yet given rise to new norms and expectations. As a result, the term "family" has become less useful as the description of a social institution. So it is harder than ever to make legislation about "the family."

Today few people want to submerge all their rights and responsibilities in a social unit, even in the family. We typically prefer people to treat us as individuals. Further, since families are so varied and unpredictable, the very possiblity of treating people as members of families is gone. We are ever less likely to think about people as spouses or parents or children of other people. More than ever in our history, we have become a society of individuals and, increasingly, our laws and social services reflect this change. In her article in this section, Margrit Eichler summarizes the more important differences between traditional and current thinking about the family.

Not only do families vary enormously from one another; they also change dramatically over time. Typically, there is a family life cycle, just as there is an individual life cycle. Like individuals, families pass through stages of functioning and well-being. At each stage the individuals involved meet new problems, try to solve them or adjust to them, then move on to another stage. For example, the stage of family life when all the children have left home — the "empty nest" stage — brings certain problems and challenges. Spouses must adjust to living alone together for another twenty or thirty years.

Lupri and Frideres (1981) have found a general, marked, lengthy decline in marital satisfaction while children are growing up; and a return to high levels of marital satisfaction after all the children have left home. This finding is no surprise when we remember that bringing up children is hard work!

And remember from the last section that women do more than their share of the family work; so women ought to express less satisfaction with marriage than men. In fact, women who have both children *and* a job to take care of ought to be the least satisfied of all. This is precisely what Lupri and Frideres find. Working women's marital satisfaction is much lower than their husbands'. Parenting has a less harmful effect on husbands' satisfaction with marriage, but then, husbands are not doing much of the work.

This reminds us of sociologist Jesse Bernard's (1973) dictum that, in every family, there are two marriages: his marriage and her marriage. His marriage demands a cozy household, a loving wife, and little children to continue the family name. Her marriage provides the cozy household, takes care of the children, provides emotional support, and brings in additional income when needed. Marriage simply benefits men more than women. For men, marriage is a support; for women, largely a burden. Many studies bear out these assertions. Recent studies show that married women run higher health risks than married men and, often, single women.

Demographer Nathan Keyfitz (1988) has also shown us the size of marriage's benefit to men, compared to women. At age twenty-five, a married man's life expectancy is about five years longer than a single man's of the same age. By contrast, a married woman's life expectancy at that age is only one and a half years longer than a single woman's. By this measure, marriage is beneficial to both sexes, but over three times healthier for men than it is for women.

For a variety of reasons, the institution of family is always changing. Some of the change is due to gender conflict; some, to the effect of changing family norms. Some is due to life cycle stresses (such as the presence of adolescent children in the home); and some is a result of economic pressures that demand two incomes, hence two careers. Some changes in the family are more narrowly demographic. In the last hundred or so years, demographic changes have produced interesting changes in family life. A longer life expectancy, combined with a shorter childbearing period, has produced a different balance of marital time.

In the past, spouses spent most of their married life in the company of children. Almost immediately after marriage, children began to arrive. No sooner had all the children grown up and left but one of the spouses died. Spouses had little opportunity to get to know each other as individuals. Today, thanks to contraception, couples wait a little longer to start a family, and they typically finish after only one or two children. Then, roughly twenty or twenty-five years after the start of childbearing, the couple is on its own again, with another twenty or thirty years of (possible) marriage ahead of them.

Yet just as these demographic changes have extended freedom from children, people have increasingly chosen to divorce their mates and start new families. As a result, few marriages today will last much longer than they would have a century ago. How do we explain this interesting substitution of divorce for death?

One possible explanation is that people divorce more often today because they cannot stand the prospect of a prolonged child-free marriage with a less than perfect spouse. When people thought married life would be short and/or filled with work and children, they may have demanded less in a spouse. Today, marriage focuses less on procreation and ever more on companionship, romance, and pleasure. Imperfections in a mate become strong motivators to divorce. People divorce in the hopes of finding more happiness in their (longer) lives.

Paradoxically, most married people today make the decision to separate and divorce when children are present and (therefore) emotional satisfaction is declining rapidly. Perhaps if they knew that satisfaction would return when their children left, and the remaining years of marriage would be happier ones, parents would not rush to divorce and remarry. By starting a new family, they go through the same upsetting process a second time.

Other parents do not remarry immediately. If they are women, they are likely to gain custody of the children after divorce and become lone parents. An article by Maureen Moore shows that this is one of three ways women become lone parents. She also shows that the three types of lone parents have different life-cycle profiles, and different experiences. Most important, lone parenting has become a very common — though often short-lived — form of family life in Canada.

Many conflictual marriages do not end in divorce but, rather, escalate into domestic violence. The prevalence of family violence, its forms and causes, is the subject of a paper by Eugen Lupri. He shows that violence between spouses is widespread and highly patterned: that is, we can predict where and when it is likely to occur. Interestingly, there is a considerable amount of violence directed by wives against husbands; although the opposite — violence by husbands against wives — is both more common and more highly publicized. Also, we cannot equate the two kinds of violence because they differ in severity and power of the perpetrator and victim.

Violence, divorce, family conflict, domestic inequality: these problems are all complex and worrisome. No one knows whether to seek solutions at home or in the political arena: as personal problems or public issues. Certainly, our family structures and family problems are more complex than they ever were.

References

Bernard, Jesse. *The Future of Marriage.* New York: Bantam Books, 1973.

Keyfitz, Nathan. "On the wholesomeness of marriage." Pp. 449–462 in Lorne Tepperman and James Curtis (eds.) *Readings in*

Sociology: An Introduction. Toronto: McGraw-Hill Ryerson, 1988.

Lupri, Eugen and Frideres, James. "Marital satisfaction over the life cycle," *Canadian Journal of Sociology,* 6 (1981), pp. 283–305.

TWENTY-ONE

Models of the Family

Margrit Eichler

MARGRIT EICHLER, Professor of Sociology at the Ontario Institute for Studies in Education, Toronto, specializes in the study of family, women's studies, and gender relations. Her books and monographs include the *Double Standard: A Feminist Critique of Feminist Social Science* (1980); *Women in Future Research* (1982); *On the Treatment of the Sexes in Research*, with Jeanne Lapointe (1985); *Canadian Families: An Introduction*, with Mary Bullen (1986); *Canadian Families Today; Recent Changes and their Policy Consequences*, 2nd edition, (1988); and *Non-Sexist Research Methods: A Practical Guide* (1988). In addition, numerous papers have been published and presented on related topics. Professor Eichler has been centrally involved in the administration of the Canadian Research Institute for the Advancement of Women, and has acted as consultant to such organizations as TV Ontario, Statistics Canada, the Secretary of State's Women's Program, and the Canadian Advisory Council on the Status of Women. Between 1984–1986, she served as Chairperson of the Sociology Department of OISE. She also has served as the President of the Canadian Sociology and Anthropology Association (1990–91), and has recently conducted a major study of Women's Studies in Canada.

INTRODUCTION

. . . It is the major thesis of this paper that within sociology a monolithic definition of the family still prevails, that this definition is not only inadequate but leads to the replacement of empirical questions with assumptions and informs our data collection process in such a manner that we remain unaware of the severity of the misfit between our assumptions and reality. In turn, this leads to a neglect of vitally important questions, and to a misperception of what constitutes "problem" families. Ultimately, such thinking results in social policies which are inadequate for meeting the needs of individual families, their individual members, and society at large.

THE MONOLITHIC MODEL OF THE FAMILY

We can conceptualize the various functions and conditions as dimensions of familial interactions which together make up the structure of the family. These dimensions can be identified as follows:
— the legal dimension
— the procreative dimension

— the sexual dimension
— the residential dimension
— the economic dimension
— the emotional dimension

Within each of these dimensions various degrees of interaction can be identified. In the following, we will explore the range of possible interactions and provide a formal definition of the monolithic family model.

Legal dimension. Legal aspects range from prescribing interaction in other dimensions (e.g., a marriage has to be sexually consummated to be legally valid, children reside by law with their parents), over leaving them legally undefined, to proscribing them (e.g., a court order restraining a violent husband from entering the matrimonial home).

Procreative dimension. Procreative interaction ranges from a couple having child(ren) with each other and only with each other, over one or both of them having child(ren) with other partners plus having child(ren) together, to having children only with other partners or having none at all.

Socialization dimension. Interaction in the socialization dimension ranges from both parents being involved in the socialization of their children, over only one of them being involved, (e.g., in the case of a divorce in which one parent has custody and the other has not even visitation rights) to neither of them being involved (e.g., when the child has been given up for adoption).

Sexual dimension. Sexual interaction ranges from a marital couple having sex only with each other, over having sex together with other partners, to having sex only with other persons or being celibate.

Residential dimension. Residential interaction ranges from all family members sharing the same residence day and night to all or some of them living in completely separate residences, with a multiplicity of intermediate arrangements.

Economic dimension. Economic cooperation can refer to a wide variety of possible relationships. As far as familial interactions are concerned, the most important economic relationship concerns support obligations and actual provision of support (e.g., a sociological rather than a legal definition of support) between family members. Economic cooperation in this sense, then, ranges from one family member being totally responsible for the support of all family members, to a family in which all members are totally economically independent. . . .

Emotional dimension. Emotional interaction ranges from all family members being positively emotionally involved with each other to being negatively emotionally involved or not being emotionally involved at all. . . .

Using these dimensions of familial interactions we can define the monolithic model of the family as a model according to which high interaction in one dimension of familial interaction is assumed to coincide with or result in high interaction in all other dimensions. This has several consequences which can be summarized as follows: (1) the assumption of congruence leads to (2) a bias in the data collection process, which leads to (3) an underestimation of the incidence of non-congruence and (4) inappropriate categorizations, which in turn, (5) lead to misdefinitions as to what constitutes "problem" families and (6) a neglect of vitally important questions. In the following, we will deal with each of the points in turn.

CONSEQUENCES OF A MONOLITHIC MODEL OF THE FAMILY

Assumption of congruence

That a family consists of two legally-married sexually-cohabiting adults who have children together whom they parent, that it constitutes an economic unit in which either one spouse (formerly always the husband-father) or both spouses (husband-father and wife-mother) are responsible for the economic support of their dependent children and each other, and that it is a social group in which all members live together and love and nurture each other is so commonly understood that it seems almost frivolous to raise any questions about this conglomeration of characteristics. Indeed, within the pertinent literature we find congruence between various separate dimensions constantly stressed. To consider just one dimension, the emotional one, there is general agreement that families (i.e., structural units which consist of spouses and possibly their children) provide love and emotional support for each other. They are presumed to constitute a "haven in a heartless world" (Lasch, 1977) although under increasing attack from outside agencies which have significantly eroded their capacity to function as a refuge. . . .

What is important to note in this context is that there is no attempt to raise the question how many of the existing structural units that we call families actually *do* provide emotional support and love for their various members? Do some families perhaps provide such support for some members but not for others? Or do they provide it part of the time but not always? Perhaps not at all? The assumption of congruence leads to the foregone conclusion: families provide emotional support and love for each other.

One would expect that one of the preconditions for positive emotional involvement would be the absence of fear. We have only very recently become aware that many families are, in fact, a dangerous place for their members to live. Bell and Benjamin have noted that "it is safe to conclude that the majority of murders in Canada occur in family and family-like relationships" (Bell and Benjamin, forthcoming, ms. p. 2). In the United States too, the Federal Bureau of Investigation estimates that over 50 percent of all murders of women are committed by men with whom they have intimate relationships (reported in Walker, 1978: 144).

Steinmetz and Straus (1974: 3) argue that ". . . it would be hard to find a group or institution in American society in which violence is more of an everyday occurrence than it is within the family." A recent Canadian study estimates that "Every year, 1 in 10 Canadian women who are married or in a relationship with a live-in lover are battered" (MacLeod, 1980: 21). This, of course, is only one form of familial violence. Child abuse is another one.

Again, we have to rely on estimates. One relevant American estimate is that as much as one-third of the population may experience some form of childhood sexual abuse (reported in MacFarlane, 1978: 86). The 1978 Ontario Report of the Task Force on Child Abuse starts out with the observation, "It is impossible to avoid the conclusion that the present arrangement of services is not effective in protecting children from child abuse." For parent assault (adult or adolescent children assaulting their parents) we do not even have estimates. It is a completely hidden crime.

The most thorough review of the literature on family violence to date concludes that "Although there are limitations in the representativeness of the samples and the precision of the methodology used in each study, the pervasiveness of physical violence between family members cannot be denied" (Steinmetz, 1978: 5). To assume congruence between the emotional dimension and the other dimensions of familial interactions is, therefore, clearly inappropriate.

The assumption of congruence concerning other dimensions of familial interaction is no less problematic. We will here only very briefly consider two other examples, one concerning the economic dimension and the other the procreative dimension.

As far as the economic dimension is concerned, the law assumes and indeed prescribes that family members are responsible for each other's support, and therefore disentitles people to access to public monies (e.g., welfare) on the basis not of their need, but of their family status. This practice is based on the concept of "family income." The notion of family income, in turn, is based on the assumptions that (a) people living in a family situation need individually less money than people not living in a family situation, and (b) that "family income" is shared in an equitable manner, thus relieving the state of responsibility for the economic welfare of individual citizens. (For a critique of the concept of family income, see Eichler, 1980.) Since "family income" is widely utilized as a basis to assess need, a great deal of real poverty thus remains hidden.

As far as the procreative dimension is concerned, the assumption of congruence demonstrates itself in two opposing ways: children who are living with two adults who are married to each other are treated as if they were the biological children of these people, whether or not they are (adoption and remarriage are two factors which lead to non-congruity in the social and biological aspects of parenting) and a parent who is not attached in marriage to the other parent who has custody of the child(ren) is treated as if (s)he (usually he) is not a parent at all. We will consider this issue further in the following sections.

Of immediate concern here is that the assumption of congruence leads to a bias in the data collection process which continually reinforces the ostensible veracity of the previously made assumption by neglecting to ask questions which would produce data that challenge the assumption of congruence. . . .

Bias in data collection

Our data collection process in effect hides the degree to which families do not conform to the model of the monolithic family. This is most obvious in the case of adoption. Adopted children are not only counted as biological children of their parents, but they are issued new birth certificates which legally declare them as such, thus making it impossible to correctly assess the number of adoptive families. We do have provincial data on the number of children who are placed in adoption every year, but since one family may adopt more than one child or children may be placed for adoption across provinces, we do not know how many families are involved. In addition, for each child that is given up for adoption whose parents are alive, there are one mother and one father who are not raising their own child themselves. Potentially, one adoption may thus create a non-congruity between the procreative and the socialization dimension for three families: the adoptive family, the family of the mother, and the family of the father.

Numerically more important in creating non-congruity between dimensions is divorce. In recent years, the divorce rates have increased sharply, from 45.7 per 100,000 population in 1965 in Canada to 222.0 per 100,000 population in 1975 in Canada (Ontario Statistics 1977, Vol. 1, Table 4.7, p. 108). The ratio of marriage to divorce was, in 1975 in Canada 1:3.9, i.e., for approximately every four marriages, there was one divorce (computed from Ontario Statistics 1977, Table 4.6, p. 107). For the United States, it has been estimated that every third marriage will eventually be dissolved in divorce (Glick, 1977: 5–13). The majority of divorced people eventually remarry. When two previously divorced people remarry, especially when their new marital partner was not previously married, the proportion of families which do not conform to the monolithic model increases further. In 1974, 10.5 percent of all Canadian marriages had a divorced bridegroom, and 3.4 percent of all marriages had a widowed bridegroom. In the same year, 9.6 percent of all brides were divorced, and 3.8 percent of all brides were widowed (Canada Yearbook, 1976–77, computed from Table 4.49). Altogether, in 1975, 21.4 percent of all marriages involved at least one previously married partner (Statistics Canada, 1977).

Divorce is especially important when children are involved. While in 1974, 41.3 percent of all divorces in Canada did not involve any *dependent* children (i.e., children under the age of sixteen living at home) 58.7 percent of all divorces *did* involve dependent children (Canada Yearbook, 1976–77, Table 4.53). In 1974 alone, about 55,000 children (computed

from Canada Yearbook, 1976–77, Table 4.53) went through the process of divorce of their parents. Whether or not these parents eventually remarry, there remains an incongruence between the biological and social parenting that these children will experience.

However, this incongruence remains largely hidden. The statistical concept of a husband-wife family with dependent children indicates merely that a woman and man are married to each other and that some dependent children live in their household. It does not tell us anything about who the biological (or, for that matter, the emotional) parents of the children are. Paul C. Glick has estimated that in the United States in 1970 "more than 30 percent of school children were *not* living with a father and mother who were in a continuous first marriage" (Glick, 1975: 22). This figure does not even include children beyond school age who nevertheless might be affected in a variety of ways by a divorce of their parents. ...

As far as the residential dimension is concerned, the unit of analysis is usually the household. Of all Canadian households in 1971, 81.7 percent were family households. The other 18.7 percent were non-family households, consisting either of one person (13.4 percent) or of two or more persons (4.9 percent) (Canada Yearbook, 1976–77, Table 4.24, p. 194). Of the family households, 8.1 percent contained, in 1971, besides the family of the household head (an)other person(s). Seventy point nine percent of all households were listed as "families of household head without additional person." Two percent of all households were two-or-more family households.

The concept of the household implies that every person lives in one household and in one household only. However, there are families in which one family member commutes regularly, or in which one or more family members spend extended periods of time elsewhere — e.g., children who attend boarding school, people whose jobs lead them to regularly spend nights elsewhere. Other cases include people who frequently and regularly have to work night shifts. Then, there is a category of seasonal jobs which takes people from their homes for extended periods of time. Lack of working opportunities in one's home region may force people to accept jobs elsewhere. Military service, extended hospital stays, prison terms, may likewise result in variations in the residential pattern.

It is a moot question to argue whether or not such people do or do not have more than one residence. What is important is that there are obviously gross variations in the way in which people who may be part of a family reside with the rest of the family. Statistics to document the extent of multiple residence or split residence patterns are unavailable.

When discussing the issue of family violence, it was noted that we have to rely on estimates which vary very substantially in order to delimit the phenomenon. This, in itself, is part of the problem we are dealing with: because of an assumption that "the" family shields its members "from physical harm, whether from natural phenomena or human violence" and satisfies the "emotional needs in family members through the provision of love, services, resources and time" (*The Family as a Focus*, 1979: 9–10) we have neglected to systematically study the incidence of family abuse and are therefore incapable of exactly assessing what proportion of families do not only fail to shield their members from harm and provide love, but actually constitute an environment within which people are exposed to greater harm than elsewhere.

As a last example of data bias, the convention of using family income as an indication of the economic status of the individuals who make up a family systematically hides inequities in the distribution of so-called family income and further hides the systematic sex differential in income security which is due to the familial roles played by women and men. As the National Council of Welfare (1979: 51) has recently concluded, "Most Canadian women become poor at some point in their lives. Their poverty is rarely the result of controllable circumstances, and it is seldom the outcome of extraordinary misfortune. In most cases, women are poor because poverty is the natural consequence of the role they are still expected to play in our society."

Underestimation of non-congruence

The assumption of congruence leads to a systematic bias in the data collection process which makes it impossible to state firmly what percentage of families actually do conform to the monolithic model of the family and what proportion deviate in some significant manner. . . .

One major type of non-congruence is found in the procreative and socialization dimensions. Incongruity between procreation and socialization may occur through death, separation, desertion, divorce, births to unwed mothers, artificial donor insemination,[1] adoption and fostering. Seen from the perspective of children, according to an American estimate, 30 percent of all school age children in 1970 were growing up in families in which there was some type of incongruity between the procreative and socialization dimensions. However, if we add to this figure the perspective of parents, the proportion of families affected by some form of this type of incongruity would increase appreciably. For every child that is raised by one parent who has custody of him or her, there is one other parent who does *not* raise this child in his or her own family. This applies to all of the factors which have been mentioned as leading to incongruity between the two dimensions under consideration, with the exception of death. In the case of adoption and fostering, three families may be potentially affected by incongruity: the adoptive or fostering family, and the families of the biological mother and the biological father, if they do have families of their own. Potentially, therefore, discrepancies between the socialization and procreation dimensions alone could conceivably affect in one way or the other more than 50 percent of all families.

Another form of discrepancy between procreation and parenting occurs when we consider the emotional dimension. Families which show no discrepancies at the structural level may nevertheless be families in which the parenting is carried on by one parent only or, in some cases of emotional and/or physical child abuse, by neither of the parents. . . .

When considering the issue of family violence, we know that it takes place, not just between parents and children but also between spouses and siblings in a significant proportion of families. Again, reliable data which would allow us to compute the proportion of families which experience some form of sustained violence against one, some, or all of their members do not exist. However, if one includes all types of family violence, including silbing violence, which seems to be very frequent (cf. Steinmetz, 1978: 5) and husband beating, the estimates for which range from 4.6 percent to 20 per-

cent of all American husbands (MacKintosh, 1978: 12), an estimate that 50 percent of all families experience some form of family violence may not be too high.

Other types of deviations from the monolithic model of the family include variant patterns in the sexual dimension, the residential dimension and the economic dimension. As far as the sexual dimension is concerned, a 1976 Canadian survey on sexual behaviors indicated that 4 percent of married men and 2.7 percent of married women never had coitus (Report of the Committee on the Operation of the Abortion Law, 1977: 329 and 331). Since it is unclear who the sexual partners of the sexually active population were, according to this survey a minimum of 4 percent of Canadian couples had no sexual relations together, but potentially the figure might be much higher. In addition, an unknown percentage of couples had one or two members who engaged in extramarital sexual relations.

As far as the residential dimension is concerned, most families form a household, which is what we would expect according to the monolithic family model. However, there are some important exceptions. We have already noted that 8.1 percent of all family households contained, in 1971, besides the family of the household head (an)other person(s). Such variations in household composition are statistically accessible; however, there are other variations on which data are not easily available. Personal experience and knowledge suggest that commuting couples, in which one spouse maintains a second residence (usually for job reasons) exist, but their number and proportion is unknown.[2] One variation within the residential dimension, however, we know to be frequent although exact figures are not available:

the number of children who attend some form of day care is very high. Until now, day care has not been conceptualized as affecting the residential dimension, its relevance — if at all considered — has been seen in terms of parent child relations and the eventual effect on the development of the child. However, it seems that day care can meaningfully be seen as partially constituting a variant pattern within the residential dimension. . . .

As far as the economic dimension is concerned, according to the monolithic model of the family, one adult, usually the husband-father, is totally responsible for the economic support of all family members. Statistically speaking, this is increasingly less frequent. In 1975, 58 percent of all wives under the age of 45 were either working full-time or part-time in the labor force (National Council of Welfare, 1979: 22, Table 4). We must further assume that the participation rate of women is underreported since women who babysit in their homes, or do other domestic services for pay, tend not to report this income in order to avoid the loss of the married exemption for their husbands.[3]

Other types of deviations from the monolithic model of the family include permanently childless couples (around 10 percent of all Canadian couples) and people living in experimental families or cohabiting (according to an American study this represents 4 percent of all adults in the United States, cf. Ramey, 1978: 1).

The various percentages and estimates that have been cited cannot be added up since we do not know to what degree they overlap. Nevertheless, it seems safe to conclude that probably only a rather small minority of families correspond to the monolithic model of the family. For the United States, for instance, "What is considered to be the traditional nuclear family, a breadwinner-father, a housewife-mother, and two children under eighteen accounted for only 7 percent of the population in 1975" (Ramey, 1978: 3). Until we change our data collection process to gather information on possible variations in familial structures, e.g., by asking people about biological children of theirs who are not living with them, by asking about the biological parents of children living within a husband-wife family, by collecting systematic and representative data on family violence, by examining the residential patterns of family members, etc., we are likely to continue to assume that families conform to the monolithic model of the family to a greater degree than they actually do. This has some serious consequences, the two most important of which probably are that we are likely to continue to ignore questions which are of vital importance in understanding the functioning of familial structures and that we create policies which are based on inadequate data. . . .

Notes

[1] Figures on artificial donor insemination are not available, but a recent newspaper article suggests that "hundreds to thousands of babies are born by this method every year in Canada" (*Thousands of babies*, 1978).

[2] Among my personal acquaintances there are several commuting couples which include spouses who have faculty positions at two different universities. One would expect this to become an increasingly frequent although statis-

tically insignificant pattern as more women are likely to seek university positions even at the price of a commuting marriage.

In addition, the labor force participation rates of women are underestimated because labor force figures include only officially unemployed people and because many women who would like to have jobs cannot find any, but nevertheless are not counted as unemployed. The under-estimation of the unemployment of women has been pegged at 65 percent (Robinson, 1978). If one were to include the "hidden unemployed," unemployment rates among women would rise from 9.4 percent to 15.6 percent for 1977 (ibid.). These figures have not been included here since, being disentitled from unemployment benefits, these women cannot contribute such benefits to the family income.

References

Anderson, Michael, ed. *Sociology of the Family*. Harmondsworth: Penguin, 1971.

Ball, Donald W. "The 'family' as a *sociological* problem: conceptualization of the taken-for-granted as prologue to social problems analysis." *Social Problems* 19(3) (1972): 295–305.

Bell, Norman W. and Benjamin, Michael. *Domestic Murders in Canada, 1961–1974*, Monograph published by the Judicial Statistics Division. Ottawa: Statistics Canada, 1979.

Boland, Madame Justice. (unpublished) "Reasons for Judgement" in the case of Baker, April 25, 1978.

Boyd, Monica, Eichler, Margrit, and Hofley, John. "Family, functions, formation, and fertility." In *Opportunity for Choice*, edited by Gail C.A. Cook, pp. 13–52. Ottawa: Statistics Canada, 1976.

Canada Yearbook, 1974.

_____, 1976–77.

Chapman, Jane Roberts and Gates, Margaret, eds. *The Victimization of Women*. Beverly Hills: Sage Publications, 1978.

Cohen, Gaynor. "Absentee husbands in spiralist families." *Journal of Marriage and the Family* 39(3) (1977): 595–604.

Cooperstock, Ruth. "Psychotropic drug use among women," *Canadian Medical Association Journal* 115 (1976): 760–763.

Coser, Rose Laub. *The Family. Its Structure and Functions*. 2nd ed. New York: St. Martin's Press, 1974.

Duberman, Lucile. *Marriage and Other Alternatives*. 2nd ed. New York: Praeger, 1977.

Eichler, Margrit. "Towards a policy for families in Canada." (mimeo) Ottawa: Status of Women Canada, 1979.

_____. "Family income — a critique of the concept." *Status of Women News*. 6 (1980): 20–21 and 24.

Elkin, Frederick and Handel, Gerald. *The Child and Society: The Process of Socialization*. 3rd ed. New York: Random House, 1978.

Eshleman, J. Ross. *The Family: An Introduction*. 2nd ed. Boston: Allyn and Bacon, 1978.

The Family as a Focus for Social Policy. Minister for Social Development, Toronto, Ontario, May, 1979.

Galper, Miriam. *Co-Parenting. A Source Book for the Separated or Divorced Family*. Philadelphia, Penn.: Running Press, 1978.

Glick, Paul C. "A demographer looks at American families." *Journal of Marriage and the Family* 35 (1975): 15–26.

———. "Updating the life cycle of families." *Journal of Marriage and the Family* 39(1) (1977): 5–13.

Lasch, Christopher. *Haven in a Heartless World: The Family Besieged.* New York: Basic Books, 1977.

Leslie, Gerald R. *The Family in Social Context.* New York: Oxford University Press, 1967.

MacFarlane, Kee. "Sexual abuse of children." In *The Victimization of Women*, edited by Jane Roberts Chapman and Margaret Gates, pp. 81–110. Beverly Hills: Sage Publications, 1978.

MacKintosh, Judy. "News from the field," *Marriage and Family Review* 1(4) (1978): 12–13.

MacLeod, Linda. *Wife Battering in Canada: The Vicious Circle.* (Advisory Council on the Status of Women). Ottawa: Canadian Government Publishing Centre, 1980.

Martin, Del. "Battered women: society's problem." In *The Victimization of Women*, edited by Jane Roberts Chapman and Margaret Gates, pp. 111–141. Beverly Hills: Sage Publications, 1978.

Meissner, Martin et al. "No exit for wives: sexual division of labour and the cumulation of household demands." *Canadian Review of Sociology and Anthropology* 12(4) (1975): 424–439.

Murdock, George Peter. *Social Structure.* New York: Macmillan, 1949.

National Council of Welfare. *Women and Poverty.* (A Report by the National Council of Welfare). Ottawa, 1979.

O'Neil, Maureen and Leonoff, Arthur. "Joint custody, an option worth examining." *Perception Now.*/Dec. 28–30, 1977.

Ontario Ministry of Treasury, Economics and Intergovernmental Affairs. *Ontario Statistics* 1977 Vol. 1, Social Series, 1977.

Petes, John F. *Divorce.* Toronto: Faculty of Education, Guidance Centre, University of Toronto, 1979.

Ramey, James. "Experimental family forms — the family of the future." *Marriage and Family Review* 1(1) (1978): 1–9.

Reiss, Ira L. "The universality of the family: a conceptual analysis." *Journal of Marriage and the Family* Nov, 1965: 443–453.

Report of the Committee on the Operation of the Abortion Law. Minister of Supply and Services. Ottawa, 1977.

Report of the Task Force on Child Abuse. Ontario, Ministry of Community and Social Services. Toronto, June, 1978.

Robinson, H.L. "Unemployment in 1977: unemployment among women is higher than among men." *Canadian Newsletter of Research on Women* 7(2) (1978): 12–13.

Roman, Mel and Haddad, William. "The case for joint custody," *Psychology Today* 12(4) (1978): 96–105.

Rosen, Edward J. "In the best interests of the child and parents." Unpublished paper, n.d.

Schlesinger, Benjamin, ed. *One in Ten: The Single Parent in Canada.* Toronto: University of Toronto Guidance Centre, 1979.

Schlesinger, Benjamin and Todres, Rubin. "Characteristics of Canadian members of 'Parents without Partners'." In *One in Ten: The Single Parent in Canada*, edited by Benjamin Schlesinger, pp. 107–112. Toronto: University of Toronto Guidance Centre, 1979.

Skolnik, Arlene and Skolnik, Jerome H., eds. *Intimacy, Family and Society.* Boston: Little, Brown and Co., 1974.

Status of Day Care in Canada. *A Review of*

the *Major Findings of the National Day Care Study* 1975. Ottawa: National Day Care Information Centre. Social Services Programs Branch, 1975.

Steinmetz, Suzanne K. "Violence between family members." *Marriage and Family Review* 1(3) (1978): 1–16.

Steinmetz, Suzanne K. and Straus, Murray A., eds. *Violence in the Family.* New York: Dodd, Mead and Co., 1974.

"Thousands of babies owe life to a lab." *Toronto Star*, Oct. 9, 1978, p. C1.

Van Stolk, Mary. "The battered and abused child." In *Marriage, Family and Society: Canadian Perspectives.* Edited by S. Parvez

Wakil, pp. 213-222. Toronto: Butterworths, 1975.

Walker, Lenore E. "Treatment alternatives for battered women." In *The Victimization of Women*, edited by Jane Roberts Chapman and Margaret Gates, pp. 143–174. Beverly Hills: Sage Publications, 1978.

Weigert, Andrew J. and Thomas, Darwin L. "Family as a conditional universal." *Journal of Marriage and the Family*, (1971), pp. 188–194.

Wheeler, Michael. *Unpublished Report on the Findings of a Study on Recently Separated Parents* (Mimeo). Hamilton: McMaster University, 1978.

TWENTY-TWO

Female Lone Parenting over the Life Course

Maureen Moore

MAUREEN MOORE is a Senior Analyst with the Demography Division at Statistics Canada, Ottawa. Now in the Current Demographic Analysis Program, she has worked on the Census, the Survey of Consumer Finance, the Family History Survey, and the quarterly *Perspectives on Labour and Income*. She continues to be interested in modern family issues and her areas of research specialty include longitudinal perspectives on the family, modern work and earnings arrangements, and family demography. Her studies include "The characteristics of dual earner families" (1989); "Wives as primary earners" (1990); and "The social rewards of family living: an analysis based on quality of life indicators" (forthcoming).

The increase in lone parenting[1] over the past few decades signals important change in the structure of our family relationships. Although these relationships have been studied at single points in time, little is known about them over the life course. Glen Elder (1981: 509)defines life courses as "age-structured pathways across settings from birth to death." Life courses are charted within patterns of family structure, and in turn, become sources of structural change. This article explores the life courses of Canadian women as they begin and end lone parenting. It uncovers dynamic attributes of lone parenting, such as when and how it begins, when and how it ends, and its duration. A retrospective sample of about 7,000 women,[2] drawn from the national 1984 Family History Survey (FHS),[3] forms the basis for the analysis. . . .

Lone parents have responsibilities for children typically shared by two parents, and because most of them are working at any given point, they are frequently overloaded. The adjustment to lone parenthood, particularly when it follows the termination of a marriage (through separation or the death of a partner), is often emotionally demanding, and may be accompanied with feelings of isolation. Of perhaps greatest concern, a high proportion of lone-parent families, especially those headed by women, are economically disadvantaged. During the recessions and inflation of the 1970s and 1980s, while more nuclear families became dual earner, the number of lone-parent families increased. It is therefore not surprising that the issue of income, its level and maintenance, is so pressing: in 1986 it was estimated that 60 percent of female lone-parent families were classified as low income (Moore, 1987).

The life course approach allows us to gain understanding of social problems . . . through time. . . . That social problems are often temporary does not alleviate the gravity of either life-long effects for the individual or their structural permanence within society. If there is a collective responsibility for the lone-parent family, it is better defined with knowledge of these transitional aspects. First, we need to discover the length of lone parenting to assess its significance in the lives of both adults and children. Second, the age at which lone parenting occurs corresponds to life cycle stages, and these are indicative of the financial need, support networks, and responsibilities of the lone parenting role. Age and other factors also contribute to the length of spells. . . .

THE LONE PARENT TRANSITION

Lone-parent families are formed through ex-nuptial birth, separation, and widowhood. Separation is often followed by divorce, but lone parenting begins at the point of physical separation. . . . Ex-nuptial births tend to occur to younger women (see Table 22-2). They . . . are often unplanned. If they involve intention, the alternatives and consequences of the decision are not always carefully weighed (Grindstaff, 1988). Ex-nuptial pregnancy presents three alternatives to lone parenting: marriage, adoption, or abortion. Despite these alternatives . . ., ex-nuptial parenting has increased. . . .

Lone parenting commonly ends with marriage or remarriage. . . . (see Table 22-1). The only other exit, children's home-leaving . . . tends to be the children's decision. Of course, these exits occur simultaneously if children decide to

leave at the point of remarriage,[4] for reasons that might iclude incompatibility with the new spouse.

The lone parenting process can thus be constructed within a chronology of six events:

1. *First birth*: The date of first birth or of first adoption, excluding dates for children who were given up at birth.

2. *First marriage*: The date of a first marriage or common-law union.

3. *First marital dissolution*: The date of death of a spouse, or of a separation, from a first marital/common-law union. . . . Separation, refers to the date at which spouses stop living together, rather than to the date of the legal decree.

4. *Second marriage*: The date of entry into a second marital/common-law union. (Marriages following common-law unions are considered as one continuous first union).

5. *Second marital dissolution*: The date of death of a spouse, or of separation, from a second marital/common-law union.

6. *Final home-leaving or death of the last child*: Some children leave home and then return, although in Canada they do this fairly infrequently. Of "first" children of female respondents, only 2 percent had ever lived on their own and then returned, according to the FHS.[5]

The sequencing of these events is based on some life cycle properties of marriage and childrearing. Marriages are linear in

TABLE 22-1   Percentage Distribution of All Women by Status of First Lone Parenting Spell Showing Current Age, Canada, 1984.

Status of First Lone Parenting Spell	Current Age						Estimated N's (All Women)
	18–24	25–29	30–39	40–49	50–65	All Ages	
All adult women[1]	100.0	100.0	100.0	100.0	100.0	100.0	7,924,000
Never a lone parent	94.2	86.1	81.9	75.2	75.6	82.4	6,527,000
Ever a lone parent	5.8	13.9	18.1	24.7	24.4	17.6	1,396,000
Because of:							
Union dissolution[2]	1.8	6.9	12.6	17.9	18.0	11.8	936,000
Separation/divorce	1.8	6.8	11.4	15.5	8.4	8.8	697,000
Ended	0.3	2.7	6.1	9.0	6.2	5.0	394,000
union re-entry	0.3	2.4	5.7	7.8	3.0	3.9	305,000
children leaving home	0.0	0.4	0.4	1.2	3.2	1.1	88,000
Unended at survey date	1.6	4.0	5.3	6.5	2.2	3.8	303,000
Death of spouse	0.0	0.2	1.3	2.4	9.6	3.0	239,000
Ended	0.0	0.1	0.7	0.9	4.6	1.4	113,000
union re-entry	0.0	0.1	0.7	0.9	2.2	0.8	67,000
children leaving home	0.0	0.0	0.0	0.0	2.4	0.6	46,000
Unended at survey date	0.0	0.1	0.6	1.5	5.0	1.6	127,000
Ex-nuptial birth[3]	4.0	7.0	5.5	6.8	6.3	5.8	460,000
Ended	2.3	5.4	4.4	6.4	6.1	4.8	384,000
union re-entry	2.3	5.3	4.4	6.3	5.7	4.7	374,000
children leaving home	0.0	0.1	0.0	0.1	0.4	0.1	10,000
Unended at survey date	1.7	1.6	1.1	0.5	0.2	1.0	77,000
Estimated numbers (all Canadian women)	1,602,000	1,102,000	2,020,000	1,317,000	1,883,000	7,924,000	

Source: Family History Survey (N = 7,228).
1. Excludes 28 cases not coded.
2. Marital or common-law from either a first or second union dissolution. Third union dissolutions are not represented.
3. Comprises women who had an ex-nuptial birth either before or after their first union.

... that a second marriage cannot be begin unless a preceding one has physically ended. Childrearing ... begins with a first birth or a first adoption, and ends when the last child leaves the parental home to attend school or to set up a new household. If parents separate, then it ends when the parent leaves the household in which all the children remain. Parents who leave might remain in contact with their children or exercise influence in their upbringing, but most of the responsibilities remain with the custodial lone parent.

Childrearing can be discontinuous. Parents who do not receive physical custody of any of their children, but have more children later ..., for example, have discontinuous parental careers.[6] According to both the FHS[7] and to central registry data, this tends to be a rare life cycle pattern among women. Throughout the 1970s, divorced mothers in Canada received physical custody of children in 85.6 percent of cases (Richardson, 1987). ...

RESULTS

... The time frame is based on Canadian women born between 1919 and 1966, so it spans life courses from 1935 (when the oldest women reached early adulthood) to 1984 (FHS date). . . .

Table 22-1[8] . . . shows how pervasive lone parenting has been among Canadian women. . . . FHS results show that of the total population, 17.6 percent, or 1.4 million women, were lone parents at some point in their lives. About 500,000 of these women were still lone parenting in February, 1984. The remaining 900,000 women had taken new paths by the survey date, 84 percent through a first or second marriage. The increase in lone parent families over the past twenty years is a reflection of these life course movements.

The frequency of women who ever parented alone increases with age, from 6 percent of women . . . 18 to 24 to 24 percent of women 50 to 65. . . . Older women are more likely to have encountered any (or all) of the life cycle events that begin lone parenting.

The precipitating causes of lone parenthood — ex-nuptial birth, separation, and widowhood — through their close connection with age, are determinants of the way in which episodes end. Women who were lone parents as a result of widowhood were most likely to exit their spells through children "vacating" the nest (40 percent), followed by women who were separated lone parents (22 percent), and women who were ex-nuptial parents (3 percent). . . . Viewed another way, ex-nuptial mothers were the most likely to end lone parenting by way of marriage, followed by separated and then widowed mothers.

DURATION OF AND AGE AT LONE PARENTING

Age at lone parenting . . . provides a clue to economic resources within the family, types of parental responsibilities, tasks that need to be completed, and internal stresses. It is also related to duration because the probability of marriage/remarriage decreases with age. One would expect, therefore, longer durations with later onsets. The home-leaving of children works in the opposite direction. . . . The older the woman, the closer her children are to home-leaving age, and hence the shorter the spell of lone parenting.

Widowed parenting tends to occur in the middle to late years of life, at an average age of 41.8 (Table 22-2). With parents at this age, children tend to be at stages of early to late adolescence (Gee, 1986), a time of potential social stress within the family (Rodgers, 1973). Economically, however, children at these ages would be old enough to take jobs to help maintain the family after the loss of the father's income.

Widowhood at younger ages is statistically less probable, but more traumatic (Elder, 1981). Only about one-tenth of widowed women become lone parents before turning 25. Some of them undoubtedly would have been lone parents as a result of World War II, married to soldiers who never returned from service overseas. These veterans' widows receive a survivor's pension, but other young widows are less likely to have accumulated assets such as life insurance, death benefits, or pensions.

Widowed parenting tends to be longer than other types of lone parenting, and lasts 7.5 years on average (including unended spells)[9] (Table 22-3). Because women become widowed parents later in life, remarriage probabilities are lower, and therefore this longer duration is expected. . . . Religious attitudes toward remarriage and bereavement might also have an effect on duration.

TABLE 22-2 Percentage Distribution of Women by First Lone Parenting Spell, Showing Age at Onset, Canada, 1984.

First Lone Parenting Spell	Age at First Lone Parenting Spell							Estimated Numbers	Average Age at Onset
	Less than 19	20–24	25–29	30–39	40–49	50 and Over	Total		
All women ever lone parents	18.0	24.6	17.7	20.7	13.2	5.8	100.0	1,396,000	29.7
Because of:									
Union dissolution									
Separation/divorce	4.0	15.6	21.8	30.2	19.7	8.6	100.0	936,000	34.2
	5.0	18.2	25.9	32.5	15.4	3.0	100.0	697,000	31.6
Death of spouse	1.2	8.2	9.6	23.6	32.4	25.0	100.0	239,000	41.8
Ex-nuptial birth	46.5	42.9	9.3	1.3	0.0	0.0	100.0	460,000	20.6

Source: Family History Survey (N = 1,307)

TABLE 22-3 Percentage Distribution of Women by First Lone Parenting Spell, Showing Duration, Canada, 1984.

First Lone Parenting Spell	Duration (Time since Lone Parenting Began)							Estimated Numbers	Average Duration
	Less than 6 Months	6–12 Months	1–2 Years	2–5 Years	5–10 Years	More than Ten Years	Total		
All women ever lone parents	10.1	10.1	11.7	29.0	22.0	17.1	100.0	1,396,000	5.5
Because of:									
Union dissolution	5.6	6.8	12.3	31.0	24.3	20.0	100.0	936,000	6.1
Separation/divorce	5.1	6.1	13.4	35.0	23.2	17.2	100.0	697,000	5.6
Ended	3.8	5.8	14.9	37.0	24.1	14.4	100.0	394,000	5.3
by union re-entry	3.5	7.4	16.3	40.9	22.8	9.1	100.0	305,000	4.3
by children leaving home	4.7	0.0	10.1	23.7	28.6	32.8	100.0	88,000	8.6
Unended at survey date	6.9	6.6	11.3	32.3	22.0	20.8	100.0	303,000	6.0
Death of spouse	7.1	8.6	9.3	19.4	27.4	28.2	100.0	239,000	7.5
Ended[1]	4.4	7.0	10.0	29.3	27.9	21.5	100.0	113,000	6.2
Unended at survey date	9.5	9.9	8.7	10.6	27.1	34.2	100.0	127,000	8.8
Ex-nuptial birth[1]	19.2	17.0	10.4	24.9	17.4	11.1	100.0	460,000	4.4

Source: Family History Survey (N = 1,307)
1. Categories collapsed due to small sample size.

Separation has been the most common antecedent to lone parenting among all women with children: some 697,000 women have been separated parents, about half now in the younger age groups (18–39). But more women currently 40–49 became separated parents (24.7 percent) than any other cohort (Table 22-1). These women were between 24 and 33 in 1968 when the first federal divorce law was introduced, so many of them would have been in the early years of marriage, which are more vulnerable to divorce....

Among six in ten (58 percent) women who became separated parents, lone parenting spells occurred between the ages of 25 and 39. The overall average age at onset is 31.6 (Table 22-2). For the period in which divorce has risen, this age represents a life cycle of early career building for working mothers (and fathers), and a preschool or early school stage of development for children. ... These lone parents generally have to deal with the financial strain of setting up and maintaining separate households, finding affordable day care, and the problems of support payments. Separated lone parenting tends to be shorter than widowed parenting, at 5.6 years on average (Table 22-2).[10] Higher expectations of remarriage due to younger ages at onset contribute to the shorter duration, although financial hardship ... would also affect willingness to remarry.

About 305,000 women who became separated parents had remarried by the survey date, beginning blended families with children from previous marriages. Their spells constituted 77 percent of all ended separated parenting spells. ...

An ex-nuptial birth is the second most common event to begin lone parenthood. It began the lone parenting paths of 460,000 Canadian women. It is somewhat surprising that 6 percent of all women aged 50 to 65 in 1984 had ex-nuptial babies (Table 22-1). The 50–65 cohort were in their childbearing years during the 1950s and earlier, when ex-nuptial births carried social disapproval. It would be interesting to study whether they began lone parenting spells that were consequently of shorter duration.

Lone parenting from an ex-nuptial birth commences at an average age of 20.6. This age corresponds to the "courtship" stage, and the historically recent stage of job training and post-secondary educational attainment. Many studies have documented the costs of early childbearing to young women (see, for example, Grindstaff, 1988). FHS data show that among women (in families) who had a child at less than age 20, only 15 percent attained post-secondary education, compared to 40 percent who had a child at age 25 or later (Pool and Moore, 1986). These births therefore, tend to block an investment that could bring more financial security in the long run.

Individuals in their late teens tend to have sporadic labour force attachment in low-wage jobs. Single mothers, however, are the most likely of all lone parents to have economic support from their parents. Some single mothers would not have left their parental homes at the time of the first birth, which occurred before the nineteenth birthdays of almost half (46.5 percent). Only 10 percent of women who became ex-nuptial parents began lone parenting after 25. It thus appears that maturity, work experience, and education diminish the chances of ex-nuptial parenting.

Most lone parenting from an ex-nuptial birth ends through a first marriage, and spells are shorter than other types; ... 4.4 years on average. This ending point would roughly correspond with age at first marriage averaged over the last twenty years. Episodes, therefore, do not seem to have postponed first marriage *on the whole.* One in three ex-nuptial mothers, however, were lone parents for over five years, periods that probably encompassed transitions to household formation and labour force entry. By cohort, duration would be expected to have lengthened, because single parenting has become more accepted, socially and legally, and there has been a broad trend toward postponement of first marriage.

SECOND SPELLS

. . . Marriages are more vulnerable if they are precipitated by pregnancy, formed at young ages, or involve children from a previous family (McKie, 1983). These factors might partly account for the finding that *three in ten women* who were once ex-nuptial mothers went through a second lone parenting episode, compared with only one in ten overall. . . . Because of the early age at onset of the first spell, there was more time for a second spell to occur . . . later . . . in life. Those (17.4 percent) that had ended their spells . . . had displayed a pattern of movement between lone and remarriage families. . . .

CONCLUSION

Female lone parenting . . . in Canada . . . lasts an average of just over five years. . . . That lone parenting is now more voluntary is suggested by the growth of the ex-nuptial and separation/divorce antecedents. Widowhood . . . has declined. Ex-nuptial mothers become lone parents at young ages and for relatively short pe-

riods that usually end in a first marriage. Separated mothers become lone parents at a critical life cycle stage financially and in terms of responsibility for children. Their episodes last five to six years on average, commonly ending in marriage. Widowed mothers become lone parents later in life when their children are older, but they are least likely to remarry, and consequently, tend to be lone parents for longer periods.

These general tendencies, of course, mask wide variations. Durations for 28 percent of ex-nuptial mothers were over five years, and 16 percent of widowed women were lone parents for less than one year. Among all women who became lone parents, 10 percent of episodes have been very short — less than six months — and 17 percent have been very long — more than ten years. . . .

Increases in ex-nuptial births and divorce have shown only slight signs of abating. But the desirability of the conjugal family is indicated by the eight in ten women who lone parented that had remarried . . . before the survey date. . . .

. . . Seven in ten Canadian women with children were still in their first nuclear families as of February 1984. Although many of them had not reached an age when separation and widowhood are statistically probable, "serial monogamy" . . . is still far off.

The lone-parent family represents the separation of marital relationships from childrearing. . . . As the adult adapts to movement between lone-parent, nuclear, and remarriage families, children provide the continuity as they grow through developmental stages. Anthropologists (see, for example, Briffault, 1927 and Manilowski, 1963) have long acknowledged the primacy of parent-child relationships as instinctive necessities . . . in determining the structure of the family. Children form the basis of the family cross-culturally. They are there-fore the primary reason for developmen-tal studies, while the life course approach continues to reveal familial diversity.

Notes

[1] The lone-parent family has also been referred to as the single-parent family, the one-parent family, and the monoparental family. The term "single parent" is very common in Canada and the United States, but because it also has a connotation of "never married," "lone parent" is preferred.

[2] The Family History Survey (FHS) asked men about children they had raised rather than children who were born to them, but the survey did not ask when they began to raise their first child. This posed a problem for constructing male lone parent spells. Consequently the article focuses solely on women, who comprise the majority of lone parents in any case.

[3] The FHS, a Labour Force Survey supplement, was conducted by telephone interview. For more information on FHS data quality, see Burch (1986).

[4] Simultaneous exits were rare, and coded as union entry.

[5] The FHS collected information on whether children ever lived away from home, the dates they returned, the dates of any deaths and the dates on which they left home for the final time. A search took place to find the date of latest leaving (which does not always involve the youngest child), or death, among all the children for up to eighteen natural children and nine adopted children. In the survey manual, a child was defined as living on their own "if the child lives independently of the respondent." Children of elderly respondents who are now support-ing their parents would have been coded as having left home and now living on their own, since a period of years likely intervened before the elderly parent joined their household. It is therefore unlikely that these would appear as lone parenting spells. This is especially true with . . . persons aged 65 and under.

[6] Joint custody arrangements are uncommon in Canada. About 8 percent of awards are joint custody awards, but in many of these cases physical custody is still with the mother (Richardson, 1987).The FHS manual instructed respondents to report children in joint custody as residing with them if the children were with them for at least six months of the year. Such arrangements would therefore appear as contin-uous parenting.

[7] Discontinuous parenting in the FHS was difficult to assess. The leaving of the first child at separation was used to indicate possible cases of discontinuous parenting. In one pattern the first child left at the point of the separation, but there were later births in a second marriage. Another pattern was similar, except women had later births without entering a second marriage; these sequences were delineated as lone parenting.

[8] Only weighted estimates are given in the tables. Where sample size is less than 100 or has a high coefficient of variation, estimates are flagged or not shown.

[9] Comparison of duration is complicated by the unended spells "truncated" by the survey. These are categorized as "Unended at survey date." Comparisons assume that unended spells are distributed fairly normally. An alternative is to compare only ended spells, but the bias here is that shorter spells, more prevalent among some types of lone parenting, will be over-represented among ended spells. Probability analysis would partially overcome these problems.

[10] This length of time parallels American findings. See Koo and Suchindran, 1980; Bumpass, 1984; Bane and Weiss, 1980; and Ross and Sawhill, 1975.

References

Bane, M. and Weiss, R. "Alone together: the world of single parent families." *American Demographics* 5 (1980): 11–15.

Briffault, Robert. *The Mothers: The Matriarchal Theory of Social Origin.* New York: Macmillan, 1931.

Bumpass, Larry L. "Children of marital disruption: a replication and update." *Demography* 21 (1984): 71–82.

Burch, Thomas K. *Family History Survey: Preliminary Findings.* Statistics Canada, Catalogue 99–955, 1986.

Gee, Ellen. "The life course of Canadian women: an historical and demographic analysis." *Social Indicators Research* 18 (1986): 263–283.

Grindstaff, Carl F. "Adolescent marriage and childbearing: the long-term economic outcome, Canada in the 1980s." *Adolescence* 23 (1988): 45–58.

Koo, H.P. and Suchindran, C.M. "Effects of children on remarriage prospects of women." *Journal of Family Issues* 1 (1980): 497–515.

Manilowski, B. *The Family Among the Australian Aborigines.* New York: Schocken Books, 1963.

McKie, D.C. *Divorce: Law and the Family in Canada.* Ottawa: Statistics Canada, Catalogue 89-502E, 1983.

Moore, Maureen. "Women parenting alone." *Canadian Social Trends* Winter, 1987: 31–36.

_____. *The Characteristics of Dual Earner Families.* Ottawa: Statistics Canada, Catalogue 13–601, 1989.

Pool, Ian and Moore, Maureen. *Lone Parenthood: Characteristics and Determinants.* Ottawa: Statistics Canada, Catalogue 99–961, 1986.

Rodgers, Roy H. *Family Interaction and Transaction: The Developmental Approach.* Englewood Cliffs: Prentice-Hall, 1973.

Sawhill, H.L. and Sawhill, I.V. *Time of Transition: The Growth of Families Headed by Women.* Washington, D.C.: The Urban Institute, 1975.

TWENTY-THREE

Why Does Family Violence Occur?

Eugen Lupri

EUGEN LUPRI, Professor of Sociology at the University of Calgary, specializes in the sociologies of the family and gender relations, and sociological theory. He has contributed numerous chapters to books and monographs and published articles in journals such as the *Canadian Journal of Sociology; Journal of Marriage and the Family; Current Sociology; International Journal of Comparative Sociology; Comparative Journal of Family Studies; Kölner Zeitschrift für Soziologie; Soziale Welt; European Journal of Sociology; Metra;* and *Revue Internationale de Sociologie.* He is author and co-author of *Soziologie der Familie* (1976), *The Changing Position of Women in Family and Society: A Cross-Cultural Comparison* (1983), and *Gender Inequality* (1990). A book, *The Dialectics of Family and Work Roles,* is nearing completion.

Data Collection

Data for this paper were derived from a national survey conducted in Canada in 1987. A probability sample of 1,834 women and men over 18 years of age was interviewed. Data on marital conflict, marital satisfaction, stress, authoritarianism, and all demographic information were derived through the interviews.[1] At the close of the personal interview, self-administered questionnaires with self-addressed, stamped envelopes were left behind for completion by those respondents who were ever married or cohabiting. A letter accompanied the questionnarie, explaining the purpose of the family life study and encouraging respondents to complete and return the instrument. Usable questionnaires were returned by 652 female and 471 male respondents, or 73.4 percent of the 1,530 eligible ever-married or cohabiting respondents. . . .

Interspousal violence was measured by a modified version of the Conflict Tactics Scales (CTS) developed by Straus (1979) and associates. The Conflict Tactics Scales . . . are considered a reliable, valid measure of the incidence of physical violence and of symbolic and verbal aggression. They are also used for assessment in clinical work. The scales contain 19 items and are prefaced by the following statement:

No matter how well spouses or partners get along, there are times when they disagree on major decisions, are annoyed with what the other person does, or are simply in a bad mood or tired. At the left below is a list of things you might have done when you had a conflict or disagreement with your partner. Please circle a number for each of the things in the list, showing how often you did it in the past year or in the last year of your marriage.

Although the Conflict Tactics Scales comprise 19 items, the findings reported here are restricted mainly to the items that involve the use of physical force. Table 23-1 delineates the eight violent or potentially violent acts to which subjects responded. . . .

TABLE 23-1   Specific Violent Acts Reportedly Committed by Legally Married or Cohabiting Women and Men against Their Partners, In Percent, 1987

During this past year of marriage or living together, I personally . . .	Husband-to-Wife Violence (n = 426)	Wife-to-Husband Violence (n = 528)
1. Threatened to hit or throw something at the other		
— once in the past year	2.5	5.0
— twice or more in the past year	6.6	10.9
2. Pushed, grabbed, or shoved the other		
— once in the past year	3.8	5.6
— twice or more in the past year	8.1	7.5
3. Slapped the other		
— once in the past year	1.9	4.3
— twice or more in the past year	3.1	3.3
4. Kicked, bit, or hit the other with fist		
— once in the past year	1.1	1.3
— twice or more in the past year	5.3	5.0
5. Hit or tried to hit the other		
— once in the past year	3.5	4.1
— twice or more in the past year	1.9	4.9
6. Beat up the other		
— once in the past year	0.0	1.7
— twice or more in the past year	2.5	4.5
7. Threatened the other with a knife or gun		
— once in the past year	1.2	0.2
— twice or more in the past year	0.9	3.4
8. Used knife or gun on the other		
— once in the past year	0.0	0.1
— twice in the past year	0.5	0.7
Overall Violence Index[1]	17.8	23.3
Severe Violence Index[2]	10.1	12.9

[1] The Overall Violence Index contains all respondents who committed at least one of the eight violent acts during the past year.
[2] The Severe Violence Index contains all respondents who committed at least one of violent acts 4 through 8 during the past year.

Although our approach is similar to that of Straus and his associates, it differs in two respects. First, in an attempt to reduce response bias, we chose to measure spousal violence by using a self-administered questionnaire rather than an interview, thereby minimizing the impact of a stranger's presence. Second, for the same reason and also to increase validity, we used self-reports of violent acts that the respondent had committed against the partner (perpetrator approach) rather than reports of victimization. This approach may minimize somewhat the risks of initiating additional abuse by blaming others.

Data Limitations

The scales contain two basic shortcomings, however: 1) The items deal with acts or incidents. Thus we do not know the context in which physical force or verbal aggression occurred or what precipitated specific acts of violence. 2) Because it was too difficult to measure accurately the outcome of the specific violent acts in a self-administered questionnaire, we do not know the severity of the injury, pain, and damage that respondents inflicted on their partners. Because we do not measure the consequences of these acts, we do not know how many husbands or wives were injured physically or were harmed emotionally, or the severity of the damage as a result of the violence. Qualitative studies show, however, that violent men cause significantly greater physical injury than violent women and that among battered women self-defence was the most common motive for their using violence against their male assailants (Saunders, 1986).[2]

Yet despite these "defects," the Conflict Tactics Scales provide a fairly sound measure of the extent to which specific acts of violence and verbal aggression take place within the home. Because these acts are based on self-reports and because respondents were asked how often they inflicted violence on their partners, the national violence rates reported here may well be underestimates. Although verbal aggression is different from physical violence, heated and angry verbal attacks can cause severe emotional damage. Furthermore, the two types of aggression often occur jointly, as we will show. . . .

Estimates of Incidence and Prevalence

Because the data presented in Table 23-1 come from a national probability sample of women and men aged 18 or older, married or living with a partner, it is possible to determine the annual incidence rate of wife abuse and husband abuse. One way to calculate this rate is to find the percentage of the total sample who reported having committed at least one of the eight violent acts against their partners during the previous year of the survey. This measure is called the "Overall Violence Index" and is presented in the lower portion of Table 23-1 together with the "Severe Violence Index." The latter includes acts that carry a high risk of serious injury: kicked, bit, or hit with a fist; hit or tried to hit the other with an object; beat up the other; threatened the other with a knife or a gun; and used a knife or a gun on the other.

The human meaning of these statistics can be understood more clearly if we translate the incidence rates into the total number of women and men affected in 1986. On the basis of approximately 5.9 million couples living in Canada in

1986, the Overall Violence Index of 17.8 for men and 23.3 for women means that conservatively speaking, over 1 million husbands and wives engaged in some form of physical violence. This staggering figure shows that domestic violence is a public issue and a social problem.

If one is inclined to dismiss the Overall Violence Index on the grounds that it casts too wide a net, the Severe Violence Index contains acts that have a relatively high probability of causing serious injury or pain. This is not to suggest that pushes or shoves cannot result in severe injuries, such as broken legs or other fractures, or that slaps cannot cause bleeding. Rather, it seems that each or any of the five physically violent acts making up the Severe Violence Index has much greater potential for causing bodily harm than do the three acts which are excluded from this index. Indeed, the Severe Violence Index measures violent acts that may well be defined as "aggravated assaults," criminal offenses that remain largely hidden in the home.

The severe violence rates of 10.1 for men and 12.9 for women translate into an absolute number of about 650,000 assaulted husbands and wives; we may estimate that these numbers include a high proportion of mutually violent couples. The growing prevalence of domestic abuse in the private confines of the home prompted an American research team to label the marriage license a "hitting license" (Straus et al., 1980). A partnership without a legal license, however, by no means guarantees the absence of violence. A comparison of cohabiting and legally married women and men under the age of 30 revealed that cohabitors appear to be as violent as their married counterparts.

Demographic Factors Associated with Domestic Violence

... The findings on violence in the Canadian home support two important generalizations. First, force appears to be an integral element of marital interaction in a fairly large segment of the population, as we showed earlier. Second, women and men who commit violent acts against their partners come from all segments of society.... No one group is free of domestic violence, but violence is not distributed equally: some women and men were found to be more likely than others to abuse their partners. The data, however, permit us to dispel the lingering myth that domestic violence is confined to the poor, the very young, or the uneducated. Specifically, the national data support the following generalizations.

Age.   Violent women and men are of all ages. On average, however, younger families (18–29) are the most violent: their rate was more than three times the rate for the age group 46 to 64 (32.9 vs. 10.8 respectively). As the age increases, the rate of violence decreases. ... Younger couples are more violence-prone because the early years of marriage or of living together require new levels of commitment and a need to redefine expectations for one another. Career and family demands often conflict, especially with the arrival of the first child. Thus younger couples have a greater need to examine and fine-tune their mutual expectations of consistency, fairness, and clarity. Younger families in Canada also are more likely than older families to experience economic hardship and unemployment.

Another possible reason why we observe more abuse among younger couples is that violent marriages are more likely to end in separation or divorce. About one-third of all couples who filed for divorce in 1986 listed "mental or physical cruelty" as grounds for the breakdown of the marriage.[3] This factor may reduce the chance of a violent marriage's enduring for more than a few years. Yet it is important to recognize that only a fraction of victimized spouses seek to leave a violent marriage; this fact underscores the seriousness of domestic violence in the home. The reasons for staying in a violent marriage are manifold, but for women economic dependency is one of the most fundamental. Therefore attempts by women to leave violent relationships or to find viable alternatives continue to be constrained by this basic gender inequality.

Education. It is believed widely that men with less formal education are more prone to engage in wife abuse, but our national data found no support for such a claim. Surprisingly, we found that the least violence occurred among the least educated men (an overall violence rate of 12.2 for those with elementary school diplomas or less) and among those with a university degree, 13.0. Another noteworthy finding concerns the rates of both women and men with some university education, who reported the highest rates of violence (30.2). This figure suggests that perhaps an incomplete university education is more stressful than none at all. Even so, education and violence are correlated only weakly . . ., and the negative association does not reach statistical significance.

Income. . . . Although spousal abuse is reported generally by respondents of all income groups, low income is associated with an increased probability of domestic violence. . . . Men who reportedly had an annual income of $20,000 or less reported a rate of violence (36.2) that was almost 300 percent greater than the rate of wife abuse in the most well-to-do families (incomes over $65,000). . . .

Employment Status. Lack of jobs, low income, and sustained economic uncertainties are risk markers that contribute to higher rates of domestic violence. American studies have found that one of the main factors associated with wife abuse in the home is the husband's employment status. The Canadian survey produced similar results: the rate of wife assault among unemployed men was more than double the rate among employed men, 37.9 percent and 16.1 percent respectively. . . . Men who were employed part time reported even higher rates, probably because they were in the worst of all possible situations — no full-time job and no eligibility for unemployment or other benefits. . . .

Stress and Violence

Some of these and other findings suggest that stress is a major contributing factor to domestic violence. In order to obtain a more direct sense of how much stress our respondents encountered in the previous year, they were asked about the type of problems they actually experienced. Each of our respondents was presented with a list of twenty problems or stressful events which a majority of people agreed produced stress in marriage. From this list the following twelve items were selected as potentially stressful events:

1. Unemployment for a period of more than one month

2. Personal bankruptcy

3. A drop in wage or salary

4. Taking an additional job to make ends meet financially

5. Working more overtime than he or she wishes in order to make ends meet financially

6. Child support or alimony payments that respondent did not have before

7. A move to a less expensive accommodation

8. Taking in a boarder to help make ends meet financially

9. One or more demotions

10. Loss of income due to going back to university

11. Some other important career setback

12. Some other important negative change in economic circumstances

Gelles's (1972) detailed study of 80 families led him to the conclusion that violence is an "adaptation or response to structural stress." . . . He proposes that structural stress produces frustration, which is often followed by expressive violence. Structural stress also produces role expectations (particularly for the husband) which, because of lack of resources, only can be carried out by means of instrumental force. The second major precondition is socialization experience. If individuals learn that violence is an appropriate behaviour when one is frustrated or angry, then "this will be the adaptation to stress employed" (Gelles, 1972: 189).

Although the validity of the original frustration-aggression hypotheses has been questioned by experimental psychologists on the grounds that frustration does not always produce aggression (Baron, 1983, 1977), the above discussion underlines the importance of con-

sidering the influence of perceived and experienced stress on the incidence of domestic abuse. This topic is addressed briefly in Figure 23-1, in which we can observe a fairly strong and statistically significant relationship between *experienced* stressful events reported by male and female respondents and the extent of reported interspousal violence. . . . Thus experienced stress accounts for 30 percent of the variance. As a close inspection of Figure 23-1 shows, each additional stressful event increased the likelihood that wife and husband abuse would occur. Men who reported eight or more stressful events, for example, had a violence rate eight times as great as that found among men who experienced only up to one stressful event. Women's rates are similar but somewhat lower for those who experienced eight or more stressful events. It seems as though the accumulation of stressful events increases significantly the risks of abuse. . . .

Interspousal Conflict and Domestic Violence

Conflict in marriage derives from opposed interests, which are inherent in the structure of the family. We may define marital conflict as a struggle over values and goals or over claims to status, power, and limited resources, in which partners act as opponents; each seeks to achieve his or her goals, usually at the expense of others (Coser, 1968; Scanzoni, 1982: 70–71). A tension may exist between the individual's need for maintaining a sense of personal identity and the couple's need for maintaining stability. In other words, couples must satisfy two inherently contradictory needs: to be close and intimate with their partners and to maintain a sense of self and privacy. These con-

FIGURE 23-1

OVERALL VIOLENCE RATE FOR MARRIED OR COHABITING WOMEN AND MEN AND EXPERIENCED STRESS, CANADA, 1987

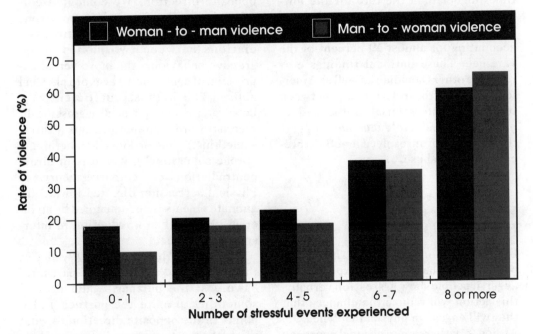

flicting needs for personal identity and couple stability constitute an ongoing dialectic process, or a process of reconciliation, in which couples must seek a balance. Thus conflict is not a zero-sum game, but may be negotiated and managed through an ongoing, interactive give-and-take process. Conflict resolution strategies can range from attempts to advance one's interest by showing the moral, logical, or factual superiority of the desired outcome to acts of verbal and physical aggression. Resolved marital conflict ... may strengthen the relationship and lead to newly defined and reconstructed exchanges from which both partners benefit (Scanzoni, 1982). Conflict resolution is very difficult, however, if the partners are at odds on basic values and cannot agree on the basic ground rules that govern the rela-

tionship. Unresolved marital conflict may accumulate gradually, become pervasive, and promote the use of emotional and physical force by one partner or both within an interactional framework of superordinate and subordinate relationships that tie husbands and wives into the domestic establishment. Thus we would expect marital conflict[4] to be related positively with violence.... This is the case: as the amount of reported conflict increases, so does the rate of violence. The strong tendency for violence to increase as the amount of conflict increases applies to both women and men. In the low-conflict marriages, 7.2 percent of the husbands reported violence, as compared to 31.9 percent of the husbands in the marriages with the most conflict. ... Wives followed the same trend, but started with a slightly higher rate of violence in the low-conflict marriages. Women with the most conflicts had a violence rate of 47.1 percent, four times higher than the rate for the low-conflict group (11.2%). Ongoing marital conflict is a major explanatory factor . . ., accounting for almost 19 percent of the variance. These national findings corroborate other Canadian as well as American reports: the relationship between frequency of interspousal conflict and reported physical violence may suggest that excessive unresolved conflict precedes mutual abuse. . . .

Verbal Aggression and Interspousal Violence

Catharsis theorists believe that angry people should be allowed to express their anger; if people show aggression verbally, this action will reduce the chances that they will engage in physical violence. . . . Although catharsis as a clinical approach to conflict resolution has been challenged empirically by several researchers, particularly by those who espouse social learning theory (Bandura, 1973, 1977, 1986; Baron, 1983), it has gained considerable support in the general public.

Of special interest here are the effects of verbal aggression and the question whether an escalation of verbal disputes is associated positively or negatively with the occurrence of physical violence. According to catharsis theory, we would expect to find that couples who engage in a great many verbal disputes have significantly lower violence rates than couples who engage in few or no verbal disputes. Similarly, couples who engage in physical aggression (against inanimate objects) would be less likely to be involved in interspousal violence than couples who engage in few or no such aggressive acts.

Our national data, however, produced little evidence to support the catharsis theory and a great deal that points in the opposite direction. We computed correlation coefficients and found strong and statistically significant positive associations between two modes of aggressive behaviour: the more verbal expression of aggression, the more physical abuse. The highest coefficient . . ., however, involves physical aggression directed toward inanimate objects ("threw something," "hit or kicked something," "broke something"), which is in direct contradiction to . . . catharsis theory. . . . Physical aggression directed toward inanimate objects is accompanied by an increase rather than a reduction in interspousal violence.

Similarly, verbal aggression ("yelled at the partner," "insulted the partner," "swore at the partner," "did or said something to spite the partner") also points in the opposite direction to what the catharsis theory predicts: verbal attacks by couples are associated with an increase rather than a decrease in domestic violence. Furthermore, women and men who engaged in a great deal of verbal aggression were six times more likely to report abusing their partners physically than women and men who engaged in few or no verbal disputes. . . .

Clearly, these findings and those reported by others (Straus et al., 1980; Brinkerhoff and Lupri, 1988) cast considerable doubt on the validity of the catharsis theory. . . . The correlational findings cannot demonstrate . . . that verbal or physical aggression "cause" interspousal violence, but they demonstrate that it does nothing to reduce violence in the home. According to an interactional model of causation (Bandura, 1986), inflicting emotional or physical pain on someone who has angered us can serve often as a positive reinforcer, and behaviour that is reinforced is likely to recur. Thus, rather than reducing subsequent physical violence, verbal or retaliatory aggression may produce reinforcers that increase the likelihood and intensity of physical violence. . . .

FAMILY LIFE IN CONTEMPORARY SOCIETY

A Dialectic Approach

. . . My dialectic approach interprets conjugal roles as an institutional network of social relationships governed by inherent contradictions that may give rise to conflict and structural change. It focuses sharply on the coexistence and unfolding of opposite forces in all social relationships, including marriage and the family. Thus proneness to conflict and incongruence are as intrinsic to the family as are affection and intimacy. . . . The question is, why is the family the most violent institution in today's society, second only to the military in wartime? . . . Although I acknowledge that not all women and men engage in domestic violence, let me sketch briefly why I think the contemporary structure of the conjugal family is highly conflict-prone.

All human groups face problems and changes. The family is no exception; it is a primary group whose members are closely bound together in the emotional sense. . . . The family can be a haven in a heartless world (Lasch, 1979), a refuge and a place of comfort, protection, and intimacy. It is also the setting within which family members define, shape, and modify their own private, meaningful world. . . .

Yet the same structural features that one can use to characterize the family as

a haven also can characterize the family as a crucible for conflict and violence. . . . Several inherently contradictory interactions characterize the contemporary family as a primary group. First, a great deal of family interaction takes place on a one-to-one basis. Many hours of the day may be spent in face-to-face interaction with other family members, and this high frequency of interaction increases the "time risk" of conflict or violence (Gelles and Straus, 1979).

Second, family interaction covers a wide range of activities: daily routine tasks, leisure-time pursuits, conversations, the expression of intimate feelings. Because numerous events take place on any given day, greater likelihood exists for disagreements, tension, or dispute over these events.

Third, marriage demands intense interaction. Couples communicate with openness and intimacy, which brings the opportunity for the development of affection, love, and deeply felt experiences. Yet there are also risks of failure and emotional injury: openness can be a one-sided affair. Intense involvement renders a partner vulnerable if the other remains uninvolved, distant, and aloof.

Fourth, dyadic relationships, such as couple interaction, contain built-in structural conflicts. As Simmel (1955, 1950) observed cogently, either member can destroy the relationship by not participating, by not becoming involved, by withdrawing. Larger groups can survive more easily the loss of one member or more without causing the group to dissolve. In addition, there is no majority rule in a couple, to which a spouse can appeal for fairness or justice. To call in outside help is defined in our society as interference, and is legitimized only as a last resort "to save the marriage." Moreover, with the addition of children, the structure of interaction changes and brings the possibility of coalition formation.

Fifth, the family is hierarchical: interaction between members is influenced by power and dependency relationships. . . . Both age and sex structures shape family relationships . . . between women and men. This situation makes the family an arena of "cultural conflict" (Straus and Gelles, 1979) because built-in control mechanisms perpetuate age and gender inequalities that amplify the potential for conflict and violence. This is captured in [the] phrase "battle of the sexes." . . .

Finally, the family is a highly privatized social group and thus is shielded from public scrutiny. This fact is epitomized in such phrases as "My home is my castle" and in former Prime Minister Trudeau's declaration, "The state has no business in the bedrooms of the nation." The norms of the nuclear family dictate that couples solve their own problems, regardless of their origin, nature, and extent. Yet many members of couples lack problem-solving abilities, interpersonal skills, and the necessary insight into their own or their partners' behaviour. . . .

To sum up, . . . modern family life consists of what Goffman (1959) calls "backstage behaviour" that evolves in a "backstage area." In contrast to the "frontstage area," the public domain, where people are obliged to perform well-defined roles, the term backstage behaviour suggests greater freedom to act without formal constraints and captures the way people act when they are relaxed, informal, uninhibited, and just being themselves. This freedom to abandon pretense . . . is also the source of considerable conflict. When partners confide in one another in the backstage area, self-disclosure, spontaneity, and easy familiarity are possible, but, . . . so are inconsiderateness, disrespect, and outright personal attacks. . . . This is the paradox of intimate relationships.

The similarities between the way in which intimates convey affection and the way they express aggression is captured eloquently in the following:

> Thus, although lovers stare at each other, so do enemies. Standing very close to a person, calling him or her "baby," remaining silent for long periods, or handling that person's possessions can signal either intimacy or hostility, depending upon the emotional context of the situation. Since lovers are used to giving one version of these signals, it seems relatively easy for them to slip into the other mode (Skolnick, 1978: 229).

These structural and interactional characteristics suggest that the modern family is likely to be the focus of more, and more serious, stresses than any other social groups. In short, the family's built-in structural inability to solve its own problems makes it far more conflict-prone than other social groups. In light of the great propensity for conflict and violence in today's marriage, it is astonishing not that so many marriages end in divorce but that so many endure. . . .

To be sure, as a culture we are "overwhelmingly committed to upholding a unified and harmonious *image* of family life" (Miller, 1990: 261). This historically evolved rhetoric serves as a powerful sense-making backdrop against which family members assess and interpret their daily activities in order to manage the inherent contradictions and inconsistencies of the ordinary domestic routine. In other words, these practices serve to integrate the image of harmony with the violent reality that many women and men face. Hence, the discrepancies between imagery and behaviour should be taken as the starting point for theoretical analysis, not as an end product. To view harmony and conflict analytically as two independent "realities," however, would be an example of what Simmel calls the "fallacy of separateness."

Notes

1 I am greatly indebted to Professor J.R. Ponting of the University of Calgary for letting me use his national probability sample of 1,834 Canadian women and men as a target population to gather information on family issues such as marital happiness, marital conflict, and domestic violence. The sampling design and the interviews for this survey were carried out by DECIMA Ltd. of Toronto and were financed through a grant from the Social Sciences and Humanities Research Council of Canada.

2 Feminists have been particularly critical of the Conflict Tactics Scales for allegedly understating victimization of women and overstating violence by women (see Breines and Gordon, 1983; Dobash and Dobash, 1979, 1983; Okun, 1986; Pagelow, 1984). Other objections centre around the fact that the CTS counts acts of violence in isolation from the circumstances under which those acts occur; that it does not measure processes and consequences; that it ignores who initiates the violence; and that the list of items is limited and restricted as it excludes many other forms of violence, most notably marital rape. It also can be argued easily that a slap or a punch by a 190 pound man is likely to be much more damaging than a slap or punch by a 125 pound woman, yet the CTS counts them as though they were the same. (For a reply to these and other criticisms, see Chapter 4, Straus and Gelles, 1990.)

3 The incidence rate of wife abuse reported by divorced and separated male respondents is almost three times as high as that reported by married or cohabiting persons (Lupri, 1989).

4 The scale of marital conflict consists of ten items regarding the frequency of disagreements about "you being tired," "irritating personal habits," "sexual relationship," "the way housework is divided," "the way money is handled," "children's behaviour," "you not showing love," "how to spend free time," "in-laws," and "time spent with friends?" . . .

References

Bandura, Albert. *Aggression: A Social Learning Analysis.* Englewood Cliffs, N.J.: Prentice-Hall, 1973.

_____. *Social Learning Theory.* Englewood Cliffs, N.J.: Prentice-Hall, 1977.

_____. *Social Foundations of Thought and Action: A Social Cognitive Theory.* Englewood Cliffs, N.J.: Prentice-Hall, 1986.

Baron, R.A. *Human Aggression.* New York: Plenum, 1977.

_____. "The content of human aggression: an optimistic perspective." *Journal of Social and Clinical Psychology* 1 (1983): 97–119.

Breines, Wini and Gordon, Linda. "The new scholarship on family violence." *Signs: Journal of Women in Culture and Society* 8 (1983): 490–531.

Brinkerhoff, M.B. and Lupri, Eugen. "Interspousal violence." *Canadian Journal of Sociology.* 13(4) (1988): 407–431.

————. "Religious involvement and spousal abuse." Paper presented at the Annual Meetings of the Society For the Study of Scientific Religion in Chicago, October 30, 1989.

Coser, Lewis A. *The Functions of Social Conflict.* New York: The Free Press, 1968.

Dobash, R. Emerson and Dobash, Russell P. *Violence Against Wives: A Case Against Patriarchy.* New York: The Free Press, 1979.

————. "Patterns of violence in Scotland." In Richard J. Gelles and Claire P. Cornell (eds.), *International Perspectives on Family Violence.* Lexington, MA: Lexington Books, 1983.

Gelles, Richard J. *The Violent Home: A Study of Physical Aggression Between Husbands and Wives.* Beverly Hills, CA: Sage, 1972.

Gelles, Richard J. and Strauss, Murray. "Determinants of aggression in the family: toward a theoretical integration." Pp. 549–581 in W. Burr *et al.* (eds.), *Contemporary Theories About the Family*, Vol. I. New York: Free Press, 1979.

Goffman, Erving. *The Presentation of Self in Everyday Life.* Garden City, N.Y.: Doubleday Anchor, 1959.

Lasch, Christopher. *Haven in a Heartless World.* New York: Basic Books, 1979.

Okun, Lewis. *Women Abuse: Facts Replacing Myths.* Albany, N.Y.: State University of New York Press, 1986.

Pagelow, Mildred D. *Family Violence.* New York: Praeger Hills: Sage, 1984.

Saunders, Daniel G. "When battered women use violence: husband-abuse or self-defense?" *Violence and Victims* I (1) (1986): 47–60.

Scanzoni, John. *Sexual Bargaining: Power and Politics in American Marriage.* Chicago: University of Chicago Press, 1982.

Simmel, George. *Conflict and the Web of Group Affiliations,* translated by Kurt H. Wolff and Reinhard Bendix. Chicago: Free Press, 1955.

————. *The Sociology of George Simmel*, edited by Kurt Wolff. New York: The Free Press, 1950.

Skolnick, Arlene S. *The Intimate Environment.* Boston: Little, Brown, and Company, 1978.

Straus, Murray A. and Gelles, Richard J. *Physical Violence in American Families.* New York: Transaction Books, 1990.

Straus, Murray A., Gelles, Richard J, and Steinmetz, Susan K. *Behind Closed Doors: Violence in the American Family.* New York: Anchor/Doubleday, 1980.

Social Change

This section is about social change. It includes articles on the political conflict between Quebec and the rest of Canada; the religious changes that led to a new, less patriarchal style of thinking about women; and the technicization of society — how technology shapes our social and cultural lives.

Social change is a difficult topic to discuss briefly, because change can come about in so many ways. Often it results from social protest; just as often, it occurs without social protest playing a part. Indeed, researchers who study social change try to discover the conditions under which inequality will, or will not, give rise to social protest and social change.

A great deal of social change occurs without plan, through the invention and spread of new technologies. Technological change inside our own society often leads to unexpected, uncontrolled social change. No one knew beforehand all the ways the telephone, automobile, and computer would transform our lives.

Social, economic, and political change that starts outside our society may change our lives. Changes in the international balance of trade, world peace, or the availability of needed resources all have major impacts on us. Historically a staple-producing country, Canada has always been particularly vulnerable to change in the demand for food and resources outside our borders. These economic changes affect our industrial and communal life, and in this way, the private lives of individual Canadians.

Another kind of change is evolutionary: it is change that does not break radically with tradition but extends it. Evolutionary change includes two main processes: differentiation and integration. Differentiation (as for example, an increasing division of labour at work) increases the complexity of the social order. The number of distinct groups and organizations, and the number of operating rules, increases. On the other hand, integration increases the coordination within a complex social order.

For example, high rates of immigration and a multicultural policy have produced a highly differentiated ethnic order in Canada. As we saw in an earlier section, many groups struggle for resources and power. Gradually, society changes in ways that moderate this competition and keep it from becoming violent. They include the growth of governmental bodies that oversee the allocation of resources among groups, and new laws that protect individual and group rights. The Canadian Charter of Rights plays an important role in this respect. It protects many kinds of minorities and regulates conflict between the majority and minority groups. Thus laws, especially constitutional laws, play an integrative role in a differentiated, changing society.

The implication is clear: the more a society differentiates, and the more rapidly it does so, the more complex integrative institutions it must develop. In turn, these institutions (like the Charter of Rights) themselves become sources of change in society. They allow certain disadvantaged groups — women, gays, and the physically disabled, among others — to press for new rights. This begins a new cycle of change. Thus, social evolution is a continuing cycle of change that works iteratively through differentiation and integration.

Other types of change are more conscious and purposeful: for example, change through collective action. Marx (see, for example, Marx and Engels, 1848) helped to found the study of social movements and social change. He theorized that all history was the working out of class conflict: a continuing struggle between subordinate and dominant classes. In this way, one social order came to replace another. Naturally, in analyzing nineteenth century capitalism, Marx wanted to understand the current condition of the working class, or proletariat. His immediate goal was to theorize about, and help set, the conditions for a successful workers' revolution. Accurately predicting the decline and overthrow of capitalism would rest on correctly understanding the working class and its mobilization.

Based on his reading of history, Marx predicted a progressive impoverishment of the working class in countries where capitalism was most advanced — England and Germany, for example. There, by mobilizing, the working class would overthrow the capitalist class and create a new, classless society. Yet, this is not what happened. Neither England, nor Germany, the United States nor France — indeed, no industrial country — produced a worker's revolution or classless society. Revolutions did occur in Russia and, then, in many Third World countries; but even here, no classless societies resulted.

Nor did Marx prove right in supposing that the working class would make these revolutions. In every instance, other classes — the urban intelligentsia, military, or peasantry (occasionally aided by small groups of workers) — were the chief agents of revolution.

Marx's predictions went wrong because he had bet that the working classes would become impoverished and, in that way, more conscious of their class interests. Through this consciousness would come a sense of community — important in the mobilization for protest. However, history shows that the working class was not impoverished. Nor will poverty always produce revolution. Neither extreme inequality nor growing inequality will always lead to protest. In fact, some evidence suggests that declining (not increasing) inequality will lead to protest if there is a "revolution in rising expectations."

People are often outraged if conditions do not improve as fast as they would like, even though they are actually improving. Less, not more, inequality makes resources available for protest: more money, food, technology, expertise, free time, and so on. People who are desperately poor have fewer of these resources for protest than relatively affluent North American college students, for example. They are too absorbed in the day to day business of sheer survival to think about challenging the government.

Though Marx was wrong about the roles of inequality, he was certainly right about the role of group consciousness in making a revolution. Social protest requires some communal, shared commitment to change. In turn, this demands geographic proximity, interaction and communication, an awareness of common experiences and problems, and a common world view. Bringing the oppressed together, whether in segregated parts of large cities, in factories or in factory towns, ought, therefore, to radicalize and mobilize them. And so it did, in nineteenth century England.

What about the French Canadian case. Why did significant protest occur in Quebec when it did, and not a decade, a generation, or a century earlier? Let's tick off the conditions. First, there was never any shortage of "community" among French Canadians in Quebec. A change in community cohesion cannot, by and large, account for the surge of nationalism, terrorism, and separatist sentiment in the 1960s and 70s. Nor is it likely that impoverishment explains it. Like the American Blacks, many French Canadians left the countryside and came to live in cities after World War I. However, there is no evidence that the French Canadian economic condition worsened as a result.

What is most striking about that fiery decade, 1966–1976, is not the change in communal organization or inequality, but the new importance of intellectuals and radical ideologies. A dominant reality of twentieth century social change is the role of intellectuals — not workers — in leading revolutions, with ideology as a weapon.

No one who reads a daily newspaper can doubt the role of ideas and idea-makers in a modern changing world. How else are we to make sense of the turmoil in the Islamic world, where religious fundamentalism — not class conflict — is the dominant force for change? Or the turmoil in the Eastern bloc, where nationalism — not class conflict — is the dominant force for change? Or the growing political role of environmentalists in pushing for change in the capitalist West? In every case, ideas and idea-makers are centrally important.

Ideas and ideologies are crucial to the success of protest movements because people are more than walking bellies. People also have hungry minds and hearts. Ideologies — whether religious, nationalistic, or secular — are food for hungry, despairing minds. They promise a better world, justify action, lower the mighty, and raise the fallen. Intellectuals are the craftsmen of ideology: they trade in ideas, words, imagery, imagination.

Intellectuals are not the only people who trade in ideology: religious leaders do too. It is no accident that political protest in Canadian history has often accompanied religious protest. And religious leaders (for example, J.S. Woodsworth of the CCF and William Aberhart of the Social Credit Party) have often been at the forefront of political protest.

Intellectuals and religious leaders have the skills, the time, and (often) the economic security to lead protests. Moreover, they have enough credibility as "people of knowledge" to be able to sell ideologies as "the truth." Not only are ideologies and intellectuals important, they also embody the interests and experiences of people who use them. Faced with a conflict between interest and ideology, people will usually come to accept changes in their interest even if it violates ideology. However, that does not mean that ideologies are nothing more than a cover-up for crude interests.

Weber (1946) recognized that every social movement goes through distinct phases. There is the "charismatic phase" of powerful emotion, communal sentiment, and blind willingness to follow a leader to the limit. Then comes the "routinization of charisma," a period when people need orderliness and established authority. In the routinization phase, typically after the charismatic leader has died, followers come to terms with the real world. They use the victories of the movement to meet the current needs of the movement members.

Quebec offers a particularly interesting case of social change in Canada that was driven by ideology. Quebec has always seen itself as a nation within a nation. Through the nineteenth century, it was a laboratory for the study of relations between two different language/culture groups, one dominant in economic affairs and the other in cultural, religious, and private affairs. In the first two-thirds of the present century, Quebec was a laboratory for studying the industrialization of a peasant people largely untouched by nineteenth century progress. Since then, Quebec has been a laboratory for the study of national self-assertion.

An article by Hubert Guindon, included in this section, was published shortly after the PQ victory in Quebec. A little later, a bare majority of Quebec voters decided against seeking sovereignty-association with Canada. In the intervening period, before that fateful vote, the air crackled with suspense; charisma was not yet fully routinized. We see the intellectual's role as ideologue in the language of Guindon's writing: it is radical, cynical, full of energy, and confidence. His paper reminds us that experiments in constitutional reform have been tried, and they have failed. Without more significant action, Canada may be headed for sovereignty-association.

The role of intellectuals and ideas is even clearer in an excerpt by Roberta Hamilton, on feminists in the academy. Here, the author gives us a short personal history of her own involvement in the development of feminist thinking. There were reasons why feminist scholarship could gain an institutional foothold in the 1980s and not in the 1960s. Success rode on other factors besides the merit of feminist ideas and high-quality scholarship. In general, this is true of all the changes we've seen in universities — and societies — in the last thirty years. Intellectuals have an important role to play in persuading publics that it is time to think new ideas. However, change does not lie in ideas alone.

Many other challenges, and opportunities, face us: among them, ecological destruction, a war that could end all wars, an enormous excess of poor people in the southern hemisphere, new health hazards and opportunities, and the chance that modern technology will perfect totalitarian rule.

In his article on the *technicisation* of society, Willem Vanderburg reminds us of the delicate interplay between people and machines. Technology becomes complex and sophisticated in certain kinds of societies, not others. Typically, technological development requires a high degree of surplus wealth, a secular and scientific orientation, and a lot of "human capital." In that sense, technology presupposes a particular kind of culture. Without it, technology cannot take off.

However, technological sophistication also changes the culture in the direction of increased concerns with rationality and efficiency. To some degree, the presence of more (and better) technology starts us putting technological concerns before human ones. How this happens, and with what result, is the subject of Vanderburg's short paper.

Like ideas and technology, demography has pushed our society in new directions. Roderic Beaujot shows in his article in this section, that declining fertility has meant — in Canada and elsewhere — population aging and an inevitable population shrinkage. Population aging and decline carry serious social and economic costs. We may choose to bear those costs, but if we cannot accept them, we shall have to enter the 21st century with a strategy for increasing fertility. In turn, this will mean lowering the "costs" of childbearing for parents, and especially mothers. It will also mean rethinking the social role of old people.

Inequality, community, ideology, intellectuals, technology, demography, charisma: all of these and so many other factors will continue to shape our collective destiny in the next century.

References

Marx, Karl and Engels, Friedrich. *The Communist Manifesto.* With an introduction by A.J.P. Taylor. Harmondsworth: Penguin Books, 1967 [1848].

Weber, Max. From *Max Weber: Essays in Sociology*, H. Gerth and L.W. Mills, eds. and trans. New York: Oxford, 1946.

TWENTY-FOUR

Quebec and the Legitimacy of the Canadian State

Hubert Guindon

HUBERT GUINDON, Professor of Sociology at Concordia University, specializes in the study of political sociology and Quebec society. He has published numerous articles on those topics and has, in addition, co-edited (with D. Glenday and A. Turowetz) *Modernisation and the Canadian State* (1978). He has taught at the University of Montreal and has served as Visiting Professor in the Institute of Canadian Studies at Carleton University. Honours include election to the presidency of the Canadian Sociology and Anthropology Association, the executive of the International Sociological Association, and the Royal Society of Canada.

THE MODERNIZATION OF QUEBEC AND THE FEDERAL STATE

... The preliminary report of the Royal Commission on Bilingualism and Biculturalism (1965: 125) began by proclaiming a state of crisis in Canada. Deep cleavages were said to exist between the francophone and anglophone components of the country. This alarmist manifesto concluded with the urgency of defining a federal language policy for the Canadian state, its state agencies, and crown corporations that could become the basis to forge a new consensus for the two "societies" sharing a common state.

Some ten years later, in the summer of 1976, the defeat of the federal state's policy was publicly consummated with the successful resistance of the Canadian Air Traffic Controllers (CATCA) and the Canadian Airline Pilots Association (CALPA) to the implementation of the official language policy.[1] For the first time in Canadian history, to my knowledge, a special interest group was able to dictate to the Crown a "free vote" in Parliament on matters that are not related to issues of personal conscience.[2] That this clause was not perceived as a direct threat to the very essence of British parliamentary democracy is quite revealing. Even more so, when one realizes that this policy had been endorsed by all political parties. Obstacles to democracy do not always come from Quebec.

Such a spectacular "crash" of federal state policy needs to be accounted for. CATCA and CALPA could not have succeeded were it not for the mobilized emotional support of English-speaking Canadians. The prime minister, in his usual somber manner, solemnly proclaimed this was a threat to national unity.[3] Other ministers of the Crown more mundanely stated that they had failed to do a good "selling job" of the official languages policy to English-speaking Canadians (Montreal *Star*, 25–8 June 1976). It might be the proper time to address oneself to the content of the policy, and to wonder whether the policy itself may have something to do with the problems it has generated for the state. Maybe it was doomed to fail.

A critique of the official languages policy might profitably start with a recall of the political and social context within which the Royal Commission on Bilingualism and Biculturalism was instituted. It was established by Prime Minister Pearson after a series of editorials by André Laurendeau in *Le Devoir* (26 August 1961 to 24 July 1963; about 48 editorials in all). His lead editorial quoted from a memorandum written by a French-Canadian federal civil servant for the attention of his French-Canadian subordinates. This memorandum was leaked to the press and in part read as follows: "Since everyone in the Department is bilingual, all reports must be written in English" (*Le Devoir*, 26 August 1961). In this civil servant's mind, this was not a political act, but a suggestion to increase internal administrative efficiency. In the larger political context, such a memo meant, if not speak white, at least write white. In the broader political scene it underlined two things: the unilingualism of the public service, the fact that anglophones could enter the civil service and be unilingual, while French Canadians could only enter government service if they were fluently bilingual.

Proceeding from this barrier to entry, it followed that French Canadians were highly underrepresented in the civil service, increasingly, so as one moved up the bureaucratic hierarchies of the public service and crown corporations (RCBB, Book III: Chap. 9). The alienating effect of these features for the French-speaking population of Canada towards the federal state was underlined. The royal commission set as a major objective to resolve this contradiction. It therefore sought to define a policy that would increase the use of French in the federal civil service and increase the proportion of French Canadians within its ranks at all levels of its bureaucratic hierarchy (RCBB, Book III: Chaps: 9–10).

Another major objective of the royal commission was also a response to a leitmotif of French-Canadian nationalism of the fifties. This leitmotif concerned the treatment of minorities. Quebec was seen as a model of majority-minority relations, a model that contrasted sharply with the way French Canadians were treated in every other province in Canada. The other provinces, dating back to the Manitoba School Question and Ontario's "Rule XVII," had severely curtailed the legal status of French within their public school systems. In the previous dispensation, when most institutions were territorially integrated within communities, locally financed and administered by local citizens, the English-speaking population of Quebec did have local autonomy and full legal status within the public school system of the state. As a consequence, Quebec was seen as the model for French-English relations, and the commission set out to exhort provincial legislatures to effect changes that would bring the status of French Canadians outside Quebec more in line with the status of anglophones in

Quebec, especially as regards the legal status of French in provincial school systems.

These two concerns — increasing the participation and the upward mobility of French Canadians within the federal state's bureaucracies and increasing the institutional support of French Canadians outside Quebec — became the major objectives of the commission's bilingual policy.

Given these objectives, the royal commission could not seriously consider a territorially based language policy (RCBB, Book I: Chap. 4). And without such a policy, it was doomed to become a political irritation in English Canada, and a political irrelevance in a modernizing French Quebec. Unfortunately, social scientists should not underestimate the state's capacity to commit itself to both.

The commissioners appointed to the Royal Commission on Bilingualism and Biculturalism were all fluently bilingual. While this may have ensured its basic commitment to bilingualism, and facilitated the efficiency of internal communications for its members, it certainly constituted a "rare event" rather untypical of what happens nationally at the level of professional associations, voluntary associations, corporations, and even federal-provincial summit conferences.

A sense of "noblesse oblige" can easily permeate a body of distinguished bilingual citizens gathering together to forge a national language policy after a proclaimed crisis in national unity. Having personally achieved the "noble" thing, such distinguished gentlemen are apt to forget that "noblesse oblige la noblesse," not the ordinary common mortal. . . .

While factually incorrect in terms of its report, as a psychological fact it is quite correct to state that the commission gen-

erated the impression in the public view that a good Canadian ought to be bilingual. This impression was further strengthened by the commission's recommendations seeking to facilitate bilingualism for federal civil servants. This cast the unilingual Canadian in a defensive moral posture he duly and rightfully resented.

No matter how lofty its ideals, the legacy of the political disaster created by the official language policy is there for anyone to see.

1/ It did not appreciably increase the francophone share of the federal state's bureaucracies (public service and crown corporations) (Posgate and McRoberts, 1976: 141–2) and yet it did give rise to the shibboleth "French power" that becomes the battle cry of the social groups who feel threatened by its implementation.

2/ It is not successful in arresting the accelerated assimilation of French Canadians outside Quebec, nor will it increase the viability of French communities outside the Sudbury-Moncton perimeter.

3/ It hinders rather than facilitates the changes needed as a consequence of the social modernization of the Québécois.

4/ It contributes to a climate of ambiguity for immigrants in Quebec and uncertainty for the large private corporate sector in Quebec.

It is a short list but a major indictment that needs some elaboration.

The Language Policy and the Promotion of French Canadians in the Civil Service and Crown Corporations

While the promotion of French Canadians to higher executive positions was one of the major aims of the royal commission, its policies, after a decade, failed to bring about any substantial changes. The number of francophones in such posts increased from 13 per cent in 1966 to 14.4 per cent in 1971. Furthermore, within that increase, it is known that Québécois are highly underrepresented (Posgate and McRoberts, 1976: 141, 142). At that rate, it would take 50 years for the number of French Canadians in executive positions to match the statistical proportion of French-speaking Canadians in the total population. Furthermore, since most of that increase is recruited from French Canadians outside Quebec and, therefore, already bilingual, its political irrelevance for Quebec becomes even clearer.

The failure of the immersion programs to increase the French competence of anglophone civil servants was admitted by the former commissioner of official languages in one of his annual reports (1976).

In short, the number of French Canadians in executive positions is not increasing significantly and the English-speaking civil servants are not becoming significantly more bilingual. Rather than questioning the validity and the nature of the whole language policy, Keith Spicer insists on remaining within a dream world and recommends that the resources be directed towards teaching French to school children. Myths die hard, especially when they are noble ones.

Given the negligible increase in the francophone representation at the various levels of the federal bureaucracy and its crown corporations, one can only wonder what would have given rise to the shibboleth "French power" that underlies the anti-French backlash the official languages policy generated across English-speaking Canada, the backlash that peaked with the CATCA and CALPA strikes.

The backlash, in my opinion, is traceable to one of the basic principles emanating from the royal commission and incorporated in the Official Languages Act. That principle, which can be labelled the 10 per cent principle, specifies that when a French or English minority is sufficiently great (roughly 10 per cent of the population), government services, in such cases, should be made available in that minority's language, whether English or French (RCBB, Book I: Recommendations). When implemented, this principle has systematically brought about ethnic tensions. . . .

The Viability of French Communities Outside Quebec

Framed in response to the Québécois nationalism of the fifties whose grievances with the Canadian political system rested, in part, on the contrast between the treatment of French minorities outside Quebec and the status of the English minority in Quebec, the royal commission, after having documented this unequal treatment, set out as its objectives, not only to redress these historical inequalities, but to insure that Canada be a bilingual country in its geographical totality. Given this objective, it could not and did not conceive a bilingual policy for the country that would be territorially based. It therefore discarded, with strikingly unconvincing reasons, serious consideration of any territorially based language policy (RCBB, Book I: 88). It opted instead to try through exhortation of the appropriate jurisdictions (mainly the provincial governments), to initiate what is called "institutional bilingualism," whose main principle has already been outlined. . . .

Institutional Bilingualism: Administrative Idealism and the Sociology of Language

With ten years of hindsight, admittedly, it nonetheless somewhat stuns the average intelligence that the royal commission managed to develop a whole series of urgent language policies without any studies on the sociology of language. What the sociology of language involves, simply defined, is a study of language interaction in different kinds of social settings at the community level, at the level of public space, at the level of voluntary organizations, at the level of institutions, etc. It raises such questions as who becomes bilingual, when, and why. How do bilingual people remain bilingual? When does language become an issue of community conflict? How do language conflicts get solved in minority/majority contexts? When and why do language conflicts become larger societal events and give rise to language movements and counter-movements? When and how do language frontiers shift? What are the consequences of such shifts on local institutions?

Since the royal commission managed to avoid all such questions in its deliberations and commissioned research, and since it did make specific recommenda-

tions, one must therefore raise the issue of what were its assumptions about the sociology of language. It is precisely these assumptions that I have labelled "administrative idealism." . . .

. . . Its administrative "idealism" as regards its language policy is witnessed by its belief in "institutional bilingualism."

Committed to reinforce the bilingual character of Canada, the commission decided on a policy of increasing francophone presence at all levels of the state bureaucracies and agencies. In this it failed as has already been shown. Acutely aware of the historical institutional deprivation of the French Canadians outside Quebec, it assumed that by increasing the institutional supports for francophone life outside Quebec, it would not only right an historical wrong but ensure the "bilingual" character of the country. Is this assumption warranted? This paper argues that it is not.

French communities have indeed managed to survive remarkably well until the recent past. Not surprisingly, the very processes that made this survival possible are becoming increasingly visible now that they are in a state of collapse. What were these processes and why are they collapsing?

The conditions that enabled the survival, indeed the growth, of French communities outside Quebec preceded the massive urbanization and industrialization that has restructured the political economy of Canada.[4] They could and did develop in a rural world of small-scale family farming, sometimes bordering on self-sufficient economies. The church was the pivotal institution of social life, around which small voluntary associations as well as elementary schools could be developed. The bilingual people in such a setting were those who dealt with the "outside" world. Those who lived most of their lives within the community lived it in French. . . .

The industrial setting under which very similar conditions could obtain is to be found at the level of the primary sector of the economy. Labour-intensive industries involved in the extraction process — mining, lumberjacking, or fishing — provided a similar basis for community survival. This Quebec demographic overflow gave rise to what Joy has called the Soo-Moncton belt (1972: chap. 4).

The days of marginal or self-subsistence farming and of labour-intensive extractive industries are over. As their relative importance in the political economy shrinks, so does the economic base of the communities they supported. The increasing productivity in farming has meant an increased need for capital, not farm-hands. Technological improvement in extractive industries equally contributes to a dwindling need for labour. In other words, economic development dooms these communities to stagnation. What made them viable, paradoxically enough, was economic underdevelopment. While one could live out one's whole life in French in St Isidore de Prescott, and many did, no one can live their whole lives in French in Cornwall. . . .

Within the urban context, French Canadians outside Quebec had to deal with an English world: the world of the market, the world of state institutions from the courts to city council, the world of higher education, as well as the world of public space. This required fluency in English. The only acknowledgment the royal commission made to the sociology of language was a casual reference to the fact that people became bilingual because of necessity (RCBB, Book I: 6). Having said this, they dropped the topic, to pursue their normative bureaucratic analysis. . . .

The Political Irrelevance of Canada's Bilingual Policy in a Modern Quebec

It becomes apparent that language has been working as a sorting device in the allocation of people in English and French workplaces. The institutions dependent on the provincial state became French workplaces and the corporate world remained an English workplace. Both workplaces expanded bureaucratically in the postwar period. The French workplace gave rise to new elites in the public and parapublic sector. These elites were created by the provincial not by the federal state. In fact, the federal state's own record within its own corporations *in Quebec* is not substantially better (definitely not in the case of airline pilots and air traffic controllers to name two politically aggressive groups) than the corporate world itself. In both cases, perfect bilingualism is the required passport for upward mobility, when not for mere entry. With such a context of a rapidly modernizing Quebec, the federal state's language policy was not only politically irrelevant but clearly reactionary. That it led to the progressive alienation of Québécois elites is a glaring fact. The consequence of prolonged and expanding elite alienation had its electoral outcome on 15 November, 1976. On 16 November, though stunned, the federal establishment was convinced that the Québécois did not want independence but good government. Undoubtedly, but from which government?

The inertia of the federal state and its irrelevance, in my opinion, can be traced to the basic thrust of the official language policy. The royal commission's frame of reference precluded it from focusing on the structurally required changes to make the Québécois true partners in the

Canadian political economy. Its objectives should have been concerned principally with the French majority in Quebec, not the French minorities outside Quebec. Secondly, it should have changed the language "rules" of the corporate game in Quebec, not imposed uneconomic French TV and radio stations on British Columbia. Its central concern should not have been to try to shore up the collapsing language frontiers upholding vanishing French communities outside Quebec, but to break down unacceptable language frontiers preventing the expanding Québécois elites from penetrating both the federal state's own corporations and the private corporate world in Quebec. Prophetic in its proclamation of an impending crisis in the legitimacy of the federal state, it provided the state with bad counsel when it cavalierly refused to give serious consideration to the forging of a bilingual Canada on a territorial basis. . . .

The royal commission's reasons for not considering a territorial definition of bilingualism for Canada are uncommonly ludicrous. In a nutshell, the commission would have us believe that as North Americans we have the unique cultural characteristic of being very mobile geographically. This, in contrast to Europeans. Mobility as a cultural trait made it impractical therefore to consider seriously territoriality as the organizing principle for bilingualism. If mobility were a cultural trait, not a consequence of economic variables, why have Maritimers been going to Ontario but not vice versa? Is it that the culture of the Maritimes has this characteristic to a much higher degree than Ontario's? That distinguished Canadians should serve such gobbledegook to the Canadian public in order to dismiss a possible basis for forging a bilingual policy is quite bewildering. . . .

Canada's Bilingual Policy and the Continuing Ambiguities: The Case of the Corporate World and Immigrants to Quebec

By refusing to adopt a territorial bilingual policy, the royal commission could not logically proclaim that the main objective of the federal state's language policy should be to make Quebec French in all societal functions, including the language of the workplace.

While the corporate world and multinational corporations may be faulted for many things, they cannot be faulted for not implementing what is not the official policy of the Canadian state. . . .

The American multinationals, in the particular instance we are concerned with, only followed the historical practice that had been initiated by the Anglo-Canadian and British corporate world years before the massive American entry in the Canadian corporate scene. The ratio of British ethnics in Quebec has been declining for more than a century (Joy, 1972: 91–109). If the anglophone proportion of the population in the greater metropolitan area of Montreal has been able to maintain itself, it was by the absorption and integration of immigrants (Joy, 1972: Tables 21 and 26, pp. 48, 59). . . .

The Case of the Immigrants: A Structural Analysis

If the federal state, not the multinational private corporate sector, can and must be faulted for refusing to define as a state policy that all sectors of societal life in Quebec should become French, much less can the immigrants in Quebec be faulted for integrating into the economic system and wanting to learn the language of the system. Here again, one sees clearly that the ambiguous situation of immigrants in Quebec is as much the consequence of the language policy of the federal government as the social and political pressures of the Québécois majority.

The thorny issue involving immigrants in Quebec revolves on the fact that roughly 80 per cent of them integrate into the English institutional system and insist on choosing the English school system (Joy, 1972: 57–63). Given the structure of the political economy of Quebec, that this choice is a rational one is not difficult to demonstrate. . . .

The Immigrant Rationality

Immigrants in Quebec had no dilemma until language became a political issue. And language did not become a political issue in Quebec until the Québécois new middle class needed further outlets, outlets blocked by the language frontier.

While the political function of immigrants in the political economy of Quebec was to ensure the institutional autonomy and the economic hegemony of the English in Quebec, this was not, obviously, their conscious motive. Consciously, immigrants to Quebec, like everywhere else in the world, were seeking to better their economic opportunities. In the case of the postwar, skilled and professionally trained immigrants, the war-ravaged economies of Europe made it difficult or impossible for them to find the same opportunities in their countries as could be found in Canada. In the case of unskilled immigrants, a self-selected group from economically underdeveloped regions within their national homeland, they were immigrating to Canada, Quebec as elsewhere, in the hopes of avoiding the urban proletariat fate or *Lumpenproletariat* fate awaiting

them in Naples, Rome, Athens, or Lisbon. While these hopes were not to materialize for the majority, the hope that their children might escape the proletarian fate by education was kept alive.

In the case of skilled and professionally trained immigrants, integration in the English workplace, where they were needed, was smooth and instant. They came equipped with a working knowledge of English, and their children could proceed through the educational system from primary school to university without interruption. Their career fate was and is linked to the fate of the anglophone workplace and the anglophone parapublic institutional sector. This for two reasons: the first being that the corporate workplace needed external reinforcement to remain English; the second that the French public and parapublic sector was being built from scratch and was not short of manpower.

In the case of unskilled immigrants, choosing the English school system for their children is rationally imperative in order to secure a twofold objective: upward mobility for their children in Quebec and Canada in the corporate world or the anglophone institutional system on the one hand; and, failing that, geographical mobility, through acquired fluency in English, in order to have access without handicap to the whole Canadian labour market. . . .

CONCLUSION: THE PRICE OF NATIONAL UNITY

This essay has argued that the political discontent of Quebec is rooted in and is a consequence of the modernization of Quebec. The provincial state created new elites in the public and parapublic domain of health, education, and welfare.

The new middle classes that emerged as a consequence of this institution-building process are confined to the public sector and, because of language, practically unrepresented in the ranks of the large private corporate economy.

While the federal state, through the Royal Commission on Bilingualism and Biculturalism and the consequent Official Languages Act, proclaimed a state of crisis in national unity, it failed to address itself to the core of the issue: the economic underdevelopment of Quebec and the Québécois. Its recommendations, by refusing to consider seriously territoriality as a basis of its bilingual policies, came forth with an institutional bilingual policy, setting forth antiquated institutional arrangements in Quebec as the model for French-English relations in Canada. Concerned with attempting to shore up crumbling language frontiers for the French communities outside Quebec, it failed to address itself to the unacceptable language frontiers in the political economy of Quebec.

The federal state has, ever since, followed a language policy that can only be characterized as a political irritation to English Canada and a political irrelevance to a modernizing Quebec.

There is a price for a new political consensus in Canada, and certain groups have to pay the price. The two unfortunate groups will have to be the French outside Quebec and the English in Quebec.

For Canada to survive, short of the use of military coercion, a new social contract will have to be negotiated. For this to happen, the unequal union, in Stanley Ryerson's apt characterization of the Act of Confederation, will have to be renegotiated. This renegotiation will have to lead to the full participation of the Québécois in their political economy. For this to happen, basic changes in the rules of the economic game as historically elaborated will have to be implemented. These basic alterations will probably have to deal, not only with Quebec, but with the regional underdevelopment of the Maritimes and the monopolization of economic growth in the "Golden triangle" to the detriment of western industrialization. . . .

Notes

1 The CATCA strike vote was held 15 June 1976; the strike began 20 June 1976 and ended 28 June 1976 (Canadian News Facts, 1976).

2 Otto Lang accepted "settlement" by air workers 28 June 1976 (Canadian News Facts, 1976).

3 P.E. Trudeau in a television address 23 June 1976 (Canadian News Facts, 1976).

4 Much of this section is based on the unheralded work of Joy, 1972.

References

L'Association des professeurs de l'Université de Montréal. *L'Université dit non aux Jesuites.* Montreal, 1961.

Clement, Wallace. *The Canadian Corporate Elite.* Toronto: McClelland and Stewart, 1975.

Commissioner of Official Languages. Annual Report for 1975. Ottawa: Information Canada, 1976.

Dion, Gérard, and O'Neill, Louis. Deux Prêtres dénoncent l'immoralité politique dans la province de Québéc. Montreal: 1956.

Drache, Daniel, ed. *Quebec, Only the Beginning: The Manifestoes of the Common Front.* Toronto: New Press, 1972.

Group de travail sur l'urbanisation. L'urbanisation au Québéc. Quebec: Ministre des Affaires Municipales et de l'Environment, 1976.

Guindon, Hubert. "Social unrest, social class, and Quebec's bureaucratic revolution." *Queen's Quarterly* LXXI (summer, 1964): 150–62.

————.
Two cultures: an essay on nationalism, class and ethnic tension." Pp. 56–9 in R. Leach, ed., *Contemporary Canada.* Toronto: University of Toronto Press, 1968.

Jackson, John D. "Institutionalized conflict: the Franco-Ontarian case." in G. Gold and M.A. Tremblay, eds., *Communities and Culture in French Canada.* Toronto: Holt, Rinehart and Winston, 1973.

Joy, Richard J. *Languages in Conflict.* Toronto: McClelland and Stewart, 1972.

Keyfitz, Nathan. "Canadians and Canadiens." *Queen's Quarterly* 70 (1963): 171–4.

Porter, John. *The Vertical Mosaic.* Toronto: University of Toronto Press, 1965.

Posgate, Dale and McRoberts, Kenneth. *Quebec: Social Change and Political Crisis.* Toronto: McClelland and Stewart, 1976.

Rioux, Marcel. *Quebec in Question.* Toronto: James Lewis and Samuel, 1971.

Royal Commission on Bilingualism and Biculturalism (RCBB) 1965 Preliminary Report. Ottawa: Queen's Printer.

————. 1969 Report. Ottawa: Information Canada.

Ryerson, Stanley. *Unequal Union.* Toronto: Progress, 1968.

Taylor, Norman W. "The French-Canadian industrial entrepreneur and his social environment." Pp. 271–95 in M. Rioux and Y. Martin, eds., *French-Canadian Society,* Vol. I. Toronto: University of Toronto Press, 1964.

Trudeau, Pierre Elliott. *Federalism and the French Canadians.* Toronto: University of Toronto Press, 1968.

————. *The Asbestos Strike.* Toronto: James Lewis and Samuel, 1974.

TWENTY-FIVE

Feminists in the Academy

Roberta Hamilton

ROBERTA HAMILTON, Associate Professor of Sociology at Queen's University, Kingston, Ontario, is particularly interested in historical sociology, Canadian and Quebec society, and feminist theory. She is the author of *The Liberation of Women: a Study of Patriarchy and Capitalism* (1978) and *Feudal Society and Colonization: The Historiography of New France* (1988); and has co-edited *The Politics of Diversity: Feminism, Marxism and Nationalism* (1986), with Michele Barrett. Also, with John McMullan, she has co-edited Hubert Guindon's essays, in *Tradition, Modernity and Nation* (1988). From 1986-1989 she was the first coordinator of Women's Studies at Queen's. She is working on a feminist introductory text to Canadian Society.

Over ten years ago I walked into the office of the chairman of the sociology department of Sir George Williams University to discuss with him my course of studies as a newly-admitted student in the department's fledgling Master of Arts program. I was nervous. It had been nine years since I had studied formally and it seemed more like a lifetime. If I had known what I came to know later, that this man had only come to full-time intellectual work when he was well into his middle years, perhaps I would have felt more comfortable. Nonetheless, when I tentatively broached my area of interest for which there was not yet a name — the sociology of women, perhaps — any ease I might have felt would have been shattered in any case. "You don't seem to understand, Mrs. Hamilton — this is a university; we do intellectual work here; there is certainly a proper and legitimate place for your interests — for which, I

might say, I have great sympathy — it is on the streets, participating in public forms of protest." "Professor," I answered, more in anger than in sorrow, "I did not come to the university to protest; I came to study the situation of women."

But looking back on it now I realize that his suspicions were not incorrect. For feminists have indeed carried their protest into the university. That is, they have challenged not only the structure of the university, and the limited place of women within it, but also the very parameters of what constitutes knowledge, and many of the assumptions underlying the traditional disciplines. In simplest terms, the feminist slogan, borrowed from the New Left, that "the personal is political" not only legitimated new areas of research, but also probed their links with broader political, economic and social relations. Indeed, the distinction between these personal — or private —

areas of life and those defined as public, has been brought under careful scrutiny. The new questions have turned on an exploration of the relationship between private and public: the relationship between forms of the family and economic structures, between the relations between the sexes and the role of the state, between socialization, education and the sexual division of labour throughout the society. The resulting analysis has concluded that the very concepts of the private and the public were historically and ideologically constituted categories, not hermetically separate areas of social life. The proverbial idea that "a man's home is his castle" has been broken down as much by feminist-informed scholarship as by overt action in the political arena. And the sin of "washing one's dirty linen in public" was transformed not only into consciousness raising — the feminist equivalent of the revolutionary Chinese process of "speaking bitterness" — but also into new areas of scholarship.

Certainly my answer to the chairman of the sociology department would be very different today. I would argue that the feminist critique belongs in the academy, belongs indeed at the centre of our questions about human society in all its aspects. For as I discovered, to be a feminist intellectual *is* to be a political subversive — subversive of knowledge that takes male domination and female subordination as given, subversive of knowledge that privileges male-public activity over female-private activity, subversive about assumptions concerning the nature of men and women, about sexuality, about the entire gamut of relations between the sexes in the family, on the streets, and in all the economic, educational, political and social institutions, not only of our society but of all other societies in the present and in the past. In

short, the intellectual importance of feminism, I would submit, has been to introduce a new paradigm of inquiry both within traditional disciplines and across disciplinary lines. The feminist critique has prompted the demystification of what has been considered "natural," the shattering of old categorizations, the turning of *assumptions* about social life into penetrating *questions* about how things came to be as they are, and in what ways, and in whose interests they are consolidated and perpetuated. It has, of course, also produced an analysis of how the processes of transformation can be understood and abetted. . . .

. . .The relationship between intellectuals and society . . . has, of course, engaged many scholars, perhaps in particular sociologists. But it is interesting that one of the least developed and most controversial areas of the discipline, despite its longevity, is that area in which scholars are called upon to be reflective about their own kind of work. If there is today at least some minimal consensus that as intellectuals we do not occupy pristine and value-free locations from which to carry on our labours, there is little understanding of precisely how intellectual schools of thought develop, why some are more successful in establishing themselves and being accepted than others, why some come to exert virtual hegemony for a time and what leads to their decline or transformation. Mannheim's hope for a virtually classless "free-floating" intelligentsia skirted these questions even if it was rather satisfying to intellectuals themselves. Marx's view that the ideas of the ruling class in any epoch come to exert hegemony was an advance but failed to explain his own intellectual trajectory, let alone its success. But Raymond Williams' recent analysis in his book *Culture* (1981) offered the outlines of a very promising approach, and certainly it sheds light on the particular group under consideration, that of feminists working in the university today.

To begin with, the very term intellectuals must be examined. Just who is included? As a synonym for "intelligent people" it is of course not only arrogant but wrong. Following Gramsci, Williams posits that "all people are intellectuals — that is they participate in the processes of cultural production — but that not all people have in society the function of intellectuals." Yet even that proviso must rest on the deeper understanding that "ideas and concepts — the specialized concerns of intellectuals in the modern sense — are both produced and reproduced in the whole social and cultural fabric."

But, if so, what decides the fate of ideas? How can we explain why some — for example that the idea that the earth is round — threaten to die with the eccentrics who mouth them while others live and become, for a time at least, part of the received wisdom — for example the streets of America are paved with gold? Williams suggests that this question be examined in terms of the social locations of those who produce them and their relative incorporation within, or distance from, what he calls the dominant networks of social relations. On these grounds we could, for example, compare the work produced by the "brain trust" of the Liberal Party and the "propagandists" of the Communist Party, the positions of the Canadian Manufacturers Association and the Canadian Labour Congress, the arguments of the Franco-Manitobans and those who oppose them.

The university has historically been a privileged location for the production of work that *can* have a certain autonomy from the dominant order. But the more interesting questions are those that address the conditions under which such autonomy is maximized or restricted. Certainly the ongoing economic crisis, and the accompanying budget restraints, as well as the political move to the right — seen especially in Canada now in British Columbia — narrow the practical range in which that autonomy can be exercised. More generally, that autonomy will also vary from discipline to discipline depending upon its contemporary relevance. The classical scholar may experience full practical independence, the social historian less, while the critical sociologist may be under attack. It is not just a question of what kind of research can be undertaken, or will be funded, or even published, but also a question of its more general reception, of its promise of becoming part of a generally accepted body of knowledge. We know that this reception is not simply linked to how sound or thoughtful or challenging the work is.

Cultural production of all kinds, from social theory and research to schools of literature, painting or dance can be analyzed in terms of its relationship to the dominant social relations. But we should not expect the relations between cultural production and the dominant order to be linear or exposed. Their underpinnings are so deeply embedded in the social structure and practices that they are assumed, not questioned, perceived as natural, not as issues for debate. For dominant relations are lived relations, they are imposed but not simply imposed. They are expressed through a society's institutions and practices, not in some reflected way, but as a dynamic and constitutive aspect of all activity. For example, in sociology a particular interpretation of the family in contemporary society was not produced and taught as some conscious tool of masculine domination but as part of a generally accepted truth about the society, a truth that was certainly confirmed by state policy, the legal system in its theory and in its practice, and church, corporate and labour union policies. But its largely uncritical reception must finally be explained through an understanding of how men, women and children internalized, and accepted as natural, the sexual division of labour within the home, in the labour force, and indeed throughout the institutions and practices of the society. Predicated upon an acceptance of the belief that men and women naturally occupied separate spheres — the woman in the home, the man in the world — with the latter mediating between them, it emphasized the functional and universal nature of the family. It comprised a primarily desciptive account of the male instrumental role and the female expressive role. At its most banal it degenerated into courses on marriage and the family which attracted mainly female students hoping for tips on their problematic task of attracting and keeping a husband — information that most instructors were ill-equipped to give even if they had been willing! Such courses were mercifully free of an historical perspective — which history at the time, and for similar reasons, could not have provided in any case. Instead there were brief evolutionary sketches showing how things had got better and better and how they would now stay like this forever — just like marriage. The findings of Margaret Mead were occasionally interjected to show how far human beings could deviate from normal standards of civilized behaviour if they lived in exotic enough environments. Certainly such courses did not include class or ethnic or regional dif-

ferences in our own society. The Moral Majority had nothing to fear in these texts: discussion of family life was, in Dennis Wrong's phrase, sufficiently desexualized to please Mrs Grundy; rape, or sex under duress, did not defile these marital beds; child abuse, incest, and wife battering did not intrude; birth control and abortion did not figure because there were no unwanted babies; couples very obligingly simply had their 3.3 children, or whatever was the going rate. What William Goode has called "the classical family of western nostalgia," minus a grandparent or two, and arranged in discreet suburbs instead of farms and villages, was alive and well in sociology classes right through the turbulent 1960s.

It is not that there were no challenges to this dominant interpretation. Gunnar Myrdal wrote an appendix to his famous *An American Dilemma* (1944) in which he analyzed the similarities and differences between the relations between the races and those between the sexes. Helen Hacker wrote an article, published in *Social Forces* in 1951, called "Women as a Minority Group." And of course Simone de Beauvoir had completed *The Second Sex* in 1949. But the point is that no one paid any attention because their analysis had no social base from which to take on the dominant interpretation. When we were sociology students in the early 1960s no one ever suggested we read them, and if we had, we might have wondered why.

In order to understand and analyze why such challenges to the dominant perspective became more than individual pieces of — primarily ignored — work we can turn to Williams' concept of *emergent* relations, a constituent part of which is work of various new kinds. Such new work can be associated with rising factions of the dominant classes — and, therefore, easily incorporated into the dominant mode — or with the struggles of underclasses, ethnic or national minorities, or movements for sexual equality.

The contemporary feminist challenge to the dominant relations and ideology, and to their constituent forms of knowledge, resulted from a convergence of social processes; first, the expansion of industry and government had drawn unprecedented numbers of women, especially married women with children, into the labour market, yet there had been no accompanying development of social support for child care, no change in the sexual division of labour in the home, and no change in the dominant ideology which held that women were first and foremost mothers and that children needed full-time mothering; second, the promise of equal education for boys and girls — the outcome of earlier feminist struggles — had not hindered either the development of a segregated work force or the perpetuation of radically unequal pay for comparable work; third, the experiences of women in the civil rights movement, in the New Left and in the anti-war movement left them reeling from a particularly painful clash between the rhetoric of equality and social justice and their actual experiences as secretaries, cooks and bed mates to the more important male theoreticians and activists. If most men in the radical movements were too polite to echo Stokely Carmichael's unfortunate phrase that "the only position for a women in the civil rights movement is prone," the statement still resonated with women: if this is what they could expect in revolutionary groups, what joys awaited them in the conventional world of marriage and family?

This extraordinary convergence of broad macro-economic processes, of a liberal education system, and of the protest movements that swept the Western world in the 1960s affected thousands of women, mostly young middle-class women with some university education. Their mushrooming protest movement converged with a quieter but sustained process through which older women were expanding their traditional organizations into pressure groups for legal and social reform. There was a lot of bravery and a lot of bravado. It is *not* apocryphal that Laura Sabia told Prime Minister Pearson through the good auspices of the *Globe and Mail* that if he did not strike a Royal Commission on the Status of Women she would bring three million women to march on Parliament Hill, and confessed afterwards that she doubted if she could have found three.

From the beginning women formed consciousness-raising groups, mobilized public and private protests, and engaged in existential acts of rebellion. At the same time they began to produce what Williams called "various new works" — polemics, critiques and analysis of the relations between men and women in our society. In language angry, direct and often moving, they began to attack the hypocrisy of the dominant ideology which offered equality and delivered patriarchy. The authors, writing both as individuals and as collectives, had several purposes: they offered interpretations for the relations of domination and subordination between the sexes; they provided strategies for their transformation and they issued a call to arms. The early contributions drew little upon previous feminist critiques. The resurrection of the Marys — Astell and Wollstonecraft — Elizabeth Cady Stanton, Nellie McClung, and all the others awaited the more systematic analysis yet to come. Primarily ahistorical, these writings emphasized issues of sexual politics, with the family now heralded as the primary location not for women's fulfilment and protection, but for their oppression. As far as I am aware, very little if any of this early work was produced by university-employed intellectuals; its genesis was with the movement's militants and supporters. Indeed their critique was gradually directed also to the kind of analysis that was produced and taught within the university, to the work that was predicated upon assumptions of the naturalness of the prevailing sexual division of labour, that accepted the separate-but-equal doctrine of male and female spheres and that left women, their interests and their activities, largely invisible.

We can see the relationshp between emergent social relations and new interpretations. The university and its personnel are part of the dominant social order and the work that was produced and taught within the academy on the relations between men and women — what little there was — was deeply embedded in that assumed order. Individual scholars might deviate, as I noted, but the consensus was clear. Yet, although the university-located intellectuals had not initiated the emerging critique, neither were they to be immune from it. As the women's movement grew, the university inevitably became one of the sites for the growing confrontation between feminist demands and analysis and prevailing social practices. For just as the university is implicated and embedded within the established order, so it is also potentially open to all the oppositional or emergent intellectual currents within the society. Some of those oppositional movements become, in however an altered form, in-

corporated within a transformed but still dominant perspective, while others never develop the social and political momentum to resound within the academy, or the opposition to them becomes sufficiently mobilized to keep them out. Let us look, then, at how the emerging feminist critique was extended from its base within a social movement to become an oppositional current within academic disciplines.

Exactly how that happened varied from country to country, university to university, and department to department. But, in some measure, all the following processes can be seen. First, we must recall the university does not just comprise professors, administrators and secretaries but must also, as a condition of its existence, open its doors to students. Depending upon what is happening in the society, these students are more or less likely to accept the content of their courses, the structures of the programmes, and the methods of pedagogy that are in place. In Canada the development of the women's liberation movement at the end of the 1960s coincided, not accidentally, as I pointed out, with a time of significant student protest, on the one hand, and with a period when public support — that is government financing — of higher education was peaking. The possibility of innovation, the funds to institute new programmes and hire more professors, and the receptivity to student interests provided a reasonably fertile ground in at least some universities for accommodating the interests of the number of students who were participating in, or being influenced by, the feminist movement. Student demand, then, was the first major pressure exerted on the universities for incorporation of women's studies courses and a feminist perspective. But it didn't stop there. For most people, being a student is a transitional role. And some of those students went on to develop their analysis, pursue their research, and apply for positions in the institutions which they had challenged for being sex-blind. These women — and a few men too — who took up feminist themes and questions in the course of their graduate work, some of whom then were accepted into academic positions, have been responsible for a great deal of the academic research and writing on women that has proliferated in the last dozen years. That they were hired in the university should certainly be attributed to their level of scholarship. But the social movement which first motivated their work also legitimated it, providing the social basis for their claims to inclusion. The sheer political success of the women's liberation movement — that is, its resonance with an increasing number of women and some men too — won for some of its adherents, and more especially for their kind of perspective, a foot in the academic door, even if there were a few broken ankles in the process.

There has been a third way: an ongoing process through which feminist perspectives have been incorporated within the established academic discourses. While women and men already in the university were clearly not the prime movers in this process, some responded, either immediately or over time, to the possibilities opened up by the new lines of inquiry. There are probably many different kinds of explanations for what amounted to almost a volte-face by some university-based intellectuals in their research interests and theoretical perspectives. My guess is that those who made sudden shifts had been, consciously or not, feminists-in-waiting. It is one thing to get up and tell everyone that you are Napoleon if no one believes you. The consequences of doing so would be quite dramatic, and not a lot of fun. But if at least some people agree that you're the man himself and treat you accordingly it's quite different. So as the times made it acceptable, some of those within the university contributed either directly, or indirectly through supporting the new interests of their new and old colleagues, to what can properly be described as a veritable avalanche of feminist-informed scholarship. By the mid-1970s the subversive feminist critique represented an oppositional — or emergent — current within many academic disciplines. . . .

Today the work of feminist-informed intellectuals is . . . dependent upon the continued presence of a broadly-based political and social movement. . . . Women's studies has become, however tenuously, institutionalized; there are departments, courses and parts of courses. Books and articles on many relevant areas are part of the usual contents of even main-line academic journals. That that work is done from many different critical perspectives is its strength. But if the continued production of that work becomes divorced from the social and political concerns and struggles which gave it birth, it will lose its critical edge; if it forgets its link with the original outrageous questions — why are things like this? how did they come to be so? how can they be changed? — it will be forced to rely once again on prescriptions and descriptions rather than upon theoretically-informed research and analysis. Students of society surely deserve challenge, not consolation, and this is especially true, I would submit, in the questions that we pose about those aspects of human relationships that we have hitherto largely taken for granted.

TWENTY-SIX

The Technicization of Society

Willem H. Vanderburg

BILL VANDERBURG, as Director of the Centre for Technology and Social Development, teaches and conducts research into the societal and ecological implications of technology and the application of this knowledge to adjust engineering theories and approaches to make technology more compatible with its human, societal, and natural contexts. He calls this preventive engineering. It integrates the methods of the social sciences and humanities into the applied sciences and engineering design. His publications include: *Perspectives on our Age: Jacques Ellul Speaks on His Life and Work* (1981); *The Growth of Minds and Cultures* (1985); "Engineering, Technology and the University" (1987); "Macro-STS: The New Frontier?" (1987); and "Political Imagination in a Technical Age (1988).

. . . Introducing industrial technology into Western European societies fundamentally disturbed the social, economic, political, legal, moral and religious dimensions of society; massive restructuring was required, which forced the various efforts at rationalization (until then largely piecemeal) into a chain-reaction transformation. Out of this emerged a diversity of societies that shared many important features and which resembled each other much more than they resembled earlier societies. They are often called *industrial* societies, but this is an oversimplification that will become particularly evident when we examine the so-called advanced industrial, or *postindustrial* societies. The transformation that produced the latter is rooted in a fundamental change in the technical knowledge base. This change, beginning ever so slowly toward the end of the nineteenth century (after the death of Marx),

became sociologically significant only after World War II. It radically changed society once again by means of a new chain reaction. The new patterns of social change were less driven by industrialization and machine technology than those of the nineteenth and early twentieth centuries.

Until the late nineteenth century, the development and application of the various techniques was largely empirical. They were passed on from one generation to the next by apprenticeship arrangements, in which one learned a technique by working with someone who had a great deal of experience. Formal education played an almost insignificant role until the end of the nineteenth century. Take technology as an example. The increasing precision and complexity of machines, as well as the growing pressure from competition to eliminate any inefficiency, required a technological knowledge base that was as much as possible scientifically founded. . . .

This was the beginning of a complete transformation of the way techological knowledge is transmitted, developed and applied. There is clearly a discontinuity between knowledge acquired from experience and knowledge acquired by formal education. No amount of experience and on-the-job training can lead to a knowledge of the applied sciences. These can only be learned in the classroom. As a result, the knowers and the doers are more and more frequently different people.

By way of example, consider a welder with many years of experience erecting high-rise buildings. One day, as the crane is bringing up another beam for the twenty-sixth floor structure, the welder may alert the crane operator and the foreman by saying, "I've never seen such a light beam being used on this large a span. Are you sure we aren't making a mistake?" The foreman may then decide to call the engineer in the field office to check the calculations. On the basis of many years of experience, the welder has obtained a certain knowledge of the strength of beams. Yet he will never learn to calculate the strength of a beam by means of stress analysis, because this it not learned from experience but from books or classroom instruction. . . .

The changes in the knowledge base of technology were accompanied by similar changes in other areas. A greater precision of one techique necessitates similar developments in other techniques. By the end of World War II, changes in the technical knowledge base had necessitated the restructuring of a variety of institutions in society. Galbraith (1978) has examined the restructuring of large corporations after World War II. Since Galbraith did not sufficiently appreciate

the interdependence of industrial technology with a whole range of other techniques, we will briefly reinterpret his findings.

At the core of the large, modern corporation, we find what Galbraith has called its *technostructure*, essentially the brain of the enterprise, in which most activities are based on knowledge acquired by the formal education of its members. Together they have an expertise in the techniques necessary for the efficient running of all parts of the corporation, such as marketing, production, engineering, management, personnel and public relations. Thus, the latest technical knowledge is applied to all aspects of the corporation. Since the expertise of each member of the technostructure is highly specialized, each task must be so subdivided that every part is coterminous with a particular body of specialized technical knowledge. A knowledge of metallurgy, for example, cannot be applied to the design of a whole automobile. It can be applied only to the selection and design of appropriate materials for its parts. Thus, technical knowledge is applied to each and every part of the task, then to each subpart in combination with another, and then in combination with still others to ensure a coherent synthesis of the whole task. All aspects of the problem must be considered at the same time. . . .

The technostructure is surrounded by the body of the corporation, in which most tasks can be performed without any advanced formal education. Most tasks can be learned on the job (such as those of assembly-line workers), while others require some technical training (such as those of the operators of word processors). In all these tasks, knowledge acquired from experience plays an essential role.

The gradual restructuring of large corporations during the first half of the twentieth century was, therefore, in part a response to the emergence of the new technical knowledge base. Without this restructuring, large corporations would not be able to take advantage of the latest developments in the natural, applied and social sciences. All corporate operations became extremely effective. The development of any new product, for example, now required the collaboration of a great many people with complementary types of expertise relevant to the task. Since these people must be paid, provided with support staff, have offices and so on, the capital investment needed to bring any new product to market skyrocketed. A competitively priced product could be produced only if this investment could be written off over a large number of units manufactured. In other words, restructuring the technical knowledge base necessitated a further acceleration in the trend toward mass production. This trend, in turn, required highly specialized production facilities. . . .

All these factors greatly increased the risk involved in developing a new product. During the considerable length of time it took to design and develop a new product and prepare the production facilities, market conditions could change. If sales fell far below the projected figures, however, the investment in design and development of the new product and the highly specialized production facilities could not be transferred to another product. In order to protect themselves from such risks, companies diversified, so that the losses in one division could be offset by profits in another and not endanger the survival of the firm.

The corporations that exploited the new technical base, therefore, required a much greater concentration of capital than did the entrepreneurial firms of the nineteenth century. This made it virtually impossible for a family or a small group of shareholders to own these new firms. A modern corporation is usually owned by a large number of shareholders, who each own only a small part of the corporation. At shareholders' meetings, they tend to approve the plans put forward and prepared by the technostructure, which essentially controls the operation of the firm as long as it earns sufficient profits to pay reasonable dividends to the shareholders and to generate enough capital to finance its own internal operations. The greatly weakened link between ownership and control also affects the economic behaviour of the large corporation, whose goals are now much more complex than a simple profit maximization. Its relationship with the market also undergoes a profound transformation. No longer can it rely on the market to supply the specialized materials and machines that may be unique to one of its products. On the output side, the corporation attempts to manage consumer demand through a variety of techniques, including advertising. It relies on the state to create the educational institutions necessary to graduate specialists for its technostructure.

The growth and development of the new technical knowledge base required an expansion in the role of the modern state. It alone could create the educational system necessary to ensure that the nation would produce specialists in the various areas of technical expertise. Before the development of the new technical knowledge base, access to higher education was typically restricted to the upper-class of society. In order to advance the development of the new technical knowledge base, access to the educational system had to be based not on social status, but on the intellectual capability of the individual. . . .

To provide the large corporation with a stable economic environment in which it could plan new products that would not come onto the market until years later, the state had to regulate the economy. It did so by creating a large public sector that it expanded or contracted to offset the fluctuations in the private sector. In the most advanced industrial nations, this public sector is in part occupied by projects not directly affecting the mainstream of society, such as defence, space programs and the development of nuclear energy. To ensure the development of the new technical knowledge base, the state also became involved in scientific and technical research. In order to efficiently carry out its new tasks, as well as to improve its effectiveness in more traditional domains, the state began to depend on the technical knowledge of experts. They brought their expertise to bear on these tasks, using patterns of collaboration very similar to the ones found in the technostructures of large corporations.

Developing the new technical knowledge base and the techniques derived from it did not only affect large corporations and the state, however. A growing number of activities in society were increasingly structured and restructured in accordance with the latest technical knowledge. In fact, all the characteristics of "postindustrialism" or "advanced industrialism" derive directly from the proliferation of techniques throughout society. . . .

THE PHENOMENON OF TECHNIQUE[1]

. . . One thing that sets modern societies apart from all others is that a wide range of activities is no longer based on custom or tradition grounded in a culture. They systematically research virtually every sphere of human activity in order to render it more effective, rational and efficient or to eliminate problems. They do this on the assumption (and this is a cultural hypothesis that underlies modern societies) that the quality of life can be improved by making all facets of our existence more efficient. Research takes the form of what we will call the *technical operation*, which is constituted of four stages.

The first stage involves studying some area of human life for a particular purpose. The study's results are used in the next stage to build a model that can range from a precise mathematical theory to a theory that is largely qualitative. In the third stage, the model is examined to determine what happens when its parameters are altered, in order to discover when it functions optimally. The technical operation concludes with the reorganization of the area of human life studied originally, to achieve the highest efficiency and rationality demonstrated to be possible by the model. It is by means of this pattern of events that modern societies seek to improve the productivity of a plant, the running of a large office or hospital, the effectiveness of classroom instruction, the performance of a professional athlete or hockey team, the functioning of a group and even the satisfaction derived from a sexual relationship. As a result, the technical operation deeply permeates the fabric of technologies or techniques. The French sociologist Jacques Ellul first drew our attention to this fact.

Increasingly in modern societies, almost every sphere of human activity is organized not on the basis of custom or tradition, but on the basis of a variety of techniques that ensure that everything is done as effectively as possible. Technology is only one part of the larger phenomenon of technique.

The reason the "industrially advanced" nations began to generate a mass of information at a certain point is now evident. When techniques increasingly began to replace tradition as the basis of human activities, much information was generated as a result of the technical operation. As these developments gained momentum, new technologies or techniques became necessary to deal with the mass of information. The computer and associated techniques were developed to meet this challenge and immediately found a wide range of applications. This in turn greatly accelerated the patterns of development described above.

The information economy, the proliferation of theoretical services, the rise of new intellectual techniques, the emergence of a new class of technical experts, the growth of the service sector and other phenomena taken to be signs of the "postindustrial age" (Bell, 1973) are simply the result of the proliferation of techniques in society. . . .

THE CONSEQUENCES OF THE TECHNICIZATION OF LIFE

. . . Techniques are not neutral; they do not merely make an activity more effective. An area of human life is studied not holistically but for a specific purpose. As a result, certain aspects of the situation will be externalized (i.e., excluded from consideration) in the technical operation. . . . Consider a simple example.

Around the turn of the century, as machines in factories became increasingly efficient, the operations carried out by human beings caused a bottleneck. It made no sense to further improve the efficiency of the machines when the workers could not keep pace. In this context, studies were done on how to rationalize human work to make it more efficient. Some of the most famous studies were done by Gilbreth (Giedion, 1969: 102–105). By fastening a small electric light bulb to the wrist of a worker performing some task, it was possible to record the trajectory traced out by the bulb with three cameras mounted along three perpendicular axes. From the photographic records, wire models were constructed that showed exactly how the worker moved his or her hand. By analysing these models, it was possible to optimize the movements, and once this was accomplished, the worker was taught to perform the task more efficiently.

Gilbreth's technique perfectly illustrates the technical operation. As expected, rationalizing traditional work by this or other techniques creates an important externality. It can readily be identified when we compare traditional with technicized work. If we observe a traditional craftsperson at work, the gestures reflect a variety of things, such as the person's state of mind, personality, previous experience (including apprenticeship training) and culture. Once the "one best way" was determined by means of the technical operation, all this had to be suppressed as much as possible by the worker. This led to the well-known consequence of physical fatigue largely being replaced by nervous fatigue in technicized work. Normally, even in the most routine movements, something of our personality comes through, as is evident in the characteristics of our handwriting. This can be explained if we recall what we said earlier about the role of culture

(Vanderburg, 1985). Since the relationship between human beings and reality is not predetermined genetically, the limited organization of the brain present at birth is expanded by experience. The mind that thus emerges in relation to the brain is the symbolic basis for mediating all relationships with reality. Since the mind is first shaped during socialization into a culture, it functions as a kind of mental man that the members of a culture use to interpret their experience and relate to one another and reality. While the mental map of each member of a culture is unique, it is sufficiently similar to those of other members to make communication possible. In traditional work, this mental map is the symbolic basis on which the craftsperson performs his or her operations.

Once work is technicized on the basis of the technical operation, the situation changes fundamentally. When workers are taught the one best way of moving their hands, they are being asked to suppress as much as possible their personality, state of mind, past experience and culture. . . .

Technique as Milieu

. . . There is a long tradition of thinking about technology as a means to accomplish human ends. This is true, of course, but it is only a part of the picture. Technology and techniques also mediate relationships between human beings or between human beings and anything in their environment. Consider the telephone. It mediates between many people who may never meet face-to-face. This is obvious, but we often forget that this mediation is not neutral. It fundamentally transforms the relationship, since many sociocultural dimensions of a typical face-to-face relationship are stripped away, requiring a change in the relationship. The culture's facial expressions, gestures and body language (Hall, 1977) are not transmitted by the telephone. Yet these dimensions play an important part in face-to-face conversation, to the point that many people are uneasy talking to a blind person face-to-face because he or she typically does not respond to or transmit all the nonverbal dimensions of conversation. Young children using the telephone for the first time will also behave as though it were a face-to-face encounter. They quickly learn, however, that the telephone does not mediate in a neutral fashion.

What is true for the telephone is equally true for television. It mediates between producer and consumer, between the politician and the voter, between events around the globe and the viewer, and so on. These mediated relations are also transformed in a nonneutral way. A politician may come across well in person but may have to rely on a media consultant to ensure that she projects the right image. Advertising is not a neutral diffusion of information about products. By linking a product to certain symbols alive in the minds of people, it affects them subconsciously on the level where these symbols have become a part of their being, thus partly displacing the culturally mediated and conscious process of choice. . . .

. . . Many relationships are technically mediated with devices playing little or no essential part. Take a large office, for example. Here organization theory is applied to large numbers of people collectively performing a variety of tasks as effectively as possible. Here again, organizational techniques have been developed to find the best way of identifying, executing and interconnecting the functions of the organization. By making use of job descriptions and organizational charts, an optimal model is created that specifies how the relationships between the people in that office are to be technically mediated. People no longer primarily behave spontaneously, on the basis of their cultural mental maps. The relationships have been transformed, as the studies of bureaucracy by Max Weber and others have shown. We are not suggesting that mediation on the basis of culture is totally eliminated in a modern office, but technically mediated relationships predominate. . . .

A society changes fundamentally once most of the relationships in which its members are engaged become technically mediated. At this point, technique becomes the primary milieu for its members. It is in relation to this milieu that life evolves. This means much more than that the members of these societies live in an urban technical environment. Human existence has known only three primary milieus: nature in prehistory, society during much of our history and technique for the "industrially advanced" nations during the past two decades. . . .

In prehistory, human beings lived in small groups totally dominated by nature. The natural milieu provided them with everything necessary for life, but it also posed the most serious threats in the form of droughts, wild beasts or storms, for example. Nature permeated almost every experience producing a unique type of consciousness characterized by a certain kind of mental map.

When human beings began to live in societies at the dawn of history the importance of the natural milieu became overshadowed by the social milieu. The latter interposed itself between the individual and nature. This made it possible

for a society to better defend itself against natural dangers, but the new primary milieu also introduced a new series of dangers, such as war and economic or political instability, that could lead to the collapse of a society or civilization. Once the social milieu became the primary and nature the secondary milieu, a new type of consciouness emerged with correspondingly different mental maps.

When the phenomenon of technique began to transform a growing number of relationships, structures and institutions within a society, the first steps toward another transition commenced. It may well be as sweeping as the one from prehistory to history. Technically mediated relationships eventually dominated culturally mediated ones, and technique displaced society as the primary milieu. Society now constituted the secondary milieu and nature moved to third place. Life in a modern society, and particularly in its large urban centres, is impossible without a variety of technical support systems, while at the same time technique presents all societies with new ultimate threats: nuclear holocaust, the destabilization and poisoning of the ecosystem and the growing inability to provide meaningful work for all people . . . .

. . . The separation of knowing from doing and knowledge from experience causes us to depend on experts in almost every domain of life. Since we have devalued daily life knowledge that is embedded in experience, we need to turn to experts who supposedly know much more about the various aspects of our lives than we can know ourselves. If we are responsible and know what is good for us, we live in accordance with the objective body of technical experience. Experts make their living by giving us access to that knowledge, which is believed to be vital for our existence. They do this personally or via the multitude of how-to-do-it books that tell us how to treat our babies, how to talk to our teenage children, how to save a marriage, improve our sex life, sleep better, eat a balanced diet, organize a good vacation, cope with stress and so on. Apparently, we cannot be trusted to do these things ourselves anymore.

We are not saying, of course, that in the past, people did not rely on experts, we are saying that the phenomenon was on a completely different scale. We have created a society in which all of us, including the experts, must rely on others in important matters to the point that we have become spectators of much of our own lives. This phenomenon is taking on new proportions as a result of the proliferation of information services accessed through personal computers. It is fundamentally alienating, whether we are exploited or not. The fact that the control over one's own life has become largely external is a threat to human freedom, and it is also very stressful. The difficulty of participating in technicized relationships and the loss of control over one's life leads to the reification of the human subject — a fact powerfully portrayed in modern abstract art, which developed as the phenomenon of technique began to manifest itself. The human subject disappeared from art.

The technicization of life produces a new kind of alienation that is superimposed on economic alienation.

During its initial phases, the web of techniques was built up in the self-interest of a specific social class. As more and more techniques linked together during the technical revolution, they became increasingly difficult to control, due to the technical alienation produced. Such alienation was experienced even by the powerful and wealthy.

The patterns of development of the "industrially advanced" world are those of the growth of technique. Many of the problems faced by present-day societies derive from these very patterns of development, yet we continue to seek new techniques in an attempt to solve the problems created by earlier ones. It is impossible, however, to solve problems by simply doing more of the kinds of things that created these problems in the first place. This approach merely replaces one problem with another, inevitably leading to a top-heavy and unstable technical order. Yet, because of the way technique as milieu influences human consciousness, societal values and myths, we continue to turn to technique to solve the problems created by it. There can, however, be no security in evermore powerful weapons, and there can be no real solution to our economic problems without addressing the challenge technique poses to human life and society. We need to create a civilization that includes technique but is based on a culture not permeated by it. This will determine the kind of world we will leave for future generations.

Note

[1] The following is largely based on W.H. Vanderburg, "Some Implications of Modern Technology for Culture and Knowledge", presented at the 1983 AAAS annual meeting in Detroit, later published under the same title in *Man-Environment Systems*, Vol. 13, no. 5, Sept. 1983.

References

Galbraith, J.K. *The New Industrial State.* 3d rev. ed. New York: Mentor, 1978.

Giedion, S. *Mechanization Takes Command.* New York: Norton, 1969.

Hall, Edward T. *Beyond Culture.* New York: Anchor Books, 1977.

Vanderburg, W.H. *Culture and Technique: I — The Growth of Minds and Cultures.* Toronto: University of Toronto Press, 1985.

TWENTY-SEVEN

The Challenge of Changing Demographics

Roderic Beaujot

RODERIC BEAUJOT, Associate Professor of Sociology and Director of the Centre for Canadian Population Studies at the University of Western Ontario, London, specializes in demography, research methods and statistics, and the study of the family. His recent books and articles include *Growth and Dualism: The Demographic Development of Canadian Society*, with Kevin McQuillan (1982); "The effect of marital satisfaction on fertility" (1985); "Population policy development in Canadian demography" (1985); "The link between immigration and emigration in Canada, 1945–1986" (1989); "The family and demographic change: economic and cultural interpretations and solutions" (1990); and "The challenge of changing demographics" (1990). His research has included work in Tunisia, Senegal and Sierra Leone, for the International Development Research Centre.

As in other modern countries, Canadian demographics are changing rather fundamentally. Looking at the long-term past, we like to refer to a demographic transition wherein mortality and fertility moved from high to low levels. For instance, in 1851, the average life expectancy was 41 years and there was an average of 7 births per woman. By 1971, we had a life expectancy of 73 years and births per woman were down to 2.2. Over this period, the population of Canada increased over eight fold.

We are now talking about a second demographic transition, as fertility persists at below-replacement levels and the population ages significantly. Since 1972, the fertility has been below the 2.1 level needed for replacement of one generation by the next, and is now about 1.7 births per woman. The average age of the population was 26 years in 1971, it is now 32 years and it is likely to be about 45 years by 2036. By then, deaths are likely to outnumber births and we are likely to be in a situation of population decline rather than the population growth that we have always experienced in the past.

We will look at these dynamics in further detail, focusing on the projections for the future, the assumptions on which these are based, and the implications especially with regard to the labor force.

FERTILITY

Among the demographic variables, fertility is the most difficult to predict, but has the largest impact. At a 1986 conference on the family and demographic change, there was a high level of consensus that certain aspects of the family have changed rather fundamentally, and that we are not likely to see a return to past patterns. These changes involve later marriage, lower proportions marrying, more cohabitation, more divorce, more single-parent families, a dominance of two-earner families and less childbearing. These changes have occurred rather suddenly, since the mid-1960s, and have affected the entire set of countries of European civilization, not only the market economies of the west but the state economies of eastern Europe.

Without going into detail on the causes of these changes, we can probably speak of two themes. Following an economic analysis, we note increases in standards of living, thus more economic independence on the part of individuals. In particular, the growth of the service sector has increased labor market opportunities for women, giving them more independence and changing the relations between women and men. This has reduced women's dependence on marriage and has significantly increased the opportunity cost of childbearing.

The second theme focuses on cultural values and notes the increased importance of individualism, along with a loosening of norms relating to sex, cohabitation, marriage, divorce and childbearing. As people especially focus on their own individual well-being, they are more likely to find that a given marriage, or children, interfere with this well-being. While most want to be in a stable relationship, they are more prone to leave relationships that are less fulfilling.

The total fertility rate, which is a synthetic measure of average in births per woman, changed from 3.145 in 1965 to 1.672 in 1986. Compared to the replacement rate of 2.1, the 1965 figure means that there were 50 per cent more people in the generation of children than in the generation of their parents. In 1986, there were 20 per cent fewer people in the generation of children than in the generation of parents. The change from 50 per cent more children to 20 per cent fewer children than parents is a rather fundamental change.

At a conference held in June 1989 called, "Facing the demographic future" several people argued that these family/fertility changes require various adaptations. Women's need for self-sufficiency, in view of marital instability, means that they need more egalitarian marriages; in particular, they want to divide childcare and domestic roles more equally so that they can devote themselves to work roles.

In effect, several people have argued that the problems of lack of equality between the sexes relate less to the labor market *per se* than to marriage and family structures. Take as an example, the need to be a "workaholic" at least for a while in order to gain the upper edge in an occupation. In order to be a workaholic, one needs either to be alone, or to have someone else looking after the other aspects of life. It is hardly possible to be a workaholic while also looking after children.

Another adaptation that was frequently called for was the need for quality child care in order to reduce the discontinuities in women's work lives, and in order for the society to absorb part of the costs of childrearing. As children are less numerous, in effect as children become a scarce resource, the argument can especially be made that we need to have quality children, by investing in child welfare.

Partly in order to simplify the presenta-

FIGURE 27-1

BIRTHS AND DEATHS, 1921–2035

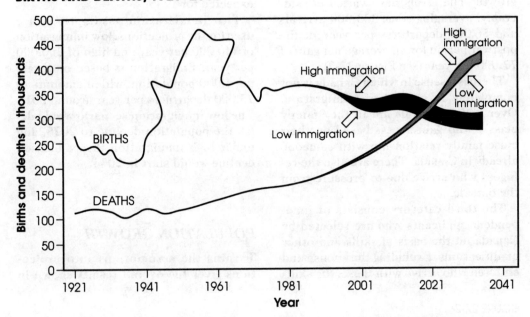

tion, the intermediate fertility assumption from Statistics Canada's latest population projections will be adopted here. Compared to the high and low projections of 2.1 and 1.2 births per woman, the intermediate scenario of 1.7 births per woman is currently accepted as the most probable assumption.

MORTALITY

Between 1971 and 1986, life expectancy increased from 74 to 77 years. There is likely to be continued slow progress in the average length of life, but this has considerably less impact on the future population. The projection used here involves a life expectancy of 81 years in 2011.

Figure 27-1 translates birth and death rates into numbers of births and deaths per year. We see the higher number of births in the 1950s and 1960s (baby boom years) and rather constant numbers since about 1971, with slightly lower levels in the future. The number of births has not declined as fast as the birth rate, because there are large numbers of people at childbearing ages. Even though they are having few births, there are sufficient numbers of people at childbearing ages to ensure a fairly constant number of births.

It can be seen from the graph that the numbers of deaths are increasing, especially after the turn of the century. By 2020 or 2022 the deaths start to outnumber the births, which is rather different from the historical experience.

INTERNATIONAL MIGRATION

The other component of population growth is international migration. Since the turn of the century, the excess of arrivals over departures has been responsible for some 22 per cent of the population growth. The levels have varied considerably, averaging some 133,000 arrivals and 56,000 departures per year in the postwar period for an average net gain of 77,000 per year (see Figure 27-2).

There is a sense in which Canada is not completely in control of immigration. Over half of arrivals are in the "family class", who gain access based on their close family relationship with someone already in Canada. There are also the refugees who arrive due to pressure from the outside.

The third category consists of independent applicants who are selected by Canada on the basis of skills and other qualifications. Excluding the spouse and children who arrive with these, the skill-

tested independent applicants constitute only 19 per cent of the total admissions expected for 1988.

Two immigration assumptions are used for the projections: low immigration of 140,000 per year and high of 200,000 per year. Emigration is based on a rate per 1,000 population, which amounts to 75,000 departures per year around 2011. The low immigration scenario would delay the population decline to 2025, and under high immigration the population decline would start in 2034.

POPULATION GROWTH

Turning the assumptions into projections gives the overall results shown in

FIGURE 27-2

IMMIGRATION AND EMIGRATION, 1921–2035

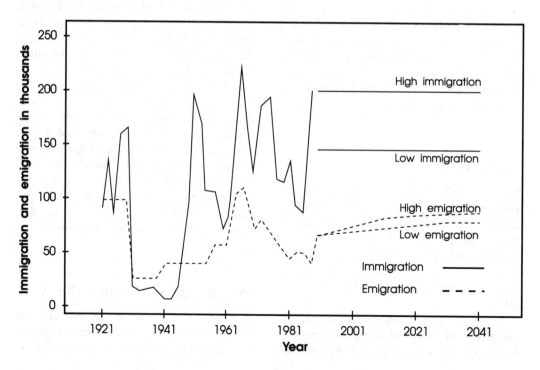

FIGURE 27-3

POPULATION PROJECTIONS TO 2036

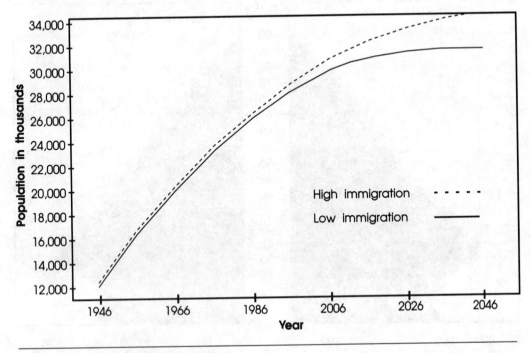

Note: Immigration assumptions high and low

Figure 27-3. Over the period 1946–1986, Canada's population increased by more than 100 per cent. Over the next 40 years, the increase would be 33 per cent under high immigration and 23 per cent under low immigration. By the turn of the century, the annual growth rate will be between 0.6 and 0.8 per cent per year. As indicated, population growth would stop in 2025 or 2034. Nonetheless, this growth is likely to be higher than those of most European countries.

AGING

The more visible results of these assumptions can be seen in the age distribution. Until the 1961 census, the age distribu-

tion involved basically a pyramid shape resulting from high birth rates. In 1988, the age structure is more like an oriental jar, narrower at the top and bottom (see Figure 27-4). The relative stability in total births is visible as a rather even base, below age 15. The baby boom bulge is now aged about 23 to 43.

The shape will gradually evolve to the one shown in Figure 27-5, projected for 2036. All persons born after 1990 are here aged under 45 years. The baby boom is here aged 65 to 85, where many, especially of the men, have died. Incidentally, we see that the immigration level has very little effect on the age structure. Immigration has a reasonable impact on the total size but not so much on the age distribution.

FIGURE 27-4

AGE PYRAMID, 1981 AND 1986

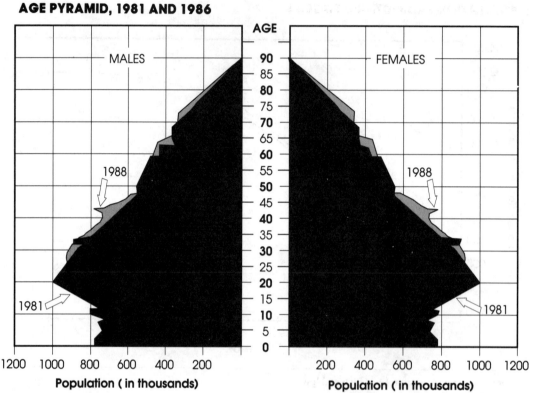

The population aged 65 and over as a proportion of the total has increased gradually over the long term, but especially since 1971. In 1986 we had 10 per cent aged 65 and over, and this would increase to some 25 per cent in the next 50 years.

LABOR FORCE

Figure 27-6 (page 340) shows how rapidly the population aged 20–64 has been growing, as the baby boom has moved into these ages. In the 10 year period 1966–1976, the population of these ages grew by more than a quarter and again by 21 per cent between 1976 and 1986. While the growth of the total population has been slowing down for some time, the growth of the population at labor force ages has continued largely to the present. The future will show much less growth, down to 7 per cent in the 10 years around the turn of the century, and becoming a decline after 2016. This is a fairly secure projection, because the population of these ages is not affected by the level of fertility for at least 20 years.

While the population as a whole has been aging, the population of labor force ages has in fact been getting younger on average. The average age of the population aged 20–64 declined from 38 in 1971 to 37 in 1986. However, the future will be rather different, showing an increase to 41 years at the turn of the century and 43 years in 2036.

FIGURE 27-5

AGE PYRAMID IN 2036, SHOWING IMMIGRATION

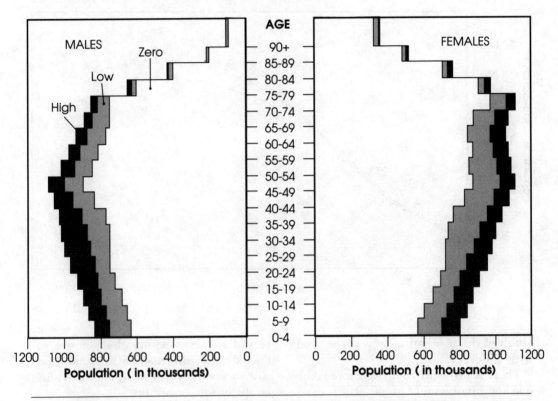

Note: Projections are based on fertility assumption of 1.7, immigration of 200,000, 140,000, and zero persons per year, and emigration of 0.25, 0.25, and 0.0 persons per 100 population per year.

It is also useful to compare the numbers of younger and older workers through the relative size of the populations aged 25–44 and 45–64. Until now, the age group 25–44 has been growing faster than that aged 45–64, but after 1991, the opposite will occur. In 1986 there were 168 people aged 20–44 for every 100 aged 45–64. By the turn of the century, there will be 125 people aged 25–44 per 100 aged 45–64, and after 2016 there will be less people aged 25–44 than the numbers aged 45–64.

In order to discuss questions of the potential for different labor market sce-

narios, it is useful to take note of the labor force participation rates by age, sex and marital status. For the single, there is not much difference between men and women. Marriage suppresses labor force participation for women. At ages 25–44 over 96 per cent of men but 71 per cent of married women are in the labor force. The differences are still there, though less marked, for the widowed and divorced. This is supported by other studies, for instance LeBourdais concludes that women's labor market involvement is discontinuous and there are little signs that this will change in the near future.

FIGURE 35-6

GROWTH OF POPULATION AGED 20–64

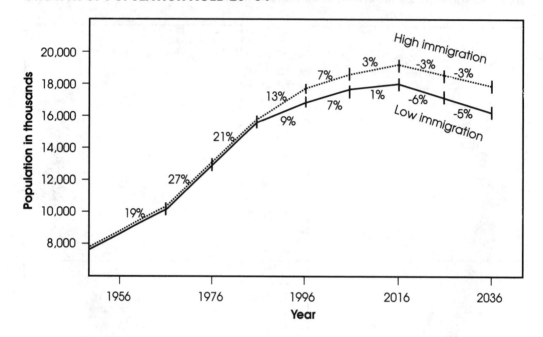

Much of the discontinuity is associated with children.

There is probably room for more labor market involvement. One study estimates that if all women participated in the labor force the way highly educated women do now, that would increase their total participation by some 20 per cent. Alternatively, if one removed the marital status suppressor, women's total labor force contribution would increase by 25 per cent. That would be a big change, requiring much adaptation on the part of men (sharing duties), the society (day care, etc.) and the workplace.

There is also room for increase in the labor market participation of older people. In fact, it has been argued that the decreased participation of older workers is as much a function of lack of labor market demand as it is a function of voluntary withdrawal. If people are to work to older ages, various changes are required, including dismantling the provisions for early retirement and providing facilities for re-training.

Regardless of the perspective for greater participation on the part of the older, and of married women, it is clear that the labor force will be undergoing a serious change in the next 20 years, in particular it will age. This itself will present various challenges in terms of ensuring continued creativity, flexibility, research and development. We have come to depend on admissions from the bottom to ensure flexibility; we will now have to depend much more on retraining.

While they have the advantage of being more experienced, in all likelihood older workers also cost more. Part of the higher salary of older workers compared to younger ones is simply a function of seniority or length [of time] in the job rather than productivity. If older workers cost more relative to their productivity, then an older labor force will mean increased labor costs.

RECOMMENDATIONS

While population growth has slowed down and the population has been aging for some time, the population at labor force ages has been growing rapidly and in fact getting younger. These trends are now changing to produce much less labor force growth and an aging of the labor force population. The labor force is likely to begin declining before population decline begins. These scenarios would tend to support recommendations in the following directions:

1. Given that children are less numerous, it is important to maintain or increase child welfare in order to increase the value of this "scarce resource".

2. Given the need and desire for women to be in the labor force, and to make equal contributions by having less discontinuities in their work lives, it is important to establish quality child care services.

3. In order to permit greater labor force participation by the elderly, it will be important to upgrade their training, and to dismantle early retirement programs.

4. Given that aging and lower growth are largely a function of fertility, it is important to sustain childbearing by having the society pay more of the costs of children.

5. Given that an additional immigration of 60,000 per year delays the population decline by eight or nine years, it is also important to sustain the level of immigration.

Copyright Acknowledgements

P. 7. From *First Sociology* by Kenneth Westhues, (New York: McGraw-Hill, 1982), pp. 20, 21–23, 26–29. By permission of the McGraw Hill Book Company.

P. 14. Robert Brym, "Foundations of Sociological Theory." Unpublished piece; by permission of the author.

P. 30. From "Historical Traditions and National Characteristics: Comparative Analyses of Canada and the United States" by S.M. Lipset in *Canadian Journal of Sociology*, 11, 2 (Spring 1986), pp. 113–155. By permission of the publisher.

P. 52. From Reginald Bibby, *Fragmented Gods: The Poverty and Potential of Religion in Canada*. Toronto: Irwin Publishing, 1987, Chapter 10. By permission of Stoddart Publishing Co. Limited.

P. 60. From Chapter 1 of M. Patricia Marchak's *Ideological Perspectives on Canada*, 3rd. ed., (Toronto: McGraw-Hill Ryerson Limited, 1988). By permission of the publisher.

P. 77. Nancy Mandell, "Role-Taking Among Pre-School Children." Unpublished piece; by permission of the author.

P. 88. From "Perceptions of Social Inequality among Public School Children" by Bernd Baldus and Verna Tribe in *Canadian Review of Sociology and Anthropology*, 15, 1 (February 1978), pp. 50–60. By permission of the publisher.

P. 98. From "The Professionalization of Medical Students" by Jack Haas and William Shaffir in *Symbolic Interaction*, 1 (Fall 1977), pp. 77–88. Reproduced by permission of JAI Press Inc.

P. 115. From John Hagan, *The Disreputable Pleasures: Crime and Deviance in Canada*, 3rd. ed. (Toronto: McGraw-Hill Ryerson Limited, 1984), pp. 46–55, 117–118, 147–149. By permission of the publisher.

P. 125. From J. Lowman, "Taking young prostitutes seriously," *Canadian Review of Sociology and Anthropology* 24(1), 1987, p.99–116. By permission of the publisher.

P. 138. Rosemary Gartner, "Patterns of Victimization." Unpublished piece; by permission of the author.

P. 154. Paul Bernard and Jean Renaud, "Les nouveau visages de l'inegalité," trans. Jack Veugelers, in *Le Devoir*, 4 February 1982, p. 18. By permission of the publisher.

P. 158. From "Teachers and the evolving structural context of economic and political attitudes in Quebec" by Raymond Murphy in *Canadian Review of Sociology and Anthropology*, 18, 2 (1981), pp. 279–295. By permission of the publisher.

P. 173. Wallace Clement, "Does class matter?" Originally in *The Challenge of Class and Analysis*. Ottawa: Carleton University Press, 1988. As edited for inclusion in Curtis and Tepperman, eds. *Images of Canada*. Toronto: Prentice-Hall (Canada), 1990. By permission of Carleton University Press Inc.

P. 189. From "Chinese immigrants on the Canadian prairie, 1910–47" by Peter S. Li in *Canadian Review of Sociology and Anthropology*, 19, 4 (1982), pp. 527–540. By permission of the publisher.

P. 199. From "Racial Discrimination in Employment" by Frances Henry and Effie Ginzberg, pp. 302–309. Originally published in James Curtis et al., (eds.), *Social Inequality in Canada*. Scarborough, Ontario: Prentice-Hall Canada Inc., 1988. Reprinted by permission of the authors.

P. 207. Jean Leonard Elliott and Augie Flevas, "From Dependency toward Autonomy: Historical Perspectives on First Nations-Government Policy in Canada." By permission of authors and Prentice-Hall Canada Ltd.

Pt. 230. From "The Domestic Economy," by Martin Meissner in *Women's Worlds: From the New Scholarship*, edited by Marily Safir, Martha T. Mednick, Dafne Izrael and Jessie Bernard. Copyright © 1985 by

Praeger Publishers. Reprinted and abridged by permission of Praeger Publishers, a division of Greenwood Press, Inc.

P. 238. From "Gender consciousness at work: modification of the male breadwinner norm among steelworkers and their spouses" by D.W. Livingstone and Meg Luxton. Appeared in Volume 26:2, May 1989. By permission of *The Canadian Review of Sociology and Anthropology.*

P. 250. Reprinted from G.S. Lowe, "The Administrative Revolution in the Canadian Office: An Overview" in K.I.P. Lundy and B. Warme (eds.), *Work in the Canadian Context: Continuity Despite Change,* 2nd ed. (Toronto: Butterworths, 1986), pp. 100–120. By permission of the publisher.

P. 269. From "Models of the Family" by Margrit Eichler in *Canadian Journal of Sociology,* 6 (1981), pp. 367–388. By permission of the publisher.

P. 280. From "Female lone parenting over the life course" by Maureen Moore in *Canadian Journal of Sociology,* 14, (3), 1989, pp. 335–351. By permission of the publisher.

P. 289. First published as "Harmonie und Aggression: Über die Dialektik ehlicher Gewalt," *Kölner Zeitschrift für Soziologie und Sozialpsychologie,* Vol. 42(3): 479–501, 1990. Used by permission of the publisher.

P. 307. From "The Modernization of Quebec and the Legitimacy of the Canadian State" by Hubert Guindon in *Canadian Review of Sociology and Anthropology,* 15, 2 (1978), pp. 227–245. By permission of the publisher and author.

P. 317. From "Feminists in the Academy: Intellectuals or Political Subversives," by Roberta Hamilton in *Queen's Quarterly,* Vol. 92(1), Spring 1985, pp. 3–20. By permission of the author and publisher.

P. 324. From Willem H. Vanderburg, "Techology and Social Change," Ch. 23 in *The Social World,* 1st ed. Edited by L. Tepperman and R.J. Richardson. Toronto: McGraw-Hill Ryerson Limited, 1986.

P. 333. Roderic Beaujot, "The Challenge of Demographics," *Policy Options,* Vol. 11, #10, 1990, pp. 19–22. *Policy Options* is published by The Institute for Research on Public Policy. Used by permission.